39.95

The Soul of a Small Texas Town

The Soul of a Small Texas Town

Photographs, Memories, and History from McDade

By David Wharton

UNIVERSITY OF OKLAHOMA PRESS : NORMAN

This book is published with the generous assistance of Edith Gaylord Harper and Bill Stott.

The paper in this book meets the guidelines for permanence and durability of the Committee on Production Guidelines for Book Longevity of the Council on Library Resources, Inc. ♾

Designed by Liz Lester

1 2 3 4 5 6 7 8 9 10

LIBRARY OF CONGRESS CATALOGING-IN-PUBLICATION DATA

Wharton, David, 1947–
The soul of a small Texas town : photographs, memories, and history from McDade / by David Wharton.
p. cm.
Includes bibliographical references and index.
ISBN 0-8061-3178-0 (cloth : alk. paper)
1. McDade (Tex.) Pictorial works. 2. McDade (Tex.)—Social life and customs Pictorial works.
3. McDade (Tex.)—History. 4. Documentary photography—Texas—McDade. 5. Oral history.
I. Title.
F394.M46W48   2000
976.4´32—dc 21   99-43612
CIP

For Marianne, Sam, and Emily
and
for my parents

Contents

Preface

This book has two parts. The first is a work of documentary photography that combines visual images and written texts to explore life in a single rural community—McDade, Texas—between 1984 and 1989. Its pictures and words attempt to draw connections between the people and events depicted and to examine issues of concern to community residents at the time. I hope it goes beyond merely showing what McDade of the late 1980s and the people who lived there looked like. The first part is divided into seven chapters, each a sequence of approximately fifteen photographs and accompanying text. When viewed and read in sequence, each chapter's pictures and texts introduce various themes, expand upon them, and sometimes relate them to people and themes introduced earlier. The first chapter is introductory; it provides a few facts about McDade and touches briefly on some of the themes explored in greater depth in later chapters. The photographs in chapter 2 are all portraits; they and their legends introduce individual members of the McDade community and tell a little about their lives. To some degree, this chapter serves as a partial cast of characters, as many of these individuals will be seen or heard from again. Chapter 3 examines public social life in McDade; civic, church, and family events figure prominently. All of the pictures in chapter 4 are of events associated with McDade's annual Watermelon Festival, always held on the second weekend in July. Their texts include information about the festivals of the late 1980s, recount anecdotes from earlier festivals, and point up the central significance of the Watermelon Festival to the McDade community. The remaining three chapters are more specific. Chapter 5 explores the role extended family life plays in the community, while chapter 6 compares the lives of men and women in McDade of the late 1980s. Finally, chapter 7 contrasts the attitudes of McDade's children toward their hometown with those of McDade's elderly.

The second part is a detailed history of McDade from its founding in 1871 through the end of the 1980s. In it I attempt to explain how McDade of the late 1980s, as portrayed in part one, came to be the way it was. The history begins with an account of McDade's early days as a Wild West railroad boomtown. It goes on to describe the town's turn-of-the-century attempts to live down its Wild West past and become more respectable; the assimilation of a nearby group of farming families, all immigrants from Germany, into the community; McDade's development as a moderately prosperous agricultural center in the years after World War I; the changes wrought in the community by World War II, especially the War Department's 1941 decision to locate a major army training camp nearby; McDade's brief resurgence in the immediate postwar years; and the town's slow decline in the decades that followed. The final chapter concerns McDade in the 1980s and includes a detailed account of a community-wide controversy, alluded to in part one, that divided the town in 1986 and 1987. Portions of this last chapter are autobiographical, describing my first visits to McDade, some of what I saw and learned there, and the evolution of some of my ideas about the community.

Like the town itself—and my awareness of it—this work has undergone an evolutionary process, developing from a small-scale photographic exercise into a decade's worth of photography, research, and writing. This preface contains a description of that process and some of what motivated it. A word of caution at the start, though: the various stages of my thinking about how to "document" McDade were not as logical or as deliberate as the following account might make them seem. Nor were many of the decisions I made about how to proceed arrived at in as orderly or as strictly chronological a fashion as the description might indicate. I have also, for the sake of brevity, ignored most of the blind alleys I stumbled down while trying to complete this project. The following, then, is considerably condensed and abridged, an approximate description at best. I offer it as a partial history of how this project came into being, in the hope that it might be worth the attention of future documentary workers and researchers, if only as a primer on some of the pitfalls to be avoided.

————————

I first went to McDade in February 1984. My only reason for going there was to take pictures. If the results of my first few visits pleased me, and if I enjoyed going there, I had vague plans to undertake a more extended photographic exploration of the community, though I had made no definite commitment to do so, either to myself or to anyone else. I certainly had no intention of spending most of the next decade photographing and writing about McDade, Texas. But that is what happened. Between 1984 and 1989, I visited McDade hundreds of times, engaged in thousands of conversations with town residents, and took an estimated twelve thousand photographs. In the years since, I have spent considerable time researching the town's past and writing about it. If I had known what the project would develop into when I began visiting McDade, I probably would not have gone there in the first place—though now, of course, I am glad I did.

I was a second-semester graduate student in photography at the time, and I went to McDade in search of something to photograph. I had entered a master's program the previous September in the Art department at the University of Texas. One of the things I hoped to gain from graduate school was the experience of working on an extended documentary project. Exactly what the focus of such a project might be I did not know, nor did I much care—to work as a documentary photographer, if only for a year or two, was all that mattered. Nothing demanded that my subject be rural or small-town life; nor did the project have to focus on the residents of a single community.

As explained in greater detail in the final chapter of part two, my decision to focus on McDade was more the result of chance than by design. The first time I visited McDade, I was with a person who lived there, someone I had met accidentally. She introduced me to several McDade residents that first day, and I took pictures of some of them. I went home to develop my film and print the pictures, and a few days later I returned to give prints away. I met more people that day and took more pictures and returned again to pass out prints. I repeated this process over and over again for a period of months, until I became something of a fixture in town. Before long, some of the town's children took to calling me "Picture Man," and no one in the community seemed to think it strange any longer that I had nothing better to do than wander around McDade taking pictures. Just that quickly and easily, I had become a documentary photographer, or so I thought.

Actually, of course, the documentary process is not so simple. Considerably more is involved than merely accumulating pictures all taken in the same place and calling the result a photographic documentary. Many complex and difficult questions arise in responsible documentary practice: What does one point the camera at in the first place? When does one trip the shutter? Which of the resulting negatives does one print? Which prints does one show? How, and to whom, does one show them? The most important question of all, though, is: What is it about the subject that compels the photographer to undertake the project in the first place? These questions and others require serious thought, if not always definite answers, from anyone who claims to be a documentary photographer. But I had little understanding of such things when I first started taking pictures in McDade, nor did I care to spend time thinking about them. I was happy enough at that point simply to have found a subject I would enjoy honing my photographic skills on. I was doubly pleased, of course, that the people of McDade seemed to welcome my doing so.

It took only a few months for me to establish McDade as a sort of personal photographic preserve, a place where I could go and "bag" a few visual trophies any time I liked. During my first year or so visiting the community, anything that happened in McDade and anyone who lived there were fair game, and I made a number of individual photographs that I liked. The fact that many of these photographs communicated little of significance about life in McDade or, worse, were sometimes so misleading about daily life there as to be untrue, did not matter. It was too easy to let myself believe that my cameras could not lie and allow that alone to justify calling the pile of pictures I was accumulating from McDade a documentary. After all, this line of reasoning went, the pictures had all been taken in McDade and thus must contain some element of truth about the town. As insubstantial as such justification seems now, it was all the license I needed during the early stages of the project to consider my growing stack of photographs from McDade a valid portrait of the community.

Fortunately, I did not continue to believe this. I may have been naive and unreflective about my early "documentary" efforts in McDade, but I soon came to realize that the mounting pile of pictures I had made there did not correspond to many of the things I knew and felt about the community. Nor, as a whole, did they make much sense; instead, they seemed a rather haphazard collection of images connected only by the coincidence of having been taken in geographic proximity to one another. There were a number of "good" photographs in the pile—pictures that were technically competent, occasionally beautiful, and that viewers found engaging—but these criteria were becoming less and less important to me all the time. I found myself wanting the people who looked at my photographs from McDade to respond to the facts and feelings, as I understood them, of life there. As I showed pictures to my wife, friends, fellow graduate students, and professors, however, I was repeatedly disappointed, and sometimes surprised, at how little they saw in them of what I knew to be true of McDade and its citizens. Often, while people looked at the photographs, I found myself telling about the circumstances in which various pictures had been taken, recounting stories about individuals in the photographs, recalling things they had said to me, or telling about their connections to people who appeared in other pictures. My compulsion to tell these things suggested that they were what I wanted those who looked at my photographs from McDade to see and know about life there. Unfortunately, they were not evident in my pictures, a fact I found increasingly discouraging.

What was happening, of course, was that I had reached the limits of what I was capable of telling about McDade in photographs alone. By keeping my eyes and ears open during the many hours I spent in the community, I had begun to learn more about the town than my pictures could show. And much of what I learned about McDade surprised me. Beneath its seemingly unremarkable surface existed a startling richness of intricately interwoven detail that amazed and fascinated me. The more I became aware of this unexpected complexity—which, while not actually hidden, was certainly not apparent to the casual observer—the more I wanted to convey it in my photographs. I thus found myself doubly frustrated, pulled in two directions. Having recently become aware of some of the shortcomings of my photography, I began to doubt my abilities as a photographer, which troubled me. At the same time, though, I was experiencing a growing sense of excitement at having discovered something about McDade that I felt compelled to communicate. The good news was that the project had taken on a life of its own and had become self-motivating; no longer was it driven merely by my detached, somewhat abstract, desire to gain experience working as a documentary photographer. The bad news was that I was failing to communicate much of what I felt was important to say about McDade, and that was a problem I did not know how to solve. I had started caring about McDade at about the same time I began doubting I could do the town justice in photographs. I make these observations in retrospect, of course. At the time—the first half of 1985 or so—my thinking about McDade was less clear. All I knew for certain was that I was not happy with my first year's photographs from McDade and that I was going to have to do something differently. Thus far, my pictures had communicated little beyond the surface appearance of various people, events, and places in McDade at select moments in time; somehow I was going to have to dig beneath that surface and make some photographs that conveyed a deeper, truer sense of what I had recently realized I wanted to say about McDade.

At roughly the same time, I started thinking that my McDade project, when finished, might best be presented in book form. Without having given the matter much thought, I had always assumed that upon completing the project I would choose the best of the pictures, print them large, matte them, frame them, and hang them on a wall. Indeed, one of the requirements of my graduate program was to mount a formal "thesis exhibition," which no doubt influenced my early thinking about how the project would look in final form. As I shuffled through my ever growing stack of work prints from McDade, though, I found myself arranging and rearranging the pictures in various thematic combinations and sequences rather than treating them as individual images. This led me to imagine them edited into book form, a notion that eventually became my goal and transformed my entire approach to the project, both in terms of what to do with the pictures I already had and the process of making new pictures. I saw several advantages to proceeding with the project as though I would eventually put it together as a book. The book format would allow me to group photographs thematically and control the order in which most viewers would see them. Most importantly, however, though I was slow to realize it at the time, thinking of the project as a book would enable me to include substantial amounts of written material along with the photographs.

The decision to include written texts with the pictures was a turning point in the evolution of the project. Not only did it free the photographs from having to communicate on a solely visual level, but it also led me to experiment with various ways of linking words and pictures. This is something many photographers resist, often because they think text dilutes the impact of pictures when the two are presented together. Whether or not that is true in any general sense is beside the point, because in the specific case of how and what I wanted to communicate about McDade, it seemed an ideal marriage. My photographs were strengthened by the addition of words, in part because I could use the written material—sometimes subtly, sometimes less so—to direct the viewer's experience of the visual images the text was paired with. Conversely, the presence of photographs relieved the written passages of having to communicate all of what I wanted to say about a particular facet of life in McDade. Each picture's "thousand words" could function as a foundation of visual "fact" on which a more deeply descriptive and freely associating verbal component could build. In short, I could now include the stories I had always wanted to tell about my pictures from McDade along with the pictures themselves.

Once I had decided to include written materials with the pictures, it did not take long to arrive at the format of sequential photographs and text in part one. I imagined the finished project as a vertically oriented book, with space beneath each photograph for a substantial paragraph of text. Because this much text can convey large amounts of information, I decided that the written pieces that went with the pictures should be more than mere captions. They should go beyond simply naming the people in the photographs and explaining what the photographs showed them doing. Instead, the text should be expansive and should reach beyond the specific circumstances of individual pictures to provide additional information about the people shown and their activities. The text could also draw connections between people in different photographs, continue stories begun earlier, and elaborate on themes introduced in previous photographs and text. The ability of written material to bridge the gap between individual pictures was especially important, not only because it discouraged the tendency to view the photographs as separate entities, but also because it reproduced one of the characteristics of life in McDade I found most striking—the ever-present, though often invisible, fabric of tightly woven interconnection. Few people in McDade lived in isolation from the rest of the community; by tying my individual pictures from McDade together with words, I was able, at least in a structural and metaphoric sense, to echo that web of mutual interconnection.

Envisioning the book also helped me isolate themes and take pictures more effectively. The process of constantly sorting through my ever expanding pile of work prints and arranging them in different combinations and sequences helped me realize that there were things about McDade I wanted to explore more fully. In several instances, these were aspects of community life that some of my photographs had already touched on, though I had yet to consciously identify them as specific areas of inquiry. Not surprisingly, these were also facets of town life I often found myself wanting to tell people about when I showed them pictures from McDade. Clearly, these were things about McDade that had drawn my attention "naturally," that is, without my deciding beforehand they were themes I "should" be looking for and trying to photograph. Many of the pictures I had taken were, in a general way, about the relationship between individuals in McDade and the community as a whole. More specifically, many of them dealt with group social life in McDade, both at public events sponsored by various community institutions—the PTA, the Historical Society, and the town's churches, for example—and at such semiprivate family affairs as reunions, weddings, and birthday parties, many of which, as a matter of course, attracted a hundred or more guests. I had also made a number of portraits, many of them of older people or children, as well as several photographs I liked that implicitly contrasted the lives of men and women in McDade. Once I became aware that these were areas of town life I had already, subconsciously, sought out to photograph, I was able to look for opportunities to photograph them in greater depth and become better informed about them. Though they all overlapped—like everything else in McDade—and thus could not be isolated from one another, each eventually came into focus in one or more chapters in part one. The particulars of what I found out about McDade can be seen there.

———————

I stopped taking pictures in McDade in 1989. I had more than enough usable photographs by then, and it seemed pointless to keep making more. It was time to gather the work together and put it into final form. Several times over the years I had compiled "dummy" books using whatever photographs I already had, but this compilation would be the last. I would have to decide which hundred or so pictures to include, group and sequence them, and write final versions of the texts that would go with them. The last step would be to write a brief introductory essay that would provide some factual information about McDade and tell a little of its history. I estimated all this might take about a year. I had completed my master of fine arts degree in 1986, at which point I entered the American Civilization program at the University of Texas as a doctoral student. By 1989, I had fulfilled that program's course and competency requirements, which left me only a dissertation to complete. The finished McDade project would be that dissertation. Once I had put it all together, which I was sure would be very soon, I would be able to put both the project and my days as a graduate student behind me.

To make a long story short, I failed to make short work of McDade's history. As I dug through newspaper archives and conducted interviews with some of the town's older residents, I became fascinated by McDade's past—the good and bad times the community had gone through; its citizens' ever changing attitudes toward McDade's relationship with other towns in Bastrop County, the rest of Texas, and the nation as a whole; and the way past events constantly seemed to presage much of what I saw happen in McDade between 1984 and 1989. Though McDade's history spanned barely more than a century, it was rich and varied and full of twists and turns that seemed to have direct bearing on the McDade I had come to know. This amazed me and made me keep digging. I had never before thought of history as anything other than a collection of isolated facts from the distant past, but to watch McDade's past, constantly in the process of becoming the future and then emerging almost seamlessly as a present I had witnessed firsthand, was a revelation of sorts and made that history come alive. This was what compelled me to continue my research despite the fact that it was taking considerably more time and would eventually require more extensive analysis than I had intended. What I had originally assumed would be a month's worth of research took the better part of a year, and what I had envisioned as ten or fifteen introductory pages on McDade's past expanded to twenty or more times that amount, eventually becoming an equal partner with the photographs and texts. This is how part two, a full-fledged local history, came about. The specifics of what I learned about McDade's past can be found there. This preface, however, seems the place for a few general observations on local history—the process of compiling it, what can be learned from it, and its significance relative to broader historical topics.

I experienced many frustrations in the process of researching McDade's past. The *Bastrop Advertiser* and the *Elgin Courier,* both weeklies, were my main sources of contemporary record. For some periods in McDade's history—the latter half of the 1920s and most of the 1940s, for example—these newspapers yielded an overabundance of material, bewildering in sheer amount, while for others—the 1930s, the late 1950s, and most of the 1970s—they contained very little. As these newspapers' fortunes ebbed and flowed through the years, so too did the quality of their content. They were quirky sources at best; more than once, for example, one or both mentioned upcoming elections in McDade but failed to report the elections' eventual results. McDade sometimes dropped out of their pages for months (occasionally years) at a time for no apparent reason and then, just as inexplicably, suddenly reappeared and started receiving regular coverage again. Most of what these papers printed about McDade appeared not as news items but in separate "News from McDade" columns, written by town residents who had no training or prior experience as journalists. With some important exceptions, their "letters" tended to focus on social goings-on in McDade and treated most other news as secondary or nonexistent. The quality of their columns varied as well. Some correspondents were remarkably conscientious, cranking out column after column every week for years. Others lasted less than a year or reported irregularly. All had different interests and styles, ranging from matter-of-fact listings of each person in attendance at particular social events to hyperbolic praise for the entire McDade community and anyone wise or lucky enough to be part of it. In short, the type and quality of information available in these columns depended on who was writing them, what the writers thought newsworthy, how much effort they put into compiling the column, and whether they had bothered to submit a column at all for any given week, as well as the specific circumstances of the writers' individual lives. Two of McDade's most informative and longest-lasting correspondents had their tenures as town columnist abruptly cut short—one by illness, the other in a fatal automobile accident—each time leaving a gaping hole in the written record. In both instances, it was years before a reliable replacement emerged. I sometimes encountered holes in the archival record as well. In the case of the *Elgin Courier*, for example, I was never able to locate more than a very few copies of the paper from the years before 1935. From that point on, though, the *Courier* had what its staff believed was a complete set of back issues, bound by year, haphazardly stored in several different back rooms. Once I started going through these volumes, however, I found that four separate years' worth of past issues—those from 1945, 1949, 1966, and 1973—were missing, with 1949 being (potentially at least) an especially important year in McDade's history.

I also conducted a number of interviews in McDade, especially among the town's older people, hoping to learn more about parts of the community's past that were still within living memory. I encountered problems in this area too and, with some exceptions, found these interviews to be less valuable as historical source material than I had hoped. I did hear several wildly variant versions of McDade's famous 1883 shoot-out, despite the fact that no one in town had been born when that incident took place. Unfortunately, people's memories of events they *had* witnessed often seemed equally unreliable, not always agreeing with other versions of the same events I had heard or read about, or not being internally consistent. Since these recollections were the products of memories that were selective at best and sometimes fading or self-serving, I found it difficult to know which of the stories people told me were accurate, which elaborated on, and which made up entirely. Nor was this problem confined to accounts of the distant past. I found the same to be true of interviews I conducted in 1989 about events that had taken place only a few years earlier. Those interviews that did provide insight into specific incidents sometimes failed to illuminate the overall tenor of times past in McDade. In others, people who spoke eloquently of general conditions at different times in the past had difficulty remembering specifics. Some topics—the root causes of several generations' worth of bad feeling between certain families in town, for example, or why there are so few African Americans in McDade—seemed off-limits; whenever I broached them, people became especially vague or forgetful and tried to change the subject. These were obviously aspects of McDade's past they did not want to share. Not surprisingly, these were also parts of town history that never made it into the pages of the *Advertiser* or the *Courier*. I do not mean to portray most of the people I interviewed as intentionally deceptive; I do not think they were. I do, however, believe that many of them unwittingly allowed certain myths—both personal myths about themselves and people they knew, as well as generally accepted local legends about McDade's past—to influence their *memories* of past events, which they then passed on to me.

The biggest problem I had with most of the information I gathered, whether from newspaper accounts or personal interviews, was deciding what was worth noting and then, of course, worth telling. Much of what I read or heard was the stuff of daily life—some of it so numbingly ordinary that I wondered why anyone would have written about it in the first place or remembered it years later to recount during an interview. Going through this mass of undigested raw material was time-consuming and sometimes extremely boring, and determining which few among the countless small details I encountered were significant was often maddening. Occasionally, I had to resort to guess-work or speculation to fill in gaps. In some instances, I had to return to material I had been through previously to locate items I had seen or heard earlier but had wrongly judged meaningless. Sometimes I could only curse at happening upon pieces of information that disproved various hypotheses I was forming. My frustration at trying to make sense out of the large amounts of undifferentiated raw data available about some parts of McDade's past was compounded by a lack of information about other times or by people's reticence to talk about certain subjects. In short, much of what I offer in part two is local history compiled by trial and error. I hope the most egregious errors have been weeded out, though a few mistakes may yet remain. Likewise, there may be important facts about McDade's past that I have missed or significant themes I have overlooked. For any such omissions, I can only apologize.

One could probably find other histories of McDade to tell, especially about the years since World War II. Oddly, as past approaches present and the facts of history are no longer obscured by the dim and distant past, the historian's job becomes more confusing. The value of raw historical material from more recent times, in its very volume and wealth of detail, becomes less certain and increasingly more formless. Stories from a century ago are that era's important stories, if only by virtue of having lasted. But much greater amounts of information are available from the more recent past, forcing the historian to pick, choose, and even guess at what is most significant. The last two chapters of part two, therefore, comprise just one history of post–World War II McDade, selected and pieced together from several possibilities. No doubt several more histories lie dormant somewhere, waiting for someone to uncover them, shake them awake, and make them take form. The history of McDade that I offer, then, especially of more recent times, is only partially true, in the sense of being only partially complete. I hope it touches upon some of the more pressing issues in McDade during those years and will provide some of the reasons why, at the end of the twentieth century, those of us who do not live in places like McDade might still find such communities worth thinking about.

Though the histories of such places may seem unimportant in comparison to events played out on larger, more central stages, they still have much to teach. If research into 120 years' worth of life in McDade, Texas—a tiny rural community of no apparent present-day distinction—reveals a past that is rich, complex, and deeply reflective of the hopes and fears of several generations of local residents, does that not argue that every small community has an equally rich, complex, and instructive history, each with its own lessons to teach? McDade's past also suggests that local histories are made by the people who live them, ordinary people motivated less by large-scale political, cultural, or intellectual concerns than by the daily circumstances of their lives. This results in local pasts, and presents, that are more often the product of emotion and gut-reaction than thought or planning. Local histories are also markedly specific, emerging from accumulations of detail about individual lives. They arise out of people's likes and dislikes, their ambitions and anxieties, and their relationships with other individuals, each of whom brings his or her own set of preferences, hopes, fears, and interpersonal relationships to an already bewildering mix. Given the almost infinite variety of factors that contribute, potentially at least, to individual local histories, it is not surprising that no theory seems adequate to account for the specifics of any one community's past. At best, one might propose a sort of sociohistorical "chaos theory," a notion so broad as to have little real value.

The relevance of individual local histories to broader interpretations of the past is thus problematic. Indeed, the ways in which local histories fail to parallel national or world events may well contain their most potentially valuable lessons. If, for example, one explains events in McDade between World Wars I and II strictly in terms of the boom-and-bust pattern of the 1920s, "hard times" in the 1930s, and recovery with the approach of World War II, then most readers would not be surprised or, probably, inclined to disagree. These are historical truisms about American life between 1918 and 1941, generally accepted by historians and students of history alike. As such, they are a form of myth—not because they are untrue, but because they are self-perpetuating and tend to generate ways of understanding the past that are often overly general and incomplete. They serve as a kind of historical shorthand, providing ready-made explanations for past events. Unfortunately, these explanations are not always accurate, especially when applied to the histories of individual places, most of which developed out of circumstances peculiarly their own. For local historians to allow these kinds of myths to predict their findings is to obscure what is most valuable about local history—the specifics of what happened in a particular place during a particular time. Indeed, the degree to which events in a given community echoed the larger history of the nation, thus lending support to standard interpretations of that history, is less important than the local historian's detailed account of how national events touched the lives of individuals within that community, thus creating the actual history of that place. Conversely, in places where events did not parallel the national experience, the local historian's task is to show how and why larger events did not affect the community, how and why they did not touch people's lives on the local level. This type of analysis is local history's greatest potential asset, since for any given period in the nation's past it can offer something of the texture of life as experienced by ordinary people in a specific local setting.

Because of their shared concern with particulars, local history and documentary have much in common. In both, relatively trivial pieces of information are selected from a wide array of potential choices, then combined and presented in ways that create greater meaning. The two genres are also similar in that each teaches by example, communicating most effectively when central themes are implicit in the material presented. In both cases, the important things they have to say should lie in the telling and are told best when they emerge directly from the tale. There are other, less obvious, parallels between local history and documentary. Because they focus on individual, usually small, places over relatively long periods of time, local histories are especially well suited to observing the transformation of past into present without the concomitant confusion of too many things happening at once. Indeed, one of the most important contributions of local history may well be that it encourages a view of the present—any present, no matter when it was, is, or will be—as little more than a momentary manifestation of an ongoing past that is constantly in the process of becoming the future. Only the historian's decision to research and write about certain events—processes that are separate from the events themselves—makes those events anything other than undifferentiated fragments of past time and turns them into history. In similar fashion, documentary—especially documentary photography—chooses isolated moments of "present" time and artificially preserves them for future examination, thus investing them with meanings the original moments may never have possessed. Fortunately, neither local history nor documentary are random processes. Instead, they are carried out by people who, presumably, are making intelligent, informed, and responsible decisions. The best local histories—those in which the particulars of time and place are used to tell about more than particular times and places—depend on good historians. Likewise, the best documentary photography depends on photographers who are knowledgeable, who care enough about their subject matter not to misrepresent it, and who constantly try to communicate about their subject in ways that add up to more than the sum of its constituent parts. As I hope what follows demonstrates, I believe that research into any given place's past, and present-time documentary photography in that place can be combined to form an effective partnership in which each method's "findings" invest those of the other with greater significance.

Strangely, when I was first visiting McDade, spending the bulk of my time there with a camera in front of my face, I often said to people there that I was trying to compile "a visual history of the present" in McDade. That was not really what I thought I was doing at the time but was just a phrase I used, with emphasis on the word "present," as a way of disavowing much interest in McDade's past. It was something I said when I sensed I was about to be told stories I did not want to listen to about "the old days," stories that would require me to take the camera away from my face. Fortunately, this tactic often did not work, and I started hearing more and more about the community's past. Eventually, I could no longer remain indifferent to the things I heard. The past sounded too strangely like the present, and vice versa, to ignore, and the lure of finding out how McDade of the 1980s had come to be grew too strong. In any event, I consider the photographs I took in McDade between 1984 and 1989, combined with the text that accompanies them, to be a valid history of the community during that time. I also believe that the history of McDade I tell in part two is a documentary of sorts, if not in terms of firsthand experience, then at least in terms of its concern with detail. As McDade grew and changed through the years, the details of how it did so were what mattered. They still are.

Acknowledgments

One accumulates a lot of debts in the course of a project such as this—so many, in fact, that it is impossible to properly acknowledge them all. First and foremost, I would like to thank the people of McDade, Texas, for opening their lives to me. Their friendliness and hospitality touched me deeply and will stay with me always. Among the many residents of the town who helped and befriended me, I would especially like to thank Laura Cayton, Adeline Eschberger, Erhard Goerlitz, Linda Haverland, Melba Skubiata, Wallace and Freda Wilson, and Dan and Evelyn Wolf. Without their help and friendship, this project would never have gotten off the ground.

I am also grateful to several members of the University of Texas faculty. Mark Goodman of the Art department helped shape my photography in McDade from the start. He never asked an easy question or accepted an easy answer, and he always made me think about what I was doing in McDade, whether I wanted to or not. Lawrence McFarland, also in Art, was helpful as well, providing common sense and good humor. Bob Crunden, Emily Cutrer, Jeff Meikle, and Mark Smith—all of the American Studies faculty—along with J. B. Colson from Journalism, all read through the manuscript, and each made numerous suggestions that improved it. I owe special thanks to Bill Stott of American Studies for his patience, support, and friendship. He was always confident that I would successfully complete the project (even when I was not) and that it would find its way to publication.

I am also indebted to the Graduate School at the University of Texas for its generous financial support in the form of several University Fellowships.

Among many others who deserve thanks are my brother, Chris Wharton, for valuable editorial assistance; Rick Williams and Julie Newton for the use of their darkroom; Ellen Browning, manuscript editor; and Randy Lewis and Jo Ann Reece of the University of Oklahoma Press for their help in shepherding this project through the publication process.

Finally, I want to thank Marianne, Sam, and Emily for their love and understanding. They were always there for me to come home to.

PART ONE

*How to Get to McDade
and What You'll Find
When You Do*

McDade is one of many small Texas towns that have seen better days. In times past, it was a thriving commercial and transportation center, but today it is little more than a dot on the map, close to—but not on—U.S. 290, one of the major east-west highways through central Texas. Very little that the rest of the world considers noteworthy goes on in McDade these days. Only twice during the mid-1980s did anyone outside of Bastrop County have reason to notice the town. For a week or so in 1986, a Hollywood production company took over McDade's dilapidated "uptown" business district to use as a backdrop for *The Texas Kid*, a sentimental made-for-TV movie about a teenage boy's efforts to prevent the annexation of his dying hometown by a larger town nearby. McDade was on television again in 1987, when Austin news crews traveled there to report on local reaction to the firing and subsequent rehiring of the McDade School's longtime principal and superintendent. The school board's flip-flop on this issue had so angered people in the community that a series of disagreements ugly enough to attract outside attention had resulted. Predictably, *The Texas Kid* used McDade's rundown appearance to evoke a stereotypically "sleepy" little country town and ignored the specific realities of life in McDade. Likewise, instead of exploring the actual issues involved in McDade's school controversy, the short pieces that aired on Austin news programs treated the town's troubles condescendingly and poked tongue-in-cheek fun at the petty resentments of small-town life. Other than these two brief appearances in the public eye, no one without prior interest in McDade had any reason to notice the community during the latter half of the 1980s. Life went on there anyway.

Approximately six hundred people live in or around McDade, about half of them within the town, the other half on small ranches or farms out in the country. Since McDade is not incorporated, no official census figures exist for the community; the United States Census Bureau counts those who live there in with all other "rural" residents of Bastrop County. McDade is in the northwestern corner of the county, twelve miles north of Bastrop, the county seat, which boasts a population of about thirty-five hundred. McDade's nearest neighbor is the even smaller community of Paige, seven miles to the east. Nine miles west of McDade is Elgin. With a population of about five thousand, Elgin is the largest town in Bastrop County. Except for business that must be transacted at the county courthouse, McDade is more closely tied—historically, socially, and economically—to Elgin than to Bastrop. Austin, a city of about half a million that is the state capital and the site of the University of Texas, is thirty-five miles west of McDade. Many residents of McDade commute to jobs in Austin. A number of others go there regularly for entertainment or to shop.

Some of McDade's older people remember the trip to Austin as an all-day undertaking. Today town residents can drive into Austin after breakfast, spend a couple of hours shopping and running errands there, and return home in time for lunch. A four-lane highway that runs between Houston and Austin, U.S. 290, passes within a mile of downtown McDade and provides the community with a speedy route into the northern part of Austin. It usually takes about forty-five minutes to drive from McDade into central Austin. During rush hour it may take an extra fifteen minutes, but rarely more than that. A large shopping mall in the northeastern part of Austin is only thirty-five minutes away.

Before the current highway was built in the years after World War II, the road heading east out of Austin—"old" State Highway 20—went through the downtown business districts of all the country towns along its route. Like McDade, these were originally railroad towns, communities whose first entrepreneurs had crowded their businesses as close to the train depot as possible, thus creating the nucleus around which each town grew. The network of roads that connected these towns with surrounding rural areas, and eventually the towns with one another, did not develop until after the town sites were fixed. The series of country roads that would eventually be consolidated into State Highway 20 closely paralleled the rail line. Because the original railroad surveyors had always chosen the highest ground they could find for laying track—in a rolling topography drained by numerous small creeks—this made for a windy, indirect route. But it also made for a route that went right down Main Street in the country towns east of Austin. A motorist traveling Highway 20 in the years before World War II had no choice but to drive through each of these communities' downtown business districts.

This is no longer the case. Today, travelers can drive an hour east of Austin on 290 before they see anything resembling a Main Street. All the way to Giddings in Lee County, a distance of almost sixty miles, the highway bypasses (though never by more than two miles) the original town centers of Manor, Elgin, McDade, and Paige. The state highway department began to straighten Highway 20 in 1941, a project that amounted to building an entirely new roadway along much of its length. World War II delayed completion of this project until 1952, at which point the road became known as "new" Highway 20. It was renamed U.S. 290 in 1953, when it was absorbed into the federal highway system. In addition to ironing out the old route's railroad-dictated twists and turns, the new road bypassed the business districts of most of the old railroad towns, skirting Manor to the north and Elgin, McDade, and Paige to the south.

Manor (pronounced MAIN-er) is a community of about twelve hundred, located seven miles east of Austin's city limit. Its old downtown is about a mile south of 290, and most of its nineteenth-century brick buildings are now empty. Manor does have several more recently established businesses: a couple of convenience-store gas stations, a cafe, a barbecue place, an auto repair shop—all located on the highway where they can cater to travelers. There is also a stoplight on 290 that helps mark Manor as a town, at least in the minds of passing motorists. Most of these highway businesses, along with several others that have since failed, opened in the early 1980s, when the Austin City Council buoyed Manor's economic hopes by selecting a tract of land along 290 near Manor as the site for a projected new airport. Purchase of the land was subject to the approval of Austin voters, however, and in a series of referenda since the city council's original announcement, the citizens of Austin rejected buying the land near Manor, then approved it, and subsequently rejected it again. By 1989, no final decision had been reached about where, or even if, Austin would build a new airport. In the interim, because Manor's leading citizens had based their vision of the community's future almost entirely on the assumption that it would host Austin's airport, the town remained in limbo. No one saw much of a future for Manor if the airport were not to be built nearby.

Ten miles east of Manor is Elgin (EL-gin, with a hard "g"). It is larger than either Manor or McDade and is the main commercial center for eastern Travis, northern Bastrop, southern Williamson, and western Lee Counties, an area of scattered small farms and ranches. In addition to a standard complement of hardware stores, feed stores, farm equipment outlets, drug stores, beauty parlors, and video rental shops, Elgin has two banks, a pair of locally owned supermarkets, a Ford dealership, and its own weekly newspaper, the *Elgin Courier*. The town is probably best known in Texas for its sausage; several local firms make "Elgin hot sausage" and market it throughout the state. Each, of course, claims its own as the original. Elgin's downtown, two miles north of U.S. 290, is much livelier than Manor's. Most of the downtown businesses that originally made Elgin a commercial center have managed to stay open, while several newer businesses, including a McDonald's, have located on 290 to cater to highway traffic. In the mid-1980s, Elgin embarked upon an ambitious "Main Street" campaign, dedicated to keeping businesses downtown and attracting shoppers there while striving to preserve the district's historic appearance. By and large, this campaign seems to have been successful. Like Manor, though, Elgin was frustrated by Austin's indecision about the airport. Many residents had foreseen a boom in Elgin with the construction of a new airport in Manor, especially as a bedroom community for people who would be employed there. But as the Austin City Council dragged its feet and started looking for alternate sites, some of those in Elgin who had banked too heavily on the airport being located in Manor lost considerable amounts of money.

Unlike Manor and Elgin, McDade has neither a cluster of businesses nor a stoplight on 290 to mark its presence. Every day, people drive by McDade without realizing that the town's old business district, just a mile or so north of the highway, even exists. A small road the Texas Highway Department designates as Loop 223 connects 290 to downtown McDade. At its intersection with the highway is a single-pump Texaco station (now closed) and the Weeping Willow Baptist Church, all of whose members are African American and, strangely, none of whom live in McDade. There is also a small sign pointing north that reads "McDade" (easily missed) and a second sign assuring motorists of a welcome at whichever of McDade's churches—Weeping Willow Baptist, McDade Baptist, Faith Lutheran, or the McDade Church of Christ—they might choose to visit. About a mile west of this intersection is the JNP Grocery—a convenience store, gas station, and beer joint owned by McDade residents Duke and Judy Mueller. That's all there is on the highway at McDade to indicate a town nearby. Even Paige, McDade's smaller neighbor to the east, has several businesses on 290. In fact, of the twelve towns along 290 between Austin and Houston, McDade is the one most completely bypassed by the highway.

Because it is no longer a place travelers pass through, people rarely wind up in McDade by chance. It's hard to get there these days without intending to. This means that very few strangers arrive in McDade. Those who do rarely find much to arouse their curiosity. Unlike many a town with a past more glorious than its present, McDade is not much to look at: it has no picturesque courthouse square with elderly men passing time on public benches; no leafy green park with a bandstand or gazebo at its center; no historic old mansions, decaying or otherwise. The fact of the matter is that McDade, at least in terms of physical appearance, is not a very attractive place.

At one time, McDade's business district took up eight city blocks, four on each side of the railroad tracks that run east-west through the middle of town. The stretch of road that was McDade's main street—it has never had an official name—ran along the south side of the tracks and was part of "old" Highway 20. The businesses on the south side faced the tracks and the depot from across the road. Likewise, the shops and hotels on the north side of the railroad faced the tracks from across an intervening roadway. Today, no trace of these north-side businesses exists except for some scattered bricks on the few lots that don't have houses on them. All that now remains of McDade's downtown business district (called "uptown" by most locals) is on the south side of the railroad tracks, in a single block of buildings facing north to the tracks across "old" Highway 20.

The two buildings on the eastern end of the block—the post office and Seigmund's General Store—are separated from the others by a narrow alleyway on the west side of Seigmund's. Mary Louise Mundine, who has worked at the McDade Post Office since 1945 and been the town's postmistress since 1967, runs the local postal service out of a small brick building that once housed the McDade Guaranty State Bank, which closed in 1934. This was the "new" bank building, the old one having been abandoned in 1914, though it still stands just behind the post office. The old bank building is now an empty brick shell; only its barred windows and a faded "GUARANTY STATE BANK" sign painted on the north wall testify to its past as a bank. During World War II, it housed a cafe. A crudely lettered sign reading "CAFE" is also visible on the cracked north wall.

The post office (ZIP code 78650) is one of the busiest places in town. Most people who live in McDade proper—as opposed to those who live outside the town—do not have their mail delivered to their homes, preferring to pick it up at the post office instead. Almost everyone checks in daily, usually stopping for a few minutes to chat with Mary Louise Mundine or her assistant, Ruth Pohler. McDade's post office also employs Forrest McDavid and Hilda Neidig, Forrest as the full-time rural route driver and Hilda as his relief. People who live in town and want to have their mail delivered have only to put a mail box up by the side of the road in front of their house and Forrest will add them to his route.

Seigmund's General Store, next door to the post office, is a rambling two-story frame structure. The building was once McDade's train depot and was located directly across old Highway 20 from where it is now. Passenger train service in and out of McDade was discontinued in 1951, and the Southern Pacific freight trains stopped taking on farm produce at McDade in 1954. Soon after that, Tom Dungan (pronounced DUN-a-gan) purchased the old depot and moved it across the highway to its current location. He ran a successful grocery business out of it until he retired in 1979. Today, George Seigmund owns the building, and he and his family have expanded their grocery business to include selling feed and seed products to local ranchers and farmers. With the exception of Duke and Judy Mueller's JNP convenience store on 290, Seigmund's is still the only place in town to buy groceries. Although the Seigmunds cannot compete with the lower prices and greater variety of supermarkets in Elgin, Bastrop, and Austin, many McDade residents buy groceries at Seigmund's. Located uptown, it is convenient, and the Seigmunds don't mind extending credit to their regular customers. Those who want beer or wine, however, have to go elsewhere, because the Seigmunds are staunch Baptists and refuse to sell alcohol. George and his wife, Jona Lee, live in a mobile home located behind the store, next to the abandoned bank building.

Across the narrow alleyway just west of Seigmund's are five small buildings joined into a continuous block. The building closest to Seigmund's is now abandoned, and George Seigmund uses it to store sacks of feed. From 1906 until the late 1950s, this building housed DeGlandon's Barbershop. Proprietor Bud DeGlandon was a popular figure in and around McDade, cutting the hair of nearly every white male in town until he was almost eighty. He has the distinction of being the first person from McDade to serve in the Texas House of Representatives. He was elected in 1936, defeating a rival from Bastrop by twenty-three votes to become state representative for District 127. He served a single two-year term, during which he continued to cut hair in McDade on weekends. In 1938, he lost his bid for reelection to another opponent from Bastrop. For several years afterwards, DeGlandon served as an assistant sergeant-at-arms for the state legislature, but remaining McDade's preeminent barber.

Next to the old barbershop is Dungan Drugs, owned and operated by Sam Earl Dungan, the younger—by thirty-six years—first cousin of former grocer and depot-mover Tom Dungan. Despite its name, Dungan Drugs has never been a pharmacy. From about 1910 until after World War II, it was S. T. Hillman's Confectionery. Poor health forced Hillman to retire in 1949, and three years later Emma Dungan, Sam Earl's mother, purchased the business. She ran it as a drugstore-style soda fountain for the next seventeen years. Since she also stocked a wide variety of patent medicines, people soon began calling her store Dungan Drugs. For years, it was a favorite meeting spot in McDade, and conversations at the store were the source for many of the items that appeared in Mrs. Dungan's "News from McDade" column that appeared weekly in the *Elgin Courier* between 1952 and 1969. Today most people refer to the store as "Sam Earl's," even though its sign still reads "Dungan Drugs." In its own way, Sam Earl's is as much a social center as it was when his mother was running the business. Sam Earl doesn't sell much other than candy, cigarettes, chewing tobacco, microwave sandwiches and pizzas, soft drinks ("soda water" in local parlance), and beer—lots of beer, much of which is consumed on the covered sidewalk in front of the store. At times, quite a crowd can gather there to drink and socialize; occasionally they are loud and rowdy. Some people in McDade don't like these uptown get-togethers, especially the "dry" Seigmunds, whose grocery store is only two doors down.

Adjoining Sam Earl's is a narrow building that had been vacant for quite some time before newcomers Hal and Nancy Metheny bought it in the early 1980s and began remodeling it as a residence. For almost forty years, beginning in 1910, this building was the site of Mabel Southern's Drugstore. Dr. G. W. Southern, Mrs. Southern's husband, was McDade's only physician for much of that time, and he usually sent his patients to his wife's pharmacy to have their prescriptions filled. After Dr. Southern died and Mrs. Southern retired, the building housed a succession of businesses, none of which lasted long. For most of the 1960s and 1970s it stood vacant. By the mid-1980s, however, the Methenys had moved in and were remodeling the interior. A successful, well-traveled couple with cultivated ideas, they built a home unlike any McDade had ever seen. They made the interior of the old drugstore seem more spacious by raising its ceiling, adding sleeping lofts, and installing skylights. They sandblasted the building's old brick facade and painted it a creamy beige. They also added a new double door, made of oak and waxed to a golden shine, that opened onto the sidewalk. The door's fittings were of polished brass, as was the antique lamp they hung next to it on the outdoor wall. Beneath the lamp, Hal hung an official-looking plaque that read: "On this spot in 1880 absolutely nothing happened." Hal died in 1989, when the small plane he was piloting crashed into a field several miles north of McDade. Nancy now lives alone and keeps to herself most of the time. She has several McDade friends she visits with, but she is not involved with the community in any public way.

Next to Nancy Metheny's home is another vacant building that George Seigmund uses as storage space. It has housed several businesses over the years, but most old-time McDade people call it the Taylor Barbershop, after the business Theo Taylor opened there in 1936, possibly thinking that new state representative Bud DeGlandon would no longer have time to cut hair. The barbershop closed and reopened several times over the years, sometimes with Theo Taylor as proprietor, sometimes with another barber leasing it from him. During the times when no one was cutting hair there, the building housed several other business ventures, including a butcher shop in the 1940s and an income tax preparation service in the 1960s. Its last occupant seems to have been barber D. D. Horton, a transplant from Houston, who cut hair there in the late 1960s.

At the western end of McDade's single-block business district, where Loop 223 intersects old Highway 20 and heads south to 290, is the infamous Rockfront Saloon. Today, most people in town refer to it as "the historical building," because it is now owned by the McDade Historical Society. In 1883, the old saloon was the site of the vigilante kidnappings that led to the hangings and subsequent gunfight that are McDade's primary claim to historic fame. On the front of the building is a plaque from the Texas Historical Survey Commission commemorating that incident and citing the building's additional importance as an early stagecoach stop. It is the oldest building in town, having been constructed by Confederate veteran Oscar Nash in the mid-1870s. He built it entirely out of stone, since two wooden saloon buildings on the same site had burned in quick succession. He built it to last as well as to resist fire: its walls have stood for more than 120 years now, and they show no sign of falling down. The McDade Historical Society has owned the building since 1964, and most of the society's financial resources—as well as the volunteer energies of its members—go into maintaining it. In recent years, the building has required a new roof and extensive work on its interior. The historical society holds meetings and fund-raisers in it and maintains a small museum there. The museum is nearly always closed, opening only for the second weekend in July, when McDade holds its annual Watermelon Festival.

That's all that remains of a once-thriving business district. A number of other enterprises dating from different times in McDade's history have disappeared with hardly a trace: several hotels and boarding houses from McDade's days as a bustling railroad town; three gas stations from when old Highway 20 was the main road between Austin and Houston; the McDade Pottery plant, which operated from 1890 until 1942 and employed twenty workers during its heyday in the 1920s and 1930s (when McDade Pottery shipped thousands of charcoal-burning clay furnaces and tens of thousands of flower pots by rail each year to markets throughout Texas and surrounding states); three cotton gins, the last of which burned in 1940; a steam-powered grist mill; a large stock pen along the tracks on the eastern edge of town; Kelton & Kunkel's McDade Mercantile, the biggest store in town from 1913 till 1961, carrying a wide range of general merchandise ("Whatever It Is, We Have It," a 1942 advertisement in the *Elgin Courier* claimed); a cannery; a broom factory; several grocery stores; a hat shop for fashion-conscious ladies; and a roller-skating rink that during the 1920s was the envy of farm kids for miles around. Today, no physical evidence remains of any of these businesses. The faded images of a few of them can be seen in old photographs that some people in McDade have saved, but for the most part they exist only in the memories of the town's oldest citizens.

For now, though, we'll save the past for later. Instead, we'll take a look at McDade of more recent times—as I found and photographed it between 1984 and 1989. Though time has not stood still in McDade since I stopped visiting the community, the texts that go with the pictures presume a "present" of 1989. A brief epilogue at the end of Part Two tells about some of the things that have happened in McDade since.

Children Waiting to Go on Stage
Coronation of the Watermelon Queens, McDade Watermelon Festival

The culminating event of McDade's annual Watermelon Festival is the coronation of new Watermelon queens. Both a Tiny Tot queen and a Teenage queen are crowned. Their reigns will last a year. The coronation ceremony is marked by a considerable degree of ritual pomp. With most of the town looking on, the previous year's queens and their attendants parade onto the raised stage at one edge of McDade's schoolyard and then surrender their crowns and watermelon scepters to the new queens. Visiting "royalty" from other rural communities in central Texas also attend, acting as courtiers. McDade's new queens and their male escorts will be expected to return this favor by attending official functions in these other towns.

CHAPTER 1

The Place and the People

1 / Freshly Plowed Garden Plot

Though McDade was originally a farming community, not many of its current residents make a living from the land. More typically, they commute to construction, service, or clerical jobs in Elgin, Bastrop, Giddings, or Austin. Many families still grow and can their own vegetables, and some raise a few beef cattle to sell at auction or to stock their freezers. A number of lots in town are vacant. Some are cultivated as garden plots—like the one in this picture—but most are grown over, many of them full of junk. Before the Texas oil economy collapsed in the mid-1980s, people who intended to build homes in McDade and commute to jobs in Austin, thirty-five miles away, had started buying a few of these vacant lots. After about 1985, however, these sales pretty much stopped. Most people in McDade hoped the slowdown was temporary, but that seemed unlikely, especially after the Austin City Council reversed an earlier decision to build a new airport just east of the city. Many local people had anticipated that the airport would fuel renewed development in the small towns east of Austin, McDade among them. Most had looked forward to this, though a few had dreaded the changes it would bring.

2 / View From the Page Family's Front Porch

McDade is a country town. There may be more domestic animals living there than people. Some local residents raise cattle, chickens, and hogs for food, and some keep horses to ride. Most of the town's animals, though, are pets whose owners generally allow them to roam free. A newcomer walking around town quickly gets to know McDade's dogs, most of whom are pretty friendly. In the background of this photograph is the town water tower, located just across the railroad tracks from McDade's tiny "uptown" business district. The water tower was erected in 1956, part of a newly built public water system. Before then, town residents used cisterns to collect rain water for drinking and washing. During the dry summer months, they either had to haul water from a public well (not far from the Pages' house) or buy it, at a dollar a barrel, from privately operated "water wagons" that came to town a couple of times each week. The water tower, painted white, is McDade's only landmark. It is visible from all over town and for several miles around.

3 / Loop 223

Loop 223 is the official designation of the road that links downtown McDade with U.S. 290, about a mile to the south. Old Highway 20, once the main road between Austin and Houston, used to run right through "uptown" (as most locals call it), but when U.S. 290 was completed in the early 1950s, it bypassed McDade's small business district. On the left of this picture, Erhard Goerlitz lends a hand with the town-wide cleanup the community undertakes each year in the weeks leading up to McDade's annual Watermelon Festival. On the right, Rachel Bright exercises one of the horses her mother, Peggy Fisher, sometimes boards and cares for. Since this picture was taken, Rachel has married and started a family. She no longer has the time to ride around town much.

4 / Peggy Fisher Training a Horse

Peggy Fisher, Rachel Bright's mother, is McDade's unofficial animal expert. She often helps people train their horses and will usually offer an opinion when an animal seems sick. Sometimes she keeps people's horses for them, even for extended periods of time. She would like to have horses of her own but says she cannot afford them. Although she is trained as a veterinarian's assistant, she has had trouble finding work. Most vets, she says, want assistants who are "young, blonde, and cute. I am neither young, blonde, nor cute." The house in the background belongs to Peggy's parents, Alton and Ruby Greenhaw. Peggy grew up in this house. Peggy and her three children now live next door. She has not seen her husband for several years, nor does she much want to. In fact, she once said, jokingly, that she might shoot him if she ever does see him again.

5 / Unloading Feed, Uptown McDade

Uptown McDade is usually pretty quiet. In this picture, Ray McDavid (left) talks with George Seigmund while one of George's hired hands unloads sacks of feed. In 1974, after twenty-eight years on the job, Ray chose early retirement from his federal civil service position in Bastrop rather than accept a transfer to New Mexico. He and his wife, Thelma, in their mid-fifties at the time, had lived in McDade all their lives and did not want to leave. Since then, Ray has supplemented his pension by raising a few cattle and supplying Austin grocery stores with produce. Cantaloupes and sweet potatoes are his biggest cash crops. George Seigmund, originally from south Texas, owns McDade's only grocery store. He also sells feed and fertilizer to local ranchers. His wife, daughter, and son-in-law all help with the business. The Seigmunds allow their regular customers liberal credit. Staunch Baptists, they do not sell beer or wine, items most small groceries make much of their money on. Nonetheless, the Seigmunds seem to do a good business. The hired hand, whose name no one remembers, is one among many of the Hispanic men who drift into town from time to time, doing odd jobs for local farmers and ranchers for a few months before moving on. Some people in McDade refer to these men as "wetbacks," in part a racial slur, in part a comment on the likelihood that these men are in the United States illegally.

6 / Drinking Beer at Sam Earl's

McDade has no bar or tavern. The only place to buy beer is Dungan Drugs, generally known as "Sam Earl's," after owner Sam Earl Dungan (third from left). There has never been a pharmacy on the premises. The name on the sign derives from the days when Emma Dungan, Sam Earl's mother, ran the business. In addition to operating a drugstore-style soda fountain, she also stocked a wide variety of patent medicines. Sam Earl took over the store after his mother's death in 1969. Although he sells a lot of beer, he does not have a tavern license, which makes it illegal for his customers to drink inside the store. There's no law against drinking out on the sidewalk, however, so a number of people—generally known in McDade as "the street people"—like to sit out front and drink. Quite a crowd can gather on summer evenings and weekend afternoons. They talk, drink, laugh, and generally have a good time. Sometimes they get loud and boisterous. Many people in town dislike these open-air parties. George Seigmund, whose grocery is two doors down and the only other business uptown, is one of those who disapprove. Some people, most of them Baptists, refuse to do business at Sam Earl's. Others, none of them Baptists, will not shop at Seigmund's. Most McDade residents, however, patronize both places. They can't buy beer at Seigmund's or get much in the way of groceries at Sam Earl's.

7 / Reverend Clifton Franks and Choir, McDade Baptist Church

Reverend Clifton Franks (seated), pastor of the McDade Baptist Church, was strongly opposed to both drinking and dancing. In 1984, when the Watermelon Festival Association instituted a Friday night street dance, an event at which beer would be sold, as part of the annual festival, he was greatly annoyed. He was angered again the following year when a member of his congregation was elected president of the Watermelon Festival Association but refused to take his advice and cancel the dance. Reverend Franks believed everything that happened in the world was part of a battle between good and evil. In one 1984 sermon, he expressed his belief that Satan had a hand in designing network television schedules, since "the best shows" were always on Wednesday and Sunday nights, the nights of his church's prayer meetings. Reverend Franks died suddenly in September 1985 of a heart attack he suffered while pushing his wife's stalled car on the shoulder of U.S. 290. He was forty-seven years old.

8 / VFW Color Guard, Watermelon Festival Parade

The high point of McDade's social year is the annual Watermelon Festival, held on the second weekend in July. Started in 1948 to raise money for McDade's school, it has grown over the years into an event that requires the year-round volunteer energies of many in the community. The McDade Watermelon Festival Association holds monthly meetings throughout the year, but as festival time approaches, it usually becomes necessary to meet more frequently. The final couple of weeks before the festival are always hectic, with some people having to take time off from their jobs to make sure everything gets done in time. Every year, it seems, tempers get short in the last-minute confusion, and some people quit, swearing they'll never work on the festival again. Usually they change their minds, but not always, especially in recent years.

9 / People Arriving, Three Oaks Cemetery Picnic

Many of McDade's older families have their own cemeteries. These cemeteries are usually in the country, on land once owned by the first member of the family to settle in the area. Three interrelated families, the Baumgartens, the Browns, and the Goerlitzes, bury their dead at Three Oaks Cemetery, located about two miles west of McDade. Members of these families have formed the Three Oaks Cemetery Association to maintain the cemetery and to determine who will be allowed burial there. Every year, on the first Sunday in June, the association holds a picnic at the cemetery, inviting friends and relatives from throughout the area. This picture shows members of the Goerlitz family—Lily (Goerlitz) Noack (in car), her daughter Wanda Pinkard, and Wanda's daughter Bridget—arriving at the 1989 picnic. The picnic provides an occasion for a major cleanup of the grounds and functions as the association's annual business meeting. At the 1989 meeting Lily's brother Erhard Goerlitz, the association president since 1977, was once again elected unanimously. He maintains the cemetery and organizes the picnic every year. He says that anyone who wishes to can be buried at Three Oaks Cemetery.

10 / **Jack and Randall Lewis**

Loud and good-natured, Jack Lewis is one of McDade's "street people"—the group that regularly gathers in front of Sam Earl's to drink beer and socialize. He works as a plumber whenever, and wherever, he can. During the early 1980s, when the Texas economy was booming, he could always "get on" at one of several large construction projects underway in Austin. Since then, however, he has worked only sporadically and has often had to travel as far as Houston, 130 miles away, to find work. During the warm summer months, Jack often stops by Sam Earl's late in the afternoon to drink a few beers. His son, Randall, sometimes meets him there. Jack is one of thirteen children, most of whom still live in or around McDade. His wife, Carolyn, is also from one of the area's large families. Randall is their only child.

11 / Tori Neidig's First Permanent

Eleven-year-old Tori Neidig had just started the fifth grade when her mother, Debbie Neidig (left), and family friend Linda Haverland gave her her first permanent. During the 1986–87 school year, the McDade PTA began sponsoring occasional Friday night dances for the school kids. These were the first dances that had ever been held at the McDade School, and some people in town objected to them. Tori's permanent was in honor of the first of these dances.

12 / **Break Dancing**

McDade is no longer as isolated as it used to be. Many of its residents, people who are still healthy and active, remember when a trip to Austin was a major undertaking. Today, you can be there and back in a morning. But even those who rarely leave McDade find their lives influenced by the sounds, images, and attitudes of modern American culture. Radio and television have given everyone access to the contemporary world. This is especially important to McDade's young people: with so little that interests them going on in their hometown, they pay close attention to what they see and hear broadcast each day. Many of them spend what money they have on the paraphernalia they need to stay current. In general, they seem to think that everything exciting, everything worthwhile, comes from somewhere other than McDade.

13 / McDade School Board, Sixth-Grade Graduation

The town's children attend school in McDade through only the sixth grade. After that, they attend middle school and high school in one of the larger towns nearby, with the McDade Independent School District paying their tuition fees. Some people, many of them newcomers to town, think McDade should give up having its own school. They say that the children's education would be better if McDade were to consolidate with the Elgin or Bastrop school districts. They also think consolidation would lower their property taxes. Most of those who have been in town for any length of time, however, are adamant about keeping the school in McDade. They believe that the education that was good enough for them should be good enough for their children. Besides, the kids have to leave McDade to go to school all too soon as it is. They also believe the school provides the community with a focal point it would otherwise lack. Being unincorporated, McDade has no mayor or city council. The school board is the closest thing there is to local government, and the school building is the town's community center and city hall. In 1987, the pro- and anti-school factions came into open and sometimes bitter conflict about whether to retain long-time superintendent and principal Thomas Baca (front row, far left). Finally, after one school board had voted not to renew Baca's contract, a newly elected board reversed that decision. Both votes resulted in a great deal of anger, some of which has yet to dissipate.

14 / Fred and Freda Wilson

Freda Wilson is not native to McDade, or even a Texan. She was born and raised in England and met her husband, Wallace, a McDade native, while he was stationed near her home during World War II. She is seen here with her son, Fred, at a CPR training session held on a Saturday afternoon in the Fellowship Hall of the McDade Baptist Church. Fred is a loyal and loving son, just as Freda has always been a devoted mother. On one occasion, at a benefit auction, he bid up an item that Freda had donated (a vase commemorating the wedding of Britain's Prince Charles) so it wouldn't sell for less than she thought it should. Fred attended the University of Texas in the late 1960s, but he was not happy there, finding campus lifestyles of the time in conflict with the values he had been raised with. After a few semesters, he quit school and moved back to McDade. He and his family now live in a handsome new home just down the road from the house he grew up in. They are active members of the McDade Baptist Church, as are Wallace and Freda. In 1985 and 1986, Fred was president of the McDade Watermelon Festival Association. He commutes daily to Austin, where he works for IBM.

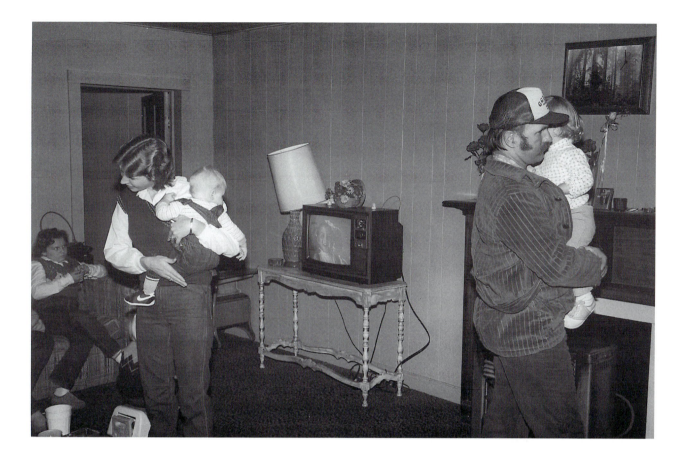

15 / Gathering Up the Kids, Randall Lewis's Birthday Party

Every January, Jack and Carolyn Lewis put on a large birthday party for their son Randall (fig. 10). Family and friends of all ages, ranging from newborn babies to people well into their eighties, gather at the Lewis's for a long afternoon and evening of eating, drinking, and talking. Some leave early, like Debbie Schkade and Roger Smith, seen here gathering up their children; others will end up spending the night. Most of the kids at this party spent the evening watching television, which is the source of many of their ideas about the world. Even though what they see on television rarely bears much resemblance to their own daily lives, they generally consider the world it depicts to be more "real" than the one they live in. Television's glamorous characters and their fast-paced adventures sometimes make the kids' own small-town lives seem dreary in comparison. Many of the children already resent the fact that "nothing ever happens" in McDade.

CHAPTER 2

Individuals

16 / **Adeline Eschberger**

Adeline Eschberger's family is among the oldest in the area. She is proud of that. The large photograph on the wall is of her grandmother, who emigrated from Germany to Texas in the 1850s. The photograph on the top right shows a man and a woman sitting in a horse-drawn buggy, the woman holding a baby. That baby is Adeline, the couple her parents. She still remembers riding in the buggy. Adeline grew up in the house her father was born in, on land her grandfather cleared before the Civil War. Her brother Dan and his family still live in that house, two miles north of McDade, where Dan still farms. Adeline now lives in a comfortable home in town, a house that her husband, Alvin, built in 1945. Adeline has multiple sclerosis and cannot walk unassisted. She uses a wheelchair around the house and a walker when she goes out. She and Alvin lead an active social life, both in McDade and in other communities nearby. Most of the people they socialize with are, like themselves, of German descent.

17 / Lucille Morrison

Before her death in 1985, Lucille Morrison lived in a tiny, one-room house near uptown McDade. During the mid-1970s, she operated a business known as The Beer Hut out of the house, in defiance of McDade's longtime town ban on the sale of alcohol. She was married to Marvin Farris for many years but took her maiden name back when their marriage broke up. Even though she lived alone after that, Lucille had little time to herself. In addition to watching her grandchildren on weekday afternoons, she also cared for her invalid mother, who lived in a mobile home next door. Lucille died suddenly, of a stroke, in 1985. Marvin's second wife, Mary, now helps look after Lucille's mother and grandchildren.

18 / George Seigmund

Though George Seigmund has recently been a controversial figure in McDade, his grocery and feed business seems to thrive. In 1984, George and several others, believing that their property taxes were too high, formed the "Ad Hoc Committee" to look into how efficiently the McDade School was being run. Eventually, several members of this committee were elected to the school board. In January 1987, after several years of sometimes bitter wrangling, a board dominated by committee sympathizers voted not to renew Superintendent Thomas Baca's contract. The following May, however, a board with four new members on it reversed that decision and rehired Baca. This resulted in an attempt by Baca's opponents to dissolve the McDade Independent School District, a move that was soundly defeated in a November 1987 referendum. This series of events caused a lot of bitterness within the McDade community, much of which still remains. Several families have transferred their church memberships to churches in neighboring towns, and others have decided not to participate in the Watermelon Festival. Some refuse to send their children to the McDade School, choosing instead to pay tuition fees to the Elgin or Bastrop school districts and drive the kids to and from school every day. George Seigmund, who has several school-age grandchildren in McDade, pays for them to attend school in Elgin.

19 / Alvin Eschberger

Alvin Eschberger makes his living as a building contractor. He has become quite successful in recent years. He and his grandson, Greg Bernhard, are partners in the business, which is based in Elgin. A descendant of one of the area's early German settlers, Alvin grew up on a farm five miles north of McDade, near the Paint Creek Lutheran Church. As a child, his first language was German, and he still speaks with a noticeable accent. In 1945, he and his wife, Adeline (fig. 16), moved into McDade, where they built a substantial new home. He used stone hauled from the original Eschberger "home place" to build the fireplace in the family room. This picture was taken in that room. Above the fireplace is an aerial photograph of his house and property. He has recently built a newer home in Elgin where he and Adeline will retire to. He has equipped it with ramps, wide doorways, and an elevator to accommodate Adeline's wheelchair. He says he's ready to move anytime. Adeline, though, is reluctant to leave the house they've lived in for so many years and the community they've been part of for so long.

20 / John and Rhode Anderson

Rhode Anderson was born in McDade in 1891. For many years, she worked as a maid in the home of A. Y. Field, long the owner of McDade's only cotton gin. Until her death in 1985, she was the oldest person in town. John Anderson, originally from east Texas, was about twenty years younger than his wife. During the last several years of Rhode's life, when she was frequently bedridden, John would cook and do the housework, as well as look after her. He is generally well liked in McDade, though he rarely participates in community events. Although surrounding towns have sizable black populations, very few African Americans live in McDade. No one will admit to knowing why that is. There were more African Americans in McDade prior to World War II. Longtime residents can readily list a dozen or so black families, all of whom lived on the southern edge of town, where "new" Highway 20 (eventually to become U.S. 290) was built in 1952. After the war, they say, only the older generation of African Americans stayed in McDade, with most of their children and grandchildren leaving in the 1950s. "They all went to California," one town resident recalls. "They had more opportunity there. There was nothing for them here." At his wife's death, John Anderson became the only member of the all-black Weeping Willow Baptist Church—located on U.S. 290 about a mile south of uptown—to live in McDade.

21 / Wallace Wilson

Wallace Wilson is married to Freda Wilson (fig. 14). He was born and raised in the rural Oak Hill community, just a few miles south of McDade. "We were poor folks and didn't know it," he says. "We had all the food we wanted to eat. We just didn't have any money." Wallace remembers his father giving him and his brothers and sisters each a penny on Sunday mornings to put in the church collection plate. In early 1942, just after the bombing of Pearl Harbor, the federal government seized more than fifty-two thousand acres just south of McDade. The War Department built Camp Swift, which eventually became one of the army's largest World War II training facilities, on this land, obliterating Oak Hill in the process. Many families, including Wallace's, had to leave their homes. Wallace's father bought a lot in McDade and built a house there, on the same site where Wallace and Freda's son, Fred, now has his house. After World War II, much of the Camp Swift land was offered for sale back to its original owners. Wallace's older brother Wendell bought the "home place" back, and for years Wallace would drive out to his boyhood home every week or so to hunt squirrels or rabbits or "just to be in nature." He would often take Fred or Fred's son, Brandon, with him. In 1988, Wendell sold the land to a doctor from Houston. Although Wallace says it was all right with him, he misses being able to walk on the land. There are other places he can go to hunt or walk, he says, but "it's just not the same."

22 / Michael Farris and Dwayne White

Before her death, Lucille Morrison (fig. 17) looked after her grandchildren, including cousins Michael Farris (in wagon) and Dwayne White, on school-day afternoons and during school vacations. Since then, Dwayne has moved to Fort Worth to be with his father, and Michael spends his afternoons watching television at the home of his step-grandmother, Mary Farris. Michael's younger brother, David, has recently returned to McDade to stay with their mother's side of the family. Before that, David had lived with their father, who is separated from their mother. Michael and David had been apart for so long that they barely remembered each other when David first returned to McDade.

23 / The Dunkin Children

Sam and Debbie Dunkin's children—Finch, Dempsey, Wallace, and Leah (oldest to youngest)—all do a share of the work on the family's small ranch, located two miles south of McDade, in what was once Oak Hill. Sam and Debbie are old-fashioned parents, believing in what they call a "family first" approach to child rearing. They are very religious, one of the few young families active in the McDade Baptist Church. Small pieces of paper with handcopied scriptural passages on them are taped up throughout their house. Debbie does not work, except for occasionally substituting at the McDade School. She would rather stay home with the kids than have the luxuries an extra income could buy. Both she and Sam think their rural lifestyle is good for their children. Even kids who live in towns as small as McDade, they believe, too often come into contact with bad influences. They prefer having the closer control over their children that the relative seclusion of ranch life provides. Their oldest child, Finch, attends junior high school in Elgin. He has made the honor roll several times since starting there. Supporters of the McDade school system often point to Finch, and other McDade students like him, as evidence that the school is providing the town's children with a good elementary education. Sam and Debbie named their youngest son, Wallace, after Wallace Wilson (fig. 21). Before he and Debbie met, Sam was briefly married to Deborah Wilson, Wallace's daughter. Although that marriage didn't last—both Sam and Deborah were very young—there were no lasting hard feelings; the Wilsons and the Dunkins are still very close.

24 / Rachel Bright

Rachel Bright is the oldest of Peggy Fisher's (fig. 4) three children. At age fourteen, when this picture was taken, she was almost grown up, or so she believed. Tall and attractive, she hoped to become a model someday. She resented her family's low economic status and the slow pace of life in McDade. She thought she would find life more exciting elsewhere and used to tell people that she was planning to leave McDade as soon as she could. At sixteen, Rachel dropped out of Bastrop High School—"to achieve her own personal freedom," her mother says. A year later she got married and in early 1988, at age seventeen, gave birth to a son. She and her family now live next door to Peggy, in a rent-house owned by her grandfather, Alton Greenhaw.

25 / Mary Farris

Mary Farris lives in a mobile home with her husband, Marvin. Marvin's first wife was Lucille Morrison (fig. 17). Michael Farris and Dwayne White (fig. 22) are his grandsons. Mary and Marvin have no children of their own. Even so, Mary often baby-sits many of the kids in the widely extended Farris family. She also does housework and laundry for some of the family's working mothers. Since Lucille Morrison's death, Mary has become especially close to Marvin and Lucille's daughter Doris, who is Michael's mother. Mary seems to enjoy her role as the central female figure in a complicated network of family interrelationships, even though she didn't marry into the family until late in life and has no blood ties to any of its members. She used to volunteer at the McDade School, chaperoning dances and helping with various fund-raisers. In 1987, however, after Thomas Baca was hired back as principal and superintendent, Mary became one of the school's most vocal critics. She will no longer have anything to do with any of its activities nor will she help with the Watermelon Festival. She wishes the family could afford to send its children to school in Elgin.

26 / Linda Haverland

Linda Haverland moved to McDade from California in 1968. Her mother, a native of McDade, was terminally ill with cancer and had come home to die, bringing her children with her. Linda was seventeen at the time. She graduated from Elgin High School in 1969, three months after her mother's death. Shortly after graduating she married Willie Haverland. She is seen here on the patio of the modern brick home she and Willie built near uptown McDade in 1984. Although they have never had any children of their own, in many ways they began their marriage as parents to Linda's much younger brother, who was born in 1966. Linda has worked for Sam Earl Dungan since 1971, minding his store on weekday afternoons and most Saturdays. This has made her a central figure in McDade, especially in the eyes of the town's children (at least those whose parents will allow them to go to Sam Earl's). She is always at the store when the kids stop by after school for a "soda water" or a microwaved cheeseburger, and several mothers trust her to keep an informal eye on their children in the late afternoons. Linda is very outgoing. She is one of the loudest of the "street people" who gather in front of Sam Earl's to drink beer. During the 1987 controversy over whether to retain Thomas Baca as superintendent and principal of the McDade School, the street people were among Baca's most vocal supporters. They felt he had done nothing to deserve being let go and that most of his opponents were "newcomers" who were trying to "change McDade." The street people often attended school board meetings as a group, and they were never shy about letting their opinions be known.

27 / Leonard Ray Kastner and Donny Kastner

Leonard Ray Kastner is from one of McDade's largest and oldest families. He married into one of the other old families in town, the Goerlitzes. Although he and his family live in Lexington, twenty-one miles away, Leonard Ray "runs cattle" near McDade, on land owned by his mother. He comes to McDade several times a week to check on the cattle, buying whatever feed he needs from George Seigmund. For a father and son, Leonard Ray and Donny get along pretty well; they share much of the work on the ranch, and they often hunt or fish together. Donny is now a student at Texas A&M University, and he expects to take over the ranch one day. He used to play football for Lexington High School, the school to which many parents in McDade—especially those of German extraction—send their children after they finish grade school in McDade. Lexington is north and east of McDade—away from Austin—and is still primarily an agricultural community. Many of its residents are of German descent, and, like McDade, Lexington has very few African American citizens. Elgin, where most of the rest of McDade's children attend junior high and high school, is nine miles west of McDade—toward Austin—and seems to become less and less of an agricultural community with each passing year. Nearly half of Elgin's residents are black or Hispanic.

28 / Mary and Laura Cayton

For most of the 1980s, Mary and Laura Cayton, mother and daughter, lived with their husbands and children on the Cayton Ranch, several miles north of McDade. Although the Cayton family had roots in the McDade area, Mary and her husband, Clyde, both grew up in Houston, and they raised their family there. Clyde retired from his job with a Houston chemical company in 1978, and soon afterward he and Mary moved onto the seven hundred-acre ranch he had purchased from his grandfather in 1942. Laura and her family moved to the ranch in 1981. After running unsuccessfully for a seat on the McDade School Board, and after being rebuffed in her attempts to reorganize the McDade Historical Society, Laura devoted herself to selling real estate. She specialized in locating rural properties for affluent Austinites who wanted to move out of the city, and she became quite successful at it. She and her husband, Mickey Maness, built a comfortable house on a wooded portion of the ranch, close to the highest hilltop on the property, where her parents had built a handsome new home. Laura's business suffered when the Texas economy crashed in the mid-1980s. Several speculative real estate investments turned out badly for her, and she eventually had to declare bankruptcy. She and Mickey broke up, and their two children went to live with him. In 1989, Laura rented out her house on the ranch and moved into a small apartment in Austin.

29 / Stella and Frank Kastner

Frank Kastner, born in 1928, has never married. He has lived most of his life with his widowed mother, Stella. "I love Mama dearly," he once said, "and I'll stay with her till she dies. But then I'm getting out." As it turned out, Frank was wrong. Because of his own poor health—he's been in and out of the hospital with diabetes-related problems several times in recent years—Frank eventually became unable to take care of his mother. In 1989, she went to live with Frank's sister in Austin, while Frank stayed in McDade. Frank once ran a beer hall and domino parlor in a "cut-and-shoot" part of Elgin. He has several knife scars on his arms and torso from those days. More recently, he worked as an orderly at the Travis State School, an institution in Austin for the mentally disabled, but he had to quit because of his health. For much of his life, Frank drank heavily, but in 1985 his doctor finally persuaded him to stop. If he didn't quit drinking, the doctor told him, he would probably die very soon. Leonard Ray Kastner (fig. 27) and Frank are first cousins.

30 / Peggy Fisher with Her Grandson David Bright

Peggy Fisher (fig. 4) enjoys playing with her grandson, David Bright, but she will not "keep" him for any length of time. She claims she doesn't have the patience to take care of a baby. "I'm still raising my own three kids," she says, "and I'm too young to be a grandmother." Peggy was born in 1943. She does not hide her irritation with her daughter Rachel (fig. 24) for becoming pregnant so early in life. She thinks that Rachel and her husband, Brian, were "careless" and have caused the whole family extra difficulties, both financial and emotional. Rachel gave birth to a second child, a boy named John, in the summer of 1989. The dog in the picture is named Mindy. She is one of several dogs that Peggy provides a home for. Peggy has so many cats that they go nameless.

31 / Doug Farris

Doug Farris is the youngest of eleven children. At age twenty-seven, he still lives at home with his mother, Minnie Lee Farris. Several of his brothers and sisters live in McDade, and none of them lives farther away than Austin. Doug has had trouble finding steady work, but he still manages to scrape together thirty-five dollars every week to pay for karate lessons in Elgin. He says he's been unlucky in his search for a job. One of his sisters says it has more to do with his "have fun all night, sleep all day" attitude toward life. Doug hopes to land a job at the Elgin-Butler Brick Company, a brick manufacturing business located halfway between McDade and Elgin. Several people from McDade, including two of Doug's brothers, work at "the brickyard." Doug and his friends spend a lot of time working on automobiles. The car in this picture is a 1975 Plymouth Doug bought for two hundred dollars at an Austin junkyard and towed to McDade. He hoped to get it running in time to be available for an upcoming opening at the brickyard that his karate teacher, "one of the bosses there," had "sort of promised" him. His oldest sister, Evelyn Wolf, says it would make their mother "happier than anything" if he could start working there.

32 / Calvin Lowery

Calvin Lowery, born on a north Texas cotton farm in 1895, has lived in McDade since 1932. "Hard times and no work" forced him to leave his native Cooke County. "There wasn't a dollar to be had in that country, no matter how hard you worked," he recalls. "Lots of folks were leaving." Along with his wife, Lorene, and their two baby daughters, he came south to Austin, where Lorene's brother-in-law, a section foreman for the Southern Pacific, had promised Calvin a job on a track maintenance crew. That job fell through, but a few months later he found Calvin a spot on the crew that worked the section of track just east of Austin. The Lowerys settled in McDade, one of the towns along that stretch of track. Calvin worked for the railroad until 1955, when his crew was consolidated with another and, at age sixty, he was forcibly retired. After that he did odd jobs in and around McDade and sold produce from his garden to supplement his pension. Until recently he worked long hours in his two-acre garden plot and keeping up his modest home. A small man, bent with age, he always worked very hard. In 1989, four years after this picture was taken, he suffered a stroke. Although he has recovered more fully than anyone had dared to hope—he still lives at home, gets around pretty well using a cane, and talks with his speech only slightly slurred—he can no longer do much work.

33 / Chris Heiser

Before moving to Austin in 1987, Chris Heiser lived in McDade with his mother and sister in a dilapidated old house owned by his grandfather, Bill Rutherford. Supposedly, the house was one of the oldest buildings in McDade, having served as a way station on the stagecoach route between Austin and Houston. Chris was seven when this picture was taken, and he was already something of a rebel. He had saved his allowance for several weeks before going to Cat Dugan's barbershop and having his hair cut into a Mohawk. Before getting started, Cat called Chris's mother, Gale Rutherford, to make sure the haircut was okay with her. She said it was. The Mohawk lasted less than a week. The other kids in town teased Chris so mercilessly that he went back to Cat and had her shave it off. She didn't charge him any extra.

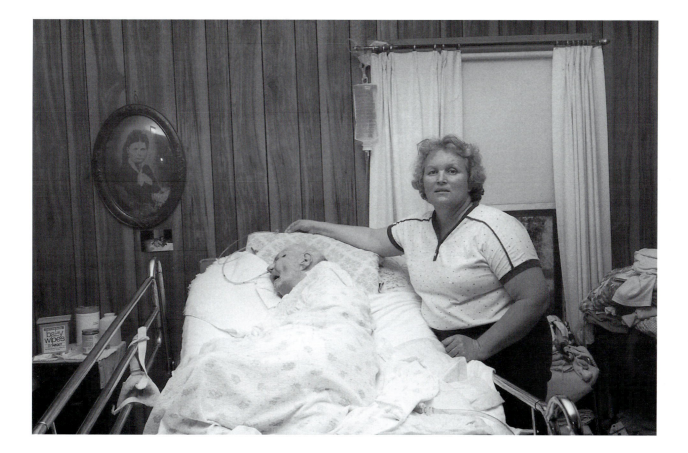

34 / Martha and Evelyn Wolf

Some families in McDade care for their infirm elderly at home. Until Martha Wolf's death in 1985, her daughter-in-law Evelyn (Farris) Wolf spent much of her time taking care of the bedridden older woman in the family's small home. All of Martha Wolf's children, including Evelyn's husband, Dan, and Adeline Eschberger (fig. 16), were born in this house. The older Mrs. Wolf and her husband both died in it. Evelyn has had a lot of practice taking care of people. She was the oldest of eleven children whose mother was often sick, so she spent much of her childhood caring for her younger brothers and sisters, including Doug Farris (fig. 31). Evelyn has also raised four children of her own. At the time of his mothers' death, Dan Wolf was working a full-time night job in Bastrop, so Evelyn had also taken on much of the responsibility for the family's small truck-farming business. After her mother-in-law's death, Evelyn no longer had to spend so much of her time at home, so she became involved with the Bastrop County Historical Society, working on a project to identify unmarked graves in the county's dozens of rural cemeteries. As a result of McDade's school controversies, however, Evelyn and the woman in charge of the project had a falling out, so Evelyn now pursues her interest in local history on her own.

CHAPTER 3

Social Life

35 / Ice Cream Social, McDade Historical Society

The McDade Historical Society occupies what was once the Rockfront Saloon in uptown McDade. The saloon was the site of the vigilante kidnappings that precipitated an infamous gun battle on Christmas Day 1883. The night before, an anonymous group of "law-abiding citizens" had seized three men who were drinking in the saloon and lynched them. These men were believed to be members of the Notchcutters, a gang of cattle rustlers and horse thieves, who usually hid out in the rugged country a few miles north of McDade. The next day, friends of the dead men came to town, and a bloody gunfight ensued, leaving three more men dead. Respectable people throughout the state were horrified, and the governor sent units of the state militia to McDade to keep the peace. Many local undesirables left town soon afterward. The old saloon is now in bad shape, requiring extensive replastering and a new roof. Most of the McDade Historical Society's funds go into maintaining the building. This ice cream social, a fund raiser featuring music by The Country Cousins from Bastrop, was held on a beautiful moonlit night. The evening ended with the band playing the traditional hymn "Amazing Grace," with most of those present singing along. In the background of this picture, Ray McDavid (fig. 5), at left, and Erhard Goerlitz (fig. 3) eat ice cream and listen to the music. Ray's grandfather, Thad McLemore, was one of the men seized out of the Rockfront Saloon in 1883 and hanged.

36 / **Bobbing For Apples, Halloween Fair**

The McDade PTA sponsors fund-raisers throughout the school year: seasonal fairs, auctions of baked goods, and hamburger suppers are typical. In addition to raising modest amounts of money for school activities, these affairs give parents a chance to socialize while the children entertain themselves. Such functions also keep people's attention focused on community concerns. In the past, nearly everyone in town attended these events, whether they had children in the school or not. More recently, though, since all the controversy over the school, fewer people participate. In this picture, David Franks, son of Reverend Clifton Franks (fig. 7), bobs for an apple while Gale Rutherford, the school custodian at the time, looks on. Gale is the mother of Chris Heiser (fig. 33.) She and her family have since moved to Austin, where she hoped to find a better-paying job. David's family also left McDade for Austin soon after his father's death in 1985.

37 / Les and Debbie Schubert, Schubert-Schulz Wedding Reception

Les Schubert and Debbie Schulz married in the spring of 1987. Both come from large German families, and their wedding was one of the year's big social events. After a traditional wedding ceremony at McDade's Faith Lutheran Church, Debbie's family hosted a reception at the Sons of Herman Hall in Giddings. More than seven hundred people attended. After a barbecue dinner and the customary toasts and speeches, the guests danced and drank beer till well past midnight. Debbie was born and raised in McDade; Les is from Lexington. They met while they were students at Lexington High School. Even though Lexington, twenty-one miles away, is considerably farther from McDade than either Elgin or Bastrop, nearly all of McDade's German families send their children to school in Lexington after they finish sixth grade at the McDade School. In part, this is because Lexington is a predominantly German community. Some say it is also because there are few African Americans in Lexington. Not surprisingly, there have been a number of McDade-Lexington weddings since so many McDade students started attending school there.

38 / Renewing Acquaintances, Kastner Family Reunion

The Kastner family holds its annual reunion in September, usually in the Fellowship Hall of McDade's Faith Lutheran Church. On the right, first cousins Hilda (Kastner) Neidig (seated) and Catherine (Kastner) Wolf exchange greetings. Both have lived in McDade all their lives. On the left is Catherine Wolf's sister, Francis (Kastner) Munson, who lives in Elgin. Beyond her, at the table, are McDade residents Morris Kastner, Frank Kastner (fig. 29), and Richard Neidig. The Kastners are one of McDade's oldest families, and they were once one of its largest. The first Kastner in McDade—Julius Kastner Sr.—came to the area in the 1880s. Most of the people in this picture are his grandchildren. He and his wife had sixteen children, nearly all of whom stayed in McDade and had children of their own. Many from that third generation still live in McDade, but most of their children left town when they reached adulthood. Today, there are only five school-age children in McDade who are descended from Julius Kastner Sr., none of whom bears the Kastner name. "It seems like we're dwindling down till there's hardly none left," says Ivy Ann (Kastner) Cronin, the family reunion's main organizer. Ivy Ann works hard at staying in touch with those family members who no longer live in McDade, and she always tries to get them to come back for the reunion. Many of them do, but others do not. Almost every year, the number of people attending the reunion decreases.

39 / Embrace, McDade Baptist Church

Reverend Jerre Guthrie (right) embraces Jack Taylor after a 1989 revival service at the McDade Baptist Church. Jerre became the full-time pastor there in June 1988. After the death of Reverend Clifton Franks in 1985, the church had a hard time finding a replacement. For much of 1986, a young minister just out of seminary served as interim pastor, but the congregation eventually decided not to "call" him on a permanent basis. After he left, the church went back to relying on a pool of substitute clergymen supplied by the Austin Baptist Association. Jerre was one of these substitute ministers and was sent to preach in McDade one Sunday in April 1988. He had never been to McDade before. Jerre and the congregation liked each other immediately. "I had a sense I fit here, that this was where the Lord wanted me," he says. Wallace Wilson (fig. 21), a member of the church's Pulpit Selection Committee, agrees: "I'm a believer in that the good Lord will have a man for us, and when we find him we'll know it. When Brother Jerre came here, there was no doubt in my mind." Jerre preached in McDade the next several Sundays and returned in midweek to lead the Wednesday night prayer meetings as well. Near the end of May, the congregation voted unanimously to "call" him to be the church's full-time pastor, and he accepted. He and his wife, Carolyn, moved to McDade the following week and took up residence in a small house owned by the church.

40 / Revival Service, McDade Baptist Church

Both Jerre Guthrie and his wife, Carolyn, believe that the controversy over the school has left McDade in need of "a healing spirit." They hope they can help provide that. In January 1989, they organized a weeklong revival at the McDade Baptist Church. An old friend, evangelist Fred McCoy, was coming to visit them in their new home, so they decided to put him to work. In the days before Fred's visit, Jerre "knocked on every door in town" to spread the word about the upcoming week of evening revival services. Both he and Carolyn encouraged everyone they ran into to attend. They emphasized that the revival was not just for church members, but for the entire community. Attendance was nonetheless modest, averaging about forty people per night, most of them from among the town's Baptists. A few members of McDade's other churches and even a couple of nonchurchgoers came to some of the services, but neither of the other two clergymen in town attended. The Guthries were disappointed but would not let themselves be discouraged. "We had three people that made a profession of faith in Christ, and two people that had a spiritual renewal," Jerre says, and he thinks they "planted some seeds" as well. Both he and Carolyn had their spirits buoyed by seeing their old friend Fred McCoy again and by organizing the revival. "In some ways," Carolyn says, "the revival was more for Jerre and me than even for the church. It gave us the pumping up that we needed."

41 / Beer Drinkers, Uptown McDade

When the weather is warm, which is much of the year in central Texas, McDade's "street people" often gather uptown on weekend afternoons or weekday evenings. Seen in this picture, as they lean on a parked pickup and "tell some lies," are Jack Lewis (fig. 10), Linda Haverland (fig. 26), John Strong, Willie Haverland, and Donnie Alanis. In the background is Henry Grimes. All of these people except Henry are regulars uptown. None except Henry goes to church. Linda attended one of the evening services during the revival at the Baptist Church—both out of curiosity and because Jerre Guthrie made a point of inviting her—but she has not been back since. She tried to get Willie, her husband, to go to the revival with her, but he refused, saying he was afraid he'd be "saved" and that would be "the end of all my fun." McDade's street people strongly supported Thomas Baca during the 1987 school controversy. They thought he was being unfairly harassed by people who did not have McDade's best interests at heart. Most of Baca's critics, they claimed, were new to town and did not understand, or respect, the feelings of most longtime McDade residents regarding the education of their children. Emblematic of the street people's support for Baca was a bumper sticker they printed up and distributed around town when tensions were at their height. The sticker read: "McDade: Love It or Leave It, but Don't Change It!" Even today, some people still proudly display this bumper sticker, identifying themselves as part of the group that successfully fought against unwanted change at the McDade School.

42 / The Grand March, Schubert-Schulz Wedding Reception

In accordance with German-Texan tradition, the dancing at Les and Debbie Schubert's wedding reception (fig. 37) began with the "Grand March"—a dance in which the newlyweds and their wedding party lead the rest of the guests in a complicated group march. Several times during the march the dancers join hands, as in this picture, and wind around the dance floor in a long, sinuous line. Each time, they regroup and march again, always with someone new. Only the newlyweds and members of the wedding party remain with their original partners. The bride and groom stay front and center for the entire dance, the focus of everyone's attention. After about half an hour, the march ends with the newlyweds dancing alone—to "their song"—in the middle of a large circle formed by the other dancers. Abruptly, and with a shout, the circle closes in on them, then pulls away. This happens several times before the bride and groom are finally left alone to dance, and usually to kiss, for the remaining few bars of the song. The wedding party waits to join them on the dance floor until the second song, usually chosen by the maid of honor. After that, the dance floor is open to everyone. The music then picks up tempo, the beer starts to flow, and the real partying begins.

43 / Fixing Dessert, Thanksgiving

One branch of the Eschberger family celebrates Thanksgiving at Laverne (Albrecht) Mattiza's home in Paige, a tiny, mostly German community seven miles east of McDade. On this Thanksgiving Day, in 1985, almost fifty people were present, and the small house seemed about to burst. As dinnertime approached, the women began getting things ready, and the men retreated to the garage to watch football and drink beer. This left the women more room to work and the kids some room to run around. In this picture, Gertrude Eschberger holds her grandson Justin Kessler, while her niece Sandy Botkin ices a cake with whipped cream. On the left, Randall Lewis (fig. 10), another of Gertrude Eschberger's grandsons, makes off with a handful of cookies.

44 / George Moore with Sausage, Griffith-Pohler Wedding Reception

The McDade Veterans of Foreign Wars Post 8313 sometimes caters local social events as a way of raising money. In this picture, George Moore carries a load of smoked sausage in to be served at the wedding reception of Jerry Griffith and Gina Pohler. Behind him are fellow VFW members James Behrend, Erhard Goerlitz, and Henry Grimes. The post's specialty is chopped barbecue beef and sausage, served in a tangy sauce. They usually cook the meat at the VFW Hall, then take it to the festivities in a pickup truck whose bed they have equipped with the specially insulated shell of an old refrigerator. This keeps the meat steaming hot. The wives of VFW members, officially known as the VFW Ladies Auxiliary, usually prepare the traditional barbecue trimmings—cole slaw, potato salad, and pinto beans. They also help serve the meal. Most of the men in the McDade VFW are veterans of World War II; others served in Korea. Even though several Vietnam veterans live in McDade, none of them belongs to the VFW.

45 / Saluting the Flag, Extension Homemaker Club Meeting

Many of McDade's middle-aged women belong to the Extension Homemaker Club, a statewide organization sponsored by the Texas Agricultural Extension Service at Texas A&M University and administered through the local offices of County Extension Agents. The McDade club meets monthly, usually
in the home of one of its members, though this meeting was held in the Fellowship Hall of McDade's
Faith Lutheran Church. At these meetings, the women trade recipes, home remedies, and other useful
information. Unless the club has scheduled a guest speaker, one of the members usually prepares a short
program for presentation to the others. At this 1988 meeting, Louise Goerlitz (right) discussed various
parasites that attack local trees and ways to combat them. Mrs. Goerlitz has written the *Elgin Courier's*
"News from McDade" column since 1976. She is married to Erhard Goerlitz (fig. 35).

46 / Boiling Crawfish, Randall Lewis's Seventh Birthday Party

Randall Lewis's birthday party—which his parents, Jack and Carolyn, put on every January (fig. 15)—has become a community event over the last few years, attracting friends and relatives from miles around. In this picture, some of Randall's cousins from east Texas boil a batch of crawfish. About two hundred people attended this party, held in 1985. They ranged in age from infants to people well into their eighties. The crowd consumed great quantities of beer and food, and a lot of money changed hands in all-night poker games. This was the last of Randall's birthday parties that Jack and Carolyn held in their home. Since then, they have rented the Paige Community Center for the party. McDade has no such public facility. Some members of the Watermelon Festival Association hope to put a portion of future festival proceeds into building one. Others involved with the festival oppose this idea.

47 / Covered-Dish Lunch, Faith Lutheran Church

McDade's Faith Lutheran Church installed Ed Steinbring (the man on the right) as its new pastor in 1985. On his first Sunday, after a special installation service, the congregation welcomed him with a covered-dish lunch. Most of the descendants of McDade's early German settlers attend Faith Lutheran. They are a tightly knit group, bound together by generations of kinship, intermarriage, and shared history. This does not mean they always get along. In fact, the 1987 school controversy severely split the congregation. With two church members, one on either side of the Thomas Baca issue, already on the school board, two others angrily opposed each other for one of the board's vacant seats. As tempers flared throughout McDade, Ed tried to get the membership of Faith Lutheran "to disagree agreeably," but to no avail. In the end, both sides accused him of improperly taking the other side, and members of three extended families (including those of both school board candidates) quit the church. These defections amounted to almost 20 percent of Faith Lutheran's active adult membership. Not everyone, though, believes that Ed's attempts to keep peace within the church, or even McDade's school controversy, were at the root of the problem. Instead, people point to the past and tell how Faith Lutheran's predecessor, the Siloah Evangelical Lutheran Church, had disbanded in 1943 after two of its members came to blows during services one Sunday. The heads of the two opposing families that quit Faith Lutheran in 1987 are the grandsons of the men who fought in 1943.

CHAPTER 4

The Watermelon Festival

48 / Preparing the Parade Float, McDade Watermelon Festival

McDade held its first Watermelon Festival in 1948 as a fund-raiser for the town's school. The festival was such a success that first year, it became established as an annual event, always held on the second weekend in July. It has grown to involve, or at least affect, nearly everyone in town. In this 1989 picture, Virgil King helps Lynn Johnson assemble McDade's parade float. Three weeks earlier, at the annual Watermelon Queens' Revue, Lynn's daughter Michelle had been elected McDade's Teenage Watermelon Queen for 1989, succeeding Virgil's daughter Becky, who was the 1988 queen. Michelle and 1989 princess Elaine Edmonson, who had placed second in the balloting, will ride on the float for the first time in the Watermelon Festival's Saturday afternoon parade. The Tiny Tot queen and princess will ride with them. On Saturday night, the outgoing queens will turn over their crowns and scepters to the new queens in an elaborate coronation ceremony. Rural communities from throughout central Texas join in the festivities by sending their parade floats along with their own "royalty" to ride on the floats and act as courtiers at McDade's coronation ceremony. McDade will respond in kind by sending its float and the Watermelon queens to these other towns when they hold their festivals. The queens' parents are responsible for getting their daughters and the float to these other communities and for pulling the float in their parades. This can become quite a chore, as nearly every small town in central Texas has an annual festival that features a Saturday afternoon parade. Virgil King was not unhappy to see his daughter's year as queen come to an end.

49 / Watermelon Auction, McDade Watermelon Festival

Watermelons were once the McDade area's main cash crop. Freight trains quit stopping at McDade in the mid-1950s, however, leaving local growers without a cost-effective way of getting their melons to market. "When you had the train cars, you could go up there and sell a pickup load," Dan Wolf remembers, "but after the train quit, you had to have enough melons where you could load an eighteen-wheeler." As a result, local farmers stopped growing watermelons commercially. Nothing as reliable has ever replaced them as a cash crop. One of the Watermelon Festival's traditional events is the auction of locally grown prize melons. In 1985, when this picture was taken, the "Grand Champion" sold for more than $1,300, and none of the top twenty melons went for less than $150. As always, a professional livestock auctioneer donated his services and kept the bidding lively. Most of those who bid for melons own businesses in nearby towns. They consider buying a melon good advertising. During election years, politicians sometimes purchase melons. Originally, all festival profits went to the McDade School. In 1984, however, the Watermelon Festival Association began distributing portions of the proceeds among other community organizations. It also started holding onto a share of the money for future uses of its own, including the possible construction of a community center. Some people in town do not approve of this. They think all the money should go to the school, as the festival's founders intended.

50 / Watermelon Float, Watermelon Festival Parade

In the early 1980s, the Watermelon Festival Association paid almost three thousand dollars to have a new parade float built. The float is bright green and red, and it is festooned with plastic watermelons, whole and sliced, of various sizes. It folds up into a self-contained travel trailer for easy storage and towing. In this picture, taken in 1985, McDade's newly elected queens and princesses—Amy Skubiata, Vicki Long, Mitzi Mundine, and Melissa Moore (left to right)—await the start of the parade. Mothers Judy Mundine and Melba Skubiata look on. Melba was McDade's Teenage queen in 1972. Mitzi, the 1985 Teenage queen, was Tiny Tot queen in 1973. Being elected queen is no empty honor: it requires the girls to appear in as many parades around central Texas as they can. The parents of the Teenage queen and the Tiny Tot queen usually take turns transporting the girls and the float. If one of the queens can't make it, her princess and the princess's family are obliged to fill in. In recent years, the Watermelon Festival Association has started paying the queens' parents for their trouble. Even so, fewer and fewer girls have been entering the competition. Many girls and their parents don't seem to think the honor of being queen is worth all the headaches that come with it. This annoys some of those involved in past Watermelon Festivals. "All they have to do now is sit up there and look pretty," says one woman. "We had to borrow a farm wagon and fix it up as a float every time our girls went to a parade. And then we had to clean it up and return it to its owner as soon as we got home, even if it was late at night."

51 / Dancing, McDade Watermelon Festival

The McDade Watermelon Festival Association held its first dance in 1984. Since then, the Friday night street dances have become a regular feature of the festival. They have been very popular and have made the festival much more profitable than it had ever been. The decision to add to the festival's traditional single-day schedule of events was a controversial one, and many people resisted it. Some simply liked the Watermelon Festival the way it had always been and saw no reason to change it. Others opposed holding a dance because its organizers planned to sell beer. Reverend Clifton Franks of the McDade Baptist Church (fig. 7) led the opposition, angrily denouncing the dance at every opportunity. Very few members of his congregation attended the 1984 dance, and some refused to be involved with the festival at all that year. Despite opposition, the first dance was a big success. By spending the money necessary to hire a band with a loyal regional following and by sticking to their decision to sell beer, dance organizers succeeded in attracting people from throughout central Texas to McDade. Nearly one thousand people paid five dollars apiece to dance on McDade's lone uptown street. Between admissions and beer sales, the dance cleared over thirty-five hundred dollars, making the 1984 Watermelon Festival a financial success. There was little opposition to holding another Friday night dance as part of the 1985 festival.

52/Children on Stage, Coronation Ceremony

The new Watermelon queens are crowned on Saturday night. The coronation ceremony, which includes the old and new queens, the other contestants, male escorts, and "courtiers" from other towns, takes place on a raised stage on the grounds of the McDade School. Some of the girls' mothers, many of whom once took part in this same ceremony, have rehearsed the children several times in the days before the coronation. Some of the younger children are always frightened, and this sometimes causes confusion onstage. Several girls from McDade, too old to be Tiny Tot candidates but not yet in their teens, help with the smaller children. The girl on the right of this picture, Tori Neidig (fig. 11), is one such helper. She was Tiny Tot queen in 1982. Tori's grandmother, Hilda Neidig (fig. 38), was McDade's first Teenage queen in 1948. The queens are chosen by vote of those in the audience at the Queens' Revue, held three weeks before the festival. It hasn't always been done this way. In 1948, the candidates for queen put jars with their names on them in public places around McDade. At the end of a two-week voting period, the girl with the most money in her jars was named queen. Some people didn't think that was fair. "Ol' Alfred Kastner wasn't gonna let anybody else's daughter have that honor of being queen," recalls one of the festival's founders. "He stuffed those jars full of money. There were a lotta poor girls around here who also would've liked to been queen. That pissed a lotta people off."

53 / Queens' Revue Rehearsal

A lot of preparation goes on behind the scenes to get ready for the Watermelon Festival. In this picture, Ernestine Schulz and Ivy Ann Cronin rehearse the Tiny Tots for their upcoming performance at the Queens' Revue. On the left, Mary Calhoun watches her daughter Katie, a reluctant participant, lift her skirt in embarrassment. Though the girls all have a chance to perform before those in the audience cast their votes, the Queens' Revue is essentially a popularity contest. The girls with the largest network of family and family friends usually win. The Revue begins with the Tiny Tot hopefuls and their escorts parading onto the stage, where they perform a short song and dance routine. (At the 1989 Queens' Revue, they pantomimed "The Itsy-Bitsy Spider" and danced "the hokey-pokey" to recorded music.) Then the teenage contestants and their escorts go onstage, and each girl gives a brief speech about why she would like to be McDade's new Watermelon queen. After that, the audience votes, using purchased ballots. Until the mid-1980s—even though it was technically against the rules—people would often buy more than one ballot, if only to contribute more money to the festival. Since then, because of a complaint, the one-vote-per-person rule has been more strictly enforced. Selecting the queen without hurting the losing candidates' feelings has always been a problem. In 1949, the Watermelon Festival tried using "impartial" judges from other communities. Adeline Eschberger (fig. 16) chaired the committee in charge of choosing the judges. "Boy, did we catch hell," she remembers. In 1950, the Watermelon Festival went back to electing the queens.

54 / Getting Ready for the Dance

Putting on the dance requires of lot work. In this picture, taken on the afternoon of the 1989 dance, Buddy Lewis puts the finishing touches on the beer stand by nailing up a county-required warning about the consequences of drunk driving. Buddy has been chairman of the Watermelon Festival's dance committee since 1985. Jack Lewis (fig. 10) is his younger brother. The dance committee is responsible for everything connected with the Watermelon Festival dance, from being sure to book a popular band well in advance to cleaning up afterward. They do a good job; the dance has always gone smoothly and been profitable. Buddy says this is because there are "a lotta folks who like to work on it, and we work real hard." The dance committee consists primarily of people in their thirties and forties for whom the more traditional Watermelon Festival events—the Queens' Revue, the parade, the coronation—don't hold much appeal. The committee includes a number of McDade's "street people." Most members of the committee say that if there were no dance for them to work on, they would probably not be involved with the Watermelon Festival at all. They are proud that the dance has become the festival's biggest moneymaker.

55 / Selling Beer, Watermelon Festival Dance

The beer stand stays busy throughout the dance. Members of the dance committee work it in shifts. Just before midnight, when county law requires that beer sales cease, things get pretty hectic. Most of the committee pitches in during those last few minutes, frantically selling all the beer they can get their hands on. In this picture, Philip Bayer fetches beer for Robin (Dungan) Sievert to pass on to a customer. Beyond them, Robin's husband, Johnny, takes orders, while John Dube gets ready to fish more beer out of the ice. Robin grew up in McDade. She and Johnny now live in Houston but often come to McDade on week-ends. They recently bought the house next door to Robin's parents' home, hoping to quit their jobs in Houston someday and move back. The dance committee is careful to stop selling beer before midnight. Even the slightest violation of county liquor laws could put next year's beer permit at risk, and there is always someone on hand from the antidance faction watching for violations. Only through the stubborn persistence of Clyde Cayton and his daughter Laura (fig. 28) was the 1984 Watermelon Festival Association able to overcome the dance opponents' influence at the county courthouse and obtain a permit. Clyde and Laura had to make several trips to Bastrop and exert political pressure of their own before the Alcoholic Beverage Commission would issue the festival a permit. They were warned that county agents would watch the dance closely and "shut it down" if necessary. There have never been any problems, though, and the dance committee wants to keep it that way.

56 / Watermelon Festival Parade

The Watermelon Festival parade is held on Saturday afternoon. Most onlookers try to find a spot in the little bit of shade cast by McDade's uptown buildings, but those in the parade have no choice but to brave the fierce July sun. In this picture, Duchess Crystal Dixon sits on a blanket to protect herself from the scorching hood of her parents' car. Only the queens and princesses—those who place first or second in the voting at the Queens' Revue—ride on the Watermelon Festival float. Those who place third or lower are given the title of duchess and have to make their own arrangements about riding in the parade. They are not expected to represent McDade at parades in other towns. Sometimes parents get upset when their daughter is not elected queen. Beginning in 1986, the same girl came in second three years in a row. Each year the disappointment of not being elected queen increased, especially for the girl's mother, until the mother got so angry that she spat at Margaret Strong, who was in charge of the Queens' Revue and coronation. The mother felt that Margaret had somehow organized the Revue to her daughter's disadvantage. Since then, Margaret Strong has refused to be involved with the festival. Almost a year later, the girl's family demanded that the Watermelon Festival Association dethrone the elected queen and replace her with their daughter. They claimed that the queen—whose house had been damaged by fire, requiring that her family temporarily stay with relatives in Bastrop—had moved out of McDade and was thus no longer eligible to be queen. After some unpleasant wrangling, the association ignored their demand.

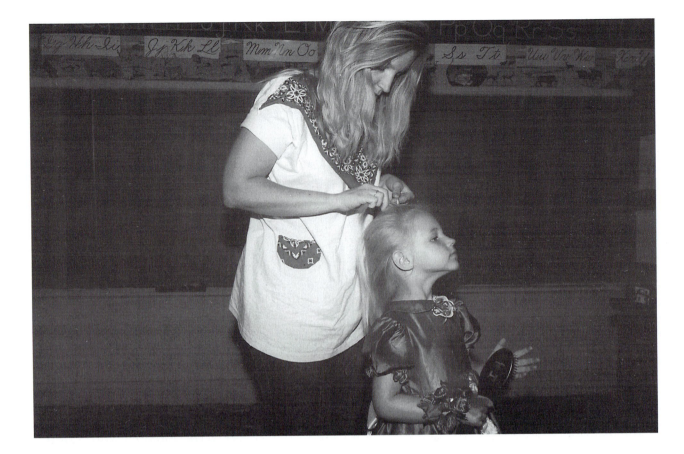

57 / **Preparing for the Coronation**

Many of McDade's more traditionally minded residents, old and young alike, view the Saturday night coronation ceremony as the highlight of the festival. In this picture, Lisa Hilcher gets her daughter Sarina ready for the 1989 coronation, using one of the school's classrooms as a last-minute dressing room. Sarina was McDade's 1988 Tiny Tot queen. In a few minutes she will be handing her crown and watermelon scepter over to the new queen, Ashlee Mills. Sarina's grandmother—Lisa's mother—is the former Inez Farris, sister of Evelyn Wolf (fig. 34) and Doug Farris (fig. 31). Lisa took part in Queens' Revues and coronations throughout her childhood. She was the princess one year, though she never became queen. She was "thrilled" when Sarina was elected queen. A lot of the children who participate, including Sarina, don't have much choice in the matter: their mothers automatically "volunteer" them year after year. Many of the mothers consider involvement in all the pageantry surrounding the Queens' Revue and coronation part and parcel of a normal, wholesome McDade childhood. They remember their own participation fondly and assume their kids will enjoy it too. This is not always true. Recently, a number of the children, though not Sarina, have been reluctant participants.

58 / **Young Dancer, Watermelon Festival Dance**

The first two dances were so successful that in 1986 the Watermelon Festival Association held an additional dance on the night of the Queens' Revue, three weeks before the festival. It was a big hit and has since become an annual event. The dance committee tries to avoid conflict with the Queens' Revue by scheduling the dance later in the evening. But voting for the queen, counting the votes, and all the Revue's ceremonial pomp take a lot of time and always make the Revue run late. Inevitably, the two events overlap and end up competing. Although most of the adults who work at the dance would not otherwise be involved with the Queens' Revue, in previous years some of their children had taken part in it. Those kids now ignore the pageantry at the school in favor of hanging around uptown at the dance, where they race around in packs and have a pretty wild time. Most of them find the dance much more fun than getting dressed up and marching around on a stage. Not surprisingly, this upsets many of the people who have always put much stock in the Queens' Revue, but they have a hard time arguing against the dances' financial success. Some have even suggested holding a third dance on Saturday night of the Watermelon Festival weekend, the night of the coronation ceremony. But that doesn't seem likely to happen. Most of the dance committee thinks the festival has achieved a good balance between ceremony and fun, and they don't want to upset it. Besides, a third dance would be too much work. "We really work our tails off as it is," Buddy Lewis says. "Another dance would be too much."

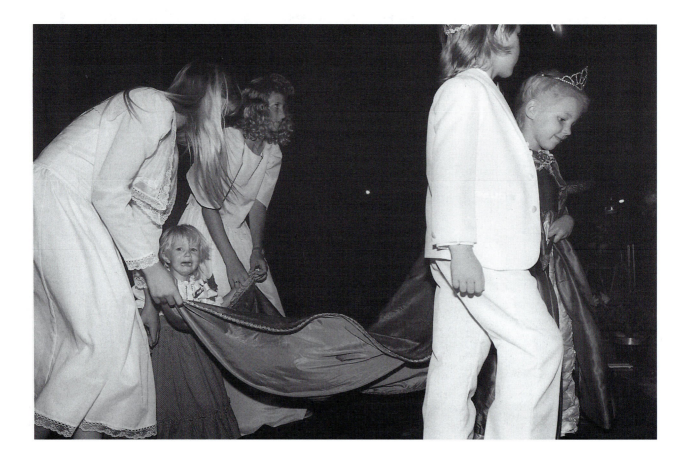

59 / Children Going Onstage

Ivy Ann Cronin (fig. 53), who was herself Teenage queen in 1950, took charge of the Queens' Revue and coronation in 1989, the year after Margaret Strong stepped down. The first thing Ivy Ann had to do was get on the phone and recruit more kids. Fewer and fewer parents had been volunteering their children in recent years, and the tension surrounding the 1988 Queens' Revue made the problem even worse in 1989. Some of the parents she talked to—and their children—were reluctant, but Ivy Ann was persistent and made it hard for them to say no. After a lot of cajoling, she enlisted five candidates for queen in each age group, as well as numerous other children to act as escorts, courtiers, and assistants. Many of the kids she recruited were from some of McDade's newer families and had never participated in the Queens' Revue and coronation before. Ivy Ann was a hard taskmaster. She spent hours rehearsing the kids and fussed over their props and costumes until everything was just right. The 1989 ceremonies came off without any major problems. In this picture, Mirriah Milburn and Kimberly Merrell help an unhappy Katie Calhoun (fig. 53) in her role as train bearer for Sarina Hilcher (fig. 57), the 1988 Tiny Tot queen. Sarina's escort is her brother Ricky. Katie was terrified throughout and refused to be consoled. Three weeks later, at the coronation ceremony, she stayed in the audience, where she watched from the comfort of her mother's lap.

60 / Celebrating the End of the Dance

Most members of the dance committee are too busy to do much partying until after the dance is over. In this picture, Shorty Calhoun, Robin Sievert, Johnny Sievert, Buddy Lewis, and Carolyn McKee celebrate the end of the 1989 Watermelon Festival dance. They have just finished working the premidnight rush at the beer stand and are happy to have that and most of their other dance-related efforts behind them. All that remains is to clean up, a job that will keep most of the dance committee uptown for several hours yet. By the next morning it will be difficult to tell that more than one thousand people had held a wild party in uptown McDade the night before. In a few weeks time, the dance committee will have a party all its own, financed in large part by money from recycled beer cans. Shorty Calhoun is Katie Calhoun's grandfather. He and Carolyn, longtime friends with Buddy and Chris Lewis, moved to McDade from Austin in 1987. Shorty's grown son and his family soon followed. Buddy and Chris, Shorty and Carolyn, plus Robin and Johnny and several other couples, most of whom are on the dance committee, often socialize together. Along with a number of others in town, they hope to someday use proceeds from the Watermelon Festival to build a community center in McDade. In 1988, the Watermelon Festival Association purchased—quite inexpensively—a small lot in town from Chris Lewis's grandfather, A. Y. Field, as a possible site for such a facility. Some people, of course, oppose building a community center with Watermelon Festival funds. The issue will probably be a source of controversy well into the 1990s.

CHAPTER 5

Family Life

61 / Four Generations, Lewis Family Reunion

The Lewis family holds its annual reunion on Easter Sunday. In this picture, taken at the 1985 reunion, Gertrude Eschberger (fig. 43) holds her grandson Justin Kessler, while Carolyn Lewis, Barry Kessler, and Alma Albrecht look on. Carolyn is Gertrude's daughter. Justin is the son of Carolyn's sister Suzanne; Barry is his father. Alma Albrecht is Gertrude's mother, Carolyn's grandmother, and Justin's great-grandmother. The Lewises are among McDade's largest and most sociable families; the Eschbergers are one of the area's oldest and most widely extended, with branches in Paige, Elgin, Coupland, Pflugerville, and McDade. Carolyn's marriage to Jack Lewis (fig. 10) is unusual in that members of the older German families do not often marry someone who is not also of German descent. Together, the two families form an extensive social network: even the most ordinary of family occasions—a baby shower or a birthday party, for example—can attract quite a crowd. There are always a lot of people at the Lewis reunion. Each year, Billy Bob Lewis (one of Jack's brothers) and Harry Eschberger (Carolyn's father) get up at dawn to start slow-smoking the meat. A little while later they tap the first keg of beer. Everyone is welcome, friends as well as family. All day long, and well into the night, people stop by to eat, drink, and talk.

62 / The Page Family

Until about 1987, the Page family lived in a large yellow house on top of a hill on McDade's eastern edge. This picture was taken on the front porch of that house. It was a friendly, welcoming place, always a mess. Nelson Page commuted to Austin, where he worked as a city building inspector. He was president of the Watermelon Festival Association in 1984, the year of the first dance. His wife, Mary Sue, taught school in Bastrop. Their children—Mary Ellen, Gilbert, and Lawrence—went to school in Bastrop, riding on the school bus Mary Sue drove back and forth each day. The older woman in the picture is Mary Stagner, Nelson's unmarried great-aunt and a lifelong resident of McDade. She enjoyed having the Pages so close and treated the kids as though they were her grandchildren. Nelson and Mary Sue have separated since this picture was taken. Nelson moved into an apartment in Austin, while Mary Sue and the children stayed in McDade. She tried to make ends meet on her teacher's salary, but she couldn't keep up with the mortgage payments and had to move out. She and the kids now live in a rented mobile home in Elgin. The big yellow house stood vacant for awhile, before a woman from Houston bought it. She painted it gray and started renovating it. But she wasn't able to keep up with the payments either, and the bank repossessed it. No one has lived there since. In 1989 a tornado tore the roof off. Even though a "For Sale" sign still stands in the front yard, no one has come around to fix the roof.

63 / Alma Kastner

Alma Kastner and her family once lived on a large ranch north of McDade. In the early 1960s, though, she and her husband divorced, and Mrs. Kastner moved into a small house in town. She has lived there alone ever since. She is seen here with one of several displays of family photographs that decorate her living room. The picture she is holding is of her mother. It was taken in a Giddings portrait studio during the 1890s. Hilda Neidig (fig. 38), McDade's first Teenage Watermelon queen, is Alma's daughter. Alma has several grandchildren and great grandchildren, including Tory Neidig (figs. 11 and 52), who live in McDade. Unfortunately, she does not get along with her children or their spouses, and this has resulted in her not having as much contact with her grandchildren and great-grandchildren as she would like. She complains that they don't come to see her and that she rarely gets invited to their homes. The only time she gets to see them, she says, is at church, family reunions, and other such semipublic events. At a 1989 wedding reception, Alma and Hilda sat together and talked for a short while. A number of people remarked upon that and expressed hope that a reconciliation had begun.

64 / Women Talking, Shorty and Ruth Bostic's Fiftieth Anniversary Party

On Shorty and Ruth Bostic's fiftieth wedding anniversary, their children hosted an open house in their parents' rural home. It was well attended, with friends and family dropping by all afternoon to offer congratulations and bring presents. The Bostics' five children gave their parents a telephone and had them fixed up with telephone service, a convenience Shorty and Ruth had never felt they needed. Their children, all of whom live nearby, wanted to be able to stay in closer touch with their parents, especially since Shorty was beginning to have some problems with his health. In this picture, taken in the Bostics' kitchen, Ruby Cain shows off a photo of her grandson to a group of younger women. With few exceptions, women do the child rearing in McDade. They also assume most of the responsibility for making sure that family gatherings go smoothly: They prepare lots of good food; they keep the children in line; and they clean up the mess when the festivities are over. Most importantly, perhaps, the women are usually the keepers of the family peace, helping to negotiate disagreements and soothe hurt feelings. While most of McDade's men are proud of their families and happy they belong to them, they do little of the work necessary to keep them going.

65 / Lisa Eschberger and Justin Kessler, Eschberger-Albrecht Family Thanksgiving

Adolescent girls often take care of the smaller children at big family affairs. In this picture, taken at the 1985 Eschberger-Albrecht Thanksgiving dinner in Paige (fig. 43), Lisa Eschberger—a teenager at the time—shows her nephew Justin Kessler (fig. 61) a picture of himself among the family snapshots tacked up on a door. Lisa is the youngest of Harry and Gertrude Eschberger's four daughters. At the time this picture was taken, she was the only one as yet unmarried. On this Thanksgiving, Lisa had one or another of the family's small children with her all day long. She carried them around, fed them, changed their diapers, entertained them, and put them down for naps. This enabled their mothers to concentrate on the large Thanksgiving meal.

66 / People Arriving, Farris Family Reunion

The Farris family holds its annual reunion on the fourth Sunday in June. There are a lot of Farrises in and around McDade. None of them has a large house, though, so in recent years the family has rented the Sons of Herman Hall in Paige as the site of its reunion. It is a big-enough place that the dancers and drinkers can enjoy themselves without disturbing those members of the family who prefer to just sit, eat, and talk. The Farris family, led in large part by Evelyn (Farris) Wolf (fig. 34), tries hard to get all its members to attend the reunion. Even though the family has several separate branches and includes individuals with markedly different lifestyles and beliefs, Evelyn has gotten most of its members to put aside their differences for this one day every year. She came up with the idea of using family funds, accumulated in part by assessing yearly dues, to purchase prizes to give away at the reunion. For the past several years, the reunion has awarded prizes to the person who has traveled the farthest to attend, to the oldest family member present, and to the parents of the youngest. There are also several randomly awarded door prizes. More and more of the Farris family's younger adults and their children have started attending the reunion in recent years. This pleases Evelyn; she hopes it is a step toward bringing the family closer together on a year-round basis.

67 / Tire Swing, Lewis Family Reunion

The Lewis family holds its Easter Sunday reunion in the yard of the tiny house that most of them call "the home place." All thirteen of Foster and Thelma Lewis's children grew up in this house. Ten of them are still living, and only one has left Texas. None of the others lives any farther away than Houston, and all of them faithfully attend the yearly reunion. Although they grew up poor, they remember being happy as children. They all speak glowingly of their mother, who died of cancer in 1974. Opal Jones, the second oldest, says: "Mama was a great lady. She had enough love to spoil every one of us rotten and make every one of us feel special." Margie Schindler, Opal's older sister, agrees: "We never lacked for love. Not ever. Not for one minute. We knew we were loved. You never doubted that. Ever." Opal lives in the house now, after living in Houston for eighteen years. During the time she "lived away," she never once missed an Easter reunion or a Watermelon Festival. She moved back to McDade in 1982, after her marriage had broken up and her only child had died. "I needed to fall back and regroup," she says. "This is where my family and friends were. I needed their support." Over the years, several of her brothers and sisters have come to stay at the old family home during times of personal crisis. It is a place they can always come back to.

68 / Waiting for Dinner, Eschberger-Albrecht Family Thanksgiving

While they waited for dinner, members of the Eschberger and Albrecht families and their Thanksgiving guests filled Laverne (Albrecht) Mattiza's small house with conversation and activity. Even though a football game was on in the living room, most of the people there didn't pay it much mind. Instead, they talked and watched the kids. The serious football fans—most of the men in the family—had another TV set in the garage, where they could watch the game in peace. In this picture, Lisa Eschberger (fig. 65), seated on the floor next to the television, keeps an eye on infant Amanda Albrecht, her second cousin. In the foreground, Randall Lewis (figs. 10 and 43) looks through a pile of photographs. The one on top is a picture of himself, taken a couple of years earlier. This branch of the family is especially keen on taking snapshots of one another and compiling family albums. Keeping the albums current is up to the women. Nearly every one of the women present had brought her most recent album to this Thanksgiving gathering. After the meal was over and they had cleaned up, the women relaxed by poring over the photo albums and drinking wine coolers. They laughed a lot and traded duplicate pictures with each other. The men watched football and drank beer.

69 / Men Talking, Three Oaks Cemetery Picnic

There are more older people in some of McDade's families than in others. Not surprisingly, these families' social occasions are calmer and quieter than those of families with more young adults and children. Their get-togethers are geared less toward watching and entertaining the kids than toward giving the older people an opportunity to "visit." A number of McDade's elderly don't see as much of each other as they once did, so many of them especially value the chance to socialize with old friends that family occasions offer. In fact, a lot of McDade's older people regularly attend their friends' family functions as well as their own. Many of them organize their lives around the annual sequence of family reunions. In this picture, taken at the 1989 Three Oaks Cemetery Picnic (fig. 9), Sonny Brown, Harold Eklund, and Herbert Smith wait for the buffet-style meal to be set out. Only Sonny belongs to one of the families that make up the Three Oaks Cemetery Association. Although there were some children at the picnic, most of those in attendance were older people. They spent the afternoon sitting in the shade of a large tent that an Elgin funeral home loans to the Cemetery Association each year. While the adults talked quietly among themselves, the kids played among the headstones.

70 / Lena Crume, Kastner Family Reunion

Although Lena (Kastner) Crume left McDade during World War I, she always returned for the annual Kastner reunion (fig. 38). Born in 1894, she was the oldest of Julius and Ida Kastner's sixteen children. All of her brothers and sisters died long before she did (as did her husband), so for many years she was the oldest living member of the Kastner family. Because of this, the family elevated her to a unique place of honor. At the 1985 Kastner reunion, where this picture was taken, everyone greeted her with special warmth and respect. Parents of small children made a point of bringing them to her: to show them off, to receive her blessing, and to impress her presence on their memories. She said the prayer before the family sat down to eat, and her meal was the first one served. A picture-taking session followed dinner. First the entire family posed together. Then people posed in smaller groups, each comprised of individuals with the same relationship to "Aunt Lena." Ivy Ann (Kastner) Cronin (fig. 53), the reunion's main organizer, kept a close eye on the photo session, because the proper groupings were sometimes hard to figure out. Mrs. Crume sat in the center of each group and thus appears in every formally posed picture taken that day. She was, after all, the Kastner family's last remaining link to its past generations, and the family revered and treasured her for that. Mrs. Crume died in 1987. Her only child, a daughter who lives in Arizona, hasn't attended the Kastner reunion for many years.

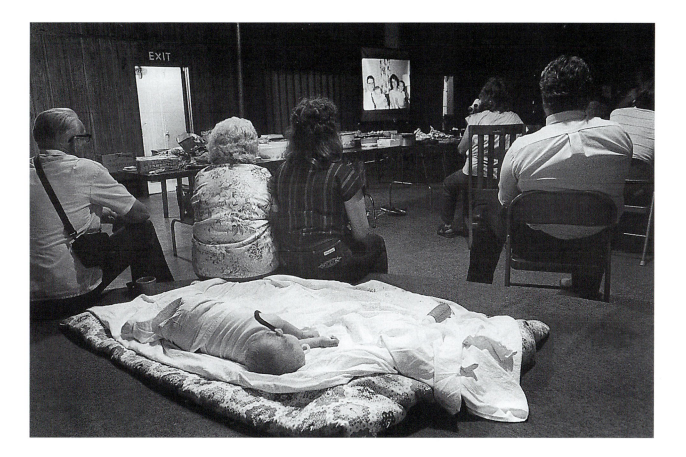

71 / Slide Show, Farris Family Reunion

Every year at the Farris family reunion (fig. 66), Evelyn (Farris) Wolf shows a set of slides she has made from old family photographs. Evelyn is fascinated by her family's largely unknown past, and she constantly tries to learn more about it. She has spent many hours in state and county archives researching one or another of her ancestors. Intent on compiling as complete a photographic record of the family as possible, she tracks down old Farris family photographs, borrows them from their owners, and makes copies of them. She copies them on both slide film and print film, so she can show slides to groups and still have negatives from which to make prints easily and cheaply. The group of slides she shows at the reunion doesn't change much from year to year. Even so, most members of the family—the adults, at least—seem to enjoy her presentation. The pictures inevitably start them reminiscing about times gone by and people who have "passed." The kids don't care for the slide show as much as the grown-ups do.

72 / Shorty and Tanya Bostic

Some of McDade's families look toward the future more than others. The Bostics are one such family. In this picture, taken at Shorty and Ruth Bostic's fiftieth wedding anniversary party, Shorty holds Tanya, the youngest of his grandchildren. Shorty and Ruth have five children, three of whom have given them a total of eight "blood" grandchildren. Their pictures are on the wall to the left, arranged by age within their separate lines of descent. The Bostics also have two adopted grandchildren, including Tanya. They are the most recent additions to the family, and at the time this picture was taken Ruth had not yet gotten around to adding their photographs to her wall display. Both Shorty and Ruth had hoped the family would continue to grow. But Shorty didn't live to see that happen. Just a few weeks after the anniversary party, he learned that he had inoperable cancer. Despite radiation treatments and chemotherapy, he died—at home—about two years later. No children were born into the family during that time.

73 / Children Playing, Three Oaks Cemetery Picnic

Before dinner was served at the Three Oaks Cemetery Picnic, Erhard Goerlitz (figs. 3 and 35) took most of the children present, several of them his grandchildren, on a tour of the cemetery. He stopped at a number of graves and told the kids a little about the people buried there and how they were related to present-day members of the Three Oaks Cemetery Association. He made a special point of telling individual children how the dead were related to them. While some of the kids listened, others fidgeted. Later, after dinner, the children went off to play in the cemetery, while the adults cleaned up and socialized. Some of the kids played games like tag or hide-and-seek and generally just raced around. Others, pretending that the cemetery was full of ghosts, did strange dreamy dances on their ancestors' graves.

CHAPTER 6

Men and Women

74 / Dan and Evelyn Wolf

Dan and Evelyn Wolf have been married since 1961. Dan was thirty-two at the time and in danger of becoming an "old bachelor." Evelyn was twenty-one. Adeline Eschberger (fig. 16) is Dan's older sister and Martha Wolf (fig. 34) his mother. Dan and Evelyn have four children, three girls and a boy, born between 1965 and 1973. The Wolfs live in the house that Dan was born in, on a small farm two miles north of McDade. The farm has been in Dan's family since 1857, and Dan is the fourth generation to work it. He is proud of that. His son, William, may become the fifth. Dan had never worked a job off the farm until 1971, when William's premature birth and subsequent hospital stay incurred medical bills the Wolfs couldn't pay without a steadier income. Dan took a job working the night shift at the Lower Colorado River Authority's hydroelectric plant at Bastrop. He stayed at that job until 1987, when he accepted an early retirement package and went back to running the farm full time. For the thirteen years Dan worked in Bastrop, Evelyn assumed much of the responsibility for running the family truck-farming business. She also raised the kids, did the housekeeping and cooking, and nursed Dan's elderly, bedridden mother till the older woman's death in 1985.

75 / Girls and Dogs

After spending their elementary years in their hometown school, McDade's children sometimes have a hard time adjusting to junior high and high school in Elgin, Lexington, or Bastrop. Wherever they go, they face teasing about being "trash" from such a tiny, "country" place as McDade. Even so, many of them look forward to leaving the McDade School. This seems especially true of the girls. By the time they have reached sixth grade, the girls have usually grown more mature than their male classmates, both physically and emotionally. Many of them have grown apart from the boys they grew up with, see-ing them as childish and having become "tired of them." They look forward to meeting some older, "cooler" boys when they enter junior high in a larger town. During their last year of school in McDade, the sixth-grade girls seem to spend their spare time with no one but themselves, forming a tight little clique exclusively their own and actively shunning the boys. Not surprisingly, the boys usually respond with increased hostility toward the girls, whom they soon come to think of as "stuck-up."

76 / Boys Playing

Major and Heath Neidig play with toy cars in Linda Haverland's garage, while their mother, Debbie Neidig, and her friend Linda give Tori Neidig, the boys' older sister, a perm in the kitchen (fig. 11). Without seeming to give it much thought, most parents in McDade segregate their sons and daughters into separate spheres of childhood activity. They encourage the girls to play at domestic things and help with household chores and the boys to do traditionally male things—play with cars or guns, or play sports. In general, they also allow the boys to roam town more freely and saddle them with fewer responsibilities than their sisters. In many ways, of course, this follows the pattern of the adults' own lives. The duties, and domains, of men and women in McDade continue to be along traditional lines. Even if women work outside the family home—as many of them do these days, once their children are in school—they are still responsible for the day-to-day welfare of the kids, for putting food on the table, and for keeping the house in order. Men are expected to be the family's main breadwinner (even if they are not), to keep up the yard and the outside of the house, and to fix whatever needs fixing. When it comes to the family car or pickup, of course, maintenance and repair are almost entirely the man's responsibility. Just as the kitchen is the woman's domain, the garage is the man's.

77 / Veterans of Foreign Wars Color Guard

Just as McDade's clergymen like to be sure that every public event in town begins with a prayer, members of the McDade Veterans of Foreign Wars Post 8313 like to assure a patriotic presence. This is a duty they take seriously. In this picture, Curtis Lacker and David Dube carry out the colors at the end of the McDade School's 1985 graduation ceremony. Both men are among the VFW's most active members and have served terms as post commander. Although some of the members' wives—organized into the VFW Ladies Auxiliary—are involved with post activities, the official membership of the McDade post remains exclusively male. The post meets once a month. The meetings are usually preceded by a social hour—attended by both men and women—during which people play dominoes and share a potluck supper provided by the Ladies Auxiliary. Once it is time for the official meeting to begin, the women and any male guests who are not members have to leave. The proceedings from that point on are secret. Sometimes the meetings last late into the night. For several members of Post 8313, these monthly meetings are the only leisure-time opportunity they have to get away from their homes and families. These men tend to be the most active in VFW affairs and rarely miss a meeting.

78 / Women with Quilt

Among older women in McDade, there are more widows than women with living husbands. Most of the widows live alone, usually in the houses where they raised their children. In many ways, they form a social set all their own, and they spend much of their time keeping one another company and helping each other. Their lives revolve around such occasions as bible study and prayer groups, club meetings, birthday parties, and family get-togethers—both those of their own family and the families of their friends. The more ambitious among them put on luncheons or teas in their homes, taking turns acting as hostess. Many get together several times a week, or even daily, in smaller, less formal groups. Those who drive will often take those who cannot, or who are "too nervous" to drive on the highway, to nearby towns to shop, or to Austin for doctor's appointments. Many of these older women share an interest in quilting. They often collaborate on quilts that will be sold at auctions benefiting the school, the Historical Society, or some other community organization. In this picture, Nora Lee Jones, Stella Kastner (fig. 29), and Hazel Creel—all of them widows—display a quilt about to be presented as a Christmas gift to me, as the photographer who "documented" the McDade community during the late 1980s. This cooperative quilting project, organized by Ivy Ann Cronin and Stella Kastner, involved over forty women in McDade. Each contributed a "block" with her name embroidered on it to the quilt.

79 / Boys Watching Girls

Generally speaking, McDade's teenage girls don't get along with the local teenage boys any better than they did as sixth-graders. At best, they treat them distantly. When they start attending school in Elgin, Lexington, or Bastrop, the girls meet boys from these other communities—boys they have no unpleasant memories of, often older boys who drive—and they start dating them. The girls don't seem sorry to leave the McDade boys behind. The boys' position is less enviable: their hometown girls aren't interested in them, but they are not yet old enough to drive, which makes it difficult for them to date girls from other towns. The boys often end up spending their weekends just hanging around McDade, while the girls they grew up with are going out to movies, parties, or dances in other towns. Sometimes this upsets the boys, and they act as though they were still in grade school, teasing and insulting the girls whenever they see them. This, of course, makes the girls think them all the more childish and all the less worthy of attention.

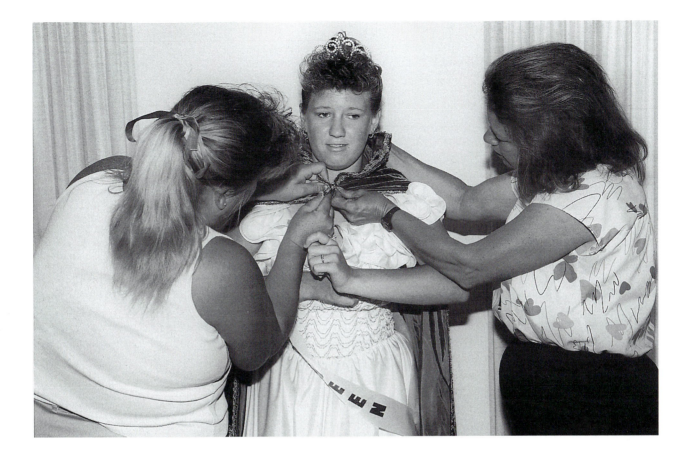

80 / Dressing the Queen

Michelle Johnson was McDade's 1989 Teenage Watermelon queen. In this picture, taken a few days after her election, Michelle's mother, Lynn Johnson (fig. 48), and Ivy Ann Cronin (fig. 53) get her ready for an official publicity photograph. This picture appeared in the *Elgin Courier*, the *Bastrop Advertiser*, and the *Giddings Times & News*, as well as in the Watermelon Festival's official program of events. Michelle had just completed her freshman year at Lexington High School when she was elected queen. Although she was pleased about having won, she was a bit overwhelmed by all the attention. She also worried about living up to people's expectations of her. Ivy Ann, in charge of the Queens' Revue and coronation, tried to reassure Michelle, telling her over and over again how much fun she would have and that she should just relax and enjoy being the center of attention. Ivy Ann has had a lot of experience in these kinds of feminine competitions, both as a contestant and as the mother of a contestant. In the early 1950s, she was McDade's Teenage Watermelon queen, won the state 4-H canning competition, and, along with Ernestine Schulz (fig. 53), was the Texas winner of a contest for original vegetable concoctions—Ivy Ann and Ernestine called their winning entry "sweet potato surprise"—sponsored by the National Vegetable Growers Association. Ivy Ann's daughter, Debra, was McDade's Teenage Watermelon queen in 1973. Debra later went on to be captain of the drill team at Southwest Texas State University, Miss Austin Aqua Beauty, and Miss Texas USA. She now sells beauty products in Austin.

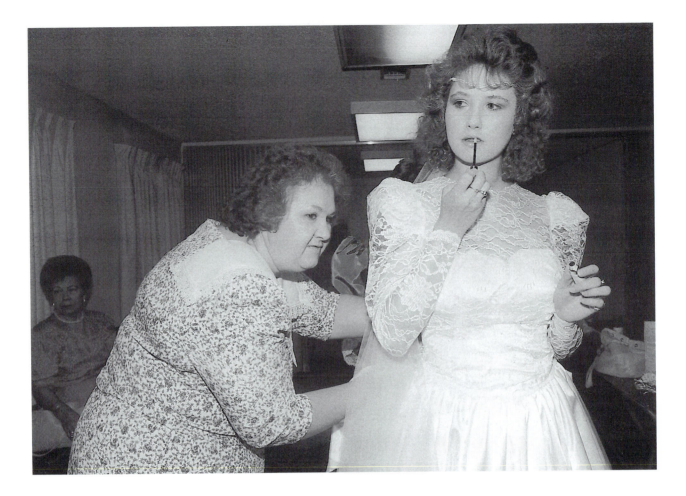

81 / Dressing the Bride, Gretchen Pohler's Wedding

A lot of McDade's young people, especially the young women, get married very early in life. Many girls marry as soon as they finish high school, typically to high school boyfriends a couple of years older than themselves. For the most part, these boys have decided against going to college and have instead started working at blue-collar or agricultural jobs right out of high school. Many of them see themselves as "working men" and think they are ready to settle down and start families. Some of the girls, of course, quit high school early to get married. Often, this is because of an accidental pregnancy. Gretchen Pohler, seen here on her wedding day with her mother, Betty, was something of an exception. She waited more than a year after graduating from Lexington High School before getting married. During that time she worked as a bank teller in Elgin and lived at home with her parents. Shortly after the wedding, she and her husband moved to North Carolina, to a town they had visited while on their honeymoon. Gretchen was McDade's 1975 Tiny Tot queen. Betty was Tiny Tot queen in 1952 and Teenage queen in 1960. She married in 1967, right after high school. Her oldest daughter, Gina Griffith, had a baby in 1988, making Betty a grandmother. She had just turned forty.

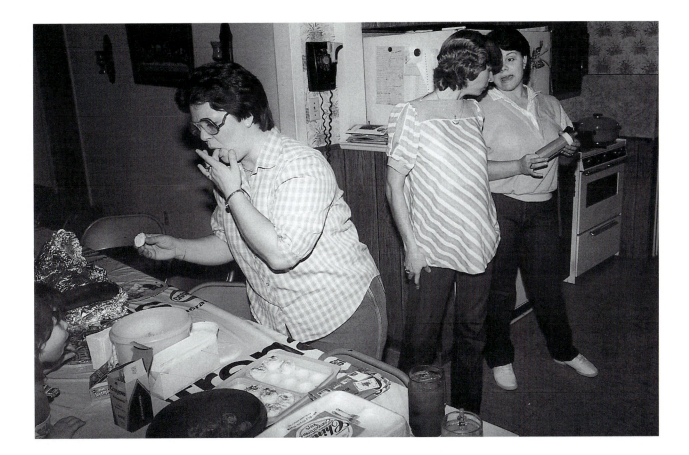

82 / Women in Kitchen, Eschberger-Albrecht Family Thanksgiving

The kitchen was a busy place at the Eschberger-Albrecht 1985 Thanksgiving dinner. In this picture, Sandy Botkin sets out the deviled eggs, while Debbie Schkade and Pam Albrecht talk about babies. Sandy and Pam are sisters; Debbie is their first cousin. Brandi Botkin (lower left) is Sandy's daughter. Once married, most couples in McDade begin families very quickly. This seems to change the women's lives more than it does the men's. Usually, the men have been out of school and working for a year or two before getting married, and parenthood doesn't have much effect on the day-to-day routines of their job-centered lives. The women, though, often have to make the transition from high school student to spouse and parent more abruptly, sometimes in less than a year. This means that many of McDade's young women set aside their own individual concerns very early in life to take care of their husbands and children. Tied down by pregnancies (sometimes one right after another) and young children, they tend to stay at home, looking neither for work nor a social life away from home and family. Their principal social contacts are often sisters or sisters-in-law who also have small children. Many develop a closer relationship with their mothers, based in large part on their common parenthood. When the daughters become parents, their mothers accept them as adults—however young they may be.

83 / Leah Dunkin

Leah Dunkin is the youngest of Sam and Debbie Dunkin's four children (fig. 23). She is their only daughter. The Dunkins live on a ranch several miles south of town. Leah's oldest brother goes to junior high in Elgin, while the other two go to school in McDade. Leah is not yet old enough to attend school, and she is a bit envious of her brothers: she would like very much to get on the school bus with them in the mornings. Instead, she spends most of her time at home on the ranch with Debbie. Sometimes she helps Debbie around the house and with some of the ranch work; sometimes she plays by herself. An outgoing, friendly child, Leah is a favorite of many of McDade's older people, especially those who see her every Sunday at the McDade Baptist Church. Several of the older church members make a point of visiting with Leah for a minute or two after the worship service is over. She almost always makes them laugh. Sometimes they give her pieces of gum or candy and tell her how cute she is. When she grows up, Leah says, she wants to be like her mother and have a family just like her own.

84 / Minnie Lee Farris

Minnie Lee Farris has eleven children. Several of them still live in McDade, and none lives any farther away than Austin. Evelyn Wolf (figs. 34 and 74), her oldest, was born in 1940, when Mrs. Farris was twenty-one. Her youngest, Doug (fig. 31), was born in 1962. He still lives with her at home. Her husband, whom she refers to as "Mr. Farris," died in 1982. Mrs. Farris collects dolls. She doesn't know how many she has, although she says she has about eighty porcelain dolls that are her favorites. She began collecting when her youngest daughter, Linda, was small. When Linda didn't seem to care much for a doll Mrs. Farris had given her, Mrs. Farris adopted the doll for herself. "That started it," she says. "I never did have no dolls when I was little." She makes all her dolls' costumes, including their underwear, from scraps of cloth her daughters bring her. The photograph on the wall above Mrs. Farris, taken in the early 1980s, includes five generations of women. Seated in front are Nanny Emerson, Mrs. Farris's mother (she is also the woman in the oval photograph to the left) and Mrs. Farris herself. Mrs. Emerson has since died. The dark-haired woman in the back row is Inez Haverland, one of Mrs. Farris's four daughters. Inez is flanked by her two daughters, Beverly Haverland and Lisa Hilcher (fig. 57). In Lisa's arms is Ricky Hilcher (fig. 59), her first child and one of Mrs. Farris's three great-grandchildren.

85 / Randall Lewis and Men

An only child, Randall Lewis (fig. 10) spends a lot of time with his father, Jack (right), and Jack's friends. In this picture, Jack pokes fun at Randall, while Bob Whitney looks on. In the background are Joe Lewis and Buddy Lewis (fig. 54), two of Randall's uncles. Jack is not overly strict when it comes to raising Randall. Although he insists that Randall does what he tells him to do, Jack is careful not to demand too much of him. "A boy oughta have a good time," Jack says. "That's more important than always doing good in school and being too much of a candy-ass. Randall ain't no candy-ass." Randall looks up to Jack and acts a lot like him. When the two of them get dressed up, they both wear cowboy boots, pressed jeans, a starched shirt, and a carefully shaped white Stetson. "I got him a real Stetson, no imitation," Jack brags. "He's a good boy. He deserves it."

86 / Gene Scott and W. C. Stevens

Both Gene Scott and W. C. Stevens, seen here at the 1989 Watermelon Festival dance, enjoy socializing over a few beers. Often, on a Friday evening or a Saturday afternoon, they can be found in the group of "street people" who gather in front of Sam Earl's. Gene is retired from more than thirty years with the Texas National Guard and now tends bar in an Elgin tavern. His wife, Elaine, cooks and washes dishes in the cafeteria at the McDade School. Gene's family is one of the oldest in town, though Gene, Elaine, and their grown son, Harry, are the last Scotts left in McDade. Linda Haverland (fig. 26), whose mother's maiden name was Scott, is a distant cousin. W. C. Stevens is a relative newcomer to McDade. He works as a lineman for the Bluebonnet Electric Cooperative, which provides most of rural Bastrop County with power. He also works as a short-order cook several nights a week at a restaurant on U.S. 290 not far from McDade. W. C. prides himself on his cooking. Before he started working at the restaurant, he would sometimes invite the whole crew of "street people" over to his mobile home for enchiladas.

87 / Men Drinking Beer, Lewis Family Reunion

McDade's men don't talk about their families much, with the occasional exception of bragging about something special one of their children has done. Instead, they talk about their jobs, the weather (especially if they're farmers or ranchers), and people they know. After a few beers, they often tell stories about their "hell-raising days." In the foreground of this picture, taken at the 1987 Lewis family reunion, are Doug Pierce, Bob Whitney, and Jack Lewis. Beyond them are Wally Mundine, Marshall Wolf, and Clyde Farris. At this event, as at most, the men stayed pretty much to themselves. With the exception of Bob, all of the men in this picture are married and have children. Most of them have to piece together a living by working more than one job or having a skill they can earn money with in their spare time. Doug drives a gasoline tanker truck full time and has a small welding business on the side. Jack and Marshall work when they can as construction site plumbers. In between jobs, Jack sometimes drives a truck, and Marshall does odd jobs around McDade. Wally has a small ranch he raises cattle on. He also sells hay and hires himself out to plow or cut hay for other ranchers. Clyde works on the state highway department road crew and is in the Texas National Guard. Bob, who has since moved away from McDade, works construction.

88 / Carolyn Lewis in front of Sam Earl's

Carolyn Eschberger was sixteen when she married Jack Lewis. He was twenty-five at the time. Randall, their only child, was born less than a year later. Carolyn doesn't always get to spend as much time with Jack as she would like. Between the demands of parenthood, Carolyn's full-time job at an Austin bank, and Jack sometimes having to travel as far as Houston to find work, their schedules often do not overlap. When Jack does "get on" at a job any distance from McDade, he usually stays in a motel near the construction site during the week, returning home only on weekends. Carolyn doesn't like his being away, but she knows she doesn't have much choice, as her salary alone is not enough for them to live on. Even when Jack is not working an out-of-town job, he is sometimes hard to find. Outgoing in the extreme, he has made lots of friends over the years, not only in McDade but in all the towns nearby. When he's not working, he likes nothing better than to get in his pickup and go visiting. These visits often involve drinking a few beers, which sometimes means that Jack does not come home when Carolyn thinks he should. This picture was taken late on a Saturday afternoon, in front of Sam Earl's. Jack was somewhere else this day—no one knew where—but Carolyn expected that sooner or later he would come looking for her at Sam Earl's. In the background are Linda Haverland (fig. 26), Opal Jones, and Chris Lewis. Opal is Jack Lewis's older sister. Chris is married to Jack's older brother Buddy (fig. 54).

89 / Velma Hoerman Peeling Potatoes, McDade Watermelon Festival

Velma Hoerman and her husband, Quintus, live on a farm just north of McDade. Quintus stays home most of the time, but Velma likes to come to town to socialize. She participates in a number of community activities. In this picture, taken during the 1987 Watermelon Festival, she helps peel potatoes for the enormous batch of potato salad that will be part of the barbecue dinner served in the school cafeteria after Saturday's parade. Peeling potatoes has been Velma's contribution to the festival for almost thirty years now. Before that—when her daughter, Juanice, was young—she worked on the Queens' Revue and coronation instead. In 1951 and 1961, the years Juanice was Tiny Tot and Teenage queen, Velma decorated Quintus's farm wagon so it could be used as a parade float. She had a budget of fifteen dollars, most of which she used on crepe paper and colored facial tissue. In recent years, however, she has peeled potatoes: she estimates she's peeled a ton of them over the years. Her close friend Adeline Eschberger (fig. 16) used to help her, but health problems now prevent Adeline from taking part in community affairs as much as she once did. She and Velma still talk on the phone almost every day, and they often play dominoes together. They have known each other all their lives. They both grew up on farms outside of town, attended grade school together in a one-room country schoolhouse, and went to high school in McDade. They both married local boys while they were still in their teens. Their husbands are also longtime friends, though the four of them rarely socialize as couples.

90 / Men Watching Women, Dungan Family Reunion

The 1985 Dungan family reunion was held at the McDade VFW Hall. The women all sat along one side of the room and the men along the other. Some of the younger people went outside and played softball, but the older people all stayed inside. The highlight of the reunion was the afternoon meal, a potluck affair that offered a variety of vegetable and meat dishes and a bewildering array of homemade cakes, pies, and puddings. All, of course, had been prepared by the women. No beer was served: most of the Dungans don't drink, and McDade's VFW post has a policy against alcohol on the premises. Nor was there any music or dancing. Most of the men seemed relieved when the meal was over and they could start thinking about going home. The women were less eager to leave: they lingered over dessert and coffee, and they took their time cleaning up. A few of the men became irritated with their wives for taking so long.

CHAPTER 7

Old and Young

91 / Young and Old, St. Andrew's Hamburger Supper

St. Andrew's Lutheran Church, better known as Paint Creek Church, is a rural congregation several miles northeast of McDade. It sponsors a hamburger supper every year at the end of June. The event is well known in the area and draws people from throughout Bastrop, Lee, and Williamson Counties. Many of the area's elderly, even those who do not get out much anymore, make a special point of attending the Paint Creek supper, arranging well ahead of time for rides and whatever other assistance they might need. For many of the older people, especially those of German descent, the supper has become a reunion of sorts, an event at which they can visit with old friends they no longer see very often. Those who do not walk well are helped to lawn chairs in the shade of the churchyard's live oak trees, while the more active circulate and renew old acquaintances. The teenagers who attend usually do so at their parents' insistence and don't seem to have much fun. They don't mix with the older people and at times seem scornful of them, especially of how much they have to rely on others. Most of McDade's teens would like to think of themselves as self-sufficient, and they don't seem to have much patience with those who are not.

92 / Mary Ellen Page and Scout

Before her family left McDade, Mary Ellen Page (fig. 62) spent much of her summer vacation just wandering around town. Some days she'd take off on her bike; other times she'd walk, often with her dog, Scout. Most days, she'd join up with other kids (and dogs), and they'd all roam town in a pack. Most of McDade's children like being free to ramble, especially early in the summer. As school vacation wears on, though, many get bored, complaining of "nothing to do and nowhere to go." In a lot of ways, they're right; McDade doesn't have many places for kids to hang out. There's a playground and crude baseball diamond at the school, but that's about it; there's no park in town, no video arcade or recreation center, no public swimming pool. Nor is there much for the kids to do in the way of organized activities. The Baptist Church offers Vacation Bible School for a few weeks each summer, but kids who want to swim, play organized baseball, or take music lessons have to go to Elgin or Bastrop. Even so, a lot of parents in town think McDade is an ideal place to raise children. They see it as a kind of preserve in which the kids can roam freely but never be far from friends or family. Parents know that adult supervision or help are always close by and that if their child misbehaves in any serious way, they will hear about it. It comforts them to know that they do not have to watch their kids all the time: the community will watch for them. As for the kids, they don't seem to care about being watched—at least not till they get older.

93 / Vlasta Walla and Smokey

Vlasta Walla and her husband, George, came to McDade in the 1950s, so George could work at the nearby Elgin-Butler brickyard. They were originally from a tiny Czech community near Smithville, thirty miles to the south. The youngest of their three children, Wilbur, grew up in McDade. He later bought a house around the corner from his parents' home and raised a family of his own there. For years, Mrs. Walla supplemented George's income by working around town as a house cleaner. "She'd clean and scrub and do the wash," one of her employers remembers, "but she always found time to bake a cake or pie. She'd just use whatever was in the house." George Walla died suddenly, of a heart attack, in 1983. This picture was taken less than a year after his death. At the time, Mrs. Walla was having difficulty adjusting to life alone. After her husband's death, she began baking and canning in quantities much greater than she, Wilbur's family, or her neighbors could consume. She would insist on feeding visitors to her home, no matter what the time of day, and most would leave with bags full of homebaked desserts, homemade pickles, and vegetables from her garden. She's been cooking less in recent years, but she still likes having someone to feed when the opportunity arises.

94 / Greeting, Shorty and Ruth Bostic's Fiftieth-Anniversary Party

At her fiftieth wedding anniversary party, Ruth Bostic—the woman with the corsage—received congratulations from a lifetime's worth of friends and family. In this picture, she greets Lida Goodwin (left) and Mabel Stewart, while Mabel's husband, J. D., looks on. In 1924, Lida Goodwin was Ruth's first teacher at the Lawhon Springs School, a one-room country schoolhouse that Ruth's father, John Wesley Lawhon, had donated the land for and helped build. Ruth cannot remember her mother, who died in 1922, when Ruth was two. She was raised by her father until his death in 1929. After that she lived with an older married sister. She still has dreams about her father's funeral. "He was the world to me," she says. In 1935, when Ruth was fifteen, she married Shorty Bostic (fig. 72). He was twenty-five at the time and already farming the land the two of them would live on for the rest of their lives together. On their first wedding anniversary, Ruth gave birth to their son Curtis.

95 / Graduation, McDade School

Eight students graduated from the McDade School in 1989. Most were planning to attend seventh grade in Elgin the following year. In this picture, valedictorian Sara Cunningham leaves the podium after delivering a short speech. Recognizable in the background are Reverend Jerre Guthrie of the McDade Baptist Church, PTA president Kathleen Bush, and Principal and Superintendent Thomas Baca. With faces obscured, are school board vice president Clyde Farris and teacher Susan Stanley. In her valedictory address, Sara said that going to school in McDade was "like being part of a big happy family" and that she was sad about having to leave. She also praised the school's small classes and its generally informal atmosphere. Sara is not from McDade, having lived most of her life in Houston. Her recently separated parents are still in Houston, but for various reasons she cannot live with either of them. At the beginning of the 1988–89 school year, Sara came to stay with family friend Susan Stanley, the fifth- and sixth-grade teacher in McDade, and to be her student. This arrangement helped Sara have a successful sixth-grade year. Unfortunately for Sara, though, Susan Stanley left the McDade area in June 1989 and could not take Sara with her. Sara was going to spend the summer with relatives in Houston, but she didn't know where she'd be attending school the following year.

96 / William Wolf

William Wolf is a 1988 graduate of Lexington High School. Dan and Evelyn Wolf (fig. 74) are his parents; Minnie Lee Farris (fig. 84) is his maternal grandmother. This picture was taken while William was still in high school, on a Saturday afternoon while he and Dan were taking a break from planting several hundred new peach trees. As an only son, William has always had to help out with the farm work. Sometimes he gets tired of it. William's high school grades were good enough that he probably could have followed his older sister Danna to Texas A&M University, but he felt he'd "been to school too long already." He now works in Bastrop as a veterinarian's assistant. He lives at home and helps with the farm some, but he devotes much of his spare time to pursuing a passionate interest in coon hunting. During certain times of year, he spends a night or two each week in the woods with the pack of hounds he's raised and trained, chasing down raccoons. On weekends he often goes to organized coon hunts, where he and his dogs sometimes tree enough raccoons to bring home prize money. He doesn't seem to think about the future much. He hasn't yet made a decision—or, if he has, he's keeping it to himself—about whether he will take over the farm when Dan gets too old to work it. Dan says he doesn't care what William decides to do about the farm, but he still tries to teach William everything he can about running the place. Except for two years in the military, Dan has spent his entire life on the farm. He graduated from ninth grade in McDade in 1943 and went on to high school in Elgin the following fall. Six weeks later, though, he quit school to help his father full time on the farm.

97 / Nellie and Homer Hudler

Nellie and Homer Hudler lived in a small house across the street from the McDade School for many years. They rented the house from Alton Greenhaw, Peggy Fisher's father. Peggy (figs. 4 and 30) was their next-door neighbor. Both of the Hudlers were born in McDade, and they lived there most of their lives. Homer made his living as a carpenter and raised a few cattle on the side. To hear him tell it, he was quite a good baseball player in his youth. One of the biggest disappointments of his life was having a cow step on his foot, breaking some bones in it, just before he was to have a tryout with a semipro team from San Antonio. This was in the early 1920s. One of Nellie's earliest memories—from 1905 or 1906, she thinks—is of a trip to Austin her family made in their covered buckboard wagon. She especially remembers lying in the back of the wagon with her brothers and sisters while it rattled down Austin's Congress Avenue. From where she lay, she could see the giant dome of the Texas State Capitol out the back of the wagon, and Nellie remembers thinking it had to be the "grandest sight in all the world." Homer suffered a debilitating stroke shortly after this picture was taken. Nellie tried to take care of him at home but wasn't able to. Even though Homer pleaded with them not to, the family finally put him in an Elgin nursing home. He died there in 1988. Nellie left McDade at about the same time, her own declining health forcing her to move in with one of her daughters in Austin. A year or so later, Alton Greenhaw allowed his granddaughter Rachel Bright (fig. 24), along with her husband and new baby, to move into the house the Hudlers had spent so much of their lives in.

98 / Selma Brown and Selma Eklund, Three Oaks Cemetery Picnic

Selma Brown (seated) was president of the Three Oaks Cemetery Association for many years. In that capacity, she organized its annual picnics, made sure everyone paid dues on time, and watched over the association's modest bank account. She delegated the maintenance of the cemetery to her son, Sonny, and her nephew, Erhard Goerlitz. In 1977, as Mrs. Brown's health began to fail, Erhard assumed the association's presidency. In this picture, taken at the 1989 picnic, Mrs. Brown talks with her niece Selma Eklund. Mrs. Eklund's mother and Mrs. Brown were sisters; their maiden name was Goerlitz. In fact, Mrs. Eklund is a "double cousin" to Erhard Goerlitz, her mother and father being sister and brother to Erhard's father and mother. Mrs. Eklund was born and raised on the site of the Three Oaks Cemetery. The house she grew up in, now abandoned and fallen down, is located in the woods in the far background of this photograph. Mrs. Eklund has a "lazy eye" that sometimes drifts off to the side when she is tired. Family legend holds that this resulted from an incident that took place shortly after World War I, in which Mrs. Eklund's mother, pregnant with her at the time, witnessed a gang of anti-German toughs beat up her husband and threaten to burn down their house and barn. Selma Brown died in 1989, two months after this picture was taken. She was buried, of course, in the Three Oaks Cemetery. Funeral arrangements were made by the same Elgin mortuary that loans the Cemetery Association the large tent it uses for its picnic every year.

99 / Graduates, 1989 Graduation Ceremony

The McDade School's 1989 graduation ceremony ended on a humorous note. A few weeks earlier, teacher Susan Stanley had quietly arranged with her sixth graders' parents to borrow some of their "cutest" family photographs of the students as small children. She had slide copies made of some of the pictures, and she showed the slides, some of which were pretty embarrassing, at the conclusion of the graduation ceremony. The students, having just heard themselves praised for achievement and maturity, howled with laughter at pictures of themselves making messes in highchairs or splashing in bathtubs. The 1988–89 school year was a happier one for the McDade School than the previous several had been. With the controversy surrounding the 1987 firing and rehiring of Superintendent Thomas Baca slowly fading into the past, and with the continued existence of the McDade School assured by a three-to-one margin in a November 1987 referendum, both staff and students at the school seemed able to concentrate on education once again. From a poor performance in standardized statewide tests administered at the end of the 1986–87 school year, students at the McDade School jumped into the top quarter for 1987–88 and the top 5 percent for 1988–89. Some of Baca's opponents hint that he manipulated the test scores, but most people seem willing to take them at face value. They would like to believe, after all, that the school prepares its students well. Its graduates' above-average performance in the Elgin and Lexington secondary schools seems to indicate that it does. Very few of the kids from McDade, though, go on to college. In general, no one seems to expect them to.

100 / **Gale Rutherford and Kids**

Gale Rutherford (fig. 36) injured her knee while working as the custodian at the McDade School in 1985. The knee eventually required surgery, and she was unable to work for several months afterward. During that time, she often sat on the front porch of the old house she lived in and talked to passersby. In this picture, she watches her daughter, Mandy, play in their front yard with Poodle, one of the family dogs. In the background, Mandy's friend Lisa Taylor, daughter of Jack Taylor (fig. 39), looks on. Chris Heiser (fig. 33) is Mandy's younger brother. Gale and her children moved to Austin in 1986. Even though she felt McDade was a good place for Chris and Mandy to grow up—the school was right across the street, and her parents lived next door—Gale couldn't find work in town once her knee had healed. The custodial position at the school had long since been filled, and there weren't many other jobs around that she could do. Using her savings and a small loan from her mother, she enrolled in an Austin business college, hoping she could eventually find office work. Since then, she's gone to school part time and held a number of night jobs in Austin, including occasional "gigs" singing in a country-and-western bar band. She often brings Mandy and Chris to McDade to spend the weekend with her mother, but Gale herself usually doesn't stay long. Now that they're used to it, Mandy and Chris prefer living in Austin to McDade. Like their mother, they have more to do there.

101 / Hazel Creel

Hazel Creel has lived in McDade all her life, more than forty years in the house in the background of this picture. The house was once the parsonage of the long-defunct McDade Methodist Church. Mrs. Creel's husband died in 1977, shortly after he retired from his job with the railroad. She has lived alone since then. She has two daughters, both of whom live within an hour of McDade. They and their families frequently come to visit her. Her sons-in-law help keep up the house, and her grandchildren do most of the yard work. Nonetheless, she often feels lonely, especially in recent years, after her older sister Nellie Hudler (fig. 97) left McDade. Although Mrs. Creel socializes a couple of times a week with some of the other older women in town, she spends most of her time at home alone. She watches a lot of television, "favoring" soap operas and game shows, and keeps the inside of her house scrupulously clean and tidy. She readily admits that she misses the days when her daughters were small and her family intact.

102 / **Lorene and Calvin Lowery**

Lorene and Calvin Lowery (fig. 32) have been married for more than sixty years. They still live in the small house where they raised their five children—four daughters and a son. Their youngest daughter, Claudine Nesselbeck, still lives in McDade. Through her, they have two granddaughters and several great-grandchildren in town. All told, they have thirteen grandchildren, more great-grandchildren than they can keep track of ("I can't count em all," Mrs. Lowery says), and one great-great-grandchild. In 1978, the Lowerys' only son, Clyde, was killed in an automobile accident. His wife was pregnant with their first child at the time. Although Clyde's wife has since remarried and moved to Austin, the Lowerys are still in close touch with his daughter, Kimberly Ann. She is the only one of their many descendants who bears the Lowery name. In 1989, at age ninety-four, Mr. Lowery suffered a stroke. Once out of the hospital, he entered a Bastrop nursing home. Most people expected he'd die there. But Mrs. Lowery spent "all day, every day" at the nursing home—feeding and bathing her husband, talking to him (even before he could respond), and helping with his physical therapy. After six weeks, his condition had improved to the point that he could come home. "The Lord changed His mind about taking him," Mrs. Lowery says. "He decided I needed him more than He did."

103 / Emma Wuensche

Emma Wuensche was born in 1906, on her parents' 140-acre farm near McDade. The land had been in her mother's family since 1869. Her maternal grandfather, August Wolf, deeded it to her parents in 1886 as a wedding gift. Emma was the youngest of ten children. Though she finished eighth grade at a nearby country schoolhouse—Alma Kastner (fig. 63) was one of her schoolmates there—she did not go on to attend the high school in McDade. Instead, she stayed home and worked on the farm. She had several suitors during her teens and early twenties, but none of them was "right," either for her or for her parents. "My parents were very particular about who I married," she remembers. "I had to marry a Christian, and he should be German. The right boy just didn't come along." In 1932, seemingly an old maid, she left the farm and went to Houston, where she found work as a governess. Nine years later, she met Harry Wuensche at a church service. They were married soon afterward and moved back to McDade, into a small house on the edge of town. Harry worked as a carpenter at Camp Swift during World War II and later truck farmed for a living. The Wuensches raised three sons in McDade, all of whom graduated from college and went on to successful business careers in Houston. Harry Wuensche died in 1984, and Emma has lived alone since. Recently, it has become difficult for her to keep the house and garden as well ordered as she once did. Her sons want her to sell the house and move in with one of them in Houston. She does not want to leave her McDade home but concedes that someday soon she may have to.

104 / Boys with Radio

This picture was taken on a quiet Saturday afternoon in 1984. McDade seemed deserted that day. These boys—Bill Jurak, David Franks, Bo Grady, Howard Walla, Jay Shannon, and Keith Grady—were almost the only people out and around. They had been playing a half-hearted game of touch football in Howard's back yard, and they didn't mind taking a break to pose for a picture. They gathered around the radio, which at the time they carried with them everywhere. The radio was tuned to an Austin Top 40 station, and the volume was all the way up. Even in 1984, when some of these boys were only eleven, none of them envisioned living in McDade when they were grown up. By 1989, four of them—Bill, David, Bo, and Jay—had left, three of them to live in large cities. Generally speaking, McDade's teenagers find life in their hometown pretty boring. As Howard once observed, "Nothing much changes in McDade except the date." Most of the teens hope to leave McDade someday. Meanwhile, many of them just mark time, not doing much of anything, while they wait for the future, which they define as when they get done with school and can go to work. In a lot of ways, they already seem to think of their lives in McDade as part of the past, and the past—whether the history of McDade, accounts of their ancestors' lives, or the roles their families have played in the community over the years—is something they have little interest in.

105 / Tom Dungan

Tom Dungan once grew watermelons for a living. In the 1950s, after the decline of melons as a cash crop, he purchased McDade's recently abandoned train depot and had it moved across the street. He opened a grocery store in the old building and made a second career out of running it. In the 1970s, Tom's health began to fail, and he sold the store to Travis McPhaul, who later sold it to George Seigmund (figs. 5 and 18). Though Tom was glad to be free of running the store, he soon found that he missed all the people he used to see there every day. He began spending a lot of time in his front yard, sometimes doing yard work, sometimes just sitting. He would invite anyone who came by to have a seat, drink some iced tea with him, and talk. In 1985, as a present for his seventy-eighth birthday, his son Jerry gave him a new television and a satellite dish. Before that, Tom had never watched much TV; the only stations available in McDade were the network affiliates out of Austin, and they didn't carry much he cared to see. After the satellite dish was hooked up, he began watching TV almost every day. He often had trouble deciding what to watch and would constantly flip back and forth between channels to be sure he wasn't missing something better than what he had on. He spent less time in his front yard and saw fewer people. Tom died in 1988, after a long illness. Cable television became available in McDade in 1989, and most of those who had satellite dishes got rid of them. Tom's is still in his side yard. Nellie Hudler (fig. 97) and Hazel Creel (fig. 101) are Tom's sisters. He also has two brothers who live in McDade.

PART TWO

McDade, Texas

Introduction
Memories and History

The preceding section of this book is a work of "present-time" documentary photography. It depicts events that took place during a five-year period, 1984–89, in the ongoing history of McDade, Texas. The accompanying text treats the entire selection of pictures as though looking back on them from the end of those five years. Together, the photographs and text comprise a "present" for both author and reader to focus on. Obviously, the designation of such a present is an artificial process. In a historical sense, the present—no matter when it is or was—is an illusion, nothing more than an imagined moment in the continuous passage of time. When selecting a specific period to study, scholars—historians and documentary workers alike—pretend to make time stand still, proceeding with their work as though that time constituted present-time reality. Actually, this is little more than convention, a convenient illusion that provides a home base for their explorations that helps them avoid bogging down in the ever-shifting historical ground around them. In truth, though, they all know that the "present" is nothing more than the cumulative product of an infinite number of prior events and that no single unit of time, therefore—be it a moment or an era—can really be isolated from the times that came before it. The photographs and text of part one constitute one such illusory "present" in the ongoing history of McDade, Texas. The chapters that follow look at McDade's past in order to learn how the community came to be the way it was during that designated late-1980s present.

The past is a frequent topic of conversation in McDade. This is especially true among the town's older residents, doubly so when they are talking to someone who is not native to the area. Generally speaking, visitors who display any curiosity at all about McDade soon start hearing about its past, often in considerable, if not entirely accurate, detail. Invariably, among the first things they hear about are the Christmas Eve hangings and the ensuing Christmas Day shoot-out that took place uptown in 1883. In the telling and retelling of this story, the number of men killed often gets stretched from the actual six to a dozen or more, and if the tale is being told uptown, the narrator will probably claim that the vigilantes hanged their victims—suspected cattle rustlers they had seized at gun point in the Rockfront Saloon—from the large live oak tree that stands by the railroad tracks across the road from Sam Earl's. In reality, the vigilantes took the condemned men into the woods outside of town to hang them; no one today seems to know exactly where. Historical accuracy aside, however, many older people in McDade enjoy talking about the past, especially to strangers. They assume it is what curious strangers want to hear about, and they are happy to accommodate.

They are less likely to tell an outsider much of substance about present-day McDade. In part, this probably reflects people's understandable qualms about sharing details of their lives, and those of their friends and neighbors, with a stranger. But even an outsider, if friendly, well mannered, and patiently persistent, can eventually overcome the reluctance of most people in McDade to talk about their lives and their community. What is more difficult to overcome is the commonly held assumption that life in present-day McDade is hardly worth the effort of talking about. Many people who live there, especially the older ones, seem to have an ingrained vision of McDade as a place whose present is a mere shadow of its past and is thus less worthy of attention. They don't understand why anyone would want to study the McDade of the present—a diminished McDade to their way of thinking, a place where life is duller and shabbier than it used to be—when the town has a past that is not only more colorful and exciting than the present but was also a time when McDade had reasonable expectations of growth and prosperity. In short, they remember the past as a time when McDade had a future. Most believe that present-day McDade doesn't have much of a future, and that is a topic they usually don't care to talk about.

It is not surprising that they feel this way. McDade has had a diverse and entertaining history, a past that belies its seemingly uneventful present. At various times, the town has been boisterously exciting (when it was a Wild West boomtown); self-consciously respectable (when it attempted to live down its Wild West past); smugly prosperous (when it was the principal mercantile center for a sizable rural area); vainly hopeful (when its leading citizens boosted it as a likely site for the discovery of oil, the perfect place to construct a lake and lake-resort complex, or the ideal location for various and sundry manufacturing enterprises); briefly resurgent (when a major World War II training camp was built nearby); and rationally "progressive" (when the town's postwar leadership embarked upon a community-wide self-improvement campaign). Throughout each of these stages, McDade has ridden the current of the times, like a tiny cork rising and falling on the surface of an ocean. It has often been in danger of sinking but has thus far stayed afloat. The town has an interesting past, one that is worth exploring in some detail.

CHAPTER 8

The Celebrated Past
The Railroad, the Bad Guys, and the Good Guys

McDade did not exist in 1869, when surveyors for the Houston and Texas Central Railroad first came through the area searching out the best rail route between Houston and Austin. A few landowners had grown cotton in the general vicinity since the 1840s, but most of these early settlers had built their homes closer to the Colorado River—near the old river-crossing town of Bastrop—twelve miles south of where the railroad would soon give birth to McDade. Two miles north of the future town site, along the upper reaches of West Yegua Creek, lived several interrelated families of German immigrants who supported themselves on the rich bottomland farms they had established there in the 1850s. As of 1869, however, there was no human habitation on the site that would soon became the town of McDade.[1]

Later that year, advance construction crews and parties of tie-cutters arrived in the area. Their appearance was the first real indication that the railroad would in fact be coming through the northern part of Bastrop County. On the spot where the projected rail line was to cross the low ridge dividing the watersheds of the Brazos and Colorado Rivers, the construction bosses established a collection point for the thousands of wooden ties their crews were busily cutting in the surrounding woodlands. This spot became known as Tie Town, or Tie City, and served as a home base for many of the railroad workers. Several tent saloons, where a man could get a tin cupful of whiskey for a dime, soon sprang up, and Tie Town quickly gained a reputation as a wild and sometimes dangerous place.[2]

The rail line was completed as far as Tie Town in August 1871, and, along with the arrival of the first train, the place got a new name. Four Bastrop land speculators registered a deed in Houston's Harris County Courthouse that same month. The deed read: "We have caused about 640 acres of land to be subdivided and laid off in blocks and have named the place McDade," after lawyer James W. McDade, a leading citizen of Brenham (sixty-five miles east of McDade, also on the Houston and Texas Central line) and a major investor in the railroad. Tie Town thus officially became the town of McDade.[3]

The town's new status and a train that ran back and forth to Houston every day brought instant prosperity. McDade became a boomtown almost overnight. For the next four months, the railroad's construction engineers directed the completion of the line to Austin from temporary headquarters in McDade, and the town continued to swarm with railroad workers. In addition, throughout autumn of 1871—until the final stretch of track was laid in late December—several stage lines ran daily coaches between Austin and the railhead at McDade, ferrying businessmen, state officials, salesmen, and other travelers back and forth, meeting them at arriving trains, and delivering them to departing trains. The stagecoach fare was a substantial six dollars each way. Travelers who missed their connection could spend the night in one of McDade's two hastily constructed hotels and could choose among several different saloons and gambling halls to amuse themselves.[4]

The completion of the Houston and Texas Central rail line to Austin had little impact on McDade's booming success. Stagecoaches operated north and south out of McDade, carrying passengers, mail, and light freight between the train depot and the surrounding countryside. To the north, the McDade stage served the communities of Knobbs Springs, Blue, and Lexington before reaching the end of the line in Rockdale, thirty-nine miles away. Residents of these landlocked farming communities were delighted to suddenly be in closer touch with the outside world. A second stage line ran south out of McDade to the Colorado River towns of Bastrop and Smithville. The leaders of these communities could not help but envy McDade's overnight success, as the train proved itself a cheaper and more reliable form of transportation than the riverboats plying the unpredictable Colorado. Due to an accident of geography—its ridge-top location on the divide between two river systems—McDade had quickly become an important place.[5]

The railhead at McDade was a busy spot, serving the surrounding rural population and several smaller towns to the north as the transfer spot for freight and agricultural produce. Day and night, workers unloaded incoming cargo, mostly manufactured goods, from the train cars onto wagons for delivery to one of McDade's new retail shops or to smaller stores in outlying communities. They would often reload the freight cars with outgoing produce from the surrounding countryside, usually livestock or cotton. McDade's first cotton gin opened in 1872, and planters from as far away as Lampasas, ninety miles to the northwest, started hauling their cotton to McDade to have it ginned and shipped. Later that year, Robert Bryce and George Lyman, the owners of the cotton gin, began operating a steam-powered corn mill in McDade. They advertised "the most modern methods" and "competitive terms" in the weekly *Bastrop Advertiser*, the county's only newspaper. "Our location upon the great (Central) railroad of Texas," their ad proclaimed, "renders us easy access from all parts of the State and will enable us to grind and deliver meal at any town or station where a customer may be found." The Houston and Texas Central Railroad had created McDade and put it on the map. A number of enterprising entrepreneurs were quick to recognize the new town's profit-making potential, and they did not hesitate to take advantage of the opportunities it offered.[6]

Less than a year after McDade officially came into being, its population topped two thousand. Many people lived in tents at first, since building materials were in short supply and the construction of commercial buildings took priority. McDade's business district soon extended four blocks on both sides of the tracks. In addition to the cotton gin and grist mill, the town boasted a number of retail businesses, two wholesale houses, a pair of hotels, two drugstores, two meat markets, a smithy, a livery stable, and several saloons and gambling joints. By July 1873, a third hotel had opened for business, as well as J. M. Cliett's lumberyard and Mrs. E. P. Crowe's "Fashionable Millinery," which supplied "Ladies Goods of all description." McDade had boomed and quickly seemed about to become civilized.[7]

Along with the railroad and commercial success, came a de facto role for McDade as something of a regional cultural center. On June 26, 1872, the first Pullman "Pioneer" sleeping car to operate in Texas—on a promotional tour sponsored by manufacturer George Pullman—traveled the Houston and Texas Central line between Houston and Austin, stopping for an afternoon at McDade.

People from miles around flocked to McDade to inspect the interior of the amazing new "moving hotel" firsthand and to marvel at its opulence. In December 1873, the railroad nearly brought John Robinson's Circus and Menagerie, advertised for weeks beforehand as "a Grand Exposition . . . the largest show ever tented in any country, [and] A Strictly Moral Circus!," to McDade. Threats of violence from a rival show in Houston, however, forced Robinson and his circus to flee the state just before the scheduled appearance in McDade. The "non-appearance" of the circus disappointed people for "25 miles around," many of whom, unaware that the show had been canceled, arrived in McDade on the afternoon of December 4 in eager anticipation of a "grand old time."[8]

Like many Western boomtowns, McDade was plagued by violence in its early years. Business there was brisk and nearly always transacted in cash. A lot of money changed hands in McDade: People traveled miles to buy things they could not raise or make themselves; merchants paid the freight agent at the depot for incoming goods to stock their shelves; and farmers and ranchers sold their produce and livestock to buyers at the railhead. In addition, McDade's thriving saloons, gambling joints, and bawdy houses helped keep considerable amounts of cash circulating. With the county sheriff's office located twelve miles away in Bastrop (and with a sheriff not overly eager to bring order to the upstart railroad town), law enforcement was virtually nonexistent. Not surprisingly, a number of shady characters soon descended upon McDade to take whatever advantage they could of the situation.[9]

The location of the Yegua Knobs just seven miles to the northeast contributed to McDade's lawlessness. The Knobs are the three highest hills on a rugged ridge line that straddles the border between Bastrop and Lee Counties. They lie roughly in a north-south line and extend for about ten miles. The tiny farming communities of Knobbs Springs and Blue are at the foot of the Knobs' western slope, but even today the land to the east of the ridge line is a wild tangle of thick woods and brush, steep rocky hillsides, and deeply cut ravines. In the years after the Civil War, the Knobs were one of central Texas's most notorious outlaw hideouts. Fugitives from justice had been hiding there since before the war, and many of them had settled in as permanent residents. During the war, a number of draft-dodgers and deserters also fled to the Knobs, some taking their families with them. By the time the railroad went through Bastrop County in 1871, a group of disaffected Civil War veterans had joined them there. Given the area's rugged terrain, its isolation, and the reputation of those who lived there, few lawmen would follow a suspected highwayman, horse thief, or cattle rustler into the Yegua Knobs. Several who did were never seen again.[10]

One can well imagine that the lawless element living near the Knobs regarded the emergence of a prosperous little railroad town just a few miles away as cause for rejoicing. Previously, the closest town of any size had been the Lee County seat of Giddings, twenty miles to the southeast and the site of the county sheriff's office. Many of those who lived near the Knobs were wanted in Lee County and could not safely go to Giddings. Thus McDade, in Bastrop County and with little in the way of law enforcement, offered them a chance to enjoy the amenities of town life as well as an opportunity to help themselves to some of the cash that was circulating freely there.[11]

McDade soon developed a reputation as a place where a man could lose his life as easily as his money. Men died over card games, in dark alleyways, and in drunken brawls. Erhard Goerlitz, born during World War I into one of the area's old German families, recalls hearing his grandfather talk about one of the professional gamblers who operated in McDade during the 1870s and 1880s. The man was a good card player and would usually win, the story went, but even if he were losing he would never cheat, preferring to maintain his reputation for honesty. Instead, for those occasions when he lost significant amounts of money, he had several hired thugs whose job was to follow the man he had lost to, relieve him of his winnings, kill him, and bury him in the woods outside of town. According to Erhard's grandfather, if a big gambling night was expected in McDade, these hired killers would sometimes go to remote locations and dig graves in advance so as to expedite the disposal of bodies. Anyone who stayed around McDade for any length of time learned not to play cards with this man: "If you lost, you were lucky; if you won, you could lose everything," Erhard remembers his grandfather saying.[12]

The roads to and from McDade were dangerous places, especially north of town, toward the Knobs. Armed highwaymen held up more than one farmer returning home from selling a crop in McDade. One man, having hidden his money in a bag of cottonseed, was tortured into telling the bandits where it was. He died of his injuries a few days later. Sometimes men were ambushed on the road out of vengeance rather than money. One night in 1876, Buck Christian, a resident of the Oak Hill community two miles south of McDade and suspected of having burned down the Oak Hill schoolhouse, was killed as he rode home from McDade. The citizens of Oak Hill would not allow him burial in the cemetery there, so his family buried him in McDade instead.[13]

Cattle rustling was also a problem. The emergence of the railhead at McDade had driven up the price of cattle in the area. This was good for local cattlemen, but few residents of McDade wanted to pay the newly inflated price for beef, a staple in the local diet. For those who were not particular about where their meat came from, a market soon developed in McDade for freshly slaughtered beeves, a situation that was tailor-made for small-time cattle rustling. Thieves could kill a few head of cattle wherever they found them, remove the hide with its identifying brand, and haul the carcasses to McDade for sale. Short of catching the rustlers in the act, there was virtually no way of preventing this kind of thievery. Sometimes rustlers did get caught, however, and with increasing frequency they wound up dead rather than in jail. In the spring of 1876, the bodies of two local toughs were found in the woods just north of McDade, each wrapped in a fresh cowhide. A wagon was tethered nearby with two skinned beeves loaded onto it. The brands on the hides indicated that the cattle had not belonged to the dead men but to brothers Jay, John, Prentice, and Jim Olive. Most people in the area served by the McDade railhead understood this incident as a warning to rustlers that local cattlemen—the Olive brothers and others—were starting to mete out their own form of justice to those caught stealing cattle. Indeed, in the months that followed, a number of suspected rustlers were found hanged. One of them had several hundred dollars in his pocket, an obvious indication that he had been killed for reasons other than robbery.[14]

The rustlers and the widely extended kin networks many of them belonged to responded in kind. By this time, they had formed themselves into a loosely organized gang known as the Notchcutters. (The source of the gang's name is unclear; some accounts claim it referred to notches the gang members cut on the handles of their guns as a tally of their victims, but others say it came from their habit of marking trails in the thick woods near the Knobs by cutting notches on trees.) In August 1876, about twenty members of the gang attacked the ranch home of the Olive brothers in southern Williamson County, killing Prentice Olive and one of his hired hands. They also stole a considerable amount of cash and burned the Olives' house and barn to the ground. The following year, a band of heavily armed, masked men seized four reputed members of the Notchcutters at a dance near Blue. After telling the fiddler to keep playing and warning the dancers to stay inside, they hanged the prisoners from a nearby tree. A vicious cycle of lynchings and retaliatory shootings, many of them fueled by family animosities, had begun. Over the next several years a number of men were found hanged in the country north of McDade. Others died in roadside ambushes, and quite a few simply disappeared.[15]

The cycle of violence came to a head in late 1883, when it erupted on the streets of McDade. The culminating sequence of events began with a robbery and double murder in the Lee County community of Fedor, a small German settlement on the eastern edge of the wild country near the Knobs. On the night of November 22, an armed man entered the general store there and demanded money at gun point. Upon being given the contents of the till, a mere fifteen dollars, he killed the elderly storeowner and his clerk. A little more than a week later, on December 1, Lee County deputy sheriff Boaz Heffington arrived in McDade. Heffington had been investigating the Fedor murders; rumor had it that he had a suspect in mind and had come to McDade to make an arrest. That night he approached someone in a dark alleyway in downtown McDade and was shot in the chest. He died the next day.[16]

The murder of Boaz Heffington shocked law-abiding people in McDade and the area served by its rail depot. As unruly a place as McDade had always been, the town had never before seen the forces of law and order so openly attacked. At no time in the community's short history had the criminal element seemed so close to controlling the town. Concerned citizens decided to organize. On the night of December 8, about two hundred people gathered in the "Union Building," constructed in 1872 to serve as McDade's schoolhouse and as meeting house for the town's two church congregations. Lee County sheriff Jim Brown "kept the door," making sure that only the "right people" gained admission. The goal of those attending was "to assist the officers of the law and use every effort to suppress lawlessness," the next day's *Galveston News* reported. "The people of this section are thoroughly aroused and seem to be determined to stop the frequent killings and robberies which have recently occurred in this vicinity." Virtually nothing of what was said that night was ever reported, though some accounts claim that saloonkeepers were ordered to cooperate by reporting suspicious talk and watching for freshly cut notches on gun handles. Nor were the names of those at the meeting ever revealed. The *Galveston News* was content to identify them only as "the very best citizens."[17]

Regardless of what was said or who was there, someone decided to act against the Notchcutters a couple of weeks later. On the night of December 24, a group of about fifty heavily armed, masked men entered McDade's Rockfront Saloon and, not wanting their voices to be recognized, handed saloonkeeper Oscar Nash a list of names to read aloud. Three of the men whose names he read—all suspected cattle rustlers and horse thieves who lived near the Knobs—were in the saloon that night, celebrating Christmas Eve. They were Henry Pfeiffer and brothers Thad and Wright McLemore. (Thad McLemore had been arrested earlier in the day for burglary, the result of a complaint sworn out by McDade shopkeeper S. G. Walker. Why he was no longer still in custody is not clear.) The vigilantes silently marched the three of them a mile or so out of town and hanged them from a tree.[18]

More killings were to follow. The next morning a group of six men rode in from the Knobs to have a Christmas morning drink at the Rockfront Saloon. Three of them— brothers Jack, Az, and Heywood Beatty—were related to the McLemores by marriage. The others—Charlie Goodman, Robert Stevens, and Burt Hasley—were related to the Beattys. Over drinks at the saloon they learned what had happened the previous night. They also learned that Heywood Beatty's name had been on the vigilantes' list, probably because a week or so earlier storekeeper George Milton had publicly accused Heywood of helping Boaz Heffington's murderer leave town by providing the fugitive with money and a horse.[19]

Accounts of exactly what happened in the next few minutes vary considerably. It seems that the Beatty brothers went looking for Milton, with Jack and Heywood entering his store and angrily confronting him. In the meantime, Az Beatty had stopped outside the store to challenge Tom Bishop, who was sitting on a bench there. Bishop was a close friend of Milton's, and he and Az had almost come to blows just a few days earlier. Either Beatty or Bishop (probably Bishop) pulled a gun, and they began wrestling for possession of it. As they rolled off the raised gallery into the street, the gun went off, wounding Az Beatty in the thigh. At the sound of the shot, Milton and the other two Beattys came rushing out of the store, Milton brandishing the shotgun he had been holding them at bay with. At that point, bullets began flying in all directions, and no one was later able to sort out the precise sequence of events. In any case, just a few moments later, Jack and Az Beatty lay dead in the street and a young man named Willie Griffin, who had rushed in trying to act as peacemaker, lay dying with a bullet in his head. Heywood Beatty was badly wounded—shot seventeen times, some accounts claim—though he did manage to escape, making it safely back to the Knobs later in the day. According to their testimony at the official inquest, Milton and Bishop then turned their guns on Goodman, Stevens, and Hasley, who they claimed had been firing at them from "across the tracks," and chased them out of town, slightly wounding Goodman and Stevens.[20]

Though written accounts of this incident have always cast Milton and Bishop as upstanding citizens defending themselves against members of the town's criminal element, the roles may have been reversed in this instance. Conflicting testimony offered at the official inquest has rendered the details of the gunfight indistinct at best. There does seem reason to believe, however, that Az and Jack Beatty were unarmed that Christmas morning and that even though they went looking for George Milton in anger, they did not intend to kill him. (Without question, Heywood Beatty was armed and fired several shots—in self-defense, he claimed—probably including the one that killed Willie Griffin.) This view is supported by the testimony of storekeeper W. A. Billingsley, who, in addition to testifying that he did not think Jack and Az Beatty were armed, also stated that Jack was "under cover of Milton's gun" when Bishop, having won the struggle for the pistol, killed Az with a shot to the head. "Bishop then whirled toward Jack Beatty," Billingsley's statement continued, "and he and Milton fired simultaneously and Jack Beatty fell." He went on to say that Jack Beatty's coat was on fire after he was shot, probably indicating a shotgun blast at close range. In addition, he testified that Burt Hasley had been in his store exchanging a pair of boots when the shooting began and thus could not have been firing at Milton and Bishop from across the railroad tracks, as they had claimed.[21]

Whatever the truth of the matter, public sentiment was solidly behind Milton and Bishop. Bastrop County sheriff Sid Jenkins came to McDade that Christmas afternoon to cut down the bodies of the men hanged the night before. He also placed Milton and Bishop under arrest for the murders of the Beatty brothers and took them to jail in Bastrop. They were released two days later. During their short stay in the county jail, there were "scores of citizens clamoring to go their bail," the *Austin Statesman* reported, and they were freed in large part because public opinion was "so unanimous that the county attorney could not find against them." Heywood Beatty was also arrested, and later tried, for the murder of Willie Griffin. Since no one could determine with any certainty whose bullet had killed Griffin, however, Beatty was acquitted. (More than fifty years later, in a statement published in *Frontier Times Magazine*, Beatty admitted to firing the shot that killed Griffin.) The *Galveston News* hailed Milton and Bishop as heroes, stating that the Beattys "had given the citizens of McDade and vicinity considerable trouble heretofore and were of that class that seemed to care nothing for the rights of property."[22]

People in McDade did not rest easy that Christmas afternoon, fearing that friends and relatives of the Beattys and McLemores would be coming into town looking for revenge. Those who stayed in McDade armed themselves and kept a close watch on the road from the Knobs. Others piled their families into wagons and fled south to Bastrop. Louis Bassist, a German-born merchant who had recently opened a business in McDade, boarded the Christmas afternoon train for Elgin, where in years to come he would be a leading member of the business community. Although he spent the rest of his life in Elgin—just nine miles away—and kept his general store in McDade open for another fifteen years, he never again set foot in McDade. Nor was reaction to the Christmas violence in McDade confined to the immediate area. Governor John Ireland, upon receiving telegraphed reports of the hangings, the shootings, and the generally tense situation in McDade, was so alarmed at the prospect of retaliation from the Knobs that he called out units of the state militia to help keep the peace. He ordered as many members of Hempstead's Johnson Guards and the Brenham Grays as could be located that Christmas Day to cut their holiday short and board the midnight train from Houston to McDade. They arrived at 4:30 the next morning.[23]

Their presence turned out to be unnecessary. Members of the Beatty and McLemore families came to town and claimed their kinsmen's bodies on the twenty-sixth without incident, and, for reasons unknown, the Notchcutters did not seek revenge. Many perceived their failure to do so as a victory for the forces of law and order in McDade. The *Galveston News* crowed that "the outlaws, having been badly whipped by the citizens . . . seem to be in no hurry to renew hostilities," and warned that "the citizens of McDade are watchful and ready for any emergency, and other law-abiding citizens of the county will aid them." In fact, many people in McDade were so encouraged by the Notchcutters' seeming weakness that they called a second public meeting for the evening of December 27. At this gathering they read aloud the names of suspected members of the Notchcutters and voted for or against each one. Those whom they voted against were warned to leave the McDade area within ten days or risk being hunted down and hanged. Many of the Notchcutters took this warning seriously and left for less hostile environs. Those who remained at the Knobs were careful to stay out of McDade. As a result, the violence in the area diminished considerably. McDade's upright citizens had apparently won their violent fight against the forces of lawlessness.[24]

CHAPTER 9

The Forgotten Past
Decline and the Search for Respectability

Ironically, McDade's fortunes began to decline soon after the community's law-abiding citizens succeeded in running the criminal element out of town. McDade's regional importance diminished markedly in the mid-1880s for reasons both obscure and obvious. On the obscure side is the likelihood that the respectable citizens of the older, more established communities of Smithville and Bastrop began to shun McDade. Even though McDade had been known as a rough-and-tumble place since railroad workers first congregated there in 1869, its reputation had been largely local. The Christmas violence of 1883, however, was of a different magnitude: it expanded McDade's notoriety and brought the region's lawlessness statewide attention. This may have so concerned citizens in the rest of the county that they decided to disassociate themselves from McDade. In any event, prior to 1884 the *Bastrop Advertiser* had carried advertisements for businesses in McDade in almost every issue. Such advertising diminished sharply immediately after the "Horrible Affray at McDade" and by 1887 had disappeared entirely. Although speculating from the distance of more than a century is risky business, one could conjecture that McDade, by bringing the violent nature of life in Bastrop County to rest of the state's attention, had so offended the area's respectable folk that they responded by shunning McDade. If this is what happened, it is ironic that their ostracism was the result of the very events that rid McDade of its most openly lawless and violent element.

A more obvious development contributing to McDade's decline was the completion of the Taylor, Bastrop and Houston Railroad in 1887. This line ran north-south through Bastrop County, intersecting the Houston and Texas Central track at Elgin, nine miles west of McDade. Now at the junction of two railroads, Elgin quickly became the main shipping point and commercial center for much of the area previously served by McDade. Within two years, Elgin outstripped McDade in population, and several businesses left McDade to relocate in Elgin or Bastrop, now both equally accessible to Austin and Houston as McDade was. The stage line between McDade and Bastrop went out of business, and the stage running north cut back its route, since the new railhead at Taylor (in eastern Williamson County) was now more convenient than the depot at McDade for most of those living in the country to the north of town. As quickly as it had risen to prominence in the northern part of Bastrop County and grown to rival the older, more staid river towns of Bastrop and Smithville for the county's commercial leadership, McDade now found itself playing fourth fiddle to Bastrop, Smithville, and Elgin. It was a hard lesson in the economics of boom and bust that plagued many communities in the American West.[1]

But McDade did not go bust. Instead, its leading citizens set about consolidating what remained into a respectable little country town. Even though the size of the region served by McDade had diminished, the town's rail depot was still the most convenient spot for many farmers and ranchers to market their produce and livestock. And for those living in the immediate area, McDade was still the obvious place to shop. In an 1890 letter to her family in Alabama, widow Dora Griffith (who worked as a bookkeeper in the Bassist General Store, McDade's largest business) described the community as a healthy little commercial town. She wrote that it had a population of about three hundred and boasted six general retail outlets, two drugstores, a pair of hotels, and two saloons. Her own employer, she wrote, kept four retail clerks busy every day and did "50,000 dollars business" a year.[2]

McDade still seemed to have trouble getting along with the rest of the county, however. A letter written by McDade's George Milton (and signed by eleven others from McDade) appeared in the *Bastrop Advertiser* of July 12, 1890, complaining of corruption within the Bastrop County Democratic Party. Milton and his cosigners claimed that "on the eve of every election," the party's leaders would gather at the courthouse in Bastrop and "go through the mockery of a republican convention . . . endorsing or nominating the candidate who puts up the most money." Milton called for a county-wide convention that would consider the wishes of people in all the county's precincts rather than catering solely to the interests of the established politicos in Bastrop. The county leadership ridiculed Milton's suggestion, however, meeting informally in Bastrop and issuing a mocking response, printed in the *Advertiser* of July 26, that concluded, "On motion, the meeting was adjourned, with the unanimous opinion that we need rain worse than [we need] a county convention." The following week, Milton replied that this gathering of the party's leaders had not been an authorized party function and had failed to take into account the opinions of Democrats in the McDade Precinct. His comments went unheeded, however, and the controversy disappeared from the pages of the *Advertiser* as though it had never occurred.[3]

During the 1890s and throughout the first decade of the new century, the *Advertiser* paid little attention to events in McDade. Occasionally, the paper printed "letters from McDade" that reported on the community's periodic attempts to become more respectable. Ironically, these pieces often referred to McDade's sinful past. One such letter reported on a two-week-long revival preached by Bastrop's Reverend B. B. Sanders in McDade during the summer of 1890. It celebrated seventy-eight "additions" to the Church of Christ there and boasted of more than seven hundred dollars pledged to the construction of a new "church house." The letter's author (an unnamed member of the congregation) expressed delight at the Reverend Sanders's inspired preaching—"such grandeur as was never seen in this part of Texas"—as well as in the revival's more tangible results. People throughout Bastrop County, the correspondent wrote, "hav[ing] heard of McDade's reputation," should be especially encouraged. "Our church is now considerable over a hundred at this place. It can truly be said that McDade has turned a new leaf."[4]

R. L. Hovis, McDade's new teacher for the 1890–91 school year, wrote of the school there in similar fashion. In the middle of September, feeling optimistic about the prospects for education in McDade, he wrote a letter to the *Advertiser* extolling the town's "progressive" attitude toward its school. After reporting that enrollment had risen from forty-three to fifty-six during the first two weeks of classes, his letter concluded: "The school has labored under many difficulties in the past, but we hope a new day has dawned for the school in this quiet little village."[5]

And perhaps it had. A letter from McDade had appeared in the *Advertiser* of August 2 proudly reporting the hiring of Hovis, "formerly principal of the public school at Jasper City, Missouri," as McDade's new schoolmaster. The same letter also mentioned that volunteers had started building a house in McDade for Hovis to live in. A few weeks earlier, another group of volunteers had dug a new cistern at the ramshackle old structure where the McDade school held its classes, the same Union Building where the vigilance committee had gathered seven years earlier to take action against the Notchcutters. They also performed other "sorely necessary improvements." At the same time, the community's leaders were trying to organize an official school district at McDade, so the town could levy taxes to finance its children's education. "The petition is signed, the boundaries are fixed, and the people are sure the measure will carry by a large majority," this letter concluded. Maybe there was reason for optimism.[6]

Further developments over the next two decades also indicate a McDade community that was striving for stability, order, and the respect of its neighbors. Three different newspapers—the *McDade Mentor*, the *McDade Keystone*, and the *Plain Dealer*—started there during the 1890s, though none lasted for more than a few issues (very few of which have survived to the present). The McDade Church of Christ followed through on the promise of its 1890 revival, purchasing a plot of land and building a meeting house of its own the following year. This freed the congregation from having to share the drafty Union Building with the Baptists, the town's schoolchildren, and traveling minstrel shows. A year later, the McDade Methodist Church opened its doors.[7]

The 1890s also saw the birth of the most successful business enterprise ever to exist in McDade—the McDade Pottery plant. Robert L. Williams, a young man from Pennsylvania with experience in the pottery business, first came to McDade in 1888, attracted by reports of large, easily accessible deposits of high-quality clay in the area. After arriving in McDade, he apprenticed himself to a local potter named Stoker. Two years later, he bought Stoker out and became sole owner of the business he renamed McDade Pottery. By 1892, Williams had built a modern new factory capable of turning out hundreds of molded clay pots every day. The new plant turned out its first pots in January 1893, and by the following year McDade Pottery was shipping freight-carloads of its various products to Houston and Austin on a regular basis. The pottery plant would be a successful enterprise for the next fifty years, employing many people in McDade and shipping countless flower pots, charcoal-burning clay furnaces (based on a patented design authored by Williams himself), and other ceramic goods to markets throughout Texas and surrounding states.[8]

During that half century, the Williams family became McDade's leading citizens, the closest thing to an aristocracy the town ever had. Robert Williams, and later his son Payne, were tireless in their efforts to improve the quality of its citizens' lives (especially the moral quality of their lives) and to make the community once again respectable in the eyes of its neighbors. As early as 1894, Williams had helped the McDade Baptist Church buy the lot occupied by the old Union Building, where the town's children attended school and where its churchgoers had gathered for Sunday worship since the 1870s. In 1900, he was instrumental in the church's purchase of the old building itself, and he paid most of what it cost to refurbish it. Williams was also a leader of the "dries" in 1902, when the McDade Precinct of Bastrop County took advantage of Texas's "local option" law and voted to ban the sale of alcohol within precinct boundaries. In 1905, he opened a general store in McDade, and two years later, he was among a group of McDade businessmen who persuaded the

Houston and Texas Central to build a "handsome, up-to-date" new depot in town. The following year, in 1908, Williams moved his general store into the abandoned Rockfront Saloon, which he had bought after succeeding in his efforts to shut the saloon down.[9]

In June 1909, the *San Antonio Express* ran an article on Bastrop County, which characterized McDade as "one of the best towns in the county," stating that it had "improved rapidly within the past few years." The best was yet to come, however. In July 1909, McDade's voters overwhelmingly approved an eight thousand dollar bond issue, as well as a "maintenance tax," to build a new school. Construction was underway in May 1910, and by the following September McDade's schoolchildren had a new two-story brick building. Large letters over the arched entrance proudly identified the building as "McDade High School" and gave the year of its construction. The new school boasted a faculty of five and offered a state-approved curriculum for first through tenth grades. In addition to the standard complement of courses in English, history, and math, McDade students had to take either Latin or bookkeeping. "Those students desiring to continue their student life are strongly advised to study Latin," warned the McDade School's *Sixth Annual Announcement* (a yearbook of sorts for the 1915–16 school year). "Our Latin course gives three entrance credits to first class universities while the bookkeeping course gives only one half credit." The first graduating class, consisting of two students, received diplomas in May 1911. One of the graduates was Robert Haden Williams, the older son of civic-minded pottery manufacturer Robert L. Williams. The younger Williams eventually went on to earn a doctorate in Romance Languages at Columbia and later taught at Brown and the University of Texas. McDade had indeed "improved rapidly."[10]

This more refined, "progressive" McDade also proved to be fertile ground for new business ventures in the years before World War I. In 1910, local entrepreneur Will Stagner installed a telephone system in McDade. When he first offered his service, his telephone exchange had only thirty subscribers, but it soon gained many more. That same year, Dr. G. W. Southern and his pharmacist wife, Mabel, moved to McDade and began their long careers serving the community's health needs. The town's first bank, a private uninsured business operated by E. F. Brown, failed in 1911, costing many in McDade considerable amounts of money. Even so, just two years later, the McDade Guaranty State Bank opened for business, in the same building the failed bank had occupied. The new bank was publicly insured and had declared capital reserves in excess of ten thousand dollars. On its board of directors were pottery entrepreneur Williams and merchant George Milton, thirty years removed from his shotgun-wielding days. This bank proved to be successful and in 1914, just a year after opening, moved out of the older bank building into handsome new quarters on the increasingly busy Houston to Austin highway. (This is the building that is now the post office, on uptown McDade's main street.) At about the same time, in 1913, partners J. S. Kelton and L. A. Kunkel established the McDade Mercantile Company. Kelton and Kunkel were enterprising young men who had become friends while working together as clerks in one of McDade's older stores. The business they founded became known as "Kelton & Kunkel" and was soon McDade's largest and most successful retail establishment, remaining so through the death of Kelton in 1942 and until Kunkel's retirement in 1961.[11]

By 1914, things were looking up in McDade. The booming railroad town of the 1870s and 1880s had weathered its bust and subsequent decline and now seemed well on the way to a modest, middle-class brand of prosperity. It was home to a successful manufacturing enterprise, new businesses were starting up, and it had its own hometown bank. Its residents included a leading family and a sizable complement of progressive, high-minded citizens who seemed intent on leading McDade into the future and establishing it as something more than a faded railroad town whose past outshone its present. The community had worked hard at becoming respectable: it could boast of three churches (two of them housed in fairly new buildings), a new high school, and an absence of saloons. No other town in Bastrop County had ever banned the sale of alcohol (and none has since); many in McDade were proud (and some still are) of that distinction. During the Christmas season of 1914—thirty-one years after six men had come to sudden, violent ends in uptown McDade—the community's churches hosted a two-day-long "old-fashioned" carol-singing convention that attracted music lovers and professional musicians from as far away as Houston. McDade was proud to be able to show the world that it was a hospitable, cultured, and morally refined little community—indeed "one of the best towns in the county."[12]

CHAPTER 10

The Other McDade
The Germans at Siloah

In 1917, a fourth church was established in McDade. Its members were not new to the area, nor was the church itself newly organized. Founded in 1882 as the Siloah (Sy-LOW-ah) Evangelical Lutheran Church, it had previously served the rural Siloah community, a tightly knit group of German immigrant families living on farms in the country to the north of McDade and Paige. It was, however, a new church to McDade, and its relocation into town enlarged McDade in ways that greatly influenced the community's future. The church's move also signaled the inability of the Siloah community to survive independently, as indicated by its residents' willingness to assimilate into the predominant American culture represented by McDade.

A number of people in present-day McDade are descended from the German immigrants who settled just north of town in the latter half of the nineteenth century. These people are arguably the dominant social group in McDade today. In a community that has no discernible upper class, moneyed or otherwise, those of German ancestry are distinctly more tradition conscious and somewhat more prosperous than most of the rest of the population. They are more tightly knit than other groups in town, and, when and if they can agree to do so, they are capable of exerting more influence upon community affairs. Nearly all of them attend McDade's Faith Lutheran Church, which grew out of the original church that moved into town from Siloah—in fact, for all practical purposes, they are the church. Most have ties by blood or marriage (often both) to several of about ten widely extended, interrelated families. Almost all of these families have been in the McDade area since before 1900, and a few have been there since before McDade existed at all. Dan Wolf, for example, who heads one of Faith Lutheran's most active families, farms land that his immigrant great-grandparents cleared in the 1850s.

Most of McDade's old German families still live in the country north of town, where their immigrant ancestors first settled the rich bottomlands of West Yegua Creek, a tributary of the Brazos flowing west to east through northern Bastrop County, a few miles north of and roughly paralleling the rail line between McDade and Paige. Sometime before 1883, the Germans' clustered farms, along with the church and school they had founded, became known as Siloah, after the Old Testament Pool of Siloam, the first reservoir constructed within the walls of Jerusalem, which supplied the city with water in times of siege. Today, the descendants of these early German farmers are so squarely in the midst of McDade's social mainstream that it is difficult to imagine the town without them. For many years, however, Siloah and McDade were separate communities that had little to do with each other. Though only a few miles apart, they developed along different lines in their early years, and while each affected the other, the residents of Siloah could not be considered members of the larger McDade community until after 1917, when they relocated their church to town.

No comprehensive account of Siloah's early days exists. Neither the *Bastrop Advertiser* nor the *Elgin Courier,* which began publication in 1890, provide a record of the German farmers at Siloah. Even though such surnames as Behrend, Ernst, Eschberger, Goerlitz, Grosse, Kastner, Rother, and Wolf—all families that have been in the area since before the turn of the century—are common in McDade today, they never appeared in the county's early newspapers. Nor was the Siloah community as a whole ever mentioned. Any account of Siloah's early years is thus a patchwork, relying on older people's fading memories, family stories, and a very brief, very fragmentary "history" of Faith Lutheran Church compiled by Reverend Alvin Bohls, the church's pastor from 1968 to 1978, from now-lost minutes of early congregational meetings. Even so, educated guesswork and inferences about issues that may have affected Siloah in its early years and brought on its eventual assimilation with McDade are possible. An exploration of such issues is central to understanding McDade's past and the evolution of the community as it exists today.

In its early days, Siloah remained separate from McDade, as the community sought to maintain an identity of its own. In 1882, the desire of the immigrant farmers at Siloah to preserve their community's cultural independence culminated in the establishment of the Siloah Evangelical Lutheran Church. Between 1882 and the World War I years, however, several factors inhibited Siloah's efforts to distance itself from McDade. Among these were the growing economic relationship between Siloah and McDade, problems internal to the Siloah community, and social and political pressures from without.

During McDade's earliest boom years, the residents of Siloah and McDade seemed to prefer staying apart from one another. Once established as a successful commercial entity, McDade showed no inclination to claim those living at Siloah as its own. The bustling, trade-oriented railroad town had little reason to care about a few rural immigrant families who came to town only sporadically. As subsistence-level dirt farmers, and foreigners, they must have seemed irrelevant to the entrepreneurial types who flocked to McDade in the 1870s and 1880s. The Germans at Siloah were a different people altogether: they spoke a different language, dressed differently, and had different customs. Nor did they play much of a role in the financial equation that was bringing McDade's merchants, saloon-keepers, and assorted go-getters success. They did not transact much business in town, and McDade's thriving businesses would hardly have missed their trade. For a short while, in fact, a few of the farmers at Siloah made a concerted effort to do their business in Paige, where several of the merchants were German. This turned out to be impractical, however, and did not last. McDade was considerably closer to Siloah than Paige was, and it had a better road leading to it from the north. In addition, McDade's cotton gin was more efficient and its shops more fully stocked.

For their part, the Germans at Siloah stayed away from McDade as much as possible during the first years of the new railroad town's existence. They may have seen their booming new neighbor to the south as a threat to the peace and stability they had sought when they left Germany and hoped to find in the fertile bottomlands of the West Yegua. The Siloah community of the 1870s and 1880s was self-contained, and those who lived there wanted to keep it that way. They spoke only German among themselves, and many, especially the women (who rarely left Siloah), spoke no English at all. Like a number of other rural German communities in nineteenth-century Texas, they seemed to believe that their tiny settlement could survive indefinitely as an island of German culture and customs in an ocean of Americans.

In 1882, the Siloah community organized a church and erected a church building that would double as a schoolhouse. Worship services and the children's lessons were conducted in German, although the school curriculum included some basic instruction in English. As the first generation of young people came of age, they tended to marry within the community and begin farms and families of their own. Those who did not wed fellow members of the Siloah community usually married residents of German settlements in neighboring Lee County—for a young German to marry an *Amerikaner* was next to unthinkable. Some brought spouses from Fedor, Giddings, or Serbin to live at Siloah; others went to live with or near their spouse's family in one of those communities. Economically, the Germans at Siloah were nearly self-sufficient. As experienced farmers with fertile land and a good supply of water, they could raise almost all of their own food. When necessary, they traded skills and labor among themselves. In short, during the early years of their community they had little need for a bustling, trade-oriented neighbor like McDade.

Little did they know, however, that within a generation's time changes in the local economy, conflicts within Siloah itself, and events being played out internationally would result in the assimilation of their community with the Amerikaners at McDade. But that is precisely what happened, as these factors, among others, combined to bring about the gradual subordination of Siloah to McDade and the Germans' eventual acceptance of town culture and the American way of life that prevailed there.

In the long run, despite their initial reluctance to become involved with McDade, the Germans at Siloah were unable to ignore the bustling little railroad town just to the south. McDade offered too much in terms of potential improvement to the material quality of their lives for them to pretend it did not exist. As accomplished farmers and husbandmen, they may have been able to raise all of the food their families needed to survive, but they could not grow such staples as sugar or coffee. Nor could their home smithies and workshops duplicate the vast array of manufactured goods that new rail-based distribution networks were making available throughout the nation. Most such goods could be had in McDade, of course, but only in exchange for cash. Accordingly, it was not long before the farmers at Siloah began to perceive McDade as more convenient than threatening. Instead of seeing its bustling commercialism as a danger to their simpler way of life, they started thinking of McDade as a handy place to buy the things they were unable to raise or make themselves.

At the same time, of course, McDade was also a convenient place for Siloah's farmers to raise the cash needed to make such purchases. As a result, a fairly typical town-country economic relationship developed: the farmers at Siloah planted cotton as a cash crop, hauled it to McDade to sell at the gin, and spent most or all of the proceeds in McDade's retail shops. This relationship afforded the German farm families a standard of living above subsistence but also, eventually, cost them their economic independence. As they became increasingly dependent on McDade as a source of goods and as a marketplace for their cotton, the linguistic and sociocultural gap between Siloah and McDade began to diminish as well. Out of fear of being cheated in their business dealings, growing numbers of Germans learned English; they also insisted that their children learn and use it.

Friendships between members of the two communities developed, including an occasional marriage or two. By the first decade of the twentieth century, the barriers that had kept Siloah and McDade separate were crumbling, and Siloah found itself inexorably falling into orbit around McDade, with market economics holding Siloah in its subordinate position. When the Siloah community relocated its church to McDade in 1917, it was the final step in an economic *pas de deux* that had started decades earlier, when Siloah's German farmers first entered McDade's retail economy to make life on the farm easier for themselves and their families.

Siloah's increasing economic dependence on McDade was not the only factor that contributed to the community's decline. The Siloah community was also subject to a number of internal tensions that weakened the ties that held it together. Many of these tensions were personal in nature and never became a matter of public record. Other than some vaguely remembered old stories, few sources for the details of these problems have survived. Some of the community's difficulties, however, involved the church, and of these, at least, a sketchy documentary record still exists.

Prior to 1882, Siloah had no church of its own. During the community's early years, clergymen from other German settlements visited Siloah several times annually to minister to the community's spiritual needs. These visiting clerics would usually stay with a local family for a week or so, conducting bible study sessions, prayer meetings, and worship services in the host family's home. They also performed whatever baptisms and weddings the community required. Their visits were high points in the life of the community, socially as well as spiritually, that helped relieve the tedium of farm work and provided the settlers an opportunity for socializing and celebrating. Some in the community, however, were not satisfied with the occasional, irregular nature of the arrangement, which was a constant reminder of Siloah's secondary status among other German settlements nearby. Both Fedor and Serbin, for example, twelve and eighteen miles away respectively, had thriving churches and resident pastors of their own, though neither community could boast many more "souls" than Siloah. By the early 1880s, a number of Siloah's residents had come to believe that their community could, and should, support a church and pastor of its own.[1]

In 1882, the heads of seven of the community's largest families founded the Siloah Evangelical Lutheran Church. August Wolf, who along with his brother Franz had been among the first German immigrants to establish farms on the upper reaches of the West Yegua in 1857, donated five acres as a building site. Most of the community helped build a meeting house, completing their work in November 1882. The new church was located two and a half miles northeast of McDade, roughly in the center of the rural population it was intended to serve. The first worship service in the new sanctuary was held in January 1883, celebrating the dawning of a new day for the Siloah community and officially installing the newly hired Reverend Michael Haag as resident pastor. Haag's duties included schooling Siloah's children, in the new church building that doubled as schoolhouse. The church was his home as well, a tiny six-by-twenty-foot apartment was partitioned off in one corner to serve as his living quarters. Haag's annual salary was "$250.00 plus," according to the official church record.[2]

It seemed a promising beginning. Less than a year before the violence in nearby McDade was to reach its bloody climax, the German farmers north of town appeared to have taken a decisive step toward assuring the future peace and stability of their community. For many of them, the establishment of a church at Siloah no doubt seemed a safeguard against the predominant culture's worldly ways, as represented by McDade, and they surely hoped the church would protect their community against such undesirable outside influences for years to come. The optimistic among them undoubtedly envisioned a future in which the church they had founded would be an ongoing presence in the lives of their children and grandchildren. With luck, it might even become the anchor Siloah needed to prevent its rural way of life and cultural traditions from being swept away in the rising tidal wave of greed and immorality that had seemingly engulfed McDade.

But Siloah would not be so lucky. The community's church had problems almost from the start. Large among them was its inability to recruit pastors or keep them for any length of time. To the congregation's disappointment, the popular Reverend Haag stayed barely more than a year at Siloah, leaving in the spring of 1884 to become pastor at Grape-Apple, an even smaller parish in the heart of heavily German Gillespie County, one hundred miles to the west. The fact that he left Siloah just when the rest of Bastrop County had started treating McDade as a public embarrassment is perhaps more than coincidence. Many residents of Siloah regarded rough-and-tumble McDade with distaste, and the pastor may have jumped at the opportunity to serve a more isolated parish in a more predominantly German area. If this were indeed the case, McDade's unsavory reputation may well have been a contributing factor to Siloah's eventual decline.[3]

Haag's departure was just the beginning of Siloah's problems. Having failed to keep its first pastor, the church had a difficult time finding a second. In fact, Siloah was without a pastor of its own until 1893, despite taking measures to make the position attractive. The community built a separate three-room parsonage, erected new fences around both the church and the parsonage, and dug new cisterns for each. These efforts were probably calculated to attract a family man who might be more inclined to stay than the young, unmarried Haag had been. Their efforts were in vain, however, because they were unable to find anyone willing to come to Siloah and be the resident pastor of their church. It is uncertain, of course, whether the reputation of nearby McDade had anything to do with this, although it would hardly be surprising if it had. In any event, between 1884 and 1893, the Siloah community again had to settle for infrequent worship services performed by visiting clergymen from parishes in Serbin, Paige, Pflugerville, and other even smaller and more distant German communities.[4]

Difficulty finding and keeping a minister plagued the Lutherans at Siloah until they relocated to McDade in 1917. Although the church's second pastor, Reverend Jakob Appel, stayed three and a half years, from the fall of 1893 till the spring of 1897, Siloah had only two other resident pastors over the next two decades, and neither stayed more than two years. Established in the hope that it would bind the community together in the present and perhaps form the foundation of a larger future community, the Siloah Evangelical Lutheran Church had not lived up to its founders' expectations. Instead, the church had been unable to convince a single Lutheran clergyman to put down roots in the Siloah community. Over a period of thirty-five years, it had persuaded only four to even try.[5]

The specifics of what was wrong are no longer available in any historically reliable form, but they almost certainly involved personal tensions within the community. The passing of the generations most directly concerned, the indistinct memories of those who were children at the time or who may have later heard accounts of the community's difficulties from their parents or grandparents, and the understandable reluctance of many people to discuss some of the more unpleasant aspects of family history have all combined to render Siloah's turn-of-the-century troubles vague. In conversation with descendants of Siloah's early settlers, one occasionally hears references to long-standing family disputes—such as the case of a young woman who married the son of her father's sworn enemy and whose parents never spoke to her again, or of property-line disputes between neighbors that sometimes led to violence—but all such accounts exist more in the realm of community myth than historically verifiable fact.

That the Siloah community experienced problems, however, is certain. Many who grew up there recall tensions between certain families. Adeline (Wolf) Eschberger, the great-granddaughter of August Wolf, is a resident of McDade who was born at Siloah in 1922 and grew up there. She recalls "bad blood" between a number of older people in the community. "It was just controversy, controversy, controversy, all the time controversy," she remembers. Her brother, Dan Wolf, who lives on land their grandparents cleared before the Civil War, agrees: "They were always fighting out here, always scrapping about one thing or another."[6]

Some of the interpersonal problems among members of the community evidenced themselves in church affairs. Though the church record is vague and incomplete about such matters (despite faithfully listing baptisms, confirmations, weddings, and funerals among the congregation, the record is otherwise sporadic, probably because Siloah rarely had a pastor to maintain the record), it occasionally alludes to tensions within the congregation. A single entry made at the end of 1902 is the most telling. This anonymous entry, apparently made to fill a gap in the record, characterizes the period between 1898 and 1900 as "years of reverses on which the Siloah congregation look[s] back with sorrow, [and] which are not easily erased from memory." It also states that the church had "stood still since 1900 [until the end of 1901], which . . . was not a pleasant experience." The same entry goes on to celebrate the fact that in late 1901 the church's membership had more than tripled, expanding from the low of seven families it had fallen to during the "troublesome time" to a new high of twenty-four families. Although this reference to the congregation's time of "sorrow" is vague at best, the entry suggests that the turn of the century was a contentious time in the Siloah community.[7]

The Siloah church also appears to have experienced problems in the years just before its 1917 relocation to McDade. In large part, these problems centered around whether, and where, to move the church. As far as Reverend Bohls's fragmentary church history reveals, the issue first arose in July 1911, when the congregation decided that the old church building was not worth improving upon. Nearly everyone wanted to build a new church instead, but they could not agree upon a location. Some wanted to remain in the country north of McDade, either rebuilding on the same site or acquiring a new piece of rural property to build on, while others advocated moving the church to McDade. Pledges made toward the cost of a new building indicate the division within the congregation: some refused to pledge if the church were to be in McDade, and others refused their support if it were to remain in the country. The pro-McDade faction carried greater financial weight at this meeting, out-pledging those opposed to the McDade site by $425 to $325, but the congregation made no final decision, instead appointing a committee to look into the church's available options.[8]

The committee reported back two weeks later. Its members had been unable to find a suitable piece of rural property—someone earlier expected to sell land to the church had changed his mind—but they had located an available lot in McDade, just three blocks north of the town's business district. The asking price was low, perhaps because newly improved McDade, befitting its status as "one of the best towns in the county," was eager to gain another church. After first voting that a simple majority vote of the congregation would be sufficient to decide the matter, the membership voted to relocate the church to McDade. However, because "there was no unity in prospect," the meeting adjourned without deciding a final course of action. Precisely why is unclear. Those opposed to moving to McDade may have threatened to leave the church, or the pro-McDade majority may have hesitated to take this potentially divisive and irrevocable step. In any case, even though the congregation had officially voted to relocate to McDade, it took no action, perhaps because of disagreements within the membership. The church stayed where it had always been, and Reverend Bohls's account mentions no further discussion, for the time being at least, of moving the church.[9]

Less than a year later, in April 1912, a group of fourteen families did leave the Siloah church. Whether their departure was connected with the issue of moving the church to McDade is unknown. It may well have been a consideration, though, because they were all from the eastern end of the area served by Siloah and lived farther from McDade than the rest of the congregation. Whatever their reasons, these families withdrew from the Siloah church and formed their own church about four miles to the east, close to where a small stream known as Paint Creek flows into the West Yegua. The church still exists. Its official name is Saint Andrew's Lutheran Church, though nearly everyone in the area refers to it as the "Paint Creek Church." Many of its members are descendants of the original founders from Siloah. The church is situated about six miles from both McDade and Paige, but most of its members maintain closer ties with Paige than with McDade. Quite a few of them, however, still have friends and relatives who attend Faith Lutheran in McDade, the eventual successor to the church at Siloah.[10]

The establishment of the church at Paint Creek drastically reduced Siloah's congregation. It also rekindled talk of moving the church to McDade. The withdrawal of most of the families living to the east of the church had altered the geographic relationship between the church and its reduced membership. In fact, the church was now on the extreme eastern edge of the community it served. Those who wanted to move the church into town could rightly argue that McDade would be a more central location for the remaining congregation. The membership reconsidered the issue in both 1913 and 1914, but both times, for reasons unknown, they voted against moving the church.[11]

Finally, on October 12, 1916, the congregation considered the matter once again. After voting unanimously to build a new church, the membership approved the McDade site previously made available in 1911 and now made available again. The vote was six to two, with several members abstaining. Another vote was taken ten days later, with six members again voting to build in McDade and all others abstaining. Although the congregation's decision was less than unanimous, they had finally made one.[12]

Things proceeded quickly from that point on. In November, the congregation sold the parsonage and three of the five acres owned by the church. They kept the church building, which continued to function as Siloah's schoolhouse, and the cemetery, which several of McDade's old German families maintain to this day, and where most of them still bury their dead. By February, the church had purchased the land in McDade and had pledged fifteen hundred dollars toward building a new sanctuary. Construction began soon afterward and was completed in the spring. The first services in McDade's new Lutheran church, still called the Siloah Evangelical Lutheran Church, were held on May 20, 1917, with a new church bell—purchased through the mail from the Sears Roebuck catalogue—ringing in the church's high steeple. Siloah's German farmers had finally come to town to stay.[13]

The timing of the Siloah church's relocation to McDade suggests one other factor that might have influenced the congregation's decision to move. The World War I years, especially as of late 1916, were not easy ones for Americans of German descent. They were most difficult for German-Americans who lived in rural communities that were predominantly or exclusively German, had churches and/or schools of their own, whose residents spoke German in their daily lives, and whose population had demonstrated a preference for remaining separate from nearby non-Germans. Siloah was such a community, and it seems unlikely that it remained unaffected by the prevailing distrust of German-Americans, which was as widespread in Texas as in the rest of the nation. While perhaps not the principal reason for the church's decision to move, it seems probable that prevailing anti-German feeling was an influencing factor, if only in providing a further argument in favor of relocation to McDade. What better way for Siloah's German farmers to demonstrate their loyalty than to move their church to town, thereby renouncing a significant portion of their cultural isolation and forging new ties with "American" McDade?

A curious break with tradition associated with the final decision to move to McDade suggests that the Siloah congregation was at least aware of, if not motivated by, anti-German sentiment in the area. According to Reverend Bohls's history, at its October 22 meeting the congregation took up the matter of financing the new sanctuary. As they usually did when raising money, the membership voted to seek pledges among themselves. In accordance with standard practice, these pledges were to be agreed upon in writing and an official record kept of them. In this instance, however, the minutes report the congregation taking the unusual step of specifying that all "paper" pertaining to securing and recording these pledges should be written in English rather than German. Given that German was the daily language of the Siloah community and that the Siloah church kept all of its records and conducted all of its services in German, the specific instruction to use only English in this instance was markedly out of the ordinary.[14]

Whether or not any specific incident led the Siloah membership to feel such a step necessary is unknown. The church's actions may have simply been a precaution. Given the tenor of the times, Siloah's congregation may have thought it imprudent to be passing documents written in German around among themselves. The pledge documents would, after all, be circulating semipublicly, and to be "caught" passing them around secretly could be disastrous. With a generalized suspicion of all things German on the rise in late 1916, such papers would be less likely to be misunderstood if they were in English. In any event, the fact that the Siloah congregation took such an unprecedented step could indicate an awareness of hostility toward themselves as members of the region's German population.

Some such hostility did exist, as occasional incidents indicated. Despite being a topic that few people today want to discuss, there is a certain amount of anecdotal evidence regarding episodes in which members of the "American" majority made life difficult for some of the ethnic Germans in the area. Details are lacking, however, and no written record of any such incident exists. It also seems likely that the Siloah congregation near McDade did not face as great a threat as German-Americans in nearby towns. Nearly everyone within McDade's present-day German community—both those old enough to remember local conditions during World War I and those who have only heard stories about them—agrees that Paige treated its German population much more poorly than McDade did. One elderly German farmer who lived near Paige was beaten to death during World War I when he couldn't convince a group of "patriotic Americans" that he had purchased as many Liberty Bonds as they thought he should.[15]

As was the case throughout the nation, much of the anti-German sentiment in McDade focused on language. Many viewed speaking German in public as suspicious behavior, un-American at best, and possibly seditious. Emilie (Eschberger) Goerlitz, born into the Siloah community in 1900, recalls that "You were not supposed to talk German in town. We did at home but never on the street." After the United States entered the war in the spring of 1917, the Bastrop County Defense Council, like similar organizations across the country, banned the use of German in churches and schools throughout the county. "Everything had to be in English," Mrs. Goerlitz remembers. Lucy (Braun) Eschberger, born in 1905, recalls the wartime funeral of a young German woman held at Siloah's new church in McDade: "They told that preacher not to say one German word, and her folks couldn't even talk English." Even as late as 1989, more than seventy years later, neither Mrs. Goerlitz nor Mrs. Eschberger would identify "they."[16]

Other elements of anti-German feeling in Texas were rooted in issues that pre-dated the war in Europe. Statewide prohibition had been the most volatile single issue in Texas politics since 1906. In election after election, the state's German population had vigorously supported "wet" candidates and had overwhelmingly opposed attempts to bring the question before the electorate. In 1911, the "dries" finally succeeded in getting the Texas legislature to submit a constitutional amendment favoring statewide prohibition to a voter referendum. The ensuing campaign has been called "one of the bitterest political fights in the history of the state." Voting was held on July 22, just a few days after the Siloah church first discussed the possibility of moving to McDade. The vote was close: the wets prevailed by about six thousand out of 468,000 votes cast. Later analysis has shown that the state's ten most heavily German counties provided approximately three times the statewide margin of victory, voting against the prohibition amendment by a cumulative total of 21,507 to 3,828. Thus, Texas's German population carried the day for the wets, foiling the best attempt the dries had mustered in five years of concerted statewide campaigning to have the state constitution amended to prohibit the sale or consumption of alcohol. Though Bastrop County was not among the ten counties analyzed, neighboring Lee County was. Many of the Germans at Siloah had close ties to Lee County, where anti-German sentiment during World War I has been characterized as "quite severe."[17]

In fact, Texas did not pass a prohibition amendment to its constitution until May 1919, a year and a half after Congress had proposed the Eighteenth Amendment to the federal Constitution. Even then, almost 90 percent of the voters in Texas's most heavily German counties opposed amending the state constitution to ban alcohol, although the amendment carried statewide with 55 percent of the vote. Since the issue was more or less moot by 1919, voter turnout was light; if voters in the German counties had turned out as heavily as they had in 1911 and maintained their 90 percent opposition, the statewide contest of 1919 would have been considerably closer than it was.[18]

In a dry community like McDade, which had exercised its "local option" to ban the sale of alcohol in 1902, such long-standing opposition to statewide prohibition may well have caused resentment among the more militant dries toward ethnic Germans in the area. Many of Siloah's farmers brewed beer at home for private consumption, which was legal, but some were rumored to illegally sell their brew on occasion. A few were even suspected of distilling and selling bootleg whiskey. As had been the case in the 1870s and 1880s, the county sheriff tended to ignore McDade, so enforcement of prohibition there was largely informal. Groups of "English-speaking" men—termed "Ku-Kluxers" by some of the area's older Germans, though whether they were literally members of the Klan is unclear—visited more than one German farmer's home to remind him of the McDade community's staunch opposition to the sale of alcohol. Occasionally, these visits turned ugly. Selma (Eschberger) Eklund, born in the early 1920s, tells of a group of men who came to her family's home shortly before she was born. The visitors roughed up her father, whom they suspected of making whiskey, and threatened to burn down the barn. Mrs. Eklund's very pregnant mother was badly frightened, and a few weeks later gave birth to a baby girl—Mrs. Eklund—with a slightly malformed eye. For the rest of her life, Mrs. Eklund's mother blamed her daughter's slight deformity on how terrified she had been that day. This appears to have been an extreme case, but these kinds of "persuasive" visits from certain people within the McDade community were not uncommon.[19]

There are other such stories, though none is pinpointed in time and all are vague. One tells of a group of citizens trying to force a young German man to marry the older "English-speaking" widow he was "seeing." He managed to escape them and avoid a forced wedding but had to leave the area for good. There are also innumerable accounts of German children from Siloah attending high school in McDade and being harassed by their "American" peers, who taunted them as "Dutchmen" and "squareheads." How much significance should be attached to these kinds of stories is questionable, but they do indicate that in the years just before, during, and after World War I anti-German feeling existed in McDade, and the German community at Siloah could hardly have been unaware of it. That the Siloah congregation's awareness of such sentiment played at least a partial role in the decision to relocate their church to town seems likely.[20]

In the final analysis, the precise reasons for the Siloah church's relocation to McDade remain obscure. When Paint Creek split off from Siloah and rendered the original church site less central than it had been previously, the congregation may have decided to move simply for the sake of convenience. Some members of the church may have felt that being part of the McDade community would serve them well economically. Others, perhaps tired of rural isolation, may have been attracted to the larger-town culture, and becoming more "American." However, they may also have felt that moving the church to McDade was necessary to preserve what they could of their cultural heritage. Even if the strain of anti-German feeling in McDade was not as virulent as in some other communities, the generalized and growing distrust of all things German may have been disturbing enough for the area's German population to have felt threatened. With or without the motivation of specific events, the residents of Siloah may have feared being seen as anything other than wholeheartedly "American" and may have concluded that becoming part of the larger whole was their only hope of cultural survival.

Whatever the precise series of events and motivating factors that prompted the church's move, its relocation to McDade marked the end of Siloah as a separate community. Its residents continued to farm for a living, and its children continued to attend elementary school in the country near their homes. When the church moved, however, the center of their social and cultural lives moved with it. In the years to come, the German families from Siloah became as fully a part of the McDade community as any other of its citizens. In many ways, in fact, as McDade declined over the years, the influence of its German community increased. Whereas McDade's business people, most of them Amerikaner, had tied themselves to the fortunes of the town, the Germans had kept their land and continued to farm. In the decade after World War II, when U.S. 290 bypassed McDade and the Southern Pacific discontinued rail service to the town, most of the community's businesses failed, forcing their owners to either retire or leave town. McDade's German families, however—rooted in the land their ancestors had settled—withstood the failure of McDade's localized economy rather well. As time passed, they became the closest thing McDade had to an upper class, able to maintain a modest prosperity that allowed them to keep up their farms and homes, buy a new car or tractor every few years, and sometimes send their children to college. No other group in McDade accomplished so much in the lean years after World War II. Eventually, the descendants of Siloah's German farmers, most of whom wanted nothing to do with McDade in the late nineteenth century, gravitated to positions of responsibility within the community, and a number of them came to be thought of as the town's leading citizens.

CHAPTER 11

Between the Wars

Imagining the Past, Remembering the Present

To this point, McDade's past has largely been the stuff of legend. Abrupt cycles of boom and bust, struggles for community control between "respectable" people and gangs of outlaws, sudden outbursts of violence, and rural immigrant populations distrustful of town and townsfolk (and vice versa, of course) are all familiar story lines to anyone who has read a Western novel or seen a Western movie. During the 1920s, however, McDade's history begins to part company with many of the cultural stereotypes associated with that decade. Late-night jazz clubs, free-flowing bootleg liquor, flappers dancing the Charleston, gangsters blazing away with machine guns from speeding cars—all images central to the myth of "the roaring Twenties"—had little in common with life in McDade in the decade after World War I. Similarly, the things most present-day Americans "remember" about the Great Depression—Hoovervilles, breadlines, ragged farm families on the road to California—bear only a slight resemblance to conditions in McDade during the 1930s. A history of the McDade community between World Wars I and II has to disentangle itself from prevailing myths about those years and concentrate instead upon presenting local events in the light of actual circumstances.

Local historians often have difficulty extricating themselves and the locales they study from legend. The ability to do so frequently depends on whether the historian has access to a regular and reliable source of local information. No such source exists for McDade before 1925. Prior to that, the town's historical record is sketchy. Only occasional community events, most of them out of the ordinary, made the pages of the weekly *Bastrop Advertiser*. In 1925, however, the *Advertiser* began printing a column of McDade news in almost every issue, dramatically increasing the quantity of information available to anyone looking into the community's past. Unfortunately, no archive exists from before 1935 for the *Elgin Courier*, the more likely of the two local papers to have been printing news of McDade.

Most of the information in the *Advertiser* is the stuff of daily life, numbingly ordinary, especially in regular weekly doses. Whether it is of historical value depends in large part on the researcher's point of view, that is, what he or she believes to be historically significant. Historians who focus their efforts on an era's most remarkable events would no doubt find little to say about McDade between World Wars I and II; to all outward appearances, nothing out of the ordinary happened there during those years. Like most of the nation, McDade prospered during the latter half of the 1920s and suffered economic setbacks during the early 1930s. By the eve of America's entry into World War II, however, the town was once again realizing a modest degree of prosperity. The Japanese attack on Pearl Harbor, though, changed the community forever, suddenly thrusting upon McDade an unexpected role in the larger affairs of the nation. Generally speaking, this could be the story of any number of

American communities in the years between 1918 and 1941. One might not expect an account of life in McDade between the wars to tell us much more than what we think we already know—that the 1920s were boom years that ended in a disastrous bust, that the nation spent the 1930s trying to pick up the pieces, and that by the end of the decade life was beginning to return to "normal," an illusion abruptly shattered by the attack on Pearl Harbor. Yet, in the specific ways that events in McDade followed these general patterns, were affected by them, and departed from them, the town's history has lessons to teach that are peculiarly its own.

With the regular inclusion of McDade news in the *Bastrop Advertiser* in 1925, a record of daily life in McDade becomes available. Having outgrown its Wild West past, the town begins to be knowable in its present, through its own specific set of activities, ambitions, and concerns. These are the kinds of details that spell the end of legend, both that of the Wild West (in McDade's case) and those of historical cliché. The same mundane, week-to-week accounts of life in McDade that testify to the town having matured beyond its early years should also caution against too readily accepting the standard historical interpretations of the 1920s and 1930s as automatically applicable to McDade. Regarding some aspects of community life, they do apply, but in reference to others they do not. Whatever historical value an account of the McDade community between World Wars I and II may have, it derives not from exploring how faithfully life there echoed trends elsewhere in the nation but instead from analyzing *specifically* how and why it either echoed them or did not. It is the details that are important; in places like McDade, the past consists almost entirely of details.

McDade changed markedly in the years between the wars. Most of the changes it underwent were neither sudden nor dramatic, although in many ways their gradual, prosaic nature belied their real significance. The pace of change was slow—so slow that many in town paid little attention. At no time during the 1920s and 1930s, however, could a citizen of McDade look back over the preceding few years and not recognize that the community had changed. When people did take notice of how their lives were changing, their reactions were mixed. Much of the time they didn't like what they saw and complained about the passing of "the good old days." In regard to some matters, however, they welcomed change wholeheartedly.

In many ways, McDade was ill prepared to deal with the transformation that life in America underwent in the years following World War I. Before the war, McDade had been a community oriented more toward the past than the present or the future. This was apparent not only in the town's sensitivity to its Wild West past (still vividly alive in the memories of many) but also in the conservative, middle-class values its leading citizens had embraced as part of living down that past. Based on unquestioning traditionalism, fundamental Protestantism, and a rigidly Victorian sense of decorum, this value system had provided McDade's "better" citizens with a blueprint for "improving" the community in the years following the embarrassing violence of 1883. With an almost evangelical enthusiasm, many of the town's turn-of-the-century leaders had felt it their duty to impart—by personal example, as well as through the community's schools, churches, businesses, and social organizations—this set of values to the rest of the population. How effective they were at "converting" their fellow citizens varied, of course, by individual and family, but in general they seem to have succeeded rather well: the McDade they created in the wake of the town's wild and woolly heyday was a surprisingly tame and proper place.

It remained so well into the 1920s. More than two decades after the turn of the century, an old-fashioned set of values and beliefs predominated in McDade to the virtual exclusion of all others. In many ways, this group of ideas constituted a brand of small-town orthodoxy more characteristic of the nineteenth century than the twentieth. Forming a complete and self-supporting system of beliefs, it encompassed every aspect of community life, including religion, politics, society, personal morality, and psychology. Moreover, it delineated the right and proper way for human beings to live their lives, or so most people in McDade seemed willing to believe. Despite a community history (experienced first hand by a number of community residents) that suggested otherwise, few in town doubted that this was the way people in McDade had "always" lived. Many among the town's most influential citizens developed an almost mystical reverence for the past (the sanitized past, that is—no gunmen need apply), and they encouraged the rest of the community to do the same. That this sanitized past was superior to the present became an article of faith in McDade, and the community soon gained a reputation, even among other small towns in the region, as a latter-day bastion of traditional values. McDade had stumbled onto an identity: by subscribing to a brand of genteel propriety that by the 1920s much of the nation had consigned to the past, McDade's leading citizens had placed their community squarely within all that was good about "the good old days." They were proud to trumpet "old-time country" values as characteristic of McDade, implicitly claiming the community's adherence to tradition as both source and proof of a native local virtue as yet uncorrupted by modern times and city ways.[1]

For McDade to remain untainted was, of course, impossible. The community may have been slow to jump on the postwar bandwagon—put off, no doubt, by modern America's seeming disregard for its small-town, rural past—but within a decade McDade had come a long way toward catching up. With the town's merchants, local farmers, the McDade Guaranty State Bank, and the Southern Pacific Railroad joining forces to cooperate on several enterprises, business activity picked up markedly during the mid- and late 1920s. Such cooperation helped establish McDade as a modest, but successful, center for truck farming, itself a new development after decades of single cash-crop cotton farming. Electricity became available in McDade in 1926, and the improving local economy soon made it possible for a number of town residents to own washing machines, radios, and refrigerators. An even greater mark of distinction was the purchase of an automobile, despite the fact that any appreciable amount of rain rendered motorcars useless on the muddy local roads. Prosperity, convenience, even luxury—all hallmarks of the emerging national culture—were, by the latter half of the 1920s, finally making their way to McDade.

For the most part, such improvements in the material quality of life were welcome. They did, after all, translate into a markedly higher standard of living for many residents of the community. A number of people, however, were less than happy about some of the unforeseen changes that accompanied modern life's amazing new advances. They especially resisted any changes that brought along new ideas or called McDade's prevailing nineteenth-century worldview into question. Oddly, much of the resistance came from those who were most responsible for bringing change to the community—the town's leading businessmen and farmers. Demonstrating considerable naiveté, they failed to realize that a rejuvenated local economy would mean not only a higher standard of living but, necessarily, a change in community values as well. They apparently believed that McDade could enjoy the material advantages of modern life without social, intellectual, or spiritual consequences. They were wrong.

Much of the information that is available about McDade during this time comes from a column of community news written by longtime McDade resident Sam Billingsley. Billingsley's column was published in both the *Bastrop Advertiser* and the *Elgin Courier*. With few exceptions, it appeared every week from the beginning of 1925 until late 1931, when failing health ended Billingsley's writing.

Sam Billingsley was born in Tennessee in 1852 and moved to Texas as a small child. His family settled in Bastrop, where he grew to adulthood. In 1871, the Billingsleys moved to McDade, Bastrop County's bustling new railroad town, where Sam and his father opened a general store. (Sam's father was W. A. Billingsley, the storekeeper whose testimony regarding McDade's 1883 gunfight, seemingly ignored at the time, called into question the official version of what happened that day.) The Billingsleys quickly became established as one of early McDade's leading families. They were founding members of the McDade Church of Christ and strong advocates of law and order in the community. Both Sam and his father were among a group of nineteen men who, in 1881, had signed an open letter to the *Bastrop Advertiser* demanding that McDade's "rowdies" mend their ways. Though they threatened no specific action, the letter stated in no uncertain terms that the town's upright citizens were not prepared to tolerate "the midnight revelry of the drunken mob" or its "vociferous yelling and firing [of] pistols" much longer.[2]

As businessman, pillar of the Church of Christ, cotton grower, land speculator, and self-proclaimed member of the local "loafers club," Sam Billingsley had been centrally involved in McDade's affairs since the town's beginnings. His knowledge of life in McDade bridged the gap between its horse-and-buggy days and those when its residents would no longer consider telephones, refrigerators, and automobiles objects of wonder. By the mid-1920s, when Billingsley's "Letter from McDade" first appeared in area newspapers, the town had begun to shake off the staid respectability of its recent past and was beginning to enjoy some of the benefits of modern life. Billingsley was not always sure this was good. He often complained about the effects of the contemporary world upon McDade's past-oriented way of life and its "old-time" value system. He was a staunch defender of the town's rural traditions and frequently used his column as a pulpit from which to shout down suggestions that the community's long-held beliefs were outmoded or in any way subject to revision. At the same time, however, he witnessed McDade's businesspeople beginning to share in the eager optimism of a resurgent national economy, and in this he rejoiced. He became an important contributor to this new attitude on the local level, testifying in many of his columns to an updated, more vibrant McDade, especially in the economic sphere. He rarely missed a chance to promote McDade in print, effusively praising his adopted hometown time and time again. With the enthusiasm of a man who truly believed McDade to be "the single best spot on God's map," he shamelessly "boosted" the community at every opportunity, boasting that its potential for future investment was unlimited.[3]

Despite his distinctive authorial voice and obvious lack of objectivity, Billingsley spoke for a significant portion of the McDade community. As a retired businessman, he empathized with local merchants: When they succeeded, he praised their energy and foresight; when they ran into difficulties, he bemoaned their bad luck. As a bona fide town founder and a member of McDade's social, commercial, and agricultural elite for more than fifty years, his opinions reflected those of McDade's most established citizens—the people whose families had been there the longest and had the greatest stake in both its past and future. As the community's semiofficial spokesman, he bore much of the responsibility for shaping outsiders' impressions of McDade. He liked to believe this meant he was responsible, to some degree, for its future as well. He earnestly wanted everyone who read his column to know that McDade was a rigorously conservative little town in its regard for the cultural, moral, and religious traditions of the past, while at the same thoroughly modern in its attitude toward economic matters and progress.

As a factual account of life in McDade, Billingsley's column leaves much to be desired. Although he never failed to list the bare facts of community life—who had visited with whom over the past week, who was "on the sick list," who had recently purchased an automobile or refrigerator, how his friends' gardens or individual farmers' crops were faring—he often neglected the kinds of items present-day readers might consider more newsworthy. He did mention, briefly, the "new" (1917) Lutheran church being struck by lightning and burning to the ground in 1925. He wrote nothing, however, about the difficulty the congregation—German families from the Siloah community—had getting a satisfactory settlement from their insurance company. And he mentioned only briefly that the "professors" of the recently opened McDade Secretarial Business College skipped town one night, "leaving behind only envelopes and stationery," as well as a number disappointed, defrauded, and no doubt embarrassed students.[4]

In general, Billingsley tended to ignore bad news, especially any hinting at conflict within the McDade community. Over the years, he wrote a number of obituaries for his column. Most, of course, were for elderly residents of McDade who had died of natural causes. In more than one instance, however, the deceased had not died naturally. In at least one such case, death was the result of violence on the part of another resident of the community. (This act of violence was not premeditated, was not intended to be life-threatening, and was never investigated by legal authorities, but it nonetheless resulted in a man's death.) In another case, the deceased had died accidentally in circumstances embarrassing to both the deceased's family and other members of the community. In both instances, people in McDade knew what had actually happened, but the obituaries Billingsley wrote gave no hint of either death being out of the ordinary. Instead, as was his usual practice, he heaped praise on the deceased, commiserated with their families, and mourned the community's loss. To do otherwise would be to publicly admit that tensions existed in McDade, and this he was plainly unwilling to do.[5]

Nor did he fully report misconduct in McDade. In 1926, for example, when a young man from McDade was arrested, tried, convicted, and eventually jailed on bootlegging charges—a case that was the talk of Bastrop County for several months—Billingsley mentioned it only in passing, remarking in one of his columns that he didn't have much news to pass on because "half the town was down at the Courthouse [in Bastrop] all last week." When the trial ended, Billingsley made note of it but did not mention the verdict; he did, however, take the opportunity to rail against the sinfulness of alcohol, calling bootlegging "the most dastardly and deadly evil of the times." At no time did he name the accused—everyone in town already knew who it was, of course—though he did seem to take a swipe at the young man's family by criticizing "fathers and mothers who are so thoughtless and blinded as to allow their children to rule the home." Other such incidents probably occurred without Billingsley mentioning them at all.[6]

In many ways, Billingsley's column is more valuable as an indication of its author's attitudes toward life in McDade than as a factual record. Much of the time, Billingsley treated news and social items as though they were of secondary importance, placing them at the end of his column, after several paragraphs of personal opinions and philosophy. Just as he often ignored news that didn't reflect his vision of what McDade should be, he frequently overemphasized stories that conformed to or promoted that vision. He also tended to exaggerate anything that hinted at good economic news for the town. Thus, a 1926 test drilling for oil near McDade became a "prospective oil gusher" that was certain to make the community "the leading business center between Brenham and Austin." Similarly, when area farmer Walter Kastner purchased seventeen hundred chicks to start a commercial chicken ranch and grocer W. H. Harvey added a self-service "Pick, Pay, and Pack" room to his store during the same week in 1927, Billingsley wrote that "McDade is soaring skyward . . . [and] will be known far and near as the livest wire in all this section of the country."[7]

Billingsley was close friends with the editors of both the *Courier* and the *Advertiser*, and they allowed him considerable latitude. They also allowed him about five times as much space as any of their other community correspondents. His style was one of hyperbole, bombast, and a sentimentality that was sometimes quite maudlin. He often quoted at length from mawkish poems glorifying selflessness, honesty, respect for one's elders, and other virtues he believed "essential to the Christian life." In most areas, Billingsley was a devoted traditionalist. Despite his booster rhetoric, he disliked the frivolity of modern life—its "foolish fashions, card parties, banquets, dances, and automobiling"— only slightly less than he despised the contemporary world's growing disdain for places like McDade. A fervent admirer of William Jennings Bryan, the "Great Commoner," Billingsley often defended the cultural and religious traditions of small-town and rural America against the modern world's more "advanced" ideas. He went about this with a passion he reserved for little else. Any idea suggesting that life in rural America was in need of improvement was suspect at best. More likely, it was dead wrong, even evil, and probably inspired by Satan himself.[8]

Billingsley desired renewed prosperity for the community, but he considered the achievement of this end more a matter of the town fulfilling its rightful destiny than changing its fundamental nature. Under no circumstances did he want the community to abandon its most basic values and beliefs in favor of more contemporary ideas. He constantly used his column as a forum for defending, and idealizing, McDade's old-fashioned, small-town way of life. Often he extolled the virtues of the past and celebrated the "common sense" displayed by most of McDade's citizens in choosing to remain close to that past. At other times, however, his writing turned angry, and he raged against the evils of modern life. On these occasions his columns became extended jeremiads in which he denounced contemporary ideas, condemned their effects on McDade, and generally anguished over the passing of "the good old days."[9]

For the most part, Billingsley's conservatism was more cultural than political, though he had old-fashioned opinions about nearly every aspect of American life. He sometimes criticized developments he perceived as new and controversial, even if they concerned issues most Americans no longer cared about. Despite the passage in 1920 of the Nineteenth Amendment, for example, he didn't believe that women—"the finishing touch of God's handywork [sic]"—should participate in the political process. They were already "the ruling queens of God's creation," he wrote in 1930;

what need did they have of the vote? Both womankind and society at large would be better served, he felt, if women would stay "at home cooking pies for a church festival" instead of worrying about politics. Their proper role, apparently, was to raise their sons to be good citizens and their daughters to be good mothers.[10]

Billingsley was equally benighted concerning matters of race. On more than one occasion he recounted crude racial jokes in his column. Invariably, the "colored" protagonists of these stories would prove themselves fools by becoming flustered at the imagined complexities of some rather simple situation and lapsing into a version of black dialect so broad and mocking as to be virtually unintelligible. The characters' inherent buffoonery, of course, was supposed to be funny in these jokes. By the end of the stories they were usually so completely confused that they made the characters on radio's *Amos 'n' Andy Show*—whose portrayal of stereotypically clownish African Americans became a nationwide sensation in 1929—seem sophisticated in comparison. Although Billingsley never mentioned the Ku Klux Klan in his column, he may well have been a member. One elderly resident of present-day McDade, a descendant of German farmers at Siloah, estimates that 80 percent of the area's "English-speaking people" (that is, non-Germans) belonged to the Klan during the 1920s. This person also mentioned several "English-speaking" families from McDade who were adamantly opposed to the Klan but did not mention the Billingsleys as being among them. No one else in McDade old enough to remember the 1920s is inclined to talk about the Klan, which makes it difficult to corroborate the claim of 80 percent local membership or to accurately assess the role the Klan may have played in McDade. In any event, whether Billingsley was a Klan member or not, he held African Americans in low regard and openly aired his prejudices in print.[11]

Billingsley did not seem to consider women's rights or matters of race to be of much importance, however. When he wrote about things he took more seriously—specifically, any idea or issue he saw as a threat to McDade's traditional way of life—he did not hesitate to prescribe extreme measures in response. In 1926, for example, concerned that subversive ideas might somehow sneak unnoticed into the minds of McDade's schoolchildren, he suggested the formation of a "Reading Committee" to screen all books proposed for use in the town's classrooms. With no hint of irony, he proclaimed that "If there is anything found that is against the [C]onstitution of our country, or that against the faith upon which America was founded, the books containing such 'rot' should not be tolerated in the schools of a God fearing and liberty loving people." He was also upset about the 1920s' sky-rocketing divorce rate. He considered "the divorce evil" to be "a menace and a curse to our civilization and religious progress." Since he believed the root cause of divorce to be "hasty up-start marriages," he suggested an amendment to the Constitution "controlling marriages and divorces alike."[12]

Billingsley's defense of rural traditionalism often focused on home and family life. As in 1926 with the family of McDade's convicted bootlegger, he sometimes scolded the community's current generation of parents for being too permissive with their children. "We often wonder what has become of all the old-fashioned fathers and mothers that used to rule in their homes with a 2 by 20 inch rawhide strap," he lamented. He believed that one of parenthood's "holy duties" was to make children "realize that father and mother are boss and that rules laid down by them must be obeyed, even if it requires the rod." Only through obedience to parental authority, Billingsley felt, could children develop into adults who would "fear God and keep His Commandments."[13]

The family home, of course, was the place specifically designed by God to impart such lessons—"the world's greatest schoolhouse and God's greatest earthly institution," Billingsley called it. Presided over by "old-fashioned saintly mothers," the home was where children learned the right and proper way to live their lives. It was also the source of love, friendship, and all other forms of human kindness, qualities which Billingsley believed were becoming ever more scarce in the modern world. In 1925, reminiscing about his own childhood in Bastrop, he recalled his family's home as the place "where we used to love, more than all else, where we at all times could find comfort, sunshine, pleasure, and love; could tell our troubles to our old-fashioned mother and with a gentle smile she wiped away our sorrows . . . in order that [we] might become honorable, up-right, God-fearing sons and daughters." He implied that such a home life had been the norm for people of his generation, which was the reason, of course, that he and his contemporaries were such good citizens and had such a clear understanding of the world's current failings.[14]

Few modern homes, Billingsley believed, were providing children with an atmosphere as wholesome or as full of loving discipline as his own had provided him. Instead, contemporary home life, even in places like McDade, had declined in recent years, because modern parents were too concerned with matters external to the home and family—chasing after money or material possessions, trying to stay current with the latest trends, or leading an overly busy social life. Such activities were "preventing [parents] from giving their children the attention they so justly deserve." That the world had changed in the sixty or more years since Billingsley had been a child was irrelevant. The proper functions of home and family, as well as the right way to bring up children, were not the kinds of things that changed, nor were they open to debate. They were founded on constant, timeless truths, Billingsley believed, truths decreed by God. As such, they were subject to neither the whims of society nor the vagaries of history; they could not change and never would. Anyone suggesting that home and family life should adapt itself to accommodate modern habits and beliefs was wrong and, whether they knew it or not, in opposition to the will of God.[15]

Billingsley presumed to know a lot about the will of God. He was an enthusiastic Christian, and he never hesitated to profess his faith in print. Christianity, he believed, was "the very salvation and bulwark of our nation," and he considered the resurrection "the greatest event ever recorded on the pages of history, an event of transcendent importance to every living soul." As a staunch fundamentalist, he was unswerving in his conviction that the bible was the literal word of God. He had no patience with those who called themselves Christians but did not accept the absolute truth of the scriptures. In his opinion, these people were hypocrites, directly responsible for the flood of uncertainty he saw eroding away "the foundation sill" of "our beloved America." He sometimes despaired that among the doubters were nationally recognized members of the clergy—leaders of the "modernists"—who, in their attempts to reconcile the beliefs of the church with the advancing discoveries of science, were willing to relegate most of Christianity's biblically revealed truths to the realm of myth. Billingsley would have none of such fence-sitting: "The man that doubts the Virgin birth of Christ," he wrote, "does something far worse, he doubts the power of God, doubts His creation of our first parents, doubts the resurrection and the future life . . . what an appalling thought."[16]

Indeed, Billingsley saved some of his most impassioned rhetoric for the defense of "old-time religion" against the onslaughts of modern rationalists. Among his favorite targets were college-trained, "modernist" clergymen, many of whom, he claimed, were "as dead spiritually as a fish after being ten days on dry land forty miles away from water." He complained that Jesus himself, should he return to earth in 1925, would have to "take a dozen or so more degrees before he would be allowed to . . . preach in our 'up-to-now,' fashionable churches." He feared that too many contemporary churchgoers were being misled by "professional" clergymen who had never received a true "call" from God and who were systematically purging the modern church of the passionate, heartfelt certainties that had traditionally formed the core of "old-time, country-pure religion"—the people's faith, their fervor, their belief in fire and brimstone justly meted out by an angry God. "Why are so many of our old preachers, like Enoch of old, who walked and talked with God," Billingsley asked, "being put out on the junk pile and college manufactured professionals being put in their places, who do not know any more about the power of God, or the love of Christ in their hearts than a Billy goat knows about a shoe shine?" Billingsley believed there was a conspiracy afoot to disrupt the nation's churches and corrupt its people, a belief he shared with conservative Christians throughout America.[17]

Among the most prominent of the nation's fundamentalists at the time, of course, was William Jennings Bryan, who spoke in 1925 of "a gigantic conspiracy among atheists and agnostics against the Christian religion." Bryan had thrice been a candidate for president and had been secretary of state under Wilson. He had been a passionate defender of rural America and fundamental Christianity throughout his long career. He had a large and extremely loyal following, especially in agricultural areas of the South and Midwest. By 1921, he had assumed a leading role in the campaign to ban the teaching of evolution in the nation's schools. As part of this effort, he traveled extensively to speak on the evils of Darwinism, authored several books and numerous articles on the subject, and wrote a syndicated column that by 1923 was appearing weekly in more than a hundred newspapers across the country. Some scholars estimate that as many as twenty-five million people may have read his column. McDade's Sam Billingsley was no doubt among them.[18]

Other than to "deplore" Bryan's unexpected death on July 26, 1925—less than two weeks after his public humiliation at the hands of Clarence Darrow in the famous Scopes "monkey trial" in Tennessee—Billingsley never mentioned Bryan in his column. Nonetheless, he often echoed his sentiments, sometimes imitating the writing of "the Great Commoner" rather closely. Just as Bryan wrote in 1924 that "it is better for one to know that he is close to the Heavenly Father than to know how far the stars in heaven are apart," Billingsley proclaimed a year later how futile he thought it to "explore space and measure the distance to the sun, moon, and stars and then teach that the miraculous birth of Christ was a myth." Naturally, Billingsley shared Bryan's disdain for the theories of Charles Darwin. He thought the notion that humankind had evolved from apes, rather than descending directly from Adam and Eve, so absurd that instead of parroting the standard arguments against evolution he simply made fun of it. "All the Darwinites and college bred egoists on earth can say that man came from the monkey if it suits them to do so," he wrote, "but . . . history will never prove that woman descended from such an ugly thing." Conservative to the core, Billingsley saw no reason for new ideas, especially of the type that might call into question the traditional, biblically based truths he and his contemporaries had grown up with.[19]

Billingsley did subscribe, however, to one currently popular strain of American religious thought—the growing belief that Christian piety, in addition to being its own reward, would result in material success for the faithful. In the wake of advertising executive Bruce Barton's runaway 1926 bestseller *The Man Nobody Knows,* which portrayed Christ as the most successful business executive in history and held his life up as a model for all who wanted to achieve such success themselves, Billingsley promised McDade's current generation of young people that if they "would be so wise" as to maintain their religious faith they too would be successful. "McDade has sent out into our business world within the last ten years," he wrote in 1927, "not less than fifteen young men, none having passed the 10th grade, holding positions to be envied, drawing salaries from $2,000.00 to $3,800.00 per annum, all of them just fools enough to believe in the divinity of Christ, while many of our university graduates [who] are anti-Christ [are] washing dishes to keep soul and body together." Until recently, Christianity had been a poor man's religion, Billingsley admitted, but now, in conjunction with the nation's rapidly improving economy, that was beginning to change. In the near future, he believed, pious Christians would be climbing to their rightful place at the top of society's economic heap. Church members who subscribed to Barton's image of Jesus as a back-slapping go-getter could reasonably expect that their faith would be rewarded with their own portion of America's growing prosperity. Billingsley wanted McDade to be at the front of the line.[20]

In Sam Billingsley's opinion, no community anywhere deserved economic success more than McDade. His adopted hometown was the best place on earth, as far as he could tell, and as such ought to be rewarded. His deep-seated love for McDade was obvious in nearly every column that he wrote. He sang the town's praises over and over again, often in absurdly excessive terms. At times he seemed to believe that God had singled McDade out for special treatment, blessing it with unparalleled natural beauty, water and soil beyond compare, and the best human beings on earth. In Billingsley's vision of McDade, the goodness of the local populace was as much a part of its natural heritage as any of its other qualities. It made perfect sense to him that the town's close ties with God and nature had resulted in a superior citizenry, almost as though the very air, earth, and water at McDade exuded a special goodness that had spread to its residents and made them better than people who lived elsewhere. As easily as he could write that McDade had more spring wildflowers than surrounding towns or the best water in the state, he could also claim that "there are more beautiful stories being lived in and around McDade than any other town in Texas." The community's natural blessings translated rather easily into moral rectitude: the town that was "the most beautiful and picturesque in all the world, a heavenly paradise for lovers, poets, and dreamers," was also "first in progressiveness, first in peace, first in heroism, first in patriotism, first in war against the devil, standing four-square for long-suffering and righteousness." Soon, he hoped, he would be able to add a bustling economy to McDade's long list of virtues.[21]

Ever the optimist, Billingsley believed the community had considerable economic potential that no one had yet tapped. "All McDade needs in development" was one of his constantly recurring themes. With this in mind, he reported local economic news more thoroughly than any other. He faithfully recorded the opening of new businesses in town, changes in ownership, and, probably with reluctance, business failures. In good booster fashion, he touted McDade as the ideal site for a number of possible business ventures. Among the more plausible were a regional creamery, a cheese factory, and a cannery. (In 1934, a canning plant did in fact open in McDade, an operation that processed local produce on a seasonal basis until 1941.) More far-fetched was his suggestion that the town enlarge its "public tank" and make it "the largest body of water between Brenham and Austin." Once that had been accomplished, Billingsley claimed, some "live wire" was sure to see the wisdom of building a resort there; it was "a sure thing," he wrote. As with McDade's previously mentioned "oil gusher," he grasped at every straw the winds of rumor blew his way; no scheme seemed too unlikely or too grandiose to succeed in the community he championed as "the best investor's opportunity in all the wide world."[22]

Billingsley also kept a close eye on local agricultural developments, rightly realizing that McDade's future depended on its farmers and ranchers. He was proud of the crops and livestock they raised and shipped out via rail to the world at large. Every year, beginning in the late summer and continuing through the autumn months, he tracked the local cotton harvest, providing a weekly tally of bales ginned in McDade. He also reported each freight carload of cattle or hogs shipped out by local stockmen, usually with a comment on the superior quality of animals raised near McDade. Just as the community produced good livestock (and good citizens), it also grew good crops. In midsummer, at the harvest of local watermelons, Billingsley was rarely able to contain himself. One year he boasted that "McDade's famous, nationally advertised melons will ere long be known and eaten in every hamlet on the continent." Another time he envisioned the town "soaring to the uttermost parts of the earth" on the wings of its watermelon crop.[23]

More significantly, Sam Billingsley was among the first in McDade to realize that the future of local agriculture lay in growing food instead of cotton. Not only was the sandy soil around McDade better suited to raising vegetables than cotton, but truck farming made economic sense for many local landowners, especially since cotton prices had fallen drastically since the end of World War I. Billingsley claimed that by raising food for markets close to home, instead of cotton for a monolithic international market whose price structure depended on decisions made in corporate boardrooms, area farmers could take greater control over their economic lives. Diversification away from cotton, he believed, would allow McDade's farmers to experiment with a variety of crops, tailor what they grew to local conditions, negotiate their own terms with buyers, and search out new markets for themselves. It would also free them from dependence on King Cotton's inflexible, quasi-feudal gin system.

Although cotton was still king in the 1920s, rumblings of discontent with its reign were occurring. By the middle of the decade, a movement was afoot in agricultural circles throughout the South that encouraged farmers to diversify. Billingsley agreed with the aims of this movement, which included a cut in cotton production to counter falling prices, regional self-sufficiency in food production, and decreased dependence on credit, long the key to the economic power wielded by King Cotton on the local level. "Cotton and credit together are two of the South's greatest enemies," Billingsley wrote in 1926, while imploring area farmers to diversify. He urged them to devote more of their land to growing food. "Corn and more corn and less cotton is what Texas needs. Having to depend on the North for our corn and packing houses for our bacon means . . . fattened corporations. By far better reverse the process and get back to raising our own living on our own farms." Unless local farmers diversified, Billingsley insisted, they would be performing "the cotton masters' bidding" forever.[24]

With the clarity of hindsight, it is obvious today that a timely switch to alternate cash crops would have saved many Southern farmers from economic disaster in 1931, when the price of cotton plummeted to levels well below the cost of production. In the mid-1920s, however, diversification was a topic of controversy. Many powerful people in the South opposed it, including a number of small-town newspaper editors, local bankers and other businessmen, and politicians. Naturally, the cotton industry supported their opposition and exerted considerable influence to discourage farmers from reducing their cotton acreage. As part of a calculated public relations campaign, the industry portrayed itself as the South's devoted, steadfast, and long-suffering soul mate and painted any attempt to diversify as not only a passing fad but an act of ungrateful bad faith as well. An editorial cartoon, entitled "Leaving His Steady Behind," that appeared in the *Bastrop Advertiser* was typical. It depicts a prosperous, overweight "Texas Farmer" driving an open car down a residential street. He is wearing his Sunday best and smiling broadly. In the car with him are five full-figured young women, all competing for his attention. The cartoon labels these women as "Livestock," "Feed Crops," "Poultry," "Fruits and Vegetables," and "Dairy Products." Looking on tearfully from her front porch is a demure young lady identified as "Cotton." The women in the car, their moral character obviously questionable, have tempted her longtime sweetheart to come away with them, at least for the moment. The question is whether he'll return before they "ruin" him.[25]

It was probably to McDade's benefit that Billingsley pushed for diversification. Although no connection between his calls for crop diversification and local farmers' decisions can be firmly established, an increasing number of McDade's farmers—many more than in surrounding towns—abandoned cotton as their main source of income and took up truck farming instead. The substitution of fruits, vegetables, and livestock for cotton probably had a greater impact upon the community's future than anything else during the 1920s. When cotton growers throughout the South were ruined by the precipitous 1931 fall in prices, a number of McDade's farmers had already switched to truck farming and were thus less affected by the cotton crash than farmers in other central Texas communities, most of whom had continued to rely on cotton.[26]

More immediately, however—in the late 1920s—truck farming brought McDade a taste of the prosperity that Billingsley and other leaders of the community had previously only dreamed of. After the town got electricity in 1926 (the result of cotton gin owner A. Y. Field guaranteeing Texas Power & Light an annual minimum electricity usage of sixteen hundred dollars at his gin), many in McDade "hooked up." Soon they were accumulating washing machines, radios, and refrigerators; ironically, those most responsible for the community's new prosperity—local farmers—would not get electricity until 1940, when the power lines were finally extended into the countryside around McDade. In 1927, the McDade Guaranty State Bank declared a ten cent dividend, leading Billingsley to describe the community as "basking in the sunlight" of resurgent good times. In September 1928, he reported "money becoming easier and easier in McDade," as evidenced by community resident Hattie Clopton "paradin' around" in a new car purchased from local Chevrolet representative J. F. Metcalfe, who was also vice president of the McDade bank. Over the next five months, Billingsley celebrated nine more new vehicles in town including top-of-the-line touring cars for barber and future state legislator Bud DeGlandon and G. W. Southern. According to Billingsley, McDade was at "the very zenith of her prosperity since Adam."[27]

To some degree, of course, the town was sharing in the prosperity enjoyed throughout the nation during the late 1920s. Specifically responsible for McDade's piece of the pie was its emergence as a center for the mercantile end of the truck farming business. Not only were local farmers planting vegetables and raising livestock instead of growing cotton, they were also taking their produce to market in McDade. This meant greatly increased activity uptown, especially around the freight depot. McDade native Grover Westbrook, one of Billingsley's close friends, had been buying large quantities of watermelons since 1914, purchasing individual farmers' crops, and combining them, if necessary, into freight carloads for shipment to wholesalers in Houston and Austin. In the late 1920s, as McDade's farmers began devoting more acreage to fruits and vegetables, Westbrook's business boomed. At the height of the 1927 watermelon harvest, for example, Billingsley reported that Westbrook had already shipped thirty-six carloads of melons from McDade, only half the crop. This was nearly three times the quantity of melons he had shipped a decade earlier. Following Westbrook's lead, other buyers, most of them from out of town, began visiting McDade at various times of year to negotiate with area farmers for their cantaloupe, corn, peanut, and sweet potato crops. Livestock agents also started frequenting McDade, purchasing cattle, hogs, goats, chickens, and, during the Thanksgiving-Christmas season, turkeys.[28]

Judging from Billingsley's column, uptown McDade was a lively place at times during the late 1920s and early 1930s. In the spring of 1927, for example, he reported increased cattle sales in town, the result of "more . . . buyers on our streets during the week." The following December, more than twelve hundred bushels of peanuts sold at the McDade depot for a dollar per bushel, a high enough price to indicate both a quality crop and stiff competition among buyers to purchase it. In July 1930, Billingsley declared McDade "the cantaloupe champion of the world—they sold here last Monday for one dollar each," also a premium price. Nor was local truck farming oriented entirely toward buyers from out of town. In fact, much of it was conducted on a smaller, less-formal basis among friends and neighbors. Kelton and Kunkel at the McDade Mercantile, for example, often bought eggs or vegetables from area farmers. In addition, by early 1928 an open-air market, held on the streets of McDade's uptown business district, had developed into a regular Saturday event. Farmers from throughout the county brought milk, eggs, and whatever else they had in surplus to sell or trade, and during the winter months several German families from Siloah peddled homemade "Yegua sausage" in town. Not surprisingly, Billingsley soon proclaimed McDade "the banner produce market in all this section, Elgin and Bastrop not excepted."[29]

Like so many of Billingsley's claims, this one too was probably exaggerated. Short of shameless hyperbole, no one can claim that during the late 1920s truck farming restored McDade to the level of prosperity and regional prestige it had known fifty years earlier. Nonetheless, the fact that area farmers moved away from total dependence on cotton earlier than farmers elsewhere seems to have benefited the community during the "hard times" to come. At the very least, no one in McDade went hungry, even those with no money, during the Depression. Food raised in the area, though it sometimes went unsold in the depths of the Depression, could still fill local stomachs. Farmers who had continued to rely on cotton, on the other hand—and this included most farmers in central Texas—were about to find themselves with a crop they could neither sell nor eat.

Even before August 1931, when the Department of Agriculture released its prediction of a disastrously large cotton harvest, the Texas cotton market had been weak. This led Billingsley, in late 1930, to pose the question that a year later would echo throughout the South: "With the bulk of the cotton crop gathered and sold leaving debts unpaid . . . how in the name of common sense can [cotton growers] expect to meet their obligations?" Unlike many farmers elsewhere, farmers in McDade had an answer to this question. With a number of area residents already experiencing modest success at truck farming, the community's business leaders embarked upon an organized, cooperative campaign to diversify local agriculture even further. Leading this movement were the McDade Guaranty State Bank and the Southern Pacific Railroad, along with McDade's merchants and several local landowners. The group's first documented action came in December 1930, when local farmers met at the bank and organized a "tomato club" to explore the feasibility of growing commercial quantities of tomatoes in the area. The following week an "Agricultural Agent" from the Southern Pacific spoke in McDade to a gathering of more than 150 farmers, seeking their promise to plant at least two hundred acres in cantaloupes. If they would do so, he said, the railroad would build a packing shed at the depot in McDade, which would enable produce to be graded and packed in town. Theoretically, this would further enhance the reputation of local crops and induce wholesalers to pay higher prices for them. The agent also brought news of a cannery in Jacksonville, 175 miles to the northeast, that would buy as many tomatoes as local farmers (and the Southern Pacific) could deliver. The cannery, the railroad, and the McDade Guaranty State Bank would provide seed, fertilizer, and ground sheeting in return for the farmers' pledge to plant a minimum number of acres in tomatoes.[30]

Both of these plans were in fact realized, though Billingsley, now almost eighty and in failing health, did not provide many details in his column. In June 1931, he reported more than five thousand pounds of local tomatoes sold at the depot in McDade. The Southern Pacific also built the promised packing shed sometime that spring, a facility that paved the way for the establishment of a seasonal canning plant in McDade three years later. Throughout this time, local stockmen continued to send regular shipments of cattle and hogs to packing houses in Fort Worth. In his column of August 6, 1931—his next-to-last—Billingsley remarked on how busy McDade was, especially in comparison to one of its larger neighbors: "With three cars of cattle shipped from here, a truckload of cantaloupes, innumerable watermelons, and plenty of chickens and eggs being sent out, the old town is moving right along while . . . Elgin is sleeping for want of energy."[31]

Thus, even as the Depression was beginning to cause hardship in much of the nation, McDade continued to produce, sell, and ship food. Many other towns in rural Texas, places where farmers were mired in the rut of raising nothing but cotton, were less fortunate. When the cotton market collapsed in late 1931, many farmers in these communities faced bankruptcy. A sizable number of McDade's farmers, on the other hand, having already begun to diversify in the 1920s, were insulated from the worst effects of the cotton crash. Moreover, having witnessed the success of truck farming, they were ready to diversify even further. Their willingness to consider new agricultural possibilities, in addition to the experience they had already gained at raising food crops and finding markets for them, gave McDade's farmers an advantage over their cotton-bound peers in other communities.

This is probably why McDade did not suffer as severely as many other rural communities during the Great Depression. The town was not untouched; few in McDade had any money during the

1930s, and several local businesses failed, including the McDade Guaranty State Bank in 1934. Nonetheless, no one today can remember a single family losing its home or its land, calamities experienced by many rural Americans of the time. Nor did anyone in McDade go hungry. Wallace Wilson, a lifelong resident of McDade, says of life there during the 1930s, "We were poor folks and didn't know it. We had all the food we wanted to eat. We just didn't have any money." He is echoed by Tom Dungan, a McDade area truck farmer during the Depression: "People around here had to go partners to get two dollar bills to rub together, but there was always plenty to eat. Some of them people over in Elgin were a lot worse off . . . [they had] nothing but black-eyed peas to eat all winter." No one today who can remember the Depression in McDade speaks of the 1930s as an overly desperate time there.[32]

The reason for this almost certainly lies in the fact that so many of McDade's farmers began producing more food than cotton in the latter half of the 1930s. How much, if any, of the credit for their doing so belongs to Sam Billingsley is difficult to determine. In the final analysis it is impossible to know for certain whether local farmers were heeding his calls for diversification or were following their own lead (or someone else's) with Billingsley merely cheering them on from the sidelines. Nor does it really matter. What does matter is that between 1925 and 1931 the McDade community displayed exactly the kind of energetic willingness to succeed (scaled down, of course, in degree) that Billingsley had bragged of so often. The town he liked to call "first in progressiveness" proved itself to be precisely that in the agricultural sphere, and this may well have saved the community from economic disaster during the Great Depression. More than one small Texas town "dried up and blew away" in the 1930s; McDade stayed well rooted in its fertile soil.[33]

Sam Billingsley concluded his column of August 13, 1931 with a pair of uncharacteristically short sentences: "This will probably be our last letter to the Courier. Good bye friends and good luck to you all." And just that abruptly, with no other indication, his exaggerated opinions and bombastic prose disappeared from area newspapers. The following October, a brief item in the *Advertiser* reported that Billingsley and his wife had left McDade for McAllen, a farming community in the Rio Grande Valley of far south Texas where their daughter lived with her husband and children. Sam Billingsley died in McAllen six years later. His obituary, which appeared in the *Elgin Courier* of December 30, 1937, stated that failing eyesight had forced him to discontinue his column and leave McDade.[34]

For several years following Billingsley's departure for McAllen, very little news of McDade appeared in the *Advertiser*. Occasionally, the paper printed a "Letter from McDade," sometimes under the byline of Mrs. J. B. Hackworth, sometimes without a byline. Rarely were these "letters" more than a listing of visits, engagements, marriages, illness, or death. In all likelihood, the *Elgin Courier* was printing these same "letters" during the early 1930s, probably with greater frequency. Unfortunately, very few issues of the *Courier* from before 1935 are available today. Thus, other than the occasional details of certain people's lives that found their way into the *Advertiser*, there is no written record of life in McDade during the worst years of the Depression.

As discussed earlier, anecdotal evidence suggests that the Depression was not as devastating to McDade as it was to many communities in rural Texas. Money was in short supply, and this caused several of the town's smaller retail businesses to fail. Food, however, was plentiful, and many of those who raised food apparently shared freely with those in need. The McDade Guaranty State Bank failed in 1934, but its depositors were reimbursed in full through an arrangement with the First State Bank of Elgin; no one in town lost their life savings. Since most of McDade's farmers had already reduced their cotton acreage, they did not benefit as much as farmers elsewhere from an Agricultural Adjustment Administration program, set up in the summer of 1933, that paid cotton growers to plow their crop under. In 1934, however, the AAA did pay local stockmen to slaughter their surplus cattle. Some ranchers in the area thought this "a sin" and refused to participate, but most herded their cattle to a spot north of town, where, under the watchful eyes of AAA representatives, the animals were shot. None of the meat from the slaughtered cattle could be sold, but local residents were allowed to take as much as they needed for their own consumption. Even with many families pickling enough beef to last them for months, there was more than enough meat to go around. Erhard Goerlitz remembers several farmers feeding the excess to their hogs.[35]

After 1934, the *Elgin Courier*'s archive is fairly complete and news of McDade becomes less scarce. Throughout 1935, and for the next decade or so, the *Courier* published a "Letter from McDade" almost every week. For the remainder of the 1930s and on into the early 1940s, these letters were usually written by Hackworth. (Her "letters" to the *Courier* were the same as those that would sometimes appear in the *Advertiser*, though the *Advertiser* printed them much less regularly.) In general, Hackworth's column is less interesting than Sam Billingsley's. Neither as flamboyant nor as opinionated as her predecessor, she was rarely subjective about McDade or the lives of its citizens. Instead, she presented the facts of community life in plainly written prose. She devoted most of her column to recording McDade's social life, especially the weekly round of activities that kept the townwomen, herself among them, constantly busy. In the process, she managed to keep her readers abreast of developments in the community's school, its churches, and such organizations as the McDade Singing Club, the McDade Cemetery Association, and the PTA. This was a side of town life that Billingsley had all but ignored. Thus, in some ways, Hackworth's account of McDade in the late 1930s is the better rounded and more complete of the two in a factual sense. Even though her writing lacks the "sound and fury" found in Billingsley's column, she nevertheless provided a good sense of what was happening in the community. Her column may be less exciting to read than Billingsley's—it is certainly less illuminating of the times in general—but it may, for all its seeming dullness, do a better job of representing life in McDade in the years just before America's entry into World War II.

Judging from Hackworth's column, the latter half of the 1930s was a fairly comfortable time in McDade. Truck farming led the local economy and continued to expand. Area farmers, who since 1934 had been selling much of their produce to McDade's part-time canning plant, saw several new markets for their fruits and vegetables open up during the latter half of the decade. Much of the credit for this belongs to longtime watermelon wholesaler Grover Westbrook. By 1938, he was advertising himself as "McDade's produce broker" and had branched into cantaloupes, green beans, peanuts, and tomatoes. Over a three-week period in 1937, Westbrook alone shipped more than two freight carloads of cantaloupes, on average, out of McDade each day. That same year, a number of area farmers, in conjunction with Kelton and Kunkel at the McDade Mercantile, entered into a "black-eye pea contract" with Benham, Incorporated, of New Orleans. The terms of this arrangement provided for Kelton and Kunkel to sell seed (supplied by Benham) to the farmers and to thresh their harvested peas, with Benham promising to buy the whole crop at a guaranteed price. By the end of July, with a sizable portion of the crop yet to be harvested, almost thirty tons of black-eyed peas had been shipped from McDade and thousands of dollars paid to local farmers. The following year was even busier. McDade was so "abuzz with activity" during the summer of 1938 that Grover Westbrook had electric lights installed in the town's packing shed so the work of grading and packing produce could go on through the night. Earlier that spring, farmers John Dube, Karlie Klemm, and A. Y. Field had purchased the area's first tractors. Over the next several years a number of McDade's farmers bought tractors of their own. Area stockmen were also increasing production. Throughout the late 1930s and early 1940s, they shipped cattle, hogs, and poultry to meat processors. In 1941, when W. H. Joiner sold four hundred head of cattle, at fifty dollars apiece, to a packing house in Tulsa, even the usually matter-of-fact Hackworth was impressed. "A twenty thousand dollar deal," she wrote, "is something unusual for our little town." In short, McDade was producing increasing amounts of food in the years just before World War II and seemed to be thriving as a result.[36]

The community's social scene was a lively one as well. In addition to attending a bewildering array of luncheons, teas, canning sessions, and sewing or quilting bees, McDade's married women organized themselves (and sometimes their husbands) into a number of different clubs. Most of these organizations were devoted to some type of community service. The PTA was one of the more active, sponsoring talent contests, seasonal carnivals, bake sales, and the like on a monthly basis throughout the school year. The money raised at these events was used to purchase such items as a radio, musical instruments, and athletic equipment for the school. In the midst of a 1938 flu epidemic, the PTA hired an Elgin doctor to come to McDade's school and "administer toxoid" to the students. That same year, the men of McDade's Chamber of Commerce built an outdoor playground at the school with materials purchased by the Ladies Home Demonstration Club. To pay for upkeep at the town's cemetery, the McDade Cemetery Association traditionally served Election Day luncheons—held on the platform of the depot in good weather, in the packing shed or the back room of Hillman's Confectionary when it rained—that attracted lovers of "fine country cooking" from throughout the county.[37]

McDade's various service organizations were constantly sponsoring some form of community entertainment. Beautiful-baby contests, husband-calling competitions ("We have some good talent here," Hackworth commented), and "Tom Thumb weddings" featuring local youngsters were typical. "Negroe minstrel shows" were also popular; a 1939 program put on by the Cemetery Association featured "the Dixie Blackbirds, the High Stepping Yellow Gals, and the Little Picaninny Chorus"— probably local citizens in black-face acting out prevailing racial stereotypes. Members of the McDade Singing Club, who advertised themselves as willing to sing "anytime, anywhere, for anybody, always free of charge," walked the town's streets singing carols during the Christmas season, visited homebound sick or elderly to perform, and put on programs in some of the smaller communities around McDade. Hackworth also kept up with events in the community's churches, faithfully reporting on baptisms, revivals, Sunday school attendance, and church picnics. In short, there seems to have been no shortage of socializing available to people living in McDade during the late 1930s and early 1940s, especially to those who were respectable, concerned members of the community.[38]

Throughout this time, McDade continued to maintain its reputation as an old-fashioned country town full of upright, God-fearing people. For the most part, this reputation seems well deserved. In a 1935 referendum on whether to continue statewide prohibition, for example, 60 percent of McDade's voters opposed repeal, even though repeal carried statewide with 54 percent of the vote. McDade was even further out of step with the rest of Bastrop County, where 63 percent of the electorate supported repeal. In 1939, an article in the *Courier* attributed McDade's unincorporated status to the high moral character its residents: "The town is [dry] and its citizens church-minded, hence no official body is needed to keep law and order." McDade lagged behind neighboring communities in other ways as well, sometimes less happily. The local phone system, for example, while it seemed to work well enough within town, constantly failed; after bad weather, people in McDade were often unable to call out of town for several weeks. The roads in and out of McDade were also a problem, becoming virtually impassable after a heavy rain. Hackworth complained, as Sam Billingsley had in earlier years, that muddy roads were crippling McDade's businessmen by preventing area farmers from getting into town.[39]

Sometimes McDade paid dearly for being behind the times. In 1935, for example, when fire destroyed a block of downtown buildings on the north side of the railroad tracks (these buildings had been empty since 1931, when Southern's Drugstore had moved out and joined McDade's remaining businesses on the south side of the tracks), fire-fighting crews from Elgin, Bastrop, and Giddings had to be called in to get the blaze under control. In her next column, Hackworth mourned the town's lack of "water-works" and seemed to indicate that if people in McDade could have fought the fire properly when it had first been detected, the damage would have been minimal.

Fire seems to have been a constant threat to the McDade community. A number of times over the years, Hackworth mentioned families being burned out of their homes. In 1940, a fire destroyed McDade's cotton gin; "another landmark of our little town gone," Hackworth lamented. Indicative of how nonessential cotton had become to the local economy, gin owner A. Y. Field did not bother to replace his ginning equipment, though he did have a state-of-the-art new peanut thresher in operation within a matter of weeks. The most damaging fire, however, occurred in February 1941, when the school building—badly underinsured, as it turned out—burned down. Improvised classrooms were set up in the canning plant and in some of the town's churches, but no one in McDade seemed to know how the community was going to be able to build a new school. Hopes were temporarily raised when Congressman Lyndon Johnson, then in his third term as representative from Texas's Tenth District, promised federal help. Six months later, though, even the indefatigable Johnson had to admit failure, citing increased defense spending as the impediment. With much of the world already at war by the summer of 1941, and with many expecting the United States to soon join in, the McDade community was once again feeling the effect of international events.[40]

The impact of world events reached McDade in other ways too. In the fall of 1941, ten of the community's young men signed on with the National Guard. Four others were among the first group of men from Bastrop County who would be drafted in case of "national emergency." In addition, during the summer of 1941, rumors circulated about the possibility of an army training camp being built near Bastrop. Supposedly, this would be a facility capable of housing thirty thousand to thirty-five thousand men and would occupy some one hundred thousand acres. Though no one wanted to seem unpatriotic by openly opposing such a camp, local feelings were mixed. No one doubted that the camp would be good for the area's economy, but people were concerned about other effects it might have. While voicing his support of any military personnel who might eventually be stationed in Bastrop County, the editor of the *Courier* warned his readers against "camp followers" in no uncertain terms. "We should begin at once to look out for these people," he wrote, "and let them know right off the bat that we do not want them and that we will not tolerate their presence. They are the ones that will corrupt the morals of Elgin people." And beyond such local fears of contamination from the outside lay one more question—an important one in the minds of most Bastrop County residents, though it remained largely unspoken: where would the camp be located? or, more precisely, on whose land?[41]

While the repercussions of international events were reaching closer to places like McDade, the cultural gap between rural America and the rest of the nation was also diminishing. People in McDade seemed to sense this happening to their community, but unlike ten to fifteen years earlier, they seemed to welcome it this time. In fact, if the eagerness with which McDade embraced Houston's "Little Jo" Cottle is any indication, the community was more than ready to participate in one of the era's most prevalent myths—that of the small-town young man or woman who goes to Hollywood and is so winningly wholesome and attractive (a "natural") that he or she becomes a star. Born near Corpus Christi in 1922, Josephine Cottle had moved to McDade with her family as a baby. She and her family moved to Houston in 1924 or 1925 and never returned to McDade. In 1939, as a seventeen-year-old high school student, Cottle won a "movie tryout" on the nationally syndicated "Gateway to Hollywood" radio program. Someone in McDade who listened to the show realized this was a girl who had been "partly reared" in McDade, and the community lost no time in claiming her as one of its own. When Cottle's Hollywood tryout was successful, she was awarded a movie contract and became "Gale Storm," the name preselected for the female winner by contest sponsor RKO. (There was a competition for male contestants as well. One Lee Bonnell from South Bend, Indiana won and became "Terry Belmont." Incredibly, Bonnell/Belmont and Cottle/Storm were married in 1941.) People in McDade, of course, were delighted at "Little Jo's" success. They wired flowers and congratulations to "Miss Storm" in Hollywood and made certain that area newspapers informed their readers that McDade was "the home of Gale Storm." The fact that Cottle had lived in McDade only briefly as a very small child—so young, in fact, that Gale Storm disclaims any memory of McDade in her 1981 autobiography—made no difference. The town insisted on claiming her as one of its own and continued to do throughout her career. (By her own admission, Storm's movie career was less than brilliant. In 1941 and 1942 she costarred with Roy Rogers in a couple of Westerns but was soon supplanted by Dale Evans. Storm did have a moderately successful television career in the mid-1950s, starring in *My Little Margie, Oh Susannah,* and *The Gale Storm Show.*) Nonetheless, for many in town, this confirmed their belief that the community was not as old-fashioned or as out of touch as it sometimes seemed; in fact, in the minds of many, it proved that McDade and places like it could still play an important role in the formation of contemporary American culture.[42]

The gap between McDade and the rest of the nation was shrinking in tangible ways as well. In late 1940, crews from the Rural Electrification Administration began erecting the power lines that would finally carry electricity to rural dwellers in the area. With characteristic understatement,

Hackworth noted that "everyone is pleased with electrification" and pronounced it "a great benefit" to local farmers. The outside world was getting closer, too. In her column of November 6, 1941, Hackworth noted that road crews working on the "new" Highway 20 running east out of Austin were getting close to McDade. "We can hear tractors beginning by six in the morning, and until six in the afternoon," she wrote. She also mentioned that some of the men on the road crew, anticipating that they would be working near McDade for the next several months, had rented houses in town for themselves and their families. Somewhat snobbishly, Hackworth remarked that she had "failed to get the names of the families."[43]

The Japanese attack on Pearl Harbor was but a month away, however, and work on Highway 20 would be discontinued for almost a decade, until after the nation had fought a second world war. In the months following December 7, however, outsiders—many more of them than previously— arrived to seek housing in McDade. These people were also construction workers and their families, but they had not come to Bastrop County to work on the highway. Instead, they were part of a massive effort to build an army training camp on more than fifty thousand acres of land near Bastrop seized by the War Department in the weeks after Pearl Harbor. This base would eventually be named Camp Swift, in honor of the recently deceased Major General Eben Swift, a Texas-born "hero" whose military career had stretched from the Indians Wars of the 1870s through World War I. The camp's main gate was located just outside Bastrop, but its northern boundary was barely a mile from uptown McDade. For the remainder of World War II and for several years thereafter, Camp Swift's nearby presence strongly influenced life in McDade, bringing the community into contact with more people from beyond rural Texas than anyone in town had ever dreamed possible. McDade was about to become an active part of the nation.

The establishment of Camp Swift had a powerful impact on Bastrop County, although it affected each of the county's communities differently. Initially, it brought economic good times unlike any the region had ever experienced. The construction effort necessary to turn fifty-two thousand acres of woods and farmland into a military base capable of feeding, housing, and training thirty-five thousand men transformed Elgin and Bastrop overnight into boomtowns. In addition, the prospect of the War Department pumping federal dollars and "dollar-spending soldiers" into the local economy for an indefinite number of years led many Bastrop County residents to believe they would soon be leading more prosperous lives than they had dreamed possible. Except during the initial burst of activity right after Pearl Harbor, however, Camp Swift turned out to be something of an economic disappointment, especially for the county's smaller towns. Other than the merchants of Bastrop and Elgin, few area residents realized much long-term benefit from the camp. In fact, by the time Camp Swift was decommissioned in 1947, many local citizens felt that the camp had so disrupted Bastrop County's traditional agricultural way of life that the county's future as a leading regional food producer, had been lost to other parts of Central Texas without a wartime army camp. This belief was especially widespread in and around McDade, where many people believed that Camp Swift's nearby presence had weakened their community. That they believed this is hardly surprising, since the camp's most apparent long-term impact on McDade was to emphasize the town's inferior status, even within rural Bastrop County. This in turn led a number of the community's citizens to finally realize just how insignificant their hometown really was. Few in McDade were happy about the realization.[1]

Opportunity Knocking: Camp Swift and Bastrop County

Camp Swift came into being very quickly. The physical transformation of more than fifty thousand acres of privately owned land into an operational military base took little more than six months. It was completed this speedily because preparations for an army camp in Bastrop County had already been underway for almost a year. In fact, by late 1941, little was left to do other than actually move people off the land and begin construction. The camp's location was the result of a cooperative effort, begun in 1940, among the Austin Chamber of Commerce, state senator Paul Page of Bastrop, and Tenth District congressman Lyndon Johnson. After studying the site, the War Department officially approved it in January 1941, although no public announcement of the decision was made at the time. Planning for the camp began soon afterward and moved ahead quickly. By the time of the attack on Pearl Harbor in December 1941, army engineers had drawn up detailed land-use plans; a team of architects had finished drawings for most of the camp's projected 2,750 buildings; government attorneys were ready to start the legal process of condemning and taking possession of 425 tracts of privately owned land (52,162 acres in all); and the War Department had approved and set aside funds for compensating dispossessed landowners. When Congressman Johnson announced on December 18 that the War Department had authorized an army training camp in Bastrop County, he claimed that "construction can begin overnight." He was not exaggerating by much.[2]

The site of the camp was triangular in shape and encompassed more than eighty square miles of land. It was bordered on the west by Highway 95 between Elgin and Bastrop (a distance of eighteen miles), on the southeast by Highway 21 between Bastrop and Paige (thirteen miles), and on the northeast by the unfinished "new" Highway 20 between Paige and Elgin (seventeen miles). Uptown McDade was a mile north of this last stretch of road, about halfway between Paige and Elgin. This configuration helped determine the camp's economic impact on Bastrop County, especially its three largest towns. Downtown Bastrop, just three miles from the main gate, was the most convenient place for soldiers or camp employees to spend their paychecks, and they did so with a regularity that made several of the town's merchants wealthy men by the end of the war. Elgin, on the main route between Camp Swift and Austin (and all points north and west), also enjoyed a business boom, while Smithville, on the road running southeast out of Bastrop toward Houston, benefited as well. McDade and Paige, however, located on an unfinished stretch of highway on the "back" side of the camp, attracted little business from Camp Swift, except during the first frantic rush in early 1942 to get the camp built.

Camp Swift's first six months were chaotic ones for Bastrop County. Early in January 1942, the War Department ordered the sixty-one tracts of land projected as the camp's central cantonment area (4,601 acres in all) vacated by the middle of the month in order that construction could begin. This resulted in a confused scramble for housing and land, as a number of families suddenly had to find new homes for themselves and new pastures for their livestock. In addition, thousands of construction workers, many of them accompanied by their families, flooded into the county hoping to find work at the camp. At chamber of commerce offices in Bastrop, Elgin, and Smithville people waited in long lines to register for employment, with "all classes and races rubbing elbows from early morning until late in the evening." By the end of March, an estimated eighteen thousand men were working on various construction projects at Camp Swift; the *Austin American* calculated that Bastrop County's population had risen from twenty-two thousand to forty-two thousand in less than three months and predicted that it would soon exceed ninety thousand.[3]

Not surprisingly, this sudden population boom taxed local resources. The number of students attending Bastrop schools doubled between Christmas and the middle of March, forcing split sessions. County sheriff Ed Cartwright told the *Austin American* that misdemeanor violations had increased "seven or eight fold . . . due to drinking, gambling, and fighting," and residents of Elgin worried that their town jail would soon prove too small. Roads throughout the county were congested "day and night" with "the heaviest traffic ever." By the middle of February, it became apparent that Bastrop's sewer system could not handle the increased demands being made upon it, so the

Public Works Administration awarded the town a $370,000 grant to build a new one. Housing was also a problem. For miles around, local residents rented out spare bedrooms and outbuildings; downtown merchants in Bastrop and Elgin invested in bunk beds and turned the empty rooms above their stores into dormitories where they could rent sleeping space on a per night basis; and hastily built trailer camps sprang up throughout the county. Even so, local roadsides were lined every night with tents, cars, and trailers full of people with no place else to sleep.[4]

This flood of people into Bastrop County spawned a number of new businesses, many of them oriented toward entertaining the Camp Swift work force and the soldiers who would follow. Reporter Jack Guinn of the *Austin American* visited Bastrop on February 6, the first payday for most of the construction workers at the camp. He found a new "honky-tonk" and four new liquor stores open for business and a newly built movie theater about to open. He also encountered a number of local citizens concerned about Bastrop's reputation, though he was "assured on every side that there are no prostitutes, there haven't been any prostitutes, and the majority of the citizenry doesn't think there will be any prostitutes." Elgin's entrepreneurs were busy as well. By the first week in March, the town had four new cafes, two new pool halls, a new theater, an "amusement parlor," a "picture gallery," and a gleaming new set of parking meters along Main Street.[5]

The first military personnel arrived at Camp Swift in early May. They were a unit of 116 quartermaster officers assigned to prepare the camp for feeding, clothing, and housing the thousands of trainees who would soon follow. Over the next several weeks, long convoys of trucks, troop transports, and armored vehicles poured into the camp, clogging local roads, and often leaving county residents unable to travel for hours at a time. On May 15, the War Department announced that all remaining owners of property within Camp Swift's boundaries were required to vacate by June 15. There were to be no exceptions; military police would be on patrol with orders to arrest "anyone caught trespassing." By mid-summer, combat training was underway, with eighteen thousand men of the 95th Infantry Division being prepared for deployment overseas.[6]

When the initial building boom was over, Camp Swift's impact on local life diminished somewhat. Most of those who had arrived in the area to work at the camp moved on when construction was complete. This left Bastrop County less crowded and the pace of life less frantic than at any time since Pearl Harbor. Although the construction workers and their families had lived among the area's civilian population—occupying every spare bed for miles around—the soldiers who came after them worked, ate, and slept at the camp, and thus had less day-to-day impact on local life. Other than in the downtown business districts of Bastrop and Elgin, where military personnel would spend considerable time and money over the next four years, much of rural Bastrop County life reverted to the more peaceful routines of prewar times. Some local residents, however, now found the old routines too slow. In early June, after construction activity at the camp had begun to taper off, Louise Metcalfe, McDade's new correspondent to the *Bastrop Advertiser* and the *Elgin Courier*, complained that the town was "too quiet, [now that] nearly everyone is gone." Some people in Bastrop County regretted the end of the initial boom, but many would change their minds.[7]

As time passed, new routines evolved that integrated Camp Swift into county life. A number of local people found work at the camp; men were employed clearing brush, as firefighters, or in the camp post office, while women worked in the kitchen or laundry. For many of Bastrop County's men, this was their first work experience other than farm work, and for most local women it was their first opportunity to work outside of their homes and to be paid for their labor. Some of Bastrop County's younger women married soldiers stationed at Camp Swift. Although the long-term impact of such marriages was to draw the women away from their family homes, they at first gave the appearance of bringing new people into local society and were for the most part welcomed.[8]

Relations between military personnel and the local populace were not always harmonious, however. Local farmers who had hoped to sell produce to the mess hall met with opposition from camp buyers, who usually considered the quantities Bastrop County's truck farmers had to offer too small to bother with. Even after organizing themselves into a marketing cooperative, area growers were unable to supply more than a fraction of Camp Swift's needs, and army purchasing agents generally ignored them in favor of large-volume wholesalers in San Antonio or Houston. This angered many of the farmers. Nor did the camp's neighbors care for the fact that stray artillery rounds sometimes landed on their property. (No one was ever hurt in these incidents, nor any buildings destroyed, though one errant shell did kill several cattle.) Local citizens had other complaints as well: They disliked the heavy traffic on the roads around the camp; they resented the constant patrols of the military police, whose power superseded that of local law enforcement agencies; and they worried that the handful of African American soldiers stationed at the camp might somehow disrupt the local peace. Later in the war, they fretted about the three thousand members of Rommel's defeated Afrika Korps who arrived at Camp Swift as prisoners-of-war. In short, as good as Camp Swift may have been for the local economy—especially for the merchants of Bastrop and Elgin—many area residents eventually resented its presence. Some even considered it a threat.[9]

With one notable exception, local people's fears for the safety of friends and family seem to have been groundless. Judging from area newspapers, there was surprisingly little violence in Bastrop County involving Camp Swift personnel. Even so, occasional incidents did occur. Shortly after the first infantry troops arrived at the camp, a military policeman shot and killed a soldier in a Bastrop drinking spot, claiming the man had pulled a knife on him. The facts that no one from Bastrop County was involved and the dead man was black and the MP white, diminished the seriousness of this incident in local eyes. This was not the case in October 1942, however, when a soldier stationed at Camp Swift raped and murdered an eight-year-old Bastrop girl. (In tragic irony, the victim was the daughter of county judge C. B. Maynard, a central figure in the effort to attract an army camp to the area.) Reflecting the sentiments of nearly everyone in the county, *Bastrop Advertiser* columnist Pete Shady demanded that military authorities "hang that beast at high noon upon the highest hill in the reservation." Otherwise, he warned, the relationship between the local populace and the military would deteriorate into "the most callous hatred that ever existed between two classes of countrymen." After a required waiting period during which the soldier—once an inmate of a Minnesota "insane asylum"—underwent a psychiatric evaluation, he was court-martialled, convicted, and sentenced to death. As tragic as these incidents were, however, they were the only reported episodes of deadly violence involving Camp Swift personnel during the camp's entire five-year existence.[10]

Camp Swift's days were numbered after the war. During the last few months of 1945, it served as a discharge center from which the army released more than twelve thousand men into civilian life. Throughout this time, newly discharged soldiers embarking on journeys home kept the train depots in Elgin and Bastrop continually busy. These men, many of them with money in their pockets and celebration on their minds, provided local eateries, drinking spots, and dance halls with a final flurry of business. This was to be the local merchants' last hurrah, however, as far as Camp Swift was concerned. Despite Congressman Johnson's efforts to keep the camp operational, he announced in April 1946 that it would be deactivated by the middle of June. "For some of us," he said, "this may mean a temporary financial sacrifice, in that we won't have the prosperity we had during the war years, but I'm confident that no one wants war again, at any price." Although Johnson promised that he would work "every day" to get the camp reopened, he was never able to do so. The last military personnel left Camp Swift in late 1946. The following January, the camp was declared war surplus and turned over to the War Assets Administration for disposal.[11]

What to do with the land Camp Swift had occupied became "a nettlesome problem" in postwar Bastrop County. Various plans had been circulating even before the end of the war. One called for the University of Texas to relocate from Austin onto a portion of the land. Another proposed a Bastrop County Community College for the site. There was also talk of establishing an experimental, large-scale agricultural cooperative at Camp Swift, while another rumor had it that one of the nation's major automobile manufacturers was considering building an assembly plant there. None of these plans ever came to anything, however.[12]

In August 1947, a group of Bastrop businessmen unveiled a proposal to form a "Bastrop County Homestead Association" that would purchase Camp Swift in its entirety—buildings and all. Their plan called for the association to divide the camp into three hundred to four hundred tracts of suitable size for farming or ranching and then offer the land for resale to veterans. Each parcel would include "a now existing and suitable [barracks] building for a house for immediate use and a sufficient number of acres of land to produce for [the veteran] and his family an American standard of living." The association would offer all this "at a price within his limited means, and upon terms he can easily meet." Obviously, the authors of this plan sensed that there was money to be made from the guaranteed home loans the government was making so readily available to military veterans. They undoubtedly hoped to slice off a healthy piece of the postwar pie—for the area in general and themselves in particular—by creating what might have amounted, if their plan had worked, to a rural Levittown in the midst of Bastrop County.[13]

This proposal met with immediate local resistance. Although the War Department had never made any legally binding promises about what it would do with the land occupied by Camp Swift when and if the camp were deactivated, the general understanding had always been that the property would be offered back to its original owners or their heirs, at the same price the government had paid for it, before being offered for sale to anyone else. The newly advanced notion that the War Assets Administration might sell the entire camp to a single buyer surprised and angered many people in the area. A September 5 public meeting held at the county courthouse passed a resolution "opposing the purchase of Camp Swift by any individual, group, or corporation." Five days later, a delegation of Bastrop County residents, including several from McDade, met with Congressman Johnson to convince him that it would be "tragic . . . now that the war is supposed to be over . . . for someone to profiteer on what had to be sacrificed by the former owners." They must have been persuasive, because later that day Johnson held a press conference to officially announce that "former landowners [at Camp Swift] will have a chance to buy their land unless federal agencies and others with priorities step in." The next day's *Austin American* reported that "all efforts to sell the camp as a block have been squashed." In October, the War Assets Administration turned the land over to the Federal Land Bank to administer the process of selling it back to its original owners.[14]

In contrast to the speed with which the government had seized the Camp Swift property in the months following Pearl Harbor, it went about the job of returning it rather slowly. One delay after another taxed the patience of people anxious to get back on their land and resume their prewar lives. Before the Land Bank would offer any of the land back to its former owners, those in charge of the program insisted that the entire tract be resurveyed, claiming that wartime activities at the camp had destroyed many of the landmarks that had defined prewar property lines. This was a time-consuming job that many locals thought unnecessary. The process of locating and contacting all of the former landowners or their heirs also took time. In addition, Congressman Johnson's efforts to prevent Camp Swift from being irrevocably shut down tended to delay land sales. On several occasions in the late 1940s, Johnson hinted at "a revival of activity" at Camp Swift, sometimes alluding to "plans that cannot [yet] be announced" for the site, sometimes suggesting that the camp be kept available for reactivation in case of "national emergency." On each of these occasions, the process of offering land back to its prewar owners was delayed. In fact, by the summer of 1950, almost four years after the War Department had declared Camp Swift war surplus, less than half of the total acreage seized by the government in 1941 and 1942 had been returned to its former owners. Some people never did get their land back, due to the Texas National Guard exercising a "priority claim" in late 1947 on almost twelve thousand acres in the northwestern part of the camp, close to Elgin and McDade. This is the present-day Camp Swift, which the Texas National Guard uses for training and maneuvers.[15]

The Land Bank's seemingly casual attitude toward returning the land at Camp Swift caused animosity in Bastrop County, both between county residents and the federal government and among different groups within the local populace. Many of the landowners wanted their land back because it was their family's home, the place they (and sometimes their parents and grandparents) had been born and always lived—in a few cases, the land had been in the family since 1836, having been granted to their ancestors by the newly established Republic of Texas in payment for service in Texas's war for independence from Mexico. For many other local people, an unoccupied army camp taking up more than fifty-two thousand acres in the middle of their county seemed a waste of good land and an unnecessary inconvenience. Residents of McDade, for example, resented the fact that several years after the war had ended they still could not get to Bastrop without traveling by way of Elgin or Paige, routes that almost doubled the distance to the county courthouse. Mrs. Edgar Owen, who had taken over as McDade's newspaper correspondent in 1942, complained in late 1947 that "due to the Camp Swift area still being closed, it's easier for us to get to Austin than Bastrop . . . Seems like if all those cattle can be turned loose in the reservation we McDade folks could at least drive through there to our county seat."[16]

Owen was referring to an issue that fanned considerable anger in postwar Bastrop County and divided many local people into opposing factions. At heart, it was an economic issue, a competition over who would benefit from the deactivation of Camp Swift and the subsequently uncertain status of the camp land. According to a brief summary of Bastrop County's postwar land difficulties that appeared in the *Austin American*, a number of Bastrop's merchants profited twice from Camp Swift—once by trading with soldiers stationed there during the war and a second time by investing their wartime earnings in cattle which they pastured at no cost on vacant camp land once the war was over. "Between the time [the War Department] 'de-activated' Camp Swift and the government began selling land [back to the original owners] thousands of livestock were turned into the reservation on a 'nester basis.' No lease money was paid, because none was asked. Many Bastrop businessmen became cowmen simply by purchasing cows and turning them out to graze on the free land in Camp Swift." Understandably, this angered many of those waiting to get their land back. A number of local people believed, and some still do, that the slow pace of returning the land at Camp Swift to its original owners was the result of collusion between Bastrop's postwar cattle barons and individuals with sufficient political clout to effect bureaucratic delay.[17]

When people regained their land, they were often unhappy with it. Although it was common knowledge that the army had razed all preexisting buildings at Camp Swift, most people did not realize the extent of damage done to the land. Returning landowners discovered wells filled in, orchards destroyed, fields and pastures overgrown with brush, and concrete foundation pillars from dismantled barracks, artillery emplacements, and other military structures scattered everywhere. The army's mistreatment of the land so discouraged some of those who had hoped to resume truck farming that they ended up selling out—often for less than they had paid the government to get their property back—to the same stockmen who had been grazing cattle on the land for free since the end of the war. As a result, between 1947 and 1950, many of the smaller pieces of Camp Swift property that had supported family truck farms before the war were consolidated into larger, more economically efficient cattle ranches, most of whose owners did not live on the land but in Bastrop, Austin, or even farther away. Thus, one of Camp Swift's effects on postwar Bastrop County was to reduce the rural population in the countryside between McDade and Bastrop, a well-watered area of sandy, fertile soil that one prewar observer had described as "the most Heavenly-blessed and bountiful truck [farming] area in all of Texas." Not surprisingly, much of this did not sit well with many Bastrop County residents. In general, the local view of what had happened with the land at Camp Swift was that the government had forcibly taken it from its rightful owners, rendered it unfit for farming, and then, once the war was over, allowed those who had most profited from the presence of Camp Swift in Bastrop County to make even more money from it, this time at the expense of the people who had owned the land to begin with.[18]

The situation became further complicated in July 1950, when, in the face of a rapidly deteriorating military situation in Korea, the Defense Department ordered all Camp Swift land sales halted. Clearly, this was a first step toward possible reactivation of the camp. Within a matter of days, Bastrop County split into opposing factions—one side enthusiastically in favor of reopening the camp, the other bitterly opposed. Just as they had in 1941, the merchants of Bastrop, Elgin, and Smithville, with additional support from the Austin Chamber of Commerce, jumped on the Camp Swift bandwagon without hesitation. The county's business leaders organized a campaign they dubbed "Operation Dollar" to push for the camp's reactivation, and the Bastrop Chamber of Commerce printed a brochure touting Bastrop County as having already proven itself an ideal site for a military training camp by virtue of its exemplary record as host of Camp Swift during World War II. At the same time, the *Bastrop Advertiser* speculated about "a possible World War III" and "the business benefits of [the] 50,000 to 75,000 dollar-spending soldiers" who might once again pour into Bastrop County.[19]

Most of the county's rural population, however, disagreed. This was especially true of those who had originally owned land at Camp Swift, whether they were once again living on their land, had gotten their land back and then resold it, or were still waiting to buy it back. Most of these landowners, who a decade earlier had been willing to give up their homes and property in support of the war effort, opposed the camp this time. Some had begun making their farms profitable again, though most were still in the process of repairing the damage the army had done to their property during the war. The owners of the Camp Swift land most recently offered for resale—the last sixty-six tracts, totaling almost nine thousand acres—were especially upset, since the Land Bank had not made their property available to them until less than three weeks before the Defense Department ordered sales of all remaining Camp Swift lands halted. This left many of these landowners in the awkward position of having paid for their land but not yet in receipt of legal title to it. With very few exceptions and regardless of their individual situations, the prewar owners of land at Camp Swift were outraged that future ownership of the land might once again be in doubt. In short, talk of reactivating Camp Swift during the Korean crisis created significant controversy and contention in Bastrop County. Those who stood to profit from a captive population of "dollar-spending soldiers" were eager to see the camp reactivated, but much of the rest of the county was not. Most strongly opposed were the owners of land at Camp Swift. Their patriotism had been sorely tried in the years since the war, and by 1950 it was beginning to wear thin. World War II had cost them their homes and many of them their livelihoods for almost a decade; they would rather see someone else host World War III.[20]

Ironically, it does not appear that the Defense Department was ever likely to reactivate Camp Swift. Most of the camp's buildings had been sold off shortly after the war—to nearby communities to use as school buildings, to several country churches in need of new sanctuaries (McDade's present-day Baptist Church was originally a chapel at Camp Swift, and one wing of its school a barracks building there), or to private citizens planning to convert them into homes or farm buildings. From the army's point of view, this made Camp Swift a less attractive prospect for reactivation than many of the other abandoned World War II training camps scattered around the country that remained more intact. Nor did the confused land situation in Bastrop County work in favor of reopening Camp Swift. Throughout the summer and fall of 1950, the Defense Department reactivated a number of World War II training facilities, including the nearby San Marcos Air Station. Austin's Bergstrom Field also underwent major renovation and expansion. Residents of Bastrop County, however, found themselves on the sidelines with little to do but watch and wait, some hopefully and others fearfully, while the army refused to commit itself one way or the other about the future of Camp Swift.[21]

Matters came to a head in Bastrop County in January 1951, largely as a result of what appears to be overoptimism on the part of those working for Camp Swift's reactivation. With the beginning of a new year and in response to more bad news from Korea, the county's business interests embarked on a renewed effort to reopen the camp. They sponsored town meetings in Bastrop, Elgin, and Smithville, so citizens of the county's "urban triumvirate" could go on record in favor of reactivation. At these meetings they urged local residents to voice their support of reopening Camp Swift by flooding the Washington offices of senators Lyndon Johnson and Tom Connally, Tenth District congressman Homer Thornberry, and various officials at the Defense Department with telegrams. The leaders of this movement wanted everyone to know that they were not acting out of self-interest but purely "in furtherance of the war effort." After all, they claimed, the government could save "several million dollars, at least" by reopening Camp Swift, though exactly how the government would save this money they did not make clear. In addition, Bastrop County was obviously, in the words of Bastrop mayor Gordon Bryson, "the best place to train soldiers." This was self-evident to those who wanted the camp reactivated.[22]

In mid-January, leaders of Bastrop County's drive to reactivate Camp Swift met with Lieutenant General Leroy F. Lutes, commander of the Fourth Army at Fort Sam Houston in San Antonio. Lieutenant General Lutes received them warmly, informed them that he was familiar with the fine work done by the people of Bastrop in hosting Camp Swift during World War II, and assured them that he was certain they would do just as good a job if the camp were reopened. He also remained steadfastly noncommittal about the future of the camp, saying only that the army would "consider" reactivating Camp Swift "if and when it becomes necessary to increase our training areas." Instead of taking this as the polite brush-off it seems to have been, local supporters of reactivation chose to take it as good news. The *Bastrop Advertiser* ran a banner headline proclaiming "CAMP SWIFT TO BE CONSIDERED IF NECESSARY!" and generally reported the meeting with Lieutenant General Lutes as a major step toward reactivation. An account of the meeting that appeared in the *Austin American* was more complete, indicating that the *Advertiser* had failed to report that Lutes had cautioned his visitors that time and money were major considerations in deciding which camps to reactivate and that "camps from which the least amount of buildings have been removed would command favorable attention." This, of course, was a factor that worked against Camp Swift, since most of its buildings had been sold as war surplus in the late 1940s. Nevertheless, in the wake of the meeting, the prevailing local belief was that the camp was about to be reactivated.[23]

This seems to have spurred those opposed to reopening Camp Swift into action. They started their own telegram-writing campaign and began circulating petitions protesting the injustice of seizing land a second time from people whose farms and livelihoods were still recovering from Camp Swift's first term in Bastrop County. They also called a mass meeting to discuss the issue and become organized. This meeting was held in McDade on January 20, a Saturday night; it was open to the public, though only owners of land at Camp Swift would be allowed to vote upon a course of action. The *Bastrop Advertiser* made no mention of this gathering, although a brief account of it did appear in the *Austin American* of January 24. Characterizing the meeting as the beginning of "an aggressive fight against [the reactivation of Camp Swift]," the article went on to list many of the landowners' grievances. It pointed out that those whose property the government had delayed offering for resale until the previous June, only to see Camp Swift land sales frozen a few weeks later, were especially bitter. These people, most of whom had paid for their land but had not yet received deeds, believed that they "could not get their money back without killing their purchase priorities." Those who had gotten their land back and begun improving it were also angry. They were furious at the prospect of seeing the improvements they had already performed go to waste and at the same time frustrated at being unable to "go ahead with development of their farms while uncertainty remains that the government may re-acquire the area for further military use." The assembled property owners voted unanimously to oppose reactivation, although the *Austin American*'s account of the meeting makes no mention of their deciding on any specific course of action. After the meeting ended, a spokesman for the landowners blamed Bastrop's "downtown business group" for the quarrelsome state of local affairs, claiming that among all of Bastrop County's citizens only its merchants stood to gain from a reactivated Camp Swift. He also pointed out that, unlike the landowners, the merchants had little to lose if the government were to once again take possession of large tracts of privately owned rural land in the county.[24]

The army never reactivated Camp Swift, although it is doubtful that the meeting in McDade affected the army's decision. After the flurry of activity in the middle of January, references to Camp Swift quickly disappeared from local newspapers. On January 28, the *Austin American* ran a final editorial in favor of reopening the camp, saying that it had been a mistake to close it in the first place and claiming that the economic benefits of a reactivated Camp Swift would outweigh whatever inconvenience it might cause local landowners. The issue was not addressed by the press again. Twice during the spring of 1951, the Bastrop Chamber of Commerce made inquiries of the Defense Department about its plans for Camp Swift; both times the answer it got was the same one Lieutenant General Lutes had given to the group he had met with in January—that the army would "consider" reactivating the camp "when and if" it needed more training sites. That is as far local supporters of reopening the camp pursued the matter. As the fighting in Korea continued without the army displaying any further interest in Camp Swift, Bastrop's businessmen seemed to resign themselves to the fact that "dollar-spending soldiers" would not be flooding back into Bastrop County. Simultaneously, local anger over the land issue began to cool. In August 1951, shortly after the opening of peace talks in Korea, the Defense Department lifted the freeze on Camp Swift land sales and offered the last of the camp properties slated for resale back to their prewar owners. World War II was finally over in Bastrop County.[25]

All camp lands slated for return to private ownership were eventually resold, most to their prewar owners or their heirs. The return of the final sixty-six pieces of property was even further delayed, but most county residents seemed more relieved to have the issue resolved than angry about the additional delay. They looked forward to "get[ting] back to normal" in the northern part of Bastrop County. Of course, "normal" was the way life had been before World War II, a time that was now more than a decade in the past. American life had changed irrevocably in those ten years, though perhaps less obviously in Bastrop County than in many other places. Even if they were not aware of it, however, the people of Bastrop County were demonstrating a fundamental postwar shift in attitude. They no longer perceived the interests of the nation to be identical to those of Bastrop County. Many of the same people who had willingly given up their homes and lands in 1941 were loathe to do so in 1951. Instead of being proud to make personal sacrifices in support of the nation's larger goals they resented being expected to make those sacrifices a second time. They directed some of this resentment toward the federal government for not promptly releasing the land at Camp Swift at the end of World War II and for appearing to take what they had sacrificed, as well as the fact of their sacrifice, for granted. They believed that the federal government had abused their trust, and they no longer implicitly believed its promises or unquestioningly assumed that its decisions were good for Bastrop County. They also resented the attempts of the county's business leaders to reopen Camp Swift. They believed that these men had acted purely out of self-interest, not only counter to the interests of those directly affected by a reactivated camp but in violation of the best interests of local people in general.[26]

In short, events involving Camp Swift in postwar Bastrop County had the effect of deflating local faith in community, the all-encompassing importance of which was one of rural America's most cherished and long-enduring myths. In the years before the war, the notion that people could (and should) live in harmony with those around them, the belief that all members of society could (and should) share common ideals, goals, and self-interests, and the conviction that what was good for the public at large was good for each individual citizen (and vice versa) had all been articles of faith in Bastrop County. People there may have been naive to believe such things, but they believed them anyway, largely because they did not want to believe otherwise. The postwar controversy over Camp Swift, however, presented too strong a challenge for their naiveté to withstand. With the interests of local businessmen obviously diverging from those of landowners, and with the federal government ignoring the wishes of both groups (as well as those of the rest of the local population), area residents concluded that their dearly held, traditional concept of community was no longer pertinent. One of society's most fundamental values appeared to have changed: No longer was cooperation in service of the common welfare the prevailing ideal; instead, a complicated set of adversarial relationships between competing interest groups had become the standard on which postwar society would model itself. In many parts of the nation, of course, this was old news, but not in Bastrop County. Area residents were disappointed to realize that they no longer lived in an idyllic rural paradise where people's first concern was to take care of each other, that their lives were no longer immune to the kind of atomistic self-interest they had previously thought confined to large cities. By the early 1950s, many local people believed that World War II, through the agency of Camp Swift, had introduced a number of bad habits and questionable values to Bastrop County, and they were beginning to realize that life there would never be the same.[27]

Opportunity Passing by: Camp Swift and McDade

In many ways, McDade's experience of Camp Swift paralleled that of the rest of Bastrop County, though some people in the community seem to have become disillusioned with the camp more quickly than people in other parts of the county. In the immediate aftermath of Pearl Harbor, however, McDade welcomed the prospect of having an army training camp for a neighbor. Like most people in the area, community residents were both proud that their home county could be of service to the nation and enthusiastic about the impact they expected the camp to have on the local economy. Many of them thought that the coming of Camp Swift to Bastrop County would allow McDade to begin growing again and to reestablish itself as the equal of Bastrop, Elgin, and

Smithville, the county's three "big" towns. They were hoping Camp Swift would put McDade "back on the map."[28]

At first, it seemed as if they might get their wish. Throughout the early part of 1942, McDade shared in the exhilarating hustle and bustle of building Camp Swift. Along with the rest of the county, the town experienced a sudden boom; not since its earliest days as a railhead had as many people spent as much time and money in McDade. Since McDade had the closest train station to the northern part of Camp Swift, where construction crews were hurriedly building a network of intracamp roads, the freight depot in town was flooded with shipments of equipment and supplies. For nearly two months, a "constant caravan" of trucks ran back and forth between McDade and camp construction sites on an almost daily basis. Many new people moved to McDade as well. According to Louise Metcalfe, who had just taken over from Mrs. Hackworth as McDade's newspaper correspondent, the newcomers from "nearly every state in the union" made McDade seem "like a small city." The only cafe in town was "rushed all the time," and rumor had it that a second cafe was about to open. A pair of "traveling picture shows" set up their tents in McDade, a number of new students enrolled in the community's schools, and the Methodist church hired its first full-time pastor in years. In March, Metcalfe estimated that 80 percent of McDade's homes were housing as many as ten extra people, and some town residents even rented out chicken coops to Camp Swift construction workers desperate for a place to sleep.[29]

McDade's merchants, of course, were delighted. Their stores had not been as busy in years, and business improved daily. Their only complaint was the difficulty they had keeping their shelves stocked. But some in town had more serious complaints. In February, for example, the Southern Pacific abruptly transferred M. B. Freeman, the longtime station master at McDade, to a less busy post in Lee County, replacing him with a man from the bustling freight yard in Houston. Freeman and his wife, both respected members of the McDade community, had little choice but to pull up stakes and leave. McDade's packing shed and cannery also fell victim to the rush to get Camp Swift built, as construction companies with contracts at the camp took over these facilities for office and storage space. The packing shed did not reopen until after the war, and the cannery, though no one knew it at the time, had shut down permanently.[30]

While the rush of new people into town put badly needed extra money into local pockets, some community residents found the sudden influx of newcomers disturbing. Louise Metcalfe quickly became overwhelmed with trying to keep up with "our new population." After marveling in late February that two-thirds of the people she saw on the street in uptown McDade were strangers to her, she lamented three weeks later that "the personals of our little town are no more." Perhaps believing that she was not adequately performing her job as community reporter, she requested news about the newcomers. When none was forthcoming, she fretted about properly welcoming them into the community and helping them get acclimated. "We only wish," she wrote, "we were able to care for them, for they too are people, just like the rest of us." In March, she resolved to compile a list of McDade's new citizens, promising to include information about their jobs at the camp, where they were from, and their family backgrounds. Such a list never appeared. Before long, she stopped writing about the newcomers, possibly because it became apparent that most of them would not be staying long. Even though some new people continued to arrive in McDade throughout the late spring and summer of 1942, most of those who had flocked to the community in January and February were leaving by the end of May, their jobs involved with getting the camp built and operational completed.[31]

Not all the new people who came to McDade in 1942 had come from "away" to work at Camp Swift. Quite a few of them, in fact, were from just down the road, people who until recently had been residents of Oak Hill, an unincorporated community of about fifty farm families gathered around a small general store, a church, and an elementary school. This cluster of buildings was situated about two miles south of McDade, just off the road to Bastrop. When Camp Swift became operational, Oak Hill ceased to exist. Both the land its "downtown" occupied and its residents' farm acreage were part of the fifty-two thousand acres the War Department condemned in late 1941. Since Oak Hill was in the northern part of the camp and thus not destined to be part of the cantonment area near Bastrop, its residents had until June 15 to vacate their homes. This gave the people of Oak Hill about five months to find new places to live—time enough, at least, to consider some alternatives.

The residents of Oak Hill dispersed throughout Bastrop County and beyond. Many had friends and relatives in towns nearby and tended to gravitate to communities where they had such ties. Many moved to McDade, not only because of friends or family but also because they wanted to remain close to their old homes and keep an eye on their property. A few chose McDade because their children attended the high school there. By this time, the McDade's Camp Swift boom was subsiding. Many of the people who had moved to Bastrop County to work on construction projects at the camp were now leaving. Other newcomers continued to arrive in the county—the families of permanent Camp Swift staff, both military and civilian, as well as a variety of entrepreneurial types hoping to profit from the soldiers who would eventually be stationed there—but most of these people preferred living in Bastrop or Smithville, close to the camp's main gate. This left housing more available in McDade than in many other parts of the county. For all of these reasons, many of the Oak Hill residents displaced by Camp Swift wound up in McDade.[32]

Among them was Mrs. Edgar Owen, a lifelong resident of Oak Hill and that community's longtime correspondent to the *Courier* and the *Advertiser*. Owen is noteworthy for two reasons. The columns she wrote from Oak Hill in the six months between December 1941, when she and her neighbors learned they would have to abandon their homes, and June 1942, when they actually had to leave them, contain the only hint of local dissatisfaction with the coming of Camp Swift to Bastrop County. They provide a brief but poignant account, written from the point of view of someone inside the community, of Oak Hill's demise. This account was sometimes angry, sometimes fearful, and sometimes deeply sorrowful, but Owen tried to maintain "a stiff upper lip" throughout. Although she never openly voiced opposition to the camp, she obviously regretted its intrusion into her and her neighbors' lives. Second, and more pertinent to a history of McDade, is the fact that soon after she moved to McDade, Owen took over from Louise Metcalfe as the town's newspaper correspondent. In her new role, she continued to complain about the impact of Camp Swift on local life. Most of Oak Hill's exresidents probably shared Owen's distaste for the camp. If so, and with so many displaced Oak Hill people having relocated to McDade, perhaps it is not surprising that McDade became a center of landowner resistance to the possible reactivation of Camp Swift in 1951.[33]

To a present-day observer, the lack of local resistance in 1942 to such a large-scale seizure of land seems extraordinary. Within a month after Pearl Harbor, the War Department had condemned 425 separate pieces of property; some of this land had been in its owners' families for more than a century. Surely not all of the landowners were so public-spirited as to be happy about signing their property over to the government, especially when sixty-one of them were given less than ten days to vacate. Not wanting to appear unpatriotic to a public with a raging case of war fever, they may have voiced their complaints only to close friends and family. Some may have thought about resisting but were unable to organize any kind of effective effort on such short notice. A few may have actually tried to fight the seizure of their land only to be ignored by a local press overwhelmingly in favor of having an army base established in Bastrop County. Whatever the truth of the matter, it seems unlikely that the displaced landowners were as unanimously selfless in their patriotism as the "old gentleman" who wrote in a letter to the *Elgin Courier* that "part[ing] with the old homestead . . . is certainly like tearing out my very heart, . . . but if my country needs it I will willingly give it up." That, however, is how the local press—to the extent the county's weeklies treated it as an issue at all—characterized the landowners' reaction to the government's seizure of their property. Citing the "old gentleman" as typical, the *Courier* proudly proclaimed that all "the good, loyal people" of Bastrop County who had sacrificed their homes and land were so full of "the spirit that built our great America and the spirit that will protect it and keep it free" that they felt honored, even privileged, to be able to aid the war effort by giving up their property. None of the landowners, according to this semiofficial version of local opinion, wished for a moment that their land had been spared. This view has persisted into the present. Interviews conducted in McDade between 1987 and 1989 contain no hint of there being any local hostility toward the War Department's seizure of land in 1942.[34]

Owen's columns between December 1941 and June 1942, her final six months at Oak Hill, indicate that not everyone in that community was enthusiastic about the new army camp. Nearly all of her writing from this period contains a barely disguised undercurrent of distaste for the changes the arrival of Camp Swift had wrought on local life. In late January, a detachment of military police arrived in the area and began patrolling Oak Hill's maze of back roads; almost overnight, Owen observed, local residents found themselves barred at times from using roads they had traveled all their lives. Soon afterward, construction of a network of camp roads began in the Oak Hill area. The road work went on day and night, further disrupting the rhythms of local life. Owen complained that the "roaring of machinery [and] cars traveling all night long" was keeping her and her neighbors awake and "gives us a feeling of uneasiness." The road work even continued on Sundays, she noted with amazement, obviously offended. "Have we as a nation forgotten God?" she asked.[35]

Most of Owen's columns from this time bear witness to the disintegration of the community around her. One Oak Hill family after another began packing up and leaving, even before June 15. Those who stayed through the spring found they had less time and fewer opportunities to socialize with their friends and neighbors than ever before. "People have no time to contact each other," Owen wrote at the end of March. "We have no neighborly visits, it's busy on every hand, all bent on getting the camp completed." In the middle of April, explaining why her columns were getting shorter with each passing week, Owen observed that "news of interest is so hard to gather, everyone is busy and our entire lives have changed so much in the past few months it's hard to express our thoughts." Sounding disoriented, she fretted that she could no longer tell one piece of land from another, what with familiar fence lines having been cleared away and houses and barns being torn down all around. When Oak Hill's church was razed, its lumber sold and hauled away, Owen seemed to feel the community was being punished. "Perhaps if we'd been more persistent . . . and not neglected our duty," she wrote, "some way may have been provided to let it stand, but now it's just a memory." As June approached, memories were about all that remained of Oak Hill; for Owen, who was one of the last to leave, those memories were preferable to the unfamiliar realities of the present and the uncertainties of the future. As the time left to her in her "beloved old home" wound down, she thought of the simpler days of the past. "No one here is living a normal life anymore," she wrote sadly. "Everything seems so different." Oak Hill, she lamented, would soon be "a thing of the past. Now a nearly complete army camp . . . take[s] its place, [and] people cannot conceive of the change that is here."[36]

With the deadline approaching, Owen tried to face the prospect of leaving matter-of-factly, confessing only to "a feeling we can't describe" at having to abandon her longtime home. She and her husband were "about the last to leave" Oak Hill, and they seem to have delayed their decision about where to relocate as long as possible. As late as June 7, "our last Sunday here in our old home" and the day she penned her final column from Oak Hill, she did not seem sure where they would be living after the fifteenth. In that final column, Owen promised to let her friends know where she had settled as soon as she knew herself. "It isn't easy, folks," she concluded, "but we will try not to look back and [will try to] fit ourselves into the activities of the community in which we live."[37]

That community turned out to be McDade. In her McDade column of June 18, Louise Metcalfe listed several Oak Hill families who had recently relocated to McDade. Among them were Mr. and Mrs. Edgar Owen, who had bought a small house and few acres of land on old Highway 20 just a mile west of uptown. As promised, Owen wasted no time becoming involved in community affairs; within six weeks, she had taken over as McDade's correspondent to the local papers. Neither Metcalfe in her final column nor Owen in her first gave any indication of why or how this came about: in the July 30 editions of the *Advertiser* and the *Courier*, the "News from McDade" column simply appeared under the byline of Mrs. Edgar Owen. It would continue to do so until 1952.[38]

In her new role as McDade correspondent, Owen did not write about Camp Swift as often as she had during her final six months at Oak Hill. When she did mention the camp, however, it was almost always with disapproval. In her early columns from McDade, she seemed unable to forget about what the coming of the camp had done to Oak Hill, and, consciously or not, she often sounded bitter. At times, she became so upset that her old farm was now part of an artillery range that she had difficulty composing her column. "Friends, if you can't make anything out of this letter," she confessed in late August, " it will be because as I write I can hear the guns booming down at the army camp. . . . We are told that the guns are set up at our old homeplace. . . . It seems as if I can just see men falling in battle; it just makes me nervous." In addition, despite feeling grateful that army bulldozers had spared the Oak Hill cemetery, she resented the military's rule that anyone wanting to visit gravesites there first had to apply for a permit at camp headquarters. Although the War Department had ruled that people with previously established family plots at the cemetery would still be allowed burial there, families were supposed to coordinate funeral arrangements with military authorities as far in advance as possible. Owen found this so absurd as to be insulting: "As if we know when Our Heavenly Father will call us Home," she huffed.[39]

The focus of her comments about Camp Swift soon shifted, however, from bitterness at the demise of Oak Hill to complaints about how the camp's nearby presence was affecting life in McDade. In the autumn of 1942, for example, she remarked upon a shortage of fresh produce in the area and expressed dismay that this could occur in the heart of one of Texas' most productive truck farming regions. She blamed the camp for the shortages: not only had it removed considerable acreage from food production, she observed, but it had also caused many local people to quit farming, in some cases by forcing them off their land and in others by offering them "high wage" employment as an alternative. The result, Owen claimed, was a county in which fewer people were producing less food, and more people, as wage earners instead of food producers, were becoming increasingly "depend[ent] on buying everything." She also blamed the camp for a troublesome shortage of local labor. As winter approached, Owen reported that there was no one to hire in the area to cut firewood and that many of those in McDade who were unable to cut wood for themselves were having to buy it—at exorbitant prices—from strangers trucking it in from other parts of the state. A similar difficulty arose the following spring, when people in McDade had trouble finding someone to plow their garden plots for them, a problem they had never encountered before. In both instances, Owen held Camp Swift responsible for disrupting long-established routines in ways that diminished the quality of life for many people in McDade.[40]

In addition, McDade's economy was once again slipping into decline. The initial economic boost McDade's merchants had received from Camp Swift was short-lived. Once construction at the camp was complete, business activity in the community slowed dramatically, soon reverting to a pace nearly as sedate as in the prewar years. Even before Owen arrived in mid-June, Louise Metcalfe had described McDade as "too quiet," as a result of many camp construction workers having left. Although some in the community expected Camp Swift personnel and their families to move in and take the workers' places, no such second wave of newcomers materialized. Nor was McDade destined to do much business with soldiers stationed at Camp Swift: the town's location on the camp's northern boundary, away from the main gate at the southern end and not on any of the commonly traveled routes to and from the camp—plus the fact that McDade was "dry"—meant that few of the "dollar-spending soldiers" had reason to spend time or money there. Thus, except during the construction boom of early 1942, most of the "good times" Camp Swift brought to the area bypassed McDade. Many people in town, well aware of handsome profits being turned in Bastrop and Elgin, resented the fact that their community had somehow missed out.[41]

McDade suffered other setbacks during the war, some of which may well have had more longterm impact on the community than simply missing out on the business of soldiers stationed at Camp Swift. When considered as a whole, much of what Owen reported from McDade during the war years testifies to a community losing cohesiveness, whose residents were realizing that in the larger scheme of things their hometown was a rather unimportant, second-rate little place. One such blow to community morale came in 1943, when the *Bastrop Advertiser* stopped carrying Owen's weekly column of news from McDade. "We didn't quit," Owen explained, "the Editor says we at McDade are too far off now, since the Camp came. But we are still on the map, just the same." Her column would continue to appear in the *Elgin Courier*, so there would still be a semiofficial record of community events, but many people in town were troubled, and insulted, that the editor of their county seat's weekly newspaper no longer considered news of their hometown worth mentioning. It was undeniably a snub and carried the implicit message that McDade, stuck way out on the far side of Camp Swift, was no longer a significant part of Bastrop County.[42]

The *Advertiser*'s decision to discontinue Owen's column was the second such slight the community had received in less than a year. In late 1942, the Postal Service had ordered one of McDade's two rural delivery routes eliminated, no doubt because the route to the south of town, which had included the Oak Hill area, was no longer necessary. This was not only a clear indication of the town's declining importance, but also left McDade native Archie Sanders, who had carried the mail on that route since 1919, out of a job. In order to remain eligible for his federal pension, he had to move to Lockhart—almost fifty miles distant—where the post office had a vacancy. His was just one in a series of forced departures from McDade. The McDade Pottery plant, long the community's only industry and largest employer, also shut its doors in 1942, a casualty of War Department restrictions on "essential materials"; several of its employees had to leave McDade to seek work elsewhere. In 1943, the Williams family, owners of the pottery plant and one of McDade's leading families since 1892, moved to Elgin. Several other of the town's smaller businesses also closed during the war, their owners either moving away or taking jobs at Camp Swift. McDade was obviously in decline: it was losing importance relative to other towns in the area; it was losing much of its economic base; and it was losing people, some of whom had been citizens of the community for years.[43]

The war years were hard on McDade area farmers as well. They were especially hurt by the shortage of labor in the region. Most of the young men the farmers had once relied on to help them during their busiest times of year had joined the military. The few able-bodied young men from the area who were not in the service now had other ways of making a living that were steadier, less back-breaking, and better paying—most of them jobs at Camp Swift. The farmers also had a hard time getting their crops to market during the war. With the military exercising strict control over all rail transport in the Camp Swift area, the freight cars local farmers had come to depend on for shipping their produce were no longer regularly available. Area growers now had to truck their crops to market themselves or hire someone else to do it. Neither alternative was as easy or as cheap as selling crops to local wholesale agents such as Grover Westbrook for further sale and delivery, as they had before the war. Many McDade area farmers found that even though they could get better prices for their produce during the war, the cost of selling their crops (in both time and money) left them working harder for less return than in the years before the war.[44]

Owen reported most such developments matter-of-factly, giving little indication of how she felt about them. She was less sanguine, however, about what she perceived as the deteriorating quality of social and community life in wartime McDade. She deplored the fact that the town was no longer as lively as in the years before the war and the coming of Camp Swift. At times, she observed that McDade seemed empty. In part, of course, this was because many of the town's men were away in the military, with more enlisting, or being drafted, all the time. ("I hope we all don't have to go in the army," Owen remarked wryly. "Seems like we will need someone to keep the home fires burning.") But a greater loss to the community, at least in Owen's estimation, was the fact that so many of the town's women now had jobs at Camp Swift. This left them with "no time to visit anymore" and brought the town's once-busy round of regular social activities nearly to a standstill. A number of the community's ladies' organizations stopped meeting during this time, eventually to fade away entirely, and such traditional events as the Cemetery Association's election-day dinners were canceled for want of people to organize or attend them. Even among the town's women who did not have jobs at Camp Swift, the practice of regularly "visiting with" one's neighbors appears to have gone out of fashion. Owen seemed to believe this lack of a social life reflected badly on the community; it certainly provided her with less to write about than she thought seemly for a town the size of McDade. She frequently mourned the passing of the social whirl, which for her was the lifeblood of belonging to a community, whether Oak Hill, McDade, or any other.[45]

She also bemoaned the fact that people in McDade were less involved than ever before in civic matters. The town even seemed to have lost interest in its school, long a focus of community concern. In April 1943, for example, only four votes were cast in the McDade school board election, in which all of the incumbents ran unopposed. Reflecting a similar degree of apathy, McDade's PTA "did not function" at all during the 1943–44 school year. There also appear to have been problems within the town's churches during World War II, although in all but one instance the details are sketchy. Three of the community's four churches had their pastors leave suddenly in the autumn of 1942. In the case of the Baptist church, the minister's departure was so unexpected that it resulted in the last-minute cancellation of a long-anticipated revival. A year later, the fourth of the town's churches—the Siloah Evangelical Lutheran Church—self-destructed in a disagreement over whether its services should be conducted in German or English. Long-standing tensions erupted into a fist fight between the heads of two of the church's founding families during a December 1943 worship service, and the congregation disbanded immediately. Those who preferred English started going to church in Elgin, while those who preferred the more traditional German began attending services in Paige. Although Owen never mentioned these kinds of internal tensions in her column, she could hardly have been unaware of them. Perhaps she considered them another symptom of the increasing paucity of community life in McDade, for which she generally blamed Camp Swift. In her view, the camp had caused too many of the town's residents to direct their energies outside their home community, and the quality of life in McDade had suffered as a result. She believed that the town's tightly woven social fabric was beginning to unravel, the victim of too much of the world from beyond rural Texas crowding too close and demanding too much.[46]

Many of the McDade's more thoughtful citizens were worried about its future. They saw their community disintegrating before their eyes—economically and socially, and in terms of what its citizens imagined the town might yet become. Having lost its packing shed, cannery, and pottery plant, as well as several of its smaller businesses, McDade's future existence as an independent economic entity seemed to be in question. Many of the social and civic activities that had once bound the community's residents together in rounds of shared activities, and in furtherance of common goals, had faded into memory. The image McDade had always projected of itself—that of a community down on its luck but in every other way the equal of Bastrop County's larger towns, a community that would certainly reassert itself in the future—was also fading, replaced by a nagging sense of doubt. Despite beginning with high hopes, at least for the quality of life on the domestic front, the war years had not been good ones for McDade. In 1945, there were fewer ways of making a living in the community than ever before, with the town unable to support even a reduced population. What would happen when the several dozen servicemen from McDade returned home was anybody's guess, but it seemed unlikely they would all be able to settle down and live "normal" lives in their old hometown. It was not the same place they had left. With the community's economic base seriously eroded and its social base fragmented, McDade's future seemed less bright at the end of World War II than at any time in recent memory.[47]

It is hardly surprising, then, that most people in McDade opposed the postwar reactivation of Camp Swift. The camp may have lined the pockets of powerful people in Bastrop and Elgin during the war, but it had diminished the quality of life in the county's more rural communities. People in these places wanted no reprise of Camp Swift's tenure in the area. They wanted to recapture the life they had known before the war. In this strangely backward way, they were looking to the future, while those who wanted Camp Swift reactivated were only hoping for a replay, on the domestic front at least, of the war years. People in McDade wanted to once again concentrate on their own community, especially since many of them felt that it was going to take a concerted effort just to keep the town alive. Owen may have been right about McDade still being "on the map," but it was not going to be easy making sure that it stayed there.[48]

CHAPTER 13

McDade, 1945–80
The Decline of Community

McDade has undergone many changes in the years since World War II. Some of these changes have been good for the community, strengthening it and making it a better place to live; some have not. Until the late 1970s, change in McDade seemed to run in cycles. Times that were good for the town, during which local residents put considerable energy into improving the quality of life there, repeatedly gave way to times during which no one seemed to care whether the community survived or not. The good times were usually the result of a concerted effort from within; the bad times were often the product of events occurring in the world beyond McDade, over which its citizens had no control. On several occasions, most notably in the early 1950s, the community seemed on the verge of becoming a ghost town, with most of its residents unable, or unwilling, to adapt to changes in the world around them. Each time, however, a small group of citizens—a different group in almost every instance—stepped forward with an idea that rekindled the community's interest in itself and spurred it to a new round of civic improvements. When these efforts had run their course, however, public enthusiasm would wane, and people in McDade would once again lose interest in community affairs. Then the cycle would begin again.

This alternating pattern predominated until the late 1970s, when several attempts at civic improvement, instead of working to unite the community, themselves became the source of spirited disagreement among town residents. These conflicts derived in part from the fact that the motivating energies for these most recent efforts to improve McDade had come from outside the group of people who, since the end of World War II, had perceived themselves as the core of the community. In the first such instance, which occurred in 1978, the impetus came from Elgin; several times since, it has come from newcomers to McDade. These disagreements over civic improvement have also derived from differing ideas about the very nature of the McDade community—how it should function, what in town needs improvement, and what in fact constitutes improvement. Almost every civic effort undertaken in McDade since 1978 has met with resistance and led to considerable dissension within the community. Some people in town see this as the result of conflict between longtime residents of McDade and newcomers to town. Indeed, as each succeeding controversy has fed on the last and provided fuel for the next, the gap between "old-timers" and "new people" has widened and been further emphasized. But the truth is more complicated, as evidenced by several tensions within the community that by the late 1980s had become so virulent as to pit a number of longtime town residents against each other. Admittedly, some of these conflicts were extensions of long-standing rivalries, but others have more recent roots and have quickly become quite bitter. In short, since about 1978, most of McDade's problems have come from within and have had their source in differing views on how, and whether, the community could be a better place to live.

Because of the conflicts they have generated, most recent attempts at community improvement have failed to make McDade a better place to live. Instead, they have diminished the quality of life there and turned McDade into a place where people have little choice between taking sides against their neighbors or dropping out of public life entirely. Indeed, by the end of the 1980s, McDade could no longer be said to have much unanimity of opinion or purpose. It had once been a community in the most literal sense, with most of its residents sharing a "common unity" of collective self-interest; in recent years, however, McDade has evolved into a collection of disparate subcommunities with little more than a telephone exchange and ZIP code in common. This marks the beginning of a new chapter in the town's history, one that hardly bodes well for its future.

How this came about is an interesting story. Beyond being interesting, however, it is also important. In many ways, the changes McDade has undergone in the years since World War II parallel postwar developments in rural America as a whole. As the distance between the nation's backwaters and its urban areas decreased—the result of a dramatic increase in automobile ownership, improved highways, the rapid growth of suburbs, and the ever-expanding influence of the mass media—many earlier distinctions between rural and urban life began to blur. Among them were differences in how country people and city people perceived the proper relationship between the individual and the community he or she lived in. With "city ways" becoming more common in America's small towns, many residents of those communities—natives and newcomers alike—became more concerned with their rights as individuals than their responsibilities to those who lived around them. Many of the towns, as corporate entities at least, suffered as a result.

In McDade, as elsewhere, the community's difficulties took various forms. Some town residents decided that, above all else, they wanted to be left alone. This led to a generalized indifference to the future of the community as a whole. Others, most of them new to the community, tried to re-create McDade according to idealized, stereotypical images of what life in America's small towns "should" be like. Unfortunately, their motivations were often more personal than public-spirited. Since the type of community they sought in McDade rarely corresponded to anyone's actual experience of the town, their efforts often caused resentment, especially among those who were native to McDade and felt they knew how the community had operated in the past and thus had a more realistic idea of how it could, and should, operate in the future. Unfortunately, in defending their town against what they saw as the meddling of outsiders, many of McDade's longtime residents ignored a number of useful suggestions and ended up entrenching themselves against change of any kind, generally preventing the community from keeping up with the times. They, too, were thus guilty of putting their own interests before those of the town. It is a story worth telling, though to give a blow-by-blow account of everything that has happened in McDade since 1945 seems pointless. Instead, this chapter will focus on selected events that took place in McDade between 1945 and 1980, events that have influenced the quality of present-day life in the community.

Postwar Renewal and the Birth of the Watermelon Festival

The fate of the land at Camp Swift and the camp's possible reactivation were not the only matters of concern to people in McDade in the years after World War II. The town had problems uniquely its own to deal with, most of which had little to do with Camp Swift. America's entry into the war had brought most efforts to better life in McDade to a halt, and civic concern had more or less stagnated since. Most of the community's more thoughtful citizens, especially among the generation of young adults starting families in the late 1940s, believed that McDade's future was in jeopardy. They feared that unless the town faced up to its problems and energetically set about finding solutions to them, it would soon cease to exist. Accordingly, a number of McDade's younger adults took it on themselves to assure their children a future in the town.[1]

In some ways, their efforts paralleled those of concerned citizens in McDade at the end of the nineteenth century, when the community was trying to live down its Wild West past. In both instances, an influential group of townspeople—influential by virtue of reputation in the 1800s and by virtue of sheer numbers (and energy) in the post-World War II years—took it upon themselves to redefine McDade and establish its reputation as a solid, middle-class kind of place. At the turn of the century, the problem had been to dilute the town's image and convince the rest of Bastrop County that McDade regretted the excesses of its recent past and now wanted nothing more than to settle into a sleepy, unexciting brand of small-town sober-mindedness. Half a century later, in the wake of World War II, the problem was different. This time around the community wanted to shake itself awake and demonstrate that it was not as sleepy or as backward as it seemed, and that it could live up to the high standards of middle-class life that postwar America was beginning to assume was the nation's birthright. Sensing the dawning of an era of new and expanded possibilities, McDade's most energetic young adults were not about to let their community drowse away the future. Instead, they were going to make every effort to ensure McDade's participation in the exciting times ahead. They were going to do this even if it meant insisting that the town exert itself in ways that, given its recent history of inactivity, might seem out of character.

Thus, at the same time that most of Bastrop County was embroiled in controversy over the future of Camp Swift, people in McDade were quietly organizing to improve their community. Part of this effort involved making McDade more attractive and more visible, at least locally, to residents of surrounding towns. It also involved attracting new residents to the area. With this in mind, Mrs. Edgar Owen (like Sam Billingsley before her, though with considerably less hyperbole) began extolling the McDade area's agricultural potential in her weekly column in the *Elgin Courier*. On several occasions, she praised truck farming as a wholesome, rewarding way of life and a good reason for anyone who was "willing to work" to consider moving to McDade. "On the farm, in the country is a good place to be" she wrote, perhaps hoping to attract new families to the area. In late 1947, after noting that almost nine hundred thousand pounds of peanuts had been shipped from McDade in the past several weeks, she remarked: "No wonder there are so many people trying to buy a home near McDade, it's a good place to live."[2]

Among the town's institutions, the McDade Baptist Church was one of the leading proponents of renewal. In August 1947, the congregation learned that the War Assets Administration had accepted its one thousand dollar bid to purchase one of Camp Swift's now unused chapel buildings. The old sanctuary, which had been McDade's original community hall—the "Union Building" in which the town's first generation of children had attended school and where McDade's law-abiding citizens had gathered in 1883 to discuss their response to the murder of Deputy Sheriff Boaz Heffington—was torn down just a few weeks later. Many people expressed relief that the ramshackle old "eyesore" was gone. The new church building, which weighed one hundred tons and cost McDade's Baptists an additional twenty-five hundred dollars to have moved from Camp Swift, was taken to McDade the following March, with most of the community looking on and cheering. "It was a real project, real big," Wallace Wilson remembers. "They had three great big old trucks grinding and grinding and straining to pull it. It was a tug of war, [the chapel] was so big and so hard to move. Took them all day to get it here. . . . Coming down the Camp Swift road, it looked like the whole country was on the move. It was a sight I'll never forget; [it] made me feel happy for the town." The chapel was set on its foundation at sunset on March 20, and McDade found itself home to a substantial, up-to-date church building that "any town anywhere would be proud of." Eight days later, on Easter Sunday, the first worship service was held in the new sanctuary. Members of all the town's churches attended, as did a number of "special guests" from as far away as Houston. Having accomplished this much, McDade's Baptists voted in June to adopt "a full-time program," and the church began sponsoring separate men's, women's, and youth groups dedicated to providing "Christian service" to McDade. Pastor T. E. Holt also installed a sound system in the new church's high steeple, which he connected to "an automatic record changer" in his office. This enabled him to play "the very best of sacred music" for the community at large anytime he felt the urge to do so. "When atmospherical conditions are favorable," he bragged, "the music can be heard from a mile away."[3]

Most of the community's postwar efforts to improve itself, though, focused on building a new school for its children. McDade had been without a proper school building since early 1941, when the old school, built in 1911, had burned down. The fact that the old building had been inadequately insured, plus the halt the war effort had brought to federal funding for most local projects, meant that the community had been unable to build a new one. In 1942, as a stopgap measure, the district had purchased a large, recently vacated private home, where the town's children attended classes for the remainder of the war years. This building, however, was in poor repair, cold and drafty in the winter, and generally unsuited to providing a "modern classroom environment." Nor did it have an auditorium that could host community-wide events, a fact that annoyed many people in McDade. Several times since the old school had burned, people had been forced to stand outside at public events (held in one of the town's churches or at the house serving as the school); other events had been canceled or not scheduled for "lack of a suitable auditorium." Therefore, one important reason for building a new school in McDade was to provide the community with a public meeting place.[4]

With the eventual construction of a new school as its goal, a revitalized PTA—under new, more youthful leadership—made a major effort in the years after the war to achieve community consensus on the issue and start raising money. The campaign began in earnest at the end of the 1945–46 school year with a PTA-sponsored "Community Rally." Bastrop County superintendent of education Fred Haynie was the featured speaker at this event, and he urged the gathered citizens of

McDade to put their individual differences aside and work cooperatively toward the goal of building a new school for the community's children. He claimed that McDade, by overcoming its "special problems," could serve as "an example" to small towns everywhere of what a group of determined, forward-looking citizens who worked together could accomplish. Several people in town remember his speech as a rousing success; it inspired a new level of public enthusiasm and more widespread participation in community affairs than had existed since well before the war.[5]

A week later, new PTA president Walter Kastner, one of McDade's more successful truck farmers, announced that the organization would soon begin sponsoring a weekly movie series. Weather permitting, the films would be shown every Friday night on an outdoor screen at the school grounds. These shows were well attended from the start and became a warm-weather institution in the community for the next several years, canceled only for rain or on those infrequent occasions when they conflicted with some other event in town. For adults and children alike, the school yard became the place to be on Friday nights during the postwar years in McDade. A number of people recall "everyone in town" attending "the movie shows." Not only did the film series provide the PTA with a constant, if modest, source of funds—all of which, plus whatever moneys could be raised at talent shows, bake sales, and the like, went into a building fund—but it also provided the community with regularly scheduled occasions to meet and socialize.[6]

In the spring of 1947, McDade took further steps toward making its new school a reality. In March, county superintendent Haynie, members of the McDade Independent School District's Board of Trustees, and several residents of the rural Siloah community met "to discuss plans for the good of the McDade School." The topic of their discussions was the possible consolidation of the Siloah and McDade school districts, a move that would provide the newly created district with a larger tax base from which to fund the construction of a new school. Because of their inability to find an "accredited" teacher for their one-room schoolhouse, residents of Siloah had been paying tuition for their children to attend school in McDade since 1942. They hoped that consolidation would enable them to hire a certified elementary teacher to teach their younger children at Siloah, with their older children continuing to attend grades six through eight in McDade but no longer having to pay tuition. (They were overly optimistic in this regard: Siloah never found a satisfactory teacher, and its school never reopened.) The 1947 consolidation proposal, which also included Fair Oaks, a one-room schoolhouse community about three miles west of McDade, went before voters in the three districts in May and passed easily in each. The newly constituted board of trustees immediately announced that building a new school in McDade would be its first priority.[7]

In less than four months, construction was underway. In a public appeal that appeared in the *Elgin Courier* of August 28, PTA president Kastner called upon all residents of McDade to give the project their whole-hearted support. Testifying to his hope that the "all for one, one for all" model of small-town life might still apply to McDade, he urged the town's citizens to work together and give freely of their time and energy. "It's going to take the full cooperation of each man, woman, boy, and girl in the community to put it over," he wrote, "so let's each one of us now pledge ourselves to any service that we are called upon to do, not that we may get pay for it, but let's work and be happy in the thought that we are working for the benefit of the boys and girls, not only for today but long after we are gone." Clearly, Walter Kastner and those he spoke for had no intention of letting McDade die.

They had started building a new school for their children, and they hoped that same school would someday serve their grandchildren.[8]

The new school was completed on schedule, in time for the 1948–49 school year. It was a one-story L-shaped brick building. In addition to its three classrooms—one for grades one and two, one for grades three through five, and one for "the seniors" in grades six through eight—it also housed a small library and an auditorium large enough to host community-wide events. Its "modern physical plant" included "individual toilets, butane gas, and proper lighting and ventilation." The board of trustees adopted the "standardized" state curriculum and hired three teachers, each "accredited [in order] to qualify us for state aid." People in McDade were proud of themselves. Stella Kastner remembers building the new school as "the best thing this town had done in a long time, and we did it all ourselves. We did something good for our youngsters and good for the town."[9]

The new school opened its doors in August 1948. In many ways, though, this was old news by then. Everyone had known since the previous spring that the school would be ready on time, and in the interim many of those who had worked so hard to make it a reality had turned their attention to a second large-scale community project. In March 1948, under the leadership of brothers Walter and Arthur Kastner, these people formed the McDade Rural Neighborhood Progress Association. Over the next several months, this group set about trying to better life in McDade on a number of different fronts. While most of what they accomplished was relatively short term in impact, they did stage the first McDade Watermelon Festival, a community event that has been an annual summertime institution in McDade ever since.[10]

The original reason for organizing the Rural Neighborhood Progress Association was to enter McDade in a contest jointly sponsored by *Farmer-Stockman Magazine* and Texas A&M University's College Extension Service. This contest called for small towns throughout Texas to undertake organized programs of community improvement during the 1948 calendar year and keep detailed records of their progress. At the end of the year, each town was to submit its "Official Record Book" to a panel of judges at Texas A&M. *Farmer-Stockman* would then award several five-hundred-dollar prizes to the communities judged to have made the greatest strides. McDade hoped to win one of the prizes and use the money to purchase playground equipment for the school grounds and books for the school's library.[11]

The first public meeting of the McDade Rural Neighborhood Progress Association was scheduled for May 21, 1948. Walter Kastner exhorted everyone in town to attend. He wanted as many people as possible to be there "to discuss our plans for building a better community in which to live and for our children to grow up in. Remember," he added, "our children are what we make them. Let's do all in our power to make our community a good clean place to grow up in. It will take the combined efforts of each one of us to do it. We can do it, if each one of us will try and brighten up our own little corner." As in the campaign for the new school, Kastner emphasized that cooperation in the present could lead to health and happiness in the future. Only by working together, he believed, could McDade's current generation of parents guarantee their children the kind of wholesome, nurturing hometown environment that would enable them to become adults who would in turn pass an improved community on to their children.[12]

At that first public meeting, Kastner revealed his vision of what he hoped McDade might someday become. He called for a community with "better kept land, more modern homes, more farm machinery, electricity, water piped to convenient places, good farms, better schools, more churches, and better cooperation." Offering McDade as representative of rural America and envisioning the role of rural America as global, even cosmic, he told those in attendance that "the whole world is looking to our land for food, . . . and God is looking to us to do our best in preserving the land. . . . Let's try to be better stewards of the little plot of land we are living on." In short, he was promoting a McDade of the near future that could serve as an example to others—a rural "city on a hill" of sorts. In his mind, the town was fully capable of demonstrating the proper way for small communities to contribute to, and prosper in, the postwar world. He envisioned a McDade that would be clean, orderly, and productive, kept that way by a population of progressive, forward-looking citizens who were well informed and selfless and who would make good decisions, always with the best interests of the community and its future at heart. He must have been persuasive that Friday night; by the following week the official membership of the McDade Rural Neighborhood Progress Association had swelled to thirty-four families. Many others who never officially joined the association also contributed time and energy over the next several months to one or another of its projects.[13]

Throughout the remainder of 1948, the McDade Rural Neighborhood Progress Association initiated more than two dozen community improvement projects. These ranged from "enter[ing] a contestant in the Bathing Beauty Revue at Bastrop" to "a community-wide drive on the eradication of rats, gophers, and crows." They also included sponsorship of a Boy Scout troop; a clean-up drive that "greatly improved the appearance of the community"; vaccination of the town's dogs against rabies; vaccination of the town's children against smallpox and typhus; spraying the business district to exterminate flies, fleas, and roaches; and demonstrations by Extension Service agents of the latest "scientific" techniques for dehorning cattle, conserving soil, and canning or freezing vegetables and meat. The association also organized a "charity drive" for a family whose home had burned down and sponsored an "amateur hour" talent show, at which several candidates for office, including a representative of Lyndon Johnson's campaign for a U.S. Senate seat, paid for the privilege of entertaining the gathered people of McDade.[14]

Almost as an afterthought, the McDade Rural Neighborhood Progress Association's "Official Record Book"—written out longhand in painstakingly neat script by secretary and treasurer Ethel Field—also mentioned the school board's acquisition of a "new" school building for the town's African American children as one of the community's accomplishments. Mrs. Field put it this way: "The colored people were having church services and school in the same building, until the School Board moved an adequate school building in and the colored people bought the old building to be used as a church. So they now have a church and a school building which makes it very nice." She mentioned this a second time as the final item in her concluding summary of the town's 1948 achievements. This latter entry read: "New building moved on colored peoples [sic] school ground. Colored school teacher has degree." There had been "colored school" held at the Weeping Willow Church since at least 1921, when County Superintendent Haynie's "Voucher Book" listed it as one of a number of rural schools under county, as opposed to local, supervision. (This despite the fact that Weeping Willow was barely a mile from uptown McDade.) The "new" school building the McDade school board provided was actually Siloah's abandoned one-room schoolhouse, unused since 1942.

Classes for McDade's black children would continue to be held in this building until the early 1960s, when the McDade School Board voted to close the school, hiring someone to drive the town's remaining black students—fewer than ten, sometimes as few as four or five, present-day old-timers estimate—to and from school in Elgin rather than letting them attend the all-white McDade School. Haynie's "Voucher Book" and Ethel Field's entries in the McDade Rural Neighborhood Progress Association's "Official Record Book" are the only instances of McDade's African American population appearing in the documentary record, an indication of the difficulty of integrating their history with that of the community at large, especially with the older members of that population dead and its younger members dispersed.[15]

Racial attitudes aside, the "Official Record Book" also listed improvements each of the association's thirty-four member families had performed on their homes and land during 1948. Indicating that some measure of postwar prosperity had arrived in McDade, fourteen families mentioned the purchase of at least one electric appliance—most often a refrigerator or "deep freeze"—while thirteen families listed buying a new tractor, truck, or automobile. Typical home improvements included the installation of electricity, the addition of extra rooms, painting, and making or buying new furniture. Five different families listed the purchase of venetian blinds for their windows as one of their accomplishments. Improvements to rural property included cleaning out old stock ponds ("tanks" in local parlance) or digging new ones, erecting new fences, and building new barns, chicken houses, or tool sheds. As well as testifying to a higher standard of living in McDade, many of the improvements helped further Walter Kastner's hope that town residents would "brighten up [their] own little corner" of the community. With the McDade Rural Neighborhood Progress Association advancing the notion that each of the town's families was an integral part of the communal whole, individual home improvements were part of community improvement. The newly modernized homes were surely more pleasant to live in and probably more attractive to look at. Since one of the association's unstated goals was for McDade to regain the respect of people in neighboring communities, the town's physical appearance was no small consideration. The people of McDade had moved a large modern church building to town, were building a new school for their children, and were now energetically trying to make their community a healthier and more attractive place to live. They were proud of what they were doing, and they wanted the rest of Bastrop County to know about it.[16]

To attract visitors to town and send them home impressed with McDade's determination to improve itself was one reason for staging a community festival. Others were to raise money for further community projects and to set aside a day for local residents to celebrate their hometown with friends and neighbors. The McDade Rural Neighborhood Progress Association also, of course, wanted to include sponsorship of a festival in the year-end list of accomplishments it would submit to the contest judges at Texas A&M. Undertaken for all these reasons, McDade's first Watermelon Festival was by far the Rural Neighborhood Progress Association's most significant and lasting achievement. With the exception of 1971, when the community sponsored a centennial celebration instead, McDade has held an annual Watermelon Festival ever since.[17]

The idea for a McDade Watermelon Festival was not entirely new. For years, some people in town had felt that Elgin's reputation as a producer of quality watermelons was based largely on melons grown in and around McDade. Sam Billingsley had complained of this several times during his tenure as McDade's newspaper correspondent two decades earlier; in 1928, for example, he asked, with characteristic overstatement, "Why, in the name of the sun, moon, and stars, is it that every [train] car of melons shipped from McDade passing within a thousand miles of [Elgin], are called Elgin's 'extraordinary, famous melons'?" More than a decade later, in 1940 and 1941, when Elgin sponsored "annual" watermelon festivals of its own, many people in McDade reacted with sarcasm and skepticism, believing that Elgin's Chamber of Commerce had overstepped itself and was claiming too much for the farmers of that community. Probably because of the war and the construction of Camp Swift, Elgin's second watermelon festival was its last. Subsequently, in 1947, after two excellent local melon harvests in a row, McDade correspondent Owen suggested that McDade sponsor a watermelon festival, primarily "to let everyone know that Elgin is not the only place they grow bountiful crops of large melons." The following year, the McDade Rural Neighborhood Progress Association incorporated her suggestion into its community improvement program and staged the first McDade Watermelon Festival.[18]

Compared to subsequent Watermelon Festivals, the first was a very small affair. Held on a Thursday afternoon and evening, it consisted of little more than a brief parade, picnicking and socializing on the grounds of the house that had served as the town's school in recent years, and the coronation of teenage and "tiny tot" Watermelon queens. The festivities got underway at four o'clock with the parade, which included twenty-one floats, Elgin's gaudily uniformed American Legion Band (an "oompah band," according to Adeline Eschberger), and McDade's children marching with their pets. Most of the floats were tractor-drawn farm wagons decorated with colored tissue paper, and all except the queens' float "depicted various rural activities and watermelon farming." Most were from McDade, with a few from Elgin. After the parade, there was a baseball game, in which the McDade team shut out a team from Paige. The focus of activity then shifted to the school grounds, where the community's teenagers operated game booths and the town's ladies served hot dogs, sandwiches, ice cream, soft drinks, and as much free ice-cold watermelon as anyone could eat. The festival ended with a dose of pomp and circumstance, as Teenage queen Hilda Kastner (the present-day Hilda Neidig, who works as the relief route driver at the McDade Post Office) and Tiny Tot queen Margie Lewis (the present-day Margie Schindler, who teaches at Elgin High School and still lives near McDade) were crowned. Numerous costumed courtiers—most of the rest of the town's children— took part in the proceedings, as did a "duke" and "duchess" representing the Bastrop Chamber of Commerce, a gesture much appreciated by people in McDade. Despite some tears from a few of the younger children, the elaborate coronation ceremony went well. The *Elgin Courier* reported that "everyone was beautifully dressed in their various costumes . . . and performed their parts in a very dignified manner."[19]

Everyone who was present that day has a favorite memory of McDade's first Watermelon Festival. Emma Wuensche tells of her husband diapering their sons' pet roosters so they could carry them in the parade without getting their clothes soiled. Freda Wilson, whose two-year-old daughter, Deborah, was to be a "seed girl" in the coronation ceremony, remembers using pipe cleaners to curl Deborah's "very fine hair" and then having "a terrible job" getting them out. She barely got the tearful Deborah to the coronation on time. Dan Wolf, a teenager at the time, still laughs when he recalls the bingo stand he had built from lettuce crates collapsing on his cousin Ernestine Wolf (now Ernestine Schulz) and several other 4-H Club girls who were running the game just as someone shouted "Bingo!" Dan's sister Adeline Eschberger remembers being embarrassed that their father rode in the parade in an old buggy drawn by the two mules he still plowed his fields with. She also remembers her younger sister Katie, who had moved away from McDade but returned for the festival, exclaiming over and over again as the parade passed that it seemed like a dream that something so exciting could be happening in McDade. It was a day Katie was unlikely to forget: later that day she met her future husband, Jim Mogonye, who had marched in the parade as a tuba player in Elgin's American Legion "oompah band."[20]

By all accounts, McDade's first Watermelon Festival was a great success. The *Elgin Courier* reported that "a grand crowd of more than a thousand persons" attended. The McDade Rural Neighborhood Progress Association's "Official Record Book" characterized the festival as "a real old-time gathering," which had drawn "old friends and old-time citizens . . . from miles away to eat melons and spend a while back home." The result, the association claimed, was the "largest crowd ever assembled in McDade." The festival was also more of a financial success than anyone had expected, with "free-will offerings," food sales, and game booth proceeds combining for a net profit of almost six hundred dollars. This was more than the Rural Neighborhood Progress Association had hoped to win as prize money and more than enough to purchase playground equipment for the new school, the organization's stated goal in entering the *Farmer-Stockman* contest. Association chairman Kastner credited all of McDade's "fine homefolk and neighbors" for the festival's success and emphasized that it was the result of "combined cooperation and hard work." He also announced that McDade would put on "an even bigger and better" festival in 1949.[21]

The panel of judges at Texas A&M awarded McDade an "honorable mention" in *Farmer-Stockman's* Rural Neighborhood Progress Contest. People in town were pleased to be recognized, and no one seemed to mind that the citation carried no cash prize. After all, the Watermelon Festival had brought in more than enough money to realize the McDade Rural Neighborhood Progress Association's original goals. In addition, most people in McDade seemed to feel that the community had received considerably more than five hundred dollars benefit from participating in the contest. As the association's "Official Record Book" succinctly stated it, "We have a better community for having entered the Rural Progress Contest." McDade had made itself a cleaner and, presumably, healthier place to live; it had improved its image; and it had generated a new, higher level of community self-confidence. People in McDade would have liked to win a cash prize as well, of course, but by the end of 1948 that had become a secondary concern. As Walter Kastner put it a couple of months after the Watermelon Festival, "We are in this contest to win money, but even if we do not win anything, we will still be winners." He was right; McDade had a lot more than a citation for honorable mention to show for its participation in the contest.[22]

With no more contests to enter, the McDade Rural Neighborhood Progress Association ceased to exist at the end of 1948. Unfortunately, many of the community improvement programs it had spawned came to a halt as well, and the town undertook few new ones in their place. The Watermelon Festival, however, continued. Just as Walter Kastner had promised, McDade put on a "bigger and better" festival in 1949. The festival has continued to grow ever since, although whether it has gotten better over the years is a matter of some current debate. In fact, by the mid-1980s there were conflicting opinions in town regarding what kinds of activities the festival should include, what its goals should be, and who should run it. Nevertheless, the Watermelon Festival has continued to be an annual presence in the lives of McDade citizens for more than forty years now. It is unquestionably the only civic activity that involves a majority of town residents on any kind of regular basis. A legacy of the postwar spirit of activism and renewal, the Watermelon Festival still plays a central role in the life of the community.

The Watermelon Festival has come to mean many things to McDade over the years. Practically speaking, it raises modest amounts of money each year for the school and other community organizations. It also provides town residents an opportunity to get together each spring to plan July's upcoming festival and work cooperatively over the next several months to bring it about. No other activity in McDade involves so much of the community on so large a scale. In addition, the Watermelon Festival gives the many people who have left McDade over the years a reason to return for a day or two each year to renew old acquaintances and relive old times. The festival is within the rural tradition of "homecoming." These functions are among the Watermelon Festival's more concrete contributions to the life of the community.

Less tangible, but no less significant, are some of the more symbolic roles the festival has played through the years. The Watermelon Festival has always, for example, functioned as a looking glass of sorts. Year after year, it has reflected McDade's fluctuating moods and fortunes and has revealed the latest shifts in the town's ever-changing image of itself. It has also at times seemed a lightning rod, attracting sparks from frictions in town. Problems internal to McDade, as well as difficulties the town has had adjusting to changes in the world around it, have both found expression in the Watermelon Festival over the years. Bad feeling among residents of McDade has often boiled over at festival time, usually over the selection of the queens or, more recently, in response to perceived attempts to change the way things have "always" been done in the festival. Rarely, however, do the root causes of such problems have anything to do with the festival. At other times, more happily, the Watermelon Festival has seemed a magnet, drawing people together from along McDade's entire social spectrum. People who would otherwise rarely have reason to encounter each other—people with school-age children and those whose children are grown and gone, people who are new to McDade and those whose families have been in town "forever," Baptists who would never dream of taking a drink and people who would rather drink beer on Sunday morning than go to church—all work closely together every year to put on another Watermelon Festival. In recent years, the festival has grown large enough to accommodate the few people in town who are sworn enemies. A person who helps organize the Friday night dance, for example, need never have contact with someone working on the Saturday night coronation ceremony, yet both are contributing to the festival.

Throughout its history, the Watermelon Festival has also functioned as a cumulative, ever-expanding cache of shared memories that help define the community and bind it together. This may well have become the festival's most important function, and it seems to grow in importance with each passing year. Many of those who run the festival today were not yet born in 1948. Others have childhood memories of that year's first festival, while a few who today still contribute time and energy were among those who got the original festival off the ground. This age disparity hardly seems to matter. Anyone who has stood onstage as part of the Watermelon queens' coronation ceremony —as nearly everyone who has been a child in McDade since 1948 has, in one role or another— shares that experience with much of the rest of the community. This includes their contemporaries, people of their parents' age, and, in some instances, members of their grandparents' generation. The same, of course, is true regarding other aspects of the festival. Such memories are the common property of anyone who has lived in McDade since 1948, and virtually no one else shares them. They add up to a local mythology of sorts, a shared community tradition that may well be present-day McDade's most defining characteristic. Few places in contemporary America are still small and intimate enough to provide such easy familiarity with the past, even if that past reaches back only forty-some years. In short, because of the common memories it has generated, McDade's Watermelon Festival may be the strongest tie binding the community together.

All in all, then, 1948 was a good year for McDade, a year during which the town's young adults created a future for the community out of little more than what they believed possible. It was during 1948 that the town replaced a ramshackle old church building with a substantial modern one, built a new school for its children, and staged McDade's first Watermelon Festival. All are institutions that continue to shape community life—the church for those of McDade's residents who are Baptists, the school for anyone who has been a child or parent there in the years since World War II, and the Watermelon Festival for nearly everyone. It is also worth noting that 1948 was the year the descendants of the old German farm families at Siloah entered McDade's mainstream in force. It was consolidation with Siloah that enabled McDade to build its new school and the participation of many from Siloah—eighteen of the McDade Rural Neighborhood Progress Association's thirty-four-member families had German surnames—that made the Watermelon Festival possible. Without their leadership and hard work, McDade's postwar accomplishments would have been considerably more modest. Siloah's German farmers and their descendants remain at the heart of the town's social structure today, even though they are now an aging population and have recently been split by internal conflict. The achievements of 1948 have never been equaled in McDade, and one is tempted to say that progress there has been stalled ever since. There is no doubt that present-day McDade could use another such infusion of its citizens' time, talent, and energy.

The 1950s: Apathy, Running Water, and Decline

During the decade or so that followed the immediate postwar years, few in McDade seemed concerned with town improvements. Other than the Watermelon Festival, little in the way of organized civic activity took place in McDade throughout most of the 1950s and early 1960s. It was almost as though the accomplishments of 1947 and 1948 had exhausted the town's energies: few of its residents seemed interested in attempting anything more in the public sphere. Most seemed satisfied with McDade as it was, apparently willing to believe that the achievements of the late 1940s were sufficient and McDade was no longer in need of improvement. Those compelled to contribute to community projects had the Watermelon Festival. The lone exception to the town's seeming apathy was a successful mid-decade campaign to build a community water system. Once this was accomplished in the spring of 1956, however, McDade seemed ready to resume its nap, despite the efforts of a few in the community to keep the town awake.

The reasons for this sudden decline in public-spiritedness are unclear. Unfortunately, the entire *Elgin Courier* archive for 1949 is missing, thus leaving no documentary record of any difficulties McDade may have experienced immediately after 1948, which had probably been the best single year in the town's existence, at least since its early days as a railhead. Nor does anyone today recall specific events that might have led to such a community-wide decline in civic-mindedness. In the absence of evidence to the contrary, one can only say that the urge to organize and improve McDade seems to have evaporated, or at least confined itself to the Watermelon Festival. In any event, as early as the middle of 1950, the community seems to have lost most of the civic momentum the town's Baptists, the PTA, and the McDade Rural Neighborhood Progress Association had generated just two years earlier.

The first half of the 1950s was not a good time for the town's citizens to be disorganized, apathetic, and generally unprepared to deal with newly emerging threats to the community's well-being. Several such challenges arose between 1950 and 1954, the most serious being the completion of U.S. 290, which bypassed uptown McDade, and the discontinuance of rail service to the community. McDade did little to face up to these and other difficulties brought on by changing circumstances in the rapidly modernizing world around it. None of these challenges was aimed specifically at McDade, of course; communities throughout rural Texas, indeed throughout all of rural America, were experiencing similar problems. Nonetheless, they constituted serious threats to the town and caused genuine hardship for many of its residents. Most of these difficulties were the result of events that occurred outside of McDade and were beyond its citizens' control. Still, one cannot help but wonder if a better organized community might not have responded more effectively. As it was, the response of many in McDade to much of the bad news the town received in the early 1950s was to hide behind the habits and traditions of the past, complain about changes in the world around it, and generally feel victimized by modern times. In the process, the town seemed once again to lose the esteem of its neighbors. McDade's postwar leadership had worked long and hard to revive respect for their town within Bastrop County, and during the late 1940s they had met with some success. The town's new respectability was short lived, however. By 1954, no one in McDade could pretend any longer that their hometown was anything but a third-rate little place that was slowly dying, a view no doubt shared by most of the county. Nor did anyone seem to think the decline in McDade's fortunes could be stopped, let alone reversed. Worst of all, no one seemed to care.

Business conditions had been deteriorating in McDade ever since the initial construction boom at Camp Swift ended in 1942. Some of the town's businesses had closed during the war. Others followed suit in the late 1940s, even as McDade's wave of postwar activism was cresting. In addition, several of the town's long-established retail businesses changed hands during this time, the result of their aging owners being unable or unwilling to keep up with changing tastes and modern business methods. By the end of 1950, McDade had only eight businesses in operation—the McDade Mercantile, a pair of small grocery stores, Bud DeGlandon's barber shop, the drugstore, the confectionery, and two gas stations. All had been in business for quite some time, though at least four of them (possibly five) had been operated by their current owners for three years or less. Only four of these eight remaining businesses would stay open through the 1950s, and one of them—the McDade Mercantile, which had been the community's largest retail establishment for many years—closed its doors in 1961. The most central of these businesses to McDade's continued survival was undoubtedly Sam Hillman's old confectionery, which Sam and Emma Dungan purchased in 1952. Though it was not a pharmacy, the business soon became known as "the Dungan Drugstore" or "Dungan Drugs." At about the same time that the Dungans bought the old confectionery, Emma Dungan took over as McDade's correspondent to the *Elgin Courier*, a job she performed until her death in 1969. Throughout that time, the "drugstore" was one of McDade's main meeting spots, a place where people could exchange news. Much of what was said there found its way into Emma Dungan's weekly columns. In its function as community bulletin board, Dungan Drugs helped hold the town together during the lean 1950s. There was little anyone could do, however, about McDade's declining business fortunes.[23]

By 1950, just two years after McDade had built a new school for its children and had staged its first Watermelon Festival, the community seemed badly down on its luck and in need of help. In her *Elgin Courier* column of June 6, 1950, Mrs. Owen mentioned that several of the town's businesses had recently been burglarized, losing varying amounts of cash and merchandise. "The burglar did not seem to feel sorry for McDade," she wrote, as though the town were in such obvious need of sympathy that only the most hardhearted of criminals could ignore its plight. Whether residents of other communities in Bastrop County felt sorry for McDade is unknown, but the town clearly seems to have lost some measure of local respect. In an article praising nearby rural communities for their contributions toward a new fire truck for the Elgin Volunteer Fire Department, the *Elgin Courier* listed McDade's contribution as "none." Even such tiny crossroads communities as Manda, Carlson, and New Sweden had managed to come up with at least one hundred dollars, and Manor, about as far west of Elgin as McDade was east, contributed more than five hundred dollars. The town was further embarrassed in 1952, when someone claiming to represent the McDade School Board began knocking on doors in Elgin soliciting donations for the community's school. No one in McDade knew anything about this person, but the board delegated Adeline Eschberger to go to the *Courier* office and deliver an apology anyway. "It was very embarrassing," she recalls. "We didn't send anybody to Elgin looking for money. We wouldn't do that. But they thought we did."[24]

The stretch of U.S. 290 between Paige and Elgin, with McDade at its midpoint, was finally completed in the summer of 1952. More than ten years had passed since McDade correspondent Hackworth, a month before the bombing of Pearl Harbor, had first mentioned hearing the roar of earth-moving equipment as construction work on the new highway approached McDade from the west. In order to accommodate traffic to and from Camp Swift, the new road running east out of Austin had been rushed to completion as far as Elgin quite early in the war. This was also true of State Highway 95 between Elgin and Bastrop. To the east of Elgin, however, work on the projected Austin-to-Houston highway had been suspended till after the war. When construction resumed in the late 1940s, it proceeded in piecemeal fashion, with road crews working on various stretches of the highway at different times rather than working progressively from one end to the other. Until 1953, when the new road was finally finished, this made for a route that alternated between a broad, modern highway that ran through open countryside and a series of narrow, poorly paved country lanes that took motorists through the business districts of the old railroad towns along the way.[25]

The seventeen miles of highway between Paige and Elgin was one of the last stretches of U.S. 290 to be finished. Generally speaking, this had worked to McDade's advantage, at least until construction was complete and the new road opened to traffic. Motorists stopping for gas, cigarettes, or a cold drink had long been a steady, if modest, source of income for the community. The regular flow of traffic through town had also brought local residents regular contact with people from other places. As long as the main route between Houston and Austin ran through the town's business district, local merchants could count on a certain amount of trade from travelers passing through. The new highway, however, bypassed the community's business district by about a mile, enough to make most motorists ignore it and keep on driving. (Ironically, the only indications on the highway that there was a town nearby were the all-black Weeping Willow Baptist Church and, next door to the church, McDade's small "colored school." Before the completion of U.S. 290, these had been at the end of a crooked unpaved street on the southern edge of town, well off the route motorists would travel through McDade.) The town's merchants felt the impact immediately. The sudden absence of passing travelers also deprived McDade of contact with outsiders, at least on any regular basis, and this led to a dawning realization in the community that not only the highway, but the rest of the modern world too, might well be in the process of passing the town by. Thus, paradoxically, the completion of U.S. 290 served in some ways to isolate McDade more than it did to link the community to the rest of central Texas. The new highway did make it a little easier for people to get out of town, cutting the driving time from McDade to other places, but its greater impact was to prevent casual traffic from passing through the community. People no longer came to McDade unless they had a specific reason to, which meant that a new face in town, once a common sight, became a rarity. When U.S. 290 bypassed McDade, the town immediately became poorer, more isolated, and more insular. This was a trend that would not soon be reversed.[26]

The biggest blow to the community in the early 1950s, however, was the Southern Pacific's discontinuance of rail service to McDade. The train had been the town's lifeblood since its founding; indeed it had been the sole reason for its founding. For decades, four passenger trains daily (two in each direction) had permitted easy travel to and from McDade, and frequent freights had provided a convenient, reliable, and economically efficient way for local farmers and ranchers to get their produce and livestock to market. The first bad news on this front came in 1950, when the Southern Pacific announced that it was eliminating its two daytime passenger trains between Austin and Houston. This left only one evening train in each direction: a westbound train that departed McDade for Austin at about eight o'clock and an eastbound train that left for Houston at about six. This meant that people who lived in McDade could no longer take the morning train to Elgin or Austin (or eastbound to Paige or Giddings) for a day of shopping or "visiting" and still return home the same evening. Many town residents, especially its older people, did not own cars; for them, the cancellation of the daytime trains in and out of McDade was truly a hardship. It not only cut them off from the rest of the world and imposed new restrictions on their lives, but it also emphasized their vulnerability in the face of changing circumstances that were beyond their control. This sense of vulnerability, even helplessness, soon expanded to include most of the McDade community. In July 1951, when the Southern Pacific petitioned the Texas Railroad Commission to allow discontinuance of all passenger service between Houston and Austin, people in McDade could do little more than wax nostalgic. After the last passenger train stopped at McDade on December 8, 1951, the *Elgin Courier* printed a short interview with "Old Man" (Dave) Sherman, who had lived in McDade since the town's founding. Born in 1862, Sherman claimed to have witnessed both the first and last passenger trains to stop at McDade. "It made me sad to watch the old train for the last time," he said. "It's like giving up an old friend. The freights still run but somehow I'm not sentimental about them."[27]

In late 1954 Southern Pacific freight trains stopped serving McDade as well. This was a significant blow to local farmers and ranchers, who had always sent the bulk of their crops and livestock to market by rail. Indeed, for anyone in the McDade area who made their living from agriculture, the easy availability of rail transport and the seasonal presence of buyers at the depot had always been crucial components in the financial equation that allowed them to profit from what they raised. Several times in the years after the freights stopped serving McDade, local growers attempted to form trucking cooperatives to get their crops to market. These efforts rarely proved successful, however, usually because of the farmers' inability to provide large enough loads or difficulties with locating suitable buyers. As a result, many of McDade's farmers were reduced to peddling their produce, in relatively small lots, to area grocery stores or, even worse, along the side of the road from the back of their pickup trucks. The time they now spent trying to sell their crops was time they had previously devoted to their farms, homes, and families. Much of their produce went unsold. Marshall Wolf, a child at the time, remembers his father donating truckloads of cantaloupes and watermelons to orphanages, reform schools, and other public institutions. Some growers fed their excess melons, worth good money until the halt in freight service, to their hogs. ("They made the meat taste sweet, unless you smoked it," Tom Dungan remembers.) Others left their melons in the fields to rot. The stoppage of freight service to McDade in the mid-1950s created considerable hardship for many rural families in the area and eventually forced some of them to quit farming altogether. A number of men and women in and around McDade who had never dreamed they would someday work for an hourly wage had to scramble for whatever jobs they could find, most of them low paying. The Southern Pacific's 1954 discontinuance of freight service to McDade was a major factor in the eventual impoverishment of many among the area's rural population, increasing their dependence on a wage-oriented economy that was beyond their control and which they knew little about.[28]

The elimination of freight service also affected business activity in town, though somewhat less drastically, given the already-reduced circumstances of most of McDade's storekeepers. Even during the doldrums of the early 1950s, the business end of local agriculture, as conducted in and around McDade's freight depot, had generated a certain amount of economic activity in town, though at a level much diminished from its pre–World War II peak. Visiting buyers, farmers with fresh cash in their pockets, and seasonal work at the packing shed had all helped sustain McDade's remaining businesses, if only modestly. After 1954, however, all of that was gone; the freights still rumbled through town several times weekly but they no longer stopped. McDade found itself even further isolated from the rest of the world. With the discontinuance of freight service, the town's strongest economic link to the rest of central Texas had been severed. From 1955 on, McDade's merchants would have to survive almost entirely on whatever business the community could generate on its own.

Despite the town's bleak prospects, several local residents decided during the mid-1950s that McDade could wait no longer for running water. The half dozen or so people most centrally involved with getting a community water system financed and built have now either died, left McDade, or do not remember the details of their effort. Nor do most others who lived in McDade at the time recall the initiative very clearly. This is probably because virtually everyone in town wanted running water, rendering the process of getting it uncontroversial and thus easy to forget. The campaign began in the summer of 1954, when a small group of citizens met to discuss the possible formation of a McDade Water District, which could then issue bonds to cover the project's cost. Soon afterward, no doubt as a result of this meeting, the Bastrop County Commissioners Court declared the creation of such a district, subject to the approval of local voters. McDade held an election in December, in which the town approved the water district by a margin of eighty-nine to five. Three months later, the newly formed district voted eighty-eight to one to issue $115,000 in bonds to finance the project. By the following September, workers had drilled a well and built a pumping station. Crews were soon digging ditches and laying pipe all over town, a process that caused chaos in the community for several months, making nearly all of its roads impassable at one time or another. Construction of a water storage tower began in late January. On April 5, 1956, the system was "turned on," providing water to anyone in town who had "hooked up," which was nearly everyone. Despite the town's other problems, McDade could once again be proud of itself. Emma Dungan was delighted: "We finally have the greatest necessity McDade has ever had," she wrote, "and that's 'city water.' . . . Those who did all of this should really feel as if they accomplished the best thing we have ever done."[29]

Although supplying people's homes with running water undoubtedly improved the quality of life in McDade, the organizational effort required to get a water system built did not, unfortunately, mark a turning point in the town's civic fortunes. For the rest of the 1950s and on into the 1960s, McDade remained remarkably inactive in the public sphere. In 1958, in a classic case of locking the barn door long after the horses had made their getaway, several local businessmen and farmers formed a McDade Chamber of Commerce. In an attempt to attract new people to the community, one of the group's first actions was to offer a free town lot to anyone willing to move to McDade and build a new house. Over the next several years the Chamber of Commerce sponsored fish fries, chili suppers, and the like, as well as annual McDade Fall Musical Festivals in 1959 and 1960. No record exists of anyone ever taking the organization up on its offer of free town real estate, and no third annual music festival took place. In fact, after January 1961, the *Elgin Courier* never again mentioned the McDade Chamber of Commerce. Obviously, the group's efforts to revive McDade were unsuccessful.[30]

Most of the energy that residents of McDade devoted to community affairs during the 1950s went into the Watermelon Festival. In keeping with the goals of the first festival, people in town generally regarded it as a showcase for the community, a yearly opportunity for McDade to put its best foot forward for others in central Texas to notice and appreciate. Consequently, and apparently in reaction to the town's declining fortunes during the 1950s, the Watermelon Festival soon developed into a mechanism for countering the community's diminished status. In one way or another, then, most of the Watermelon Festivals of the 1950s emphasized current trends, advancing the notion that McDade had not lost touch with the world around it and that the town was as able as any other small community to keep up. Thus, even as the cultural gap was widening between places like McDade and the nation's increasingly urban and suburban mainstream, the Watermelon Festival promoted McDade as a place that was both aware of contemporary developments and eager to incorporate them into the lives of its citizens.

Several new trends within the Watermelon Festivals of the 1950s demonstrate the community's desire to appear energetic, confident, and up-to-date. In 1951, the festival boasted its first guest celebrity, Texas secretary of state Joe Ben Sheppard, who presided over the coronation of the new Watermelon queens. Several times over the next decade or so, locally famous personalities, usually politicians or entertainers, attended McDade's Watermelon Festival in one or another official capacity. In 1953, in an attempt to drum up more visitors to the festival, the Watermelon Festival Committee sponsored its first "booster tour," in which a group of McDade's more gregarious male citizens traveled to other towns in the area during the weeks before the festival to perform humorous musical skits in those communities' downtown business districts. This, too, became a tradition of sorts; the sillier the boosters' performance, the more fun they seemed to promise at the festival itself. Not to be left behind by one of the era's most far-reaching innovations, the 1954 Watermelon Festival offered a "21-inch Philco television set" as a raffle prize, despite the fact that Austin's lone television station was not yet broadcasting a signal strong enough to be received in McDade. Nor did festival planners ignore the power of the new medium to reach potential visitors. A few days before the 1954 Watermelon Festival, McDade's newly elected Watermelon queens appeared on Austin's noontime *Town & Country* television show, cutting melons on the air and inviting viewers to "come out and have some fun" that weekend in McDade. Several representatives of the Watermelon Festival—royalty and otherwise—appeared on local radio and television over the next few years touting the festival. In 1955, McDade's reputation traveled even farther afield, when Tenth District congressman Homer Thornberry purchased the festival's first-prize watermelon for a hundred dollars and announced his intention to take it to Washington and present it to President Eisenhower. Several weeks later, Watermelon Festival Chairman Otto Moore received a thank-you note from the president, who claimed that he had never eaten a better watermelon. The following year, apparently having developed a taste for national exposure, the Watermelon Festival shipped its prize-winning melon to the popular *Gary Moore Show* in New York, where Moore served it to his on-air guests, making McDade resident Stella Kastner, who had grown the melon, "mighty proud." Obviously, McDade was no shrinking violet when it came to publicizing the Watermelon Festival.[31]

Given the town's limitations—its economic difficulties, the makeup of its population, and its inherent conservatism and defensiveness—this may, in retrospect, seem to have been an absurd undertaking. In fairness, though, we must remember that the Watermelon Festival's various attempts to make McDade seem up-to-date were probably less the product of conscious design than the result of festival planners following the path of least resistance and going along with the general tenor of the times. To appear too old-fashioned in the mid-1950s was unfashionable. American society was rapidly modernizing—for the better, most people seemed to think—and any community that allowed itself to appear too out of step with contemporary trends was in danger of seeming hopelessly mired in the past and irredeemably old fashioned. Even tradition-bound McDade did not want to seem that far out of touch with modern times. Thus, even though events occurring outside of McDade during the 1950s frequently led to hardship in the community, the Watermelon Festival tried to maintain McDade as a functioning part of the contemporary world. These attempts continued, perhaps as a form of denial, long after the increased isolation brought on by the completion of U.S. 290 and the Southern Pacific's discontinuance of local train service had emerged as a serious threat to the town's future existence. As the organization in charge of the only civic enterprise in the community, the Watermelon Festival Association was determined to pretend that McDade was surviving, and that the rest of the world might well have a hard time getting along without it. The stubborn refusal of Watermelon Festival planners to be anything but blindly optimistic may well have been the strongest glue binding the community together during the 1950s, and the festival may have been the only thing that kept McDade functioning at all.

Without question, the 1950s were a low point in McDade's history, possibly the lowest ever. Despite the newly gained luxury of running water and the Watermelon Festival's efforts to promote an image of McDade as energetic and up-to-date, the community could not keep up with the rapidly changing modern world. Too inconsequential to protect itself from the impact of contemporary events, McDade found itself again in decline, unnoticed from a highway that bypassed its business district and freight trains that roared through town without stopping. With the community's economic base depleted, most of its businesses closed. Those that remained open struggled to survive as the town's population dwindled and local incomes diminished. Fifteen years after the end of World War II, and only twelve years after its own remarkable burst of postwar energy, McDade found itself poorer than it had been since the Depression and more isolated than ever. As a result, the community became more insular, more distrustful of strangers, and more suspicious of new ideas. With the 1960s about to begin, McDade would soon have change thrust upon it, primarily by the arrival of new people in town. How the community would react would help determine whether or not it would have a future.

The 1960s: Newcomers, the Discovery of the Past, and Progressive Ranching

Public involvement in community affairs increased somewhat in McDade during the 1960s, especially around the middle of the decade. In large part, this was the result of new people moving into the area, many of them from places less removed from the social mainstream than McDade and some of them actively seeking a community whose public life they could take part in. Led by one family in particular, several of the newcomers became involved in the town's social life, creating new opportunities for a brand of genteel public socializing that had never before existed in McDade. Wealthy and sophisticated by local standards, the leading newcomers succeeded in rekindling, if only briefly, a renewed sense of civic concern among a number of previously disinterested town residents. Though McDade's old-timers did not particularly welcome these new people, neither did they resent them. Fewer than ten families arrived over a period of several years, and even though some of the town's longtime residents might have thought them a bit silly at times, the newcomers did not seem to pose much of a threat to local customs or beliefs. Eventually, however, the newcomers' influence on McDade would prove to be much greater than their small numbers had originally suggested. Beginning in about 1962, they sparked the community's first fledgling interest in its past, helped start several new social organizations in town, and, most significantly, changed the face of local agriculture. In the longer run, they also paved the way for the much larger influx of newcomers who came to the area in the 1970s and 1980s. This latter group would eventually effect even greater changes in town.

The 1960s began in McDade much as the 1950s had ended—with the town continuing its downhill slide. A major blow to community self-esteem came in early 1961, when the McDade Mercantile, long the town's largest retail business, closed because of owner L. A. Kunkel's advancing age and declining health. Unable to find anyone willing to purchase the business in its entirety, Kunkel was forced to sell out piecemeal at public auction, "regardless of price." The sale included the remaining stock on the shelves, the store's fixtures, the buildings that housed Kunkel's store and warehouse, and the lots they sat on. People in McDade were saddened to see this longtime local institution close, especially in such an undignified manner. Emma Dungan understated public sentiment when she wrote in her *Elgin Courier* column that the Mercantile "ha[d] been a popular trading place for almost half a century as well as a meeting place for friends and neighbors to pass the time of day. It will be missed from McDade's Main Street, as will the gentle octogenarian proprietor and his friendly wife."[32]

Nor were McDade's farmers faring well in the early 1960s. Drought years in 1960 and 1962 resulted in poor harvests, and the lack of wholesalers and truckers coming to town to purchase and haul local produce made it difficult for area growers to make much of a profit from whatever crops they were able to harvest. "It was tough times," Dan Wolf recalls. "If you couldn't fill an eighteen-wheeler, you had to haul and peddle [your crop] yourself, and there weren't many good places to do that. You spent more time driving than working on the farm." Basically, local truck farmers still had not recovered from the Southern Pacific's elimination of freight service in 1954. Most of them would not until the introduction of small-scale cattle ranching to the area in the mid-1960s.[33]

McDade's school, which had remained relatively trouble free throughout the 1950s, also became a worrisome source of uncertainty in the early 1960s. Fred Britt, the popular principal at the school since 1954, resigned at the end of the 1960–61 school year, and McDade's Board of Trustees had difficulty finding a replacement. Just in time for the opening of school the following September, the board hired Mrs. Mac Bane, wife of McDade's Baptist preacher at the time, to drive the school bus and act as principal. She stayed only a year, however, leaving town when her husband was reassigned in the spring of 1962. This was the start of a disturbing pattern: over the next nine years, McDade's school would have seven more principals, two of whom would be the wives of clergymen assigned to congregations in town on a temporary basis. The reasons for this high turnover rate are unclear, but McDade's inability to attract and keep a qualified principal indicates that the job must have been a thankless one, probably accorded little respect and no doubt poorly paid. It also suggests that a quality, up-to-date education for its children was not one of the community's higher priorities.[34]

On a more positive note, the early 1960s witnessed the establishment of Faith Lutheran Church in McDade. The new church was a direct descendant of the old Siloah Evangelical Lutheran Church, which had relocated to McDade from the rural Siloah community in 1917. Despite having disbanded in 1943 because of personal conflicts within the congregation, the old church had retained ownership of its small sanctuary and the town lot it stood on. Given an opportunity to sell this property in 1960, a majority of the congregation members who had once worshipped there met officially for the first time since 1943 and voted to keep the land and building. This meeting and the decision not to sell seem to have sparked interest in reestablishing a Lutheran church in McDade. According to Erhard Goerlitz, a central figure in the founding of Faith Lutheran, most of the community's old German families "wanted to have church at home" again after almost twenty years of spending their Sunday mornings at Lutheran churches in Elgin, Paige, or Paint Creek. In the belief that "If we're gonna live in McDade, keep our town going, we're gonna have to start going to church in this town," most of the old Siloah church's former members voted in early 1962 to organize a new congregation. Despite being refused help from the district office of the American Lutheran Church—probably because of their contentious history—they forged ahead, refurbishing and adding to their old sanctuary and securing a part-time preaching commitment from the pastor of the Lutheran church in Paige. The new congregation's first worship service was held in March. A month later, they officially reorganized themselves as Faith Lutheran Church, their choice of name reflecting their pride in having founded the new church "on faith alone," that is, without the help of outsiders. Within two years, Faith Lutheran had a full-time resident pastor, and by 1968 the church could boast a membership of more than one hundred (including a number of people from among McDade's non-German population) and a handsome new sanctuary, paid for and built by the church membership.[35]

By late 1962, there were other signs as well that McDade was emerging from its lethargy. In September, Emma Dungan reported in her *Elgin Courier* column that three new homes were currently under construction in McDade. All were being built by longtime rural residents of the area who were moving into town, two of them after selling their land to people from other parts of Texas who planned to move in and try their hand at ranching. A year later, two more new houses were underway, probably for similar reasons. In a separate 1963 development, one that hints at increasing respect for the community among its neighbors, McDade's Freda Wilson, whose daughter, Deborah, attended Elgin High School, was elected president of the Elgin PTA. After more than a decade of backsliding, McDade was becoming respectable again.[36]

In the autumn of 1962, the discovery of a prehistoric Native American burial site in the area briefly attracted the attention of the outside world to McDade. For several weeks in November, the town was host to numerous amateur relic seekers, as well as, belatedly, a team of anthropologists from the University of Texas. Probably hoping to sell a few extra "soda waters," Emma Dungan advertised in her *Elgin Courier* column that anyone needing directions to the site could stop by the "drugstore" in uptown McDade and get them from her. The site was located about three miles east of town, on property recently purchased by Mr. and Mrs. C. J. McCormick, people of means from Houston who planned to raise cattle there. The McCormicks were building "a modern hilltop mansion" on their land. In fact, it was during the construction of the McCormicks' new home—the likes of which the McDade area had never seen—that a bulldozer operator had uncovered skeletal human remains and artifacts indicating that sometime within the past thousand years or so a band of Tonkawa Indians had frequented the hilltop where the McCormicks were building their home.[37]

Surprisingly, the McCormicks did not seem to mind Emma Dungan giving strangers directions to their new home. Indeed, they and she soon became friends, and over the next few years all three were centrally involved in getting the fledgling McDade Historical Society off the ground. The historical society was founded just a few weeks after the discovery of the Tonkawa burial site at "the McCormick Ranch." The organization's first meeting was held at Emma Dungan's drugstore in November 1962. After electing officers, the first order of business was a discussion of how to raise enough money to buy the old Rockfront Saloon from the Williams family, once owners of the McDade Pottery Plant who had since moved to Austin. Located three doors from the Dungan Drugstore, the old saloon had been the site of the Christmas Eve vigilante kidnappings that sparked McDade's famous 1883 shoot-out. Long abandoned, the building had fallen into serious disrepair. By 1962, it consisted of little more than four sturdy stone walls, its roof having collapsed many years earlier and its interior having become choked with trash and weeds.[38]

Even though the historical society's first officers were all longtime residents of McDade, the McCormicks were undoubtedly the organization's most indispensable members, especially in its early years. Their fundraising efforts ensured the society's survival and enabled it to purchase and refurbish the old saloon building. Between 1963 and 1965, the McCormicks hosted a number of events at their ranch—barbecues, "old-time" songfests, a small rodeo, a Christmas pageant, even "a Hawaiian luau"—to benefit the Historical Society. Most of these events attracted hundreds of paying guests and, all told, must have raised several thousand dollars. Thanks largely to the McCormicks, the McDade Historical Society was able to purchase the Rockfront Saloon from the Williams family in May 1963. By July 1964—in time to house a modest local history exhibit during the Watermelon Festival—the building had a new roof and concrete floor, and had been wired for electricity. Without the efforts of the McCormick family, all this would not have been so quickly possible.[39]

Several other community organizations sprang up in McDade during the mid-1960s. The McCormicks were involved to some extent in almost all of them, as were members of several other families that were new to the area. These organizations included the McDade Youth Posse, a horseback riding club for the town's young people, and the McDade Town and Country Garden Club, which periodically—though not monthly—named a "Yard of the Month" in town. This group also helped Mrs. McCormick prepare her home for some of the historical society fundraisers she and her husband hosted; Emma Dungan found the garden club's decorations for the 1965 "Hawaiian Luau" especially impressive: "[It] made you think you were in Hawaii the way it was decorated with all the tropical green plants," she wrote. "[It] made you feel like you had gone to another country."[40]

From 1965 to 1967, the McCormicks also hosted Easter Sunday sunrise worship services at their home. These were nondenominational Protestant services, open to anyone, with the pastors of McDade's Baptist and Lutheran churches and Paige's Methodist church presiding. Colorfully robed choirs from these congregations, a profusion of flowers (both cut flowers and the site's naturally occurring April wildflowers), the McCormicks' spectacular hilltop view, and good weather all combined to make the 1965 Easter service a success. Almost two hundred people attended and stayed for coffee and doughnuts afterward, according to Emma Dungan. Things apparently did not go as well in 1966 and 1967, however, and the nascent tradition died out. Exactly why is unclear. Adeline Eschberger, a charter member of McDade's Faith Lutheran Church, remembers some people in the community not being comfortable with an Easter service that attempted to embrace such disparate styles of worship. Speaking from her own Lutheran point of view, she recalls that "the Baptists were big on giving their 'testimony.' That's not a part of our service at all. . . . We have a liturgy, . . . you don't get up and say 'I was saved' and all this, never. . . . It's just not the way we do things." Some of McDade's Baptists were probably just as put off by the Lutherans' seeming spiritual reserve. In any event, whether such religious differences were responsible or not, there were no more Easter services at the McCormicks' after 1967.[41]

Although no one in McDade today claims to remember any specific incident, something may have occurred around this time to sour the relationship between the McCormick family and the community. Whatever the reason, Emma Dungan's announcement of 1967's upcoming third annual Easter sunrise service was the last reference to the McCormicks in the *Elgin Courier*'s McDade column until late 1970, when they hosted a small Christmas party for the Baptist Church's Sunday School. Dungan did not even offer a retrospective of the 1967 Easter service in her column. Prior to that, of course, she had mentioned the McCormicks with great frequency, obviously because of their involvement in so many of McDade's social activities. After March 1967, however, their name disappears for nearly four years, almost as though they had ceased to exist. They received two more passing mentions in early 1972, but then they vanish altogether. Thus, just as abruptly as they appeared on the local social scene, making their "debut" with the 1962 discovery of Native American remains on their property, the McCormicks virtually disappeared from McDade society in the spring of 1967. No one today seems able, or willing, to remember why or how this happened. Some people vaguely recall that the McCormicks sold their property and moved away sometime during the 1970s, but no one seems to know exactly when they left or where they went. Although most of the social organizations the McCormicks were involved with in McDade faded away as well, the historical society managed to continue without them, though at a much reduced level of activity.[42]

Whatever the reasons for the McCormicks' sudden withdrawal from community affairs, their influence on McDade extended well beyond the merely social. In fact, the McCormicks and several other rural landowners, most of whom were also new to the area, had an impact on local agriculture, and thus the local economy, that continues to be felt today. By clearing brush from their newly purchased land, much of which they had been able to buy inexpensively because it was so heavily overgrown, and then planting a recently developed, higher-yield hybrid strain of Bermuda grass, these new landowners were able to profitably raise cattle on acreage most longtime area residents had considered worthless. The process was, of course, a gradual one, but by the mid-1960s it had become apparent that the new grass was thriving under local conditions and that cattle were thriving on the new grass. People in other parts of Bastrop County soon took notice. In early 1964, members of the Bastrop and Elgin Chambers of Commerce toured three of the area's new ranches —those of the McCormick, Ramsey, and Cayton families. They returned from their visits favorably impressed, crediting these and other "progressive ranchers" in the vicinity with bringing about "a complete transformation" of the McDade community. The ranchers had accomplished this, according to the *Elgin Courier*, by staying abreast of the "latest scientific developments" and "employ[ing] the most progressive ranching methods."[43]

To claim in 1964 that this new trend had produced "a complete transformation" in McDade was an exaggeration, but over a period of years the emerging new style of ranching did, in fact, alter the face of local agriculture, changing rural land use patterns and traditional notions of land value in the process. According to Clyde Cayton, one of McDade's first "progressive" ranchers, these changes did not occur without a certain amount of local skepticism and resistance. "The people here were reluctant to take on new ideas," he recalls. "It took people from the outside to come in here and do this. . . . The people [who were] born and raised here really haven't contributed to the growth of the area." He remembers that when he first seeded a portion of his newly cleared land with coastal Bermuda grass in 1957, some of his neighbors gathered at the fence line to watch, commenting all the while on how foolish it was to consider raising cattle on such "sorry" land. Within several years, Cayton was growing coastal Bermuda grass for profit, selling root sets to commercial planters who made their living sodding ranches throughout the central and eastern parts of Texas with the new grass. Their list of clients eventually included one of Cayton's once-skeptical neighbors.[44]

Unlike most of the other newcomers, Clyde Cayton had family ties to McDade, his maternal grandparents having lived in the community since its early days as a railhead. His grandfather, John Smith, had operated one of the town's first cotton gins as well as its only grist mill, which he powered every Saturday morning by means of an old steam boiler salvaged from a wrecked locomotive. Though born and raised in Houston, Cayton spent considerable time during his childhood with his grandparents in McDade, both at their home in town and at his grandfather's hunting cabin, located on seven hundred acres of land he owned five miles northeast of town. During Prohibition, Cayton's grandfather operated an illegal still on this land, which "the Feds shot up" during a late-1920s raid, an incident entirely ignored by then newspaper correspondent Sam Billingsley. One of Clyde Cayton's childhood memories is of his mother receiving "a wire on Western Union that Grandpa Smith was in jail for bootlegging, and she needed to send some money to bail him out."[45]

This was the land that Clyde Cayton eventually cleared and planted in coastal Bermuda grass and where he and his wife, Mary, now live. In partnership with his father, Cayton purchased the property from his grandfather in 1942. No one in the area considered it to be worth much, primarily because only about twenty of its seven hundred acres were free of woods or heavy brush. In fact, much of the rural land to the northeast of McDade had become so heavily overgrown during the war years that when Cayton first brought Mary to see the property in 1945 "we had to ride a horse from about halfway between here and McDade, and even then we could hardly ride, it was so thick in brush." Even though the Caytons continued to live in Houston, where Clyde worked as a chemical engineer, they spent most weekends and whatever other time they could on the ranch, working to clear the land and building a small house. In 1957, they planted their first coastal Bermuda grass, starting with a set of roots they had purchased from the experimental station in Georgia where the grass had been developed. Within three years, they were selling root sets themselves and channeling the profits into clearing and improving the rest of their land. Once that was finished, in about 1963, they "got out of the grass business" and began raising cattle. Though they spent considerable time on the ranch over the years, the Caytons did not start living there full time until 1978, when Clyde retired from his job in Houston. One of their daughters, Laura Maness, and her family joined them there in 1981.[46]

Clyde Cayton believes that the new breed of cattle ranchers who came to the area in the late 1950s and early 1960s were the economic salvation of McDade. By investing time and money to clear land that had previously been considered useless and by planting a new higher-yield strain of grass, they made cattle the area's primary cash crop. Previously, commercial cattle ranching had been feasible only for those with very large amounts of property. "The way the land was," Cayton claims, "it would take fifty acres for one cow. But like it is now, you can have five cows to the acre if you have the proper moisture and fertilizer on it." The repercussions were enormous, especially in a community where individual rural land holdings were more typically measured in hundreds of acres than thousands. The area's smaller acreages had been well suited to truck farming, but that economy was now in shambles, having never recovered from the 1954 discontinuance of local rail service. Suddenly, with the introduction of coastal Bermuda grass, it was possible to make a living from cattle, even on the McDade area's relatively small acreages. With the land once again able to support people, land values rose and, eventually, so too did local property tax revenues, providing the sorely strapped McDade Independent School District with an unaccustomed influx of funds. Small-scale cattle ranching remains the predominant form of agriculture in the McDade area today. A few rural landowners still grow seasonal fruits and vegetables to sell—most often cantaloupes, tomatoes, or blackberries ("dewberries" in local parlance)—but nearly everyone with acreage raises at least a few head of beef cattle. Except in the most extreme of drought years, they continue to be a reliable source of income.[47]

Despite the "progressive" tendencies of the mid-1960s, the decade did not end well for McDade. After the McCormicks' sudden withdrawal from public affairs, the number and variety of social events taking place in the community declined sharply. There also appears to have been some bad feeling among certain town residents at about this time. In an anonymous letter to the *Elgin Courier*, a person who signed him- or herself as "A Disgusted Citizen" complained of a "McDade Gossip Club" whose members "love[d] to hurt people." Whether or not there was any connection to the circumstances that had prompted this letter is unclear, but just a few weeks later, the community was shocked to learn that only one girl had signed up to compete for the privilege of serving as McDade's 1967 Teenage Watermelon Queen. This had never happened before. (Nor has it happened since.) The lack of contestants deprived the community of its usual atmosphere of anticipation and suspense in the days before the 1967 Queen's Revue. Embarrassingly, it also left the queen without a princess or courtiers to ride with her and pay her homage in the Watermelon Festival parade. It also meant that McDade had no official stand-in to substitute for the queen when she was unable to attend parades and other festivities in other towns. Worst of all, it made McDade appear contentious and apathetic. The community may well have been contentious and apathetic in 1967, but most people in McDade felt that the town's problems should not be put so obviously on display. The following year, even Emma Dungan, normally the soul of grace and good humor in her column, allowed her own sense of irritation to show when someone from a recently deceased man's family inserted an amusing anecdote about their loved one into an obituary Dungan had written for the *Elgin Courier*. "I don't ever write up things like that . . . in a person's death," she fumed in the paper's next issue. "I'm not use[d] to people changing the things I write and I don't appreciate it."[48]

If 1967 and 1968 were marked by people in McDade squabbling among themselves—and, surely, any such spats that found their way into the *Elgin Courier*, however obliquely, were merely the tip of an iceberg—1969 turned out to be much worse, a year of serious misfortune for the community. In January, the town lost another of its landmark old buildings when L. A. Kunkel's abandoned uptown warehouse, which had gone unsold at Kunkel's 1961 going-out-of-business auction, burned to the ground. Six months later, a tornado roared through McDade's already depleted business district, tearing the roof off the Dungan Drugstore. These misfortunes paled, however, in comparison to the human toll exacted on McDade in 1969. In addition to the usual round of funerals among the town's elderly population, the community was rocked by several untimely deaths, some from illness, others by accident. Among the latter was Emma Dungan's death in a car wreck on U.S. 290 that stunned the town. Dungan's son, Sam Earl Dungan, who had recently returned from two years in the military, took over the daily operation of the store. He could not, however, take his mother's place in the hearts of McDade's townspeople. In her seventeen years at the drugstore, "Miss Emma" had become a McDade institution and her store a favorite gathering place for town residents, young and old alike. Well loved by everyone, she was sorely missed.[49]

Emma Dungan's death closed out an era in McDade's history in more ways than one. Not only did it occur at the end of a decade that had witnessed many changes in the community, but her final column also marked the last time for almost ten years that news of McDade would regularly appear in print. Since 1952, the Dungan Drugstore had functioned as an unofficial clearing house for community information, much of which Emma Dungan had included in her weekly columns. Sam Earl may have had the opportunity, but he had neither the temperament nor the inclination to follow in his mother's footsteps as town newsgatherer and spokesperson. Several people tried to fill her shoes over the next several years, but, typically, their attempts at writing a weekly McDade column deteriorated rapidly, becoming biweekly, then occasional, before, in most cases, disappearing altogether. In short, Emma Dungan was irreplaceable, both as the person who defined the McDade community— to itself, as well as to the rest of the world—and as the figure who recorded town doings for posterity. Never again would the written record from McDade be so constant or so full of the small details of town life.

The 1960s were a time of transition in McDade. It was also the last decade from which the weekly rhythms of community life are discernible in the public record. Since then, most of the "news" that has come from McDade has concerned itself with various town crises rather than the day-in, day-out realities of small-town life. Almost by definition, by the time such crises had come to public attention they had already been blown out of proportion. Thus, most of what the *Elgin Courier* printed about McDade in the 1970s and 1980s pointed up the contentious side of town life rather than a happier vision of a mutually supportive, inter-involved community of loving family and friendly neighbors. As we shall see, the realities of life in McDade during the past twenty years lie somewhere in between. Throughout the 1970s and 1980s, various groups within the community have consistently wanted what they thought best for the town, but they have often been unable to agree on exactly what that was. At times, they fought bitterly over how to approach, and live in, the future.

The 1970s: Little News That Was Fit to Print

Emma Dungan died in April 1969. Throughout the remainder of that year, the *Elgin Courier* printed a total of five news items from McDade, all of them quite brief. This was a pattern that would continue until late 1976, when the next reliable community correspondent emerged. In fact, between

April 1969 and September 1976, when Louise Goerlitz started writing her column of news from McDade (which she still writes today), the *Elgin Courier* made mention of events in McDade a mere fifty-one times—considerably less often, on average, than once a month. Very few of these items are of historical interest, most of them announcements of births, deaths, weddings, family reunions, church picnics, and the like. Twice during these years, in 1969 and 1973, the *Courier* did not even note McDade's Watermelon Festival; when it did mention the festival, it usually only reported who had been selected Watermelon queen or how much the festival's prize melons had sold for at auction.[50]

A few items of McDade news from the *Elgin Courier* during these years testify to a small amount of continuing civic activity in town. In November 1969, McDade's Veterans of Foreign Wars Post 8313 was founded; this organization is still active in McDade today. In April 1971, the McDade Baptist Church, the Ladies Home Demonstration Club, and the local 4-H Club sponsored a town-wide "community clean-up." The *Elgin Courier* termed this effort "a tremendous success," probably an indication that McDade had become unsightly over the years. The following month, the Veterans of Foreign Wars and the McDade Historical Society put on a "McDade Loyalty Day," at which VFW commander Bill Standifer presented the historical society with an American flag. At a well-attended ceremony, Standifer spoke of McDade's "priceless heritage" and urged local people to "continue to stand strong and free." After offering a prayer, singing "The Star Spangled Banner," and pledging allegiance to the newly raised flag, the crowd paid tribute to several young men from McDade who had returned home from tours of duty in Vietnam in the past few years. Also of note was the 1972 establishment of the McDade Volunteer Fire Department, with Henry Grimes as fire chief and Sam Earl Dungan and Jerry Dungan, Sam Earl's second cousin and son of watermelon-farmer-turned-grocer Tom Dungan, as captains. In 1974, the town received a pleasant surprise when McDade native Debra Cronin was chosen Miss Texas USA and went on to compete in the Miss USA Pageant in Niagara Falls, New York. Strangely, Cronin had failed in two of three attempts to be elected McDade's Watermelon Queen. Nonetheless, the town hastened to erect a sign along U.S. 290 proudly proclaiming McDade as the home of Miss Texas USA for 1974.[51]

The written record from McDade for the first two-thirds of the 1970s is obviously on the sparse side, and most town residents do not seem to enjoy talking about those years. Several new trends developed during the 1970s that many of the community's old-timers found objectionable. Among the more disturbing was McDade's emerging reputation as a latter-day "outlaw town." Perceived as having no law other than occasional patrols by Bastrop County sheriff's deputies, the McDade area began attracting a new kind of outlaw. These were people who dressed, lived, and acted in ways unlike anything most town residents had ever seen, except possibly on television news programs or in the pages of *Life*, *Time*, or *Newsweek*. Most of them were young; most had come to McDade from Austin or Houston; and most were seeking refuge from an urban environment they variously found too crowded, too complicated, or overly intrusive. Nearly all of them smoked marijuana; some used harder drugs. Renting vacant houses in or around McDade, they often lived in groups whose numbers fluctuated. Most of those who lived as couples were not married. Many did not hold regular jobs, seeming to prefer spending their time cultivating large vegetable gardens and sitting on front porches. In short, they were hippies, come to McDade as part of the "back-to-the-land" movement of the late 1960s and early 1970s.[52]

Some among this new population were peaceful, friendly sorts of people who were simply looking for a place to live that was quieter and less complicated than the cities they had come from. A few of them continue to live in McDade today and have integrated themselves into community life and become well accepted over the years. Others, however, were attracted to McDade less by the peace and quiet of small-town life than in the hope of avoiding the notice of organized law enforcement. Though impossible to document with any degree of precision, it seems that several marijuana farms operated in the McDade area during the 1970s, as did a couple of "speed labs," one of which was supposedly run by one of Texas's more infamous motorcycle gangs. In 1975, there was a sizable "bust" in McDade, at which the Bastrop County Sheriff's Department made several arrests, uprooted and destroyed more than six hundred marijuana plants, and confiscated in excess of five hundred pounds of cured marijuana. In spite of this raid, illegal drugs seem to have remained something of a problem in the community, at least through the end of the decade. In 1979, a member of a group calling itself "Concerned Parents of McDade" wrote to the *Elgin Courier* to warn people about "the danger" posed to local children by marijuana, which "is readily available in our town." There do not appear to be many, if any, drug users left in McDade today, though one still occasionally reads of marijuana farms and drug manufacturing labs being raided in rural parts of Bastrop and surrounding counties. A couple of these raids have not been far from McDade.[53]

It was also during the mid 1970s that Lucille Morrison opened her "Beer Hut," in defiance of McDade's traditional, but only quasi-legal, ban on the sale of alcohol. Located across the road on the west side of the old Rockfront Saloon (generally known in McDade as "the historical building" by this time), the Beer Hut was a tiny sheet metal structure with a service window cut in one side. It was barely large enough to hold the person tending it and a large cooler full of beer. For years, McDade's beer drinkers had congregated along the railroad tracks just east of uptown to drink and socialize, their favorite spot under a couple of large live oak trees at a place known as "the scales," the site of the old weighing platform during the days when McDade's farmers shipped their produce by rail. Though they had openly consumed large amounts of beer at the scales for years, the town's beer drinkers had always driven to Elgin or Paige to buy their beer. With the sudden appearance of the Beer Hut, they could now get cold beer in uptown McDade. The town's "dries" were outraged, of course, and tried to get the Beer Hut shut down. They failed, however, to mount a serious legal challenge, in large part because the state's "local option" law regarding alcohol sales in unincorporated communities was antiquated and unclear. Even though the Beer Hut operated for only a couple of years, beer had come to McDade to stay. Sam Earl Dungan began selling beer at his store in the late 1970s. By the mid-1980s, to the chagrin of most of the town's more "respectable" folk, the sidewalk in front of his store had become the favorite hangout of local beer drinkers.[54]

Not all of McDade's problems during the 1970s, however, were related to changing times and the town's changing population. Several of the community's long-established institutions ran into difficulty, as did portions of its aging infrastructure. In 1977, for example, the main water pump failed and could not be repaired. McDade was left without running water for almost two weeks before the town could raise the money to buy a new pump. Later that year, Tom Dungan put his grocery business up for sale. Remembering that L. E. Kunkel had been unable to find a buyer for the McDade Mercantile in 1961, many townspeople feared that the community would soon be left without a place to purchase anything but beer, "soda water," and snack foods. Dungan eventually sold the store to Travis McPhaul in 1979. A year later, McPhaul sold it to George and Jona Lee Seigmund, who continue to operate it today. Some of the town's social organizations were having a hard time as well. In 1978, McDade Historical Society president Jewell Hudler pleaded in the *Elgin Courier* for more people to join and become active in the society. Less than half the membership, she complained, attended meetings and only about five of those who did were willing to put any further time or effort into the organization and its functions. The historical society was about to die, she feared, for lack of interest.[55]

Problems such as these, however, were minor in comparison to some of the other difficulties that cropped up in the late 1970s. Conflicts arose within the town's Watermelon Festival, over its school, and concerning the possible inclusion of McDade in a proposed Elgin Hospital Taxation District. A brief look at these problems will help explain the much more bitterly divisive difficulties that McDade experienced in the 1980s. Dissension within the Watermelon Festival during the late 1970s and concerns over the cost and quality of local education were simpler, smaller versions of battles the community would fight in the decade to follow, precursors of more troublesome times to come. In addition, reaction in McDade to the question of including the town in an Elgin-instigated attempt to create a taxation district to fund Elgin's financially ailing hospital indicated the depth of anger McDade residents were capable of when they felt themselves infringed upon and their hometown's autonomy threatened. A similar spirit of irritability, defensiveness, and hostility would predominate throughout much of the 1980s.

Since its inception, the McDade Watermelon Festival had been an institution the community could point to with pride. Other than a few minor squabbles, usually related to the selection of the queen, the festival had always gone smoothly, providing a good time for visitors and residents alike. It was something that people from across McDade's social spectrum could work on together, regardless of differences in age, economic class, religious affiliation, or ethnic background. The festival had become quite successful over the years, raising ever-increasing amounts of money for the McDade School annually. In early 1979, what to do with the proceeds of the upcoming festival became an issue, apparently for the first time. One faction, led by Watermelon Festival Association chairman Andy Blaschke, felt that the board of directors should be able to distribute the money among various community organizations, as well as retain some funds for the Watermelon Festival Association itself to use as seed money for future projects. Others believed that the association should automatically turn over all festival proceeds to the PTA, as it had always done, for that organization to spend on behalf of the school. For a brief while, the issue became rancorous, with Chairman Blaschke threatening to resign unless the association's directors would be allowed, as he claimed was "originally specified in the Charter, . . . [to] hear requests for funds for worthy projects in McDade rather than be directed to turn the proceeds from the Festival over to the PTA." Blaschke eventually got his way, though not without having to override strenuous objections. The issue was complicated by the fact that no one could find a copy of the original charter, drawn up in 1950. Believing that the first charter's bylaws specified that all Watermelon Festival profits should go to the McDade School, those in favor of continuing to turn the money over to the PTA searched attics, barns, garages, and closets all over town, but to no avail—the original was never found. (A new charter, specifying that festival directors could distribute funds within the community at their discretion and specifically allowing the association to retain money for future operating expenses and the possible purchase of property, was officially adopted in 1985.) For better or worse, change had come to one of McDade's most long-standing and successful traditions. Many of those who had helped found the Watermelon Festival in 1948 were not pleased to see the torch they had lit passed on to a generation that wanted to do things differently. The festival would become increasingly politicized throughout the 1980s, even to the point that some people refused to participate.[56]

McDade's school also became a source of concern in the late 1970s. Faced with the possible loss of state accreditation for its "intermediate" program in the fall of 1976, the McDade Board of Trustees considered eliminating grades seven and eight from the school's curriculum. This would mean having to pay additional tuition fees to send the district's seventh- and eighth-graders to Elgin Junior High School. For reasons that are not entirely clear, the board took no action on this issue at the time, despite being assured by the Texas Education Association that it would have "no problem" accrediting the McDade School for a standard kindergarten through sixth-grade elementary program. There were no announced candidates for the following spring's school board election, possibly because no one in town relished the thought of being directly involved in the difficult and potentially unpopular decisions the new board would probably have to make in the very near future. Three new members elected by write-in vote, none of them incumbents, eventually filled the vacant seats on the board. Just a month later, concluding that the town's adolescents "need[ed] larger group activities and more specialized subjects" than the McDade School could offer, the new board "regretfully" voted to discontinue grades seven and eight. Though the trustees had little real choice in the matter, McDade had once again been diminished.[57]

Funding the school was also becoming a problem. Despite a nearly four-fold increase in tax revenues between 1972 and 1978, the McDade Independent School District was finding it difficult to operate the school with the moneys it had available. At the same time, a number of area residents felt that their property taxes were unnecessarily high. In 1978, only a year after publishing a list of delinquent taxpayers and hiring an attorney to pursue collections, the McDade School Board of Trustees raised the local property tax rate by 25 percent, the maximum allowed by state law. The board also purchased a set of aerial photographs from the state highway department to ensure that improvements to rural properties in the district—new barns, additions to houses, newly cleared or fenced pasture lands, etc.—did not go unassessed. Many area residents found these measures intrusive and insulting. For the first time, the relationship between a sizable portion of the local electorate and McDade's school board, which had always been the town's only elected body, had become adversarial. Just a few years later, in the mid-1980s, the linked issues of school funding and taxation would flair into open and bitter conflict in McDade.[58]

McDade's biggest political flap of the 1970s, however, came over whether the town would be included in a newly proposed Elgin Hospital Taxation District. Most people in McDade used one of Elgin's several doctors as their personal physician and generally visited its small, privately owned Fleming Hospital for minor surgeries or in cases of emergency. In 1978, with the hospital in financial difficulty, its board of directors decided to seek public funding by proposing that local voters create a new taxation district to help support the hospital. They hoped to include McDade in this district, though they feared the impact of a large negative vote there. Accordingly, their original plan called for Elgin and McDade to vote separately, a strategy they believed might minimize the effect of an overwhelming rejection in McDade. They also proposed that the tax rate in McDade be smaller than in Elgin, a tactic they hoped might induce people in McDade to vote in favor of the district. From its supporters' point of view, the proposal was poorly timed, especially for securing the participation of McDade. First suggested in March 1978, it came just six months after McDade's 25 percent property-tax rate hike and just as the first voices of tax rebellion were being raised at McDade School Board meetings. Coming when it did and calling for an additional 14 percent raise in the local tax rate, the proposal was probably doomed from the start in McDade. In retrospect, it also seems to have postponed some of the internal conflicts that were brewing in McDade over higher property taxes and funding for the town's school. Already in a cantankerous mood, people in McDade did not have to fight among themselves for most of 1978; they could fight with Elgin instead.[59]

And fight they did. The proposed hospital taxation district dominated local politics throughout the spring and summer of 1978, its various twists and turns becoming a new chapter in the history of McDade's often testy relationship with Elgin. In early April, an unsigned letter appeared in the *Elgin Courier* claiming that most people in McDade preferred the newer hospitals in Bastrop and Giddings to Elgin's Fleming Hospital and wondered why the citizens of Elgin thought McDade property owners should help pay for what was obviously an inferior and outdated facility. Accurate or not, this letter ruffled many feathers in Elgin and set the tone for nearly six months of bickering to follow. In early May, sensing that the issue had already become overly emotional, Chairman W. W. Cottle of the Elgin Hospital Taxation District Steering Committee tried to defuse the situation, pleading with citizens of both communities "to forget any past irritations that are affecting present thinking." The last thing the committee wanted was for the issue to break down along Elgin-versus-McDade lines.[60]

But it was to no avail. As the issue became increasingly more complex, tensions mounted. A major complication arose at the end of May, when the Fleming Hospital's Board of Directors announced that the hospital would close on June 17. This was an unexpected and shocking announcement; few people had realized the hospital was in such immediately dire financial straits. This development redoubled public concern in Elgin and increased the pressure to have the proposed taxation district approved by local voters. It also intensified the rhetoric surrounding the issue and the potential for resentment toward anyone who opposed the plan. Shortly after the hospital closed, to make matters even worse, the steering committee was advised by its attorney that the original plan to have Elgin and McDade vote separately and for the two communities to have different tax rates was probably illegal; the taxation district would have to be voted on in a single comprehensive election, and everyone in it would have to be taxed equally. This was the final straw for many in McDade. At the next meeting of the steering committee, several "McDade dissidents," as the *Courier* termed them, showed up with lawyers in tow, implying the threat of legal action if they felt their interests violated.[61]

Finally, the steering committee set a public hearing for the latter part of August. Anyone who lived within the proposed taxation district's boundaries would be allowed to speak at this hearing, after which the committee would decide upon a future course of action. The "McDade dissidents" came to this meeting prepared to fight. They claimed that the new district's taxpayers would be responsible for the current debts of the Fleming Hospital and that they would have to pay the medical bills of the district's indigent no matter where they went for care. They also pointed out that the Bastrop County Tax Office would charge the new taxation district a fee of 1.5 percent to administer, collect, and disburse the newly raised tax moneys. Even though members of the steering committee disputed these claims, taxation district opponents, most of them from McDade, painted a picture of endless obligation and "big government" inefficiency so frightening that nearly everyone in McDade was convinced that their community should want no part of such an enterprise. When the hearing was over, the steering committee proposed holding separate, nonbinding straw polls in Elgin and McDade to get a direct reading of public sentiment in the two communities. The following week, Elgin's voters indicated their support of the taxation district by a decisive tally of 330–107; voters in McDade, however, rejected the idea even more decisively, by a margin of 220–19. At its next meeting, the steering committee voted to exclude McDade from the proposed Elgin Hospital Taxation District. McDade resident Henry Grimes, who had served as the committee's vice chairman and had campaigned tirelessly among his neighbors for the establishment of the district, resigned, saying he was "very disappointed."[62]

————————————

The people of McDade had indicated in no uncertain terms that they would tolerate no threat, real or imagined, to their sense of the town's independence. They had reacted decisively and angrily to Elgin's attempt to form even the most limited kind of civic partnership. This, of course, was no real surprise, as cooperation with others had never been one of McDade's strengths. More serious, however, were the first rumblings of discontent within the Watermelon Festival and dissatisfaction with the town's school, both of which hinted at more serious problems to come. As the 1970s ended with McDade's open decline, many local residents seemed to become increasingly touchy about their town's situation. They also became increasingly defiant toward anyone who presumed to think they knew how to make things better, whether the "do-gooders" had roots in McDade or were new to town. As a result, the community's hypersensitivity and sense of hostility would turn inward during the 1980s, as various issues that challenged the validity of long-standing local traditions made suspect the notion that McDade could solve its own problems. They also called into doubt whether the term "community" still had much meaning in McDade. With an increasing percentage of the town's population having no past local ties, no one knew any longer precisely who comprised the community, who should make the town's decisions, and whom its institutions should serve. By the late 1980s, the most important question in McDade was probably one that usually went unasked: what was there left of the town that could still legitimately be considered a community? It is a question that no one has yet had a good answer for. A number of people in McDade have voiced their opinions, but nearly always to angry disagreement from others. In fact, as of 1989, no one in McDade seemed able to agree on much of anything. How things got that way is the story of the 1980s.

CHAPTER 14

McDade in the 1980s
Of Change and Resistance

The decade of the 1980s, of course, is when I started going to McDade. I mention this not because it was an important moment in the history of the town, but because it was an important moment for me. I visited McDade hundreds of times between 1984 and 1989, engaged in thousands of conversations there, and made an estimated twelve thousand photographs. In the years since, I have spent considerable time researching the town's past and writing about it. With the story of that past on the verge of becoming the present, however, this history of McDade has come to the point where these disparate ways of looking at the community must merge. In ways that are irrelevant to what happened in McDade during the 1980s—but indispensable to this account of what happened—the historian becomes part of the history, if only as an actively curious observer. The following account of McDade in the 1980s, then, is pieced together from my own observations; from a sizable body of common community knowledge; from other people's recollections of events; from hearsay; from personal opinion; and, occasionally, from written accounts of events that appeared in area newspapers. Whenever possible, I have attributed factual material, individual surmise, and quotations to their appropriate sources. In some cases, though, this has not been possible. A few of the people I spoke with about events in McDade during the 1980s would talk to me only if I promised not to identify them. In other instances, the material I present derives from more than five years' accumulated knowledge about the community, much of which I cannot attribute to individual sources with any pretense of accuracy. This, no doubt, is one of the shortcomings of a participant-observer trying to act as historian as well. So be it; the story of what happened in McDade during the 1980s is worth telling anyway.

————————

I first went to McDade in February 1984, at the start of my second semester as a graduate student in photography at the University of Texas. This visit was the result of a chance meeting with Laura Cayton (then Laura Maness) in Elgin about six weeks earlier. I had spent much of the previous few months driving around the central Texas countryside and taking pictures in some of the region's many small towns. Having lived most of my life in the Northeast and Pacific Northwest, Texas was new to me when I moved to Austin in the summer of 1983, and it excited my curiosity. As a way of exploring this strange new environment, I undertook to photograph a portion of it. I chose to concentrate on the rural, small-town culture that surrounds the city of Austin as an ocean surrounds an island. For reasons that are no longer important, I expected to find a way of life in these places that was more purely "Texan" than the urban hustle and bustle of rapidly expanding Austin.

I put a lot of miles on my car that fall, getting out of Austin at least once a week to take pictures in rural communities. Shortly before Christmas, one such trip took me to Elgin, twenty-six miles east of Austin. As I habitually did when visiting a new place, I parked in the downtown business district and began walking, carrying a tripod over my shoulder and two cameras around my neck. I had been there only a few minutes when a short, round-faced woman burst out of a laundromat and, with a friendly smile on her face, demanded to know what I was doing. This was Laura Maness. She startled me at first, but after I told her who I was and explained my interest in small-town Texan culture, we ended up talking for quite some time. Among other things, Laura told me that Elgin, with a population of about five thousand, was a big town, not a small town, and if I wanted to see a "*real* small town" I should visit the community she lived in, a place called McDade, nine miles east of Elgin. We also talked about Texas in general, about Austin and the rapid changes it was undergoing, and about some of the advantages and disadvantages of living in a rural area. Before going our separate ways, Laura gave me her phone number, saying I should call her after the holidays and she would take me around McDade and introduce me to some people.

The more I thought about her offer over the next few weeks, the better it sounded. I saw it as an opportunity for me to broaden and deepen my photography, which I had sensed was becoming repetitive and superficial. Most of the pictures I had taken during my visits to small towns that autumn had been landscapes, or, more accurately, townscapes, and nearly all of them had been devoid of people. I had enjoyed driving around the central Texas countryside, learning the back roads and the way the land fit together, and I had liked walking around exploring new towns, but I wasn't pleased with the pictures I had been taking. They were handsome enough photographs, as well done black-and-white landscapes often are, but they seemed cold and distant, lacking life and spark. Most of them had been taken from a distance, a distance I now realize was emotional as well as physical. Though I certainly wouldn't have said so at the time, they depicted the towns of central Texas as inanimate objects. It was as though they were museum pieces, sucked dry of life and incapable of growth or change, that existed only for me to point a camera at. Unintentionally, I had portrayed these places as having no meaning or importance except as empty stage sets, visual raw material, for me to photograph. I wasn't able to understand all this till later, but I'm reasonably certain that, on a subconscious level, this was a main reason I found most of the pictures I had taken during my first few months in Texas unsatisfactory.

There were a few pictures I was happier with, though, even if they were not as "good" by most external photographic standards. Occasionally, when I walked the streets of the towns I visited, I ran into people who, like Laura, were good-naturedly curious about what I was doing. Whenever I encountered such people, I would stop and talk awhile, and would usually end up taking some pictures of them. Thus, sprinkled among the many townscapes that showed up on my contact sheets, there were also a few portraits. In general, these portraits were not as technically accomplished or as studied as the townscapes, but they seemed warmer and somehow more satisfying. These were often the photographs I found myself wanting to spend time in the darkroom printing. Less happily, though, these pictures also reminded me of how much of an outsider I was in the communities I had been visiting. They made me wish I could get to know some people in one or more of the towns and develop relationships with them that would allow me to return there to photograph over and over again without feeling like an intruder. Unfortunately, being a bit shy and never having developed much social grace, I didn't really think there was much likelihood of such a thing ever happening.

This was why Laura's invitation to visit McDade and have her introduce me around the town seemed worth pursuing. I can't claim that I was ready at that point to make the kind of longterm commitment an in-depth documentary project requires. Nor had I planned how I would go about such a project. The door Laura had opened for me, though, seemed too inviting to pass up, not without at least stepping inside and taking a look around. So, despite continued misgivings from the more reticent side of my personality, I called Laura sometime in the middle of January 1984.

We arranged to meet on February 1 at Kastner's Drive-In (later to become the JNP Grocery), a couple of miles west of McDade on Highway 290. I think Laura wanted to talk some more and make sure she would not later regret taking me uptown and showing me around. I did a lot more talking that first day than picture taking. Laura introduced me to the owners of McDade's three retail businesses—Kelly Wayne Kastner at the Drive-In, Sam Earl Dungan at Dungan Drugs, and George and Jona Lee Seigmund at Seigmund's Grocery. I also met Postmistress Mary Louise Mundine and her assistant, Ruth Pohler, at the post office, as well as a number of other people who were uptown that day getting their mail, trading at Dungan's or Seigmund's, or just visiting with one another on the benches facing the street from the raised sidewalk in front of the stores. I mentioned my interest in starting an extended photographic project in a rural Texas community to each person I met and asked them if they thought McDade would be a good place to do that. Just about everyone said they thought it would, though most didn't seem to understand why anyone would want to do such a thing in the first place. I also asked them if they thought there would be many people who would object to a stranger wandering around taking pictures a couple of times each week. No one seemed to think that would be a problem as long as I was polite and respected people's privacy. I did manage to snap a couple of quick pictures of some of the people I met, mainly so I could have some prints in hand to show and give away the next time I came to town. This would give me an excuse for searching these same people out a second time and might help generate some good will.

I returned to McDade the following Saturday. The local Veterans of Foreign Wars post was barbecuing chickens that morning and would start selling them to the public at midday. According to Laura, the VFW did this four or five times yearly, and their barbecues had become something of a town tradition. Through long practice, they had cooking and selling the chickens down to a science. A few men got up before dawn to start the fires to make the cooking coals, while the rest of the post membership arrived a bit later at the barbecue pit, located next to the school grounds, to begin marinating and slow-smoking several hundred half-chickens. The chickens they cooked were always tender and delicious, Laura said, and nearly everyone in town ordered a few, some to eat that day, others to freeze for later. A little before noon, people would start coming by to pick up and pay for their chickens. Members of the PTA would also be there selling baked goods. Laura thought it would be a good opportunity for me to meet a lot of town residents. She was right. I must have met a hundred people that morning. With people coming and going all the time, I was constantly shaking hands, explaining who I was, and talking about what I hoped to do in McDade. On the whole, people were very friendly and seemed receptive to my visiting to take pictures. Several individuals invited me to stop by their homes sometime. I also took a few more photographs that morning, again so I could have some prints with me to give away the next time I was there.

That's how the project started. Over the next several months I visited McDade at least twice a week. Often, I just walked around town, sometimes taking pictures, sometimes not. I was constantly on the lookout for new people to meet, whether they were out and about uptown or at home doing yard work or sitting on their porches. Though I sometimes found it difficult, I always tried to initiate conversations with the people I encountered, introducing myself and talking about the photographic project I was trying to get started. Some people knew who I was by this time, largely because of my presence at the VFW chicken barbecue, and some did not. If I sensed people were at ease with me, I would take some pictures of them then and there. If they seemed uncertain, I would ask if I could call them sometime to arrange another visit, at which time I might or might not try to make a portrait of them. By never being pushy about the picture-taking process and by always being polite and friendly, I was usually able to allay most people's distrust of me as a stranger. I soon started accumulating a mental list of names and faces and a written list of telephone numbers. It was a slow process, though. There were many days that I walked around McDade and saw no one, and on these occasions I would return to Austin feeling discouraged.

I also met people at various social and community events that Laura and some of her friends in McDade invited me to. I attended a Boy Scout camp-out in the woods outside of town with Scoutmaster Nelson Page and a group of a dozen or so boys; a couple of Boy Scout meetings at the old house on a hilltop that Nelson and his wife, Mary, had recently bought and were fixing up; a quilting bee at David and Barbara Carson's elegantly modern new home on the edge of town; and a party five miles north of McDade on the Cayton Ranch, owned by Laura's parents, Clyde and Mary Cayton, where Laura and her family—husband Mickey Maness and sons Jared and Chad—also lived. I took a lot of pictures at these events, and though none of them is among the better photographs I took during my five years in McDade, they kept me supplied with prints to give away. I also photographed the McDade School's athletic field day in early May and the sixth graders' graduation ceremony at the end of the school year. In the process, I met Superintendent and Principal Thomas Baca, most of the teachers at the McDade School, a number of the town's children, and some of their parents. Several of the parents were quite pleased when I gave them pictures of their children. If nothing else, then, I had succeeded in expanding my base during those first few months. I was constantly meeting more people, and by giving away hundreds of black-and-white prints I was generating good will. These prints also served to legitimize and solidify my position in the community. As word got around that I was okay and as people who were unable to remember my name started calling me "Picture Man," I began to realize that I was becoming increasingly accepted in town. In the sense that it enabled me to carry the project into the future, this was undoubtedly the most important thing I accomplished in McDade that spring. As the summer of 1984 started, I was no longer a complete stranger in town. In some circles I was even becoming something of a familiar face.

I made a special effort to get to know some of McDade's older people. Several times that spring I attended one of the lunches for senior citizens that a group called McDade Community Action had begun sponsoring in January. These lunches were held twice weekly in the Fellowship Hall of the McDade Baptist Church, which Reverend Clifton Franks had volunteered despite the fact that none of McDade Community Action's organizers belonged to his church. In and of themselves, these lunches were not especially good photographic opportunities. They did, however, give me a chance to meet some of McDade's older people and take more pictures I could later give away. After I had been to several of these lunches, some of McDade's seniors were comfortable enough with me to give me their phone numbers so we could arrange a time for me to come to their homes and take portraits of them. I began making appointments in early May. The first of the pictures I took in McDade that I still consider successful—the portraits of John and Rhode Anderson (fig. 20) and Vlasta Walla (fig. 93)—were made during this first series of home visits to people I met at the McDade Community Action lunches.

More important than specific photographs, however, were some of the things I learned about McDade as a result of these visits. Two lessons in particular stand out. The first grew directly out of the events of a single afternoon, though the day is memorable less for the specifics of what it taught me than for how it made me realize, in a general way, that just beneath McDade's surface there existed a depth and breadth of interconnection that a casual observer might easily miss. Thinking back on that day, I consider it an especially lucky one, both in the sense that I stumbled onto this realization by chance and that what it taught me about McDade made me resolve to be a less casual observer.

It was a weekday late in May. I had scheduled four portrait appointments that afternoon, one right after the other, allowing about an hour for each. They were with Amanda Haverland, Hazel Creel, Nellie Hudler, and Emilie Goerlitz, all ladies I had met at the senior lunches. All were in their seventies or eighties, and all but Mrs. Hudler were widows. My first appointment was with Mrs. Haverland at her small farmhouse a mile or so west of town. I took some pictures of her both inside the house and out front in her flower garden, but she was obviously uncomfortable in front of the camera, so we cut the photography short and spent the rest of the time talking. We had a pleasant conversation and enjoyed each other's company. I then drove back into town to Mrs. Creel's house, near the McDade School. Once again, the company and conversation were enjoyable, but the photography uninspired. Feeling a bit discouraged, I proceeded to Nellie and Homer Hudler's house, across the street from the school playground. We spent most of the hour sitting on their small front porch, drinking iced tea, and talking. The few pictures I took did not seem very promising. What I remember about my visit with the Hudlers, though, is that when I mentioned that I had just come from Mrs. Creel's house, Mrs. Hudler told me that she and Mrs. Creel were sisters. Their maiden name had been Dungan. They had been born and raised in McDade and had three brothers who still lived in town, including Tom Dungan, longtime owner of the grocery business now operated by George and Jona Lee Seigmund. Sam Earl Dungan, owner of Dungan Drugs, was their first cousin despite being about forty years younger. Mr. Hudler then listed his local "kinfolk" for me, including his distant cousin Clyde Cayton, Laura Maness's father and owner of the Cayton Ranch. Cayton's mother, a native of McDade and kin to Mr. Hudler's mother, had left town years earlier, before she married. Her son Clyde and his family had returned in 1978 to take up residence on seven hundred acres of wooded land her father had owned a few miles north of McDade. Mr. Hudler told me this almost apologetically, as though he felt badly for not knowing his distant cousins any better than he did.

By this time I was running late for my next appointment, so I hurried off and didn't think much about what the Hudlers had told me. This last appointment of the day was with Emilie Goerlitz, at her rural home several miles northwest of McDade. Once again, I did more talking than photography. When I mentioned the people I had already visited that day and my surprise at learning that Mrs. Creel and Mrs. Hudler were sisters, Mrs. Goerlitz laughed and told me that she and Amanda Haverland were also sisters. Their maiden name had been Eschberger, and they too had several siblings in the area, as well as numerous cousins, nieces, nephews, children, grandchildren, and great-grandchildren. Surprised, I mentioned that it seemed quite a coincidence that I had unknowingly made appointments on a single day with two pairs of sisters. She didn't seem to think it especially remarkable, though, saying something to the effect that nearly everyone whose family had been in McDade for any length of time was related in one way or another. She seemed genuinely puzzled, and a bit amused, that I thought I had stumbled onto something unusual.

As I drove back to Austin that day, my mind was in a whirl. It had not occurred to me that tiny McDade might be such a complicated place. I was struck less by the specifics of who was related to whom than by the sudden realization that just beneath the present-day surface of McDade there no doubt existed countless such interrelationships, each one imprinting the present with its own particular stamp of the past. Unless one was on the lookout for it, I realized, this dynamic would remain largely invisible and unspoken, assumed as common knowledge by those who were familiar with the local past and ignored by those who were not. Yet it was a vitally important process, central to understanding places like McDade: while it might not be apparent to a casual observer—or even to many of the town's current residents—McDade's present was in large part defined by a complex set of interrelationships among individuals and families that grew directly out of the community's past and which still drew much of their meaning from past events. Without an awareness of the local past, especially the histories of certain individuals and families, someone new to McDade like myself would never be able to understand more than a fraction of how the community fit together and functioned in the present. This made me realize that unless I wanted my photography to reflect nothing more than the surface appearance of life there in the 1980s, I would have to become more knowledgeable about the local past, in particular about how that past had influenced people who were now shaping the community's present.

My visits with some of the older people I had met at the McDade Community Action lunches also led me to realize that McDade was not the happily united community I had presumed it to be. In fact, as I would later find out, the lunches themselves had been a source of minor controversy from the start, reflecting some of the divisions within McDade that colored so many aspects of life there. One example will suffice: a woman who attended one of the first Community Action hot lunches served at the Fellowship Hall of the McDade Baptist Church did not think the moment of silent prayer observed before the meal sufficiently Christian enough, and she complained to Reverend Franks. He agreed with her and a few days later, in the company of several church members, paid an unannounced visit to the home of David and Barbara Carson, the primary organizers of the Community Action lunch program. He told the Carsons in no uncertain terms that unless a specifically Christian prayer were spoken aloud before each meal, McDade Community Action would no longer be able to use church facilities for its program. Believing that the service they were providing was more important than what kind of prayer was said at the lunches, the Carsons acquiesced, though Barbara Carson later characterized this episode as "disenchanting" and "disturbing."[1]

The McDade Community Action lunch program experienced other problems as well. I soon realized that the people who attended the lunches with any regularity represented considerably less than half of McDade's elderly population. Many of the town's seniors, in fact, adamantly refused to have anything to do with McDade Community Action or its hot lunch program. Their reasons varied. Some were put off by the prospect of attending a function at a church not their own, while a few specifically objected to participating in an activity held at the Baptist church. Others considered the lunches "a charity program" intended for poor people, despite the fact that McDade Community Action made it easy for individuals to pay whatever they wished for the lunches, or not pay at all, and remain entirely anonymous about how much, if anything, they had paid. This group stayed away from the hot lunch program out of pride and urged others to do the same. That some of McDade's elderly might have benefited from an inexpensive, or free, hot meal seems not to have been an issue. Others who refused to attend the lunches seemed to do so out of distrust of the program's organizers—David and Barbara Carson, Clyde and Mary Cayton, Kenneth and Catherine Wainscott, and a few others, most of whom had come to McDade within the past several years. Though they could not say how, a number of longtime community residents believed that these "newcomers" stood to benefit from the program, probably at local expense. They also suspected them of having some sort of hidden agenda for the community as a whole, which, given some of the other things that were going on in McDade at the time—things I did not become aware of till later—was no great surprise. Nor did those attending the lunches do so without mixed feelings. While they welcomed the social opportunities the twice-weekly lunches offered, they worried about others in the community perceiving them as accepting charity. In addition, they did not fully trust the program's organizers either; they were essentially strangers, and most of McDade's older people were accustomed to being around people they had known all their lives. With each passing week during the spring of 1984, attendance at the lunches dwindled. By May, fewer than ten people were showing up with any regularity, a turn of events the program's organizers found discouraging. After "temporarily" discontinuing the lunches for the summer, McDade Community Action did not renew the program the following fall.[2]

The distrust with which so many of McDade's seniors regarded the Community Action lunches was one of the first indications I had of how fragmented McDade really was. Over the months, then years, that followed, I slowly came to understand that what I had originally assumed to be a happily unified little town actually consisted of a number of small subcommunities that often had little to do with each other. When they did, there was sometimes conflict. Membership in some of these groups could overlap but frequently did not. In regard to certain issues, McDade's internal divisions could quickly make themselves apparent, and differences of opinion within the community could become quite heated. Some of the dividing lines were obvious; others were not.

Religious affiliation was one of the most clear cut, and thus least controversial, criteria by which people in McDade divided themselves. The community's Baptists, its Lutherans, and members of the McDade Church of Christ each formed their own separate social set in town. Membership in one of these churches did not mean that one refused to socialize with members of the town's other churches, though it sometimes resulted in certain people not coming into contact with certain others. There were also a number of town residents who attended church in surrounding communities:

Presbyterians (most of them "newcomers" to McDade), Methodists, and those Lutherans who preferred the more conservative Missouri Synod brand of Lutheranism drove to Elgin to worship; Seventh Day Adventists and McDade's few Catholics went to church in Bastrop. (In a curious reversal of this trend, a number of African Americans, most of them from Elgin, came to McDade on Sunday mornings to attend services at the all-black Weeping Willow Baptist Church, located on U.S. 290 where Loop 223 connected the highway to uptown. Strangely, John and Rhode Anderson were the only members of Weeping Willow's congregation who lived in McDade.) There were also a number of people in town, most of them middle-aged or younger, who did not go to church at all, and they too formed a distinct social group.

Closely allied with people's religious convictions were their attitudes toward alcohol. This was an issue in McDade precisely because McDade had no bar or tavern. The town's beer drinkers congregated uptown in front of "Sam Earl's," where they could buy beer by the can and carry it out front to drink. These were McDade's self-styled "street people," so called because their impromptu get-togethers could sometimes take over McDade's single uptown street. Most of the street people had been born and raised in McDade, though few of them belonged to any of the town's more established families. Most had jobs in Elgin, Bastrop, or Austin. They ranged in age from twenty-one (occasionally younger) to about fifty. Very few attended church. As long as the weather was not too cold or wet, there were usually at least a few of the street people drinking beer in front of Sam Earl's in the late afternoon or early evening, no matter what day of the week it was. On weekends, their spontaneous gatherings could expand to include thirty or more people, and they sometimes erupted into full-blown parties that lasted late into the night and became quite loud and boisterous. Not surprisingly, those with religiously based objections to alcohol—such as the Seigmunds, devout Baptists who owned the only other business uptown and lived in a mobile home behind their store—despised these open-air drinking parties. Others in town, even if they had no objections to drinking, felt that these uptown beer parties gave McDade a bad name, and they wished they would stop. A number of the newer people in town felt this way.

Ethnicity was another dividing line in McDade, though it usually manifested itself as loyalty to one's own group rather than as hostility toward others. Practically speaking, the only meaningful ethnic distinction in McDade was between those who were of German descent and those who were not. Hispanics and African Americans, significant minorities (often majorities) in many parts of rural Texas, were all but absent from McDade. The few Hispanics in town at any given time during the 1980s were nearly all Mexican nationals in the United States temporarily, and sometimes illegally, to work. For the most part, they were young men who rarely stayed in McDade more than a few months at a time, usually renting one of several run-down mobile homes on the western edge of town. Most of them performed day labor on some of the larger ranches in the area, many of whose owners lived in other parts of the state. They socialized almost exclusively among themselves, rarely had children with them to enroll in the McDade School, and had virtually no influence or impact on the life of the community as a whole. Nor were there enough African Americans in town to constitute a significant subcommunity. Though a number of blacks had lived in McDade before World War II, most had moved away, many to California, in the 1950s. During the latter half of the 1980s, in fact, there were only three African American families in town. Of these, only John and Rhode

Anderson had been in McDade for any length of time. Because there were so few minority residents in McDade, racial matters were not of much concern to the community as a whole. This is not to suggest that some of the town's citizens did not exhibit racist attitudes at times—many of them did—but the kinds of racial tensions that plague many rural communities in the South did not exist within McDade during the 1980s.

It did make a difference, though, if a person was ethnically German. This was especially true if he or she belonged to one of the dozen or so interconnected families descended from the German immigrants who settled the countryside north of McDade in the late nineteenth century. If, a hundred years later, McDade could be said to have an aristocracy, it was this group of families. They formed the core of McDade's Faith Lutheran Church, indeed had founded the church in the 1960s. Most still lived in the country north of town, many of them earning modestly prosperous livings at small-scale farming or ranching. On the whole, they were less religiously conservative than McDade's Baptists or members of the McDade Church of Christ, and most of them had no ingrained antipathy to drinking, dancing, or otherwise letting loose and having fun. Most did not care for the sometimes uproarious antics of McDade's street people, though, even if a few of their number were street people themselves and several others might occasionally be found uptown drinking a beer. Nor did McDade's Germans always agree among themselves. Over the course of years, religious and political differences, family squabbles, and various interpersonal conflicts had all taken a toll on the group's solidarity. Even though many members of McDade's German community were inter-related, attended the same family and social functions, were acquainted with the same people, and knew and shared a common history—or perhaps in part because of these things—they did not all like each other. Most of the time they kept such feelings out of the public eye, but during times of conflict in McDade, old wounds would reopen.

Many of McDade's non-German population also belonged to extended kinship networks. In fact, a considerable portion of the town's social and political life amounted to little more than a complex system of family alliances. At times, this detracted from community cohesiveness by emphasizing loyalty to one's family over the interests of the town at large. Most of McDade's extended families held regularly scheduled annual reunions: the Dungans, for example, always held their reunion on the first Sunday in June. In addition, many families spent Thanksgiving, Christmas, Easter, the weekend of McDade's Watermelon Festival, and various birthdays together, thus giving their members' social lives a predictable year-round regularity. They also provided a social support system, both routinely, as in the case of a family's women sharing child care or its men sharing work, and in times of financial difficulty, sickness, or death. While these family networks usually worked to their members' benefit, they were exclusionary by nature and tended to fragment people's responses to certain issues of concern to the McDade community as a whole. Their importance for so many of the town's residents also meant that those who did not belong to one of McDade's extended family networks led social lives that were markedly separate from the social lives of those who did. This made for two distinct groups of people in McDade, each with a qualitatively different set of assumptions about the basic nature of social interaction. Sometimes these belief systems clashed, causing social misunderstandings that were difficult, if not impossible, to reconcile.

People in McDade also tended to segregate themselves by age and gender. Not only were the town's school children and adolescents often at odds with its adults over the usual matters of authority, but the town's adult population also seemed divided at times between the young, the middle-aged, and the old. Differences of opinion among these groups often surfaced over matters concerning the McDade School—how it should be funded, the level at which it should be funded, how the students should dress and act, who should teach them, and what they should be taught. Gender was also a fundamental dividing line, especially among those who were native to McDade. Almost without exception in this population, women took care of children, home, and food. The fact that many of them also worked full-time jobs outside their homes seemed to have little bearing on their domestic responsibilities. Men were expected to be the family's primary breadwinner (even though many of them were not), to take care of the property and maintain the outside of the house, and to operate and repair machinery. Very rarely did they cook (except, of course, to "burn some meat" over a barbecue pit) or do any kind of housework. McDade's children learned what was expected of them in their separate roles as boys or girls at a very early age.

Probably the most visible, and potentially problematic, division within McDade during the 1980s was the gulf separating those who were native to the area from those who had come to town more recently. A number of new people had come to live in McDade over the past decade, many of them from Austin or Houston. Some bought older houses in town to renovate, though most built new homes on the edge of town or out in the country. Some were retirees, while others were families with young children whose breadwinners commuted to jobs in Austin. In general, these people were more affluent and better educated than the population they were joining. Old and young alike, they had consciously chosen to move to a place where they assumed life would be simpler and less stressful than in the places they had left. Once settled into McDade, however, many of them found their adopted hometown lacking, and several of them set about trying to "improve" it. McDade Community Action, with its hot lunch program, the CPR workshops it sponsored, and its successful campaign to get the county to erect street signs in McDade, was only the most visible example of newcomers to town attempting to remake the community in accordance with their own expectations of how a small town "should" function. They also tried to revitalize ("take over," some said) the McDade Historical Society, become active in the Watermelon Festival, and be elected to the McDade Independent School District's Board of Trustees.

Not surprisingly, they ruffled a lot of local feathers in the process. Most of McDade's longtime residents did not see anything wrong with their hometown, except possibly the presence of many new people who seemed to think it inferior. Why, many of the town's old-timers wondered, had these people come to McDade in the first place if they thought it in such bad shape? Other local people, perhaps willing to admit that McDade could stand some improvement, were offended by what they perceived as a high-handed, superior attitude on the part of many of the newcomers. They seemed to be trying to change the community without bothering to find out what the native population thought and appeared to consider themselves, with their broader experience of the contemporary world, their more extensive educations, and their generally greater sophistication, as the only group in town capable of "saving" McDade. This, of course, caused resentment among the town's old-timers and made many of them doubt whether the "improvements" the newer people sought were really in the best interests of the community as a whole. Some suspected the newcomers of having a "secret agenda" for McDade that might not be good for, and indeed might harm, others in town. At best, many of the old-timers saw the newcomers, especially those who had retired to McDade, as "do-gooders" with too much time and money on their hands and nothing better to do than stick their noses into other people's business. (On the other side of the coin, of course, those newcomers who kept to themselves were often dismissed as snobbish and criticized for not getting involved in community affairs.) The arrival of so many new people in McDade during the late 1970s and early 1980s represented a considerable infusion of talent, energy, and money into the area. Unfortunately, much of what the new people had to offer went to waste, either rejected out-of-hand by obstinate old-timers who felt themselves insulted, or dissipated by the strain of repeated conflict. The gulf between newcomers and natives in McDade was undoubtedly the most potentially explosive of the town's divisions, capable of polarizing opinion throughout the community and often dividing McDade's various subcommunities among themselves. Tensions that were in part the result of this split caused open and bitter conflict in McDade during 1986 and 1987.

I don't mean to characterize McDade as an unusually contentious place. In general, it was probably no more or less so than most other small communities, which, by their very nature, are places where people's long-standing familiarity with each other can sometimes become a source of friction. More specifically, McDade underwent a crisis in the mid-1980s, a complex series of events that led to considerably more turmoil in town than was normal. As is often the case in small communities beset by internal conflict, McDade's crisis magnified the differences that already existed among its citizens. But civic crises are a normal part of small-town life. All communities go through them at one time or another, and, inevitably, each town's preexisting factions choose opposing sides, thus incorporating the specifics of their crisis into the more general circumstances that constitute the larger, longer-standing differences between them. McDade was not, therefore, unusual in this regard either.

What does set the town apart, at least for present purposes, is that its crisis came to a head during the time that I was a frequent visitor to town and could take the time to observe McDade's difficulties, ask questions about them, think about them, research their background, and later write about them. Some of my more naive expectations about small-town life to the contrary, I discovered that the people of McDade were no more (or less) altruistic or noble in the midst of crisis than most other modern-day Americans. Many of the people who lived there were among the finest people a person could ever want to know, and some were distinctly otherwise; most, of course, fell somewhere in between. But observations such as these are overly general, too vague to be either interesting or useful. The real story lies in the specifics.

By the summer of 1984, I had been visiting McDade long enough to be looking forward to my first Watermelon Festival with great anticipation. I was sure the weekend's slate of activities would offer some excellent opportunities for picture-taking as well as a chance to observe the community consciously trying to function as a whole. The 1984 festival was the first of six Watermelon Festivals I attended in McDade. If I had known what to look for that first year, I probably could have witnessed most of the town's factional rivalries at work, both during the festival itself and during the weeks of preparation leading up to it. As chance would have it, though, a single controversy dominated the festival that year, and this tended to obscure most of McDade's other internal differences, at least to my untrained eye. The conflict arose out of the Watermelon Festival Association's decision to hold a Friday night street dance, an event at which beer would be sold, as part of the 1984 festival. The very thought of a dance in McDade scandalized some people in town, and a number of others had serious doubts about the wisdom of allowing the Watermelon Festival to sponsor an event that would probably end up as a gigantic beer bash. This was a dispute obvious enough even for me to notice and understand, or so I thought at the time.

The Watermelon Festival had never sponsored a dance before. In fact, no one in town could remember a public dance ever being held in McDade for any reason. Not surprisingly, there was opposition from the start. Much of it came from people who objected to dancing and drinking on religious grounds—some of McDade's Baptists, a few members of the Church of Christ, and others. After unsuccessfully trying to block the Watermelon Festival Association's application for a license to sell beer at the dance, Reverend Clifton Franks of the McDade Baptist Church urged his congregation to boycott the festival, both by withholding their volunteer energies (traditionally, nearly everyone in town worked on the Watermelon Festival in some capacity) and by refusing to attend any of its functions. To his displeasure, however, few among his congregation were willing to withdraw from the festival entirely. Most refused to have anything to do with the dance, but they did not let the dance prevent them from participating in their usual festival activities. This was something of a shock to Reverend Franks. Having only been in town a couple of years, he had not yet learned that in McDade tradition was sometimes an even more powerful force than religion. This was especially true in regard to the town's Watermelon Festival.

Which was precisely why so many other people in town had doubts about holding a dance—it broke with almost forty years' worth of hard and fast tradition. Prior to 1984 (and with the exception of the first Watermelon Festival), official festival activities had always been confined to Saturday. The festival would get underway in the morning with a panel of judges choosing a "Grand Champion" watermelon, a "Reserve Grand Champion," several runners-up , and a dozen or so honorable mentions from among a large selection of melons submitted by local growers. An "old-time" country string band, in recent years a group from Bastrop called the Country Cousins, usually provided musical accompaniment for the melon judging. Many of McDade's older people enjoyed the traditional, mostly religious, music they played, and they would sometimes sing along, though no one ever dared dance. Saturday afternoon's slate of activities would include a parade through uptown that would end up at the school; games, crafts, carnival rides, and several hours visiting at the school grounds; and a barbecue supper served in the school cafeteria. After people had eaten, the prize melons were auctioned off, usually to the owners of businesses in neighboring communities for whom spending several hundred dollars on one of McDade's prize watermelons was an effective, and tax-deductible, form of advertising. There was also a smaller auction of donated local handicrafts—quilts, crocheted afghans, and the like. After sunset, the coronation ceremony to install McDade's new Watermelon queens got underway. Many of the town's children had parts in this elaborate ceremony, entertaining the audience—most of the town plus numerous out-of-town friends and relatives—with songs, cute little skits, and a sizable dose of pomp and circumstance. In many ways, the coronation was the climactic event of the entire festival, its never-varying rituals perhaps assuring the McDade community that its traditions were alive and well, tying present to past and promising to continue doing so in the future. After the coronation, the festival concluded with a free, "all-you-can-eat" watermelon feast that sent everyone home overly full of watermelon but generally relieved that the festival was over for another year.

The Friday night of Watermelon Festival weekend had always been reserved to prepare for Saturday's busy slate of activities: erecting game booths, craft booths, and carnival rides on the school grounds; preparing much of the food for the next evening's dinner; and rehearsing many of the town's children for their parts in the coronation ceremony. Thus, in addition to their misgivings about sponsoring an enormous beer blast uptown, many people involved with the Watermelon Festival feared that a Friday night dance would siphon off too much of the work force needed to prepare everything for Saturday. The dance might also mean a shortage of children available to participate in the queens' coronation, which threatened to rob the ceremony of much of what the town's more traditionally minded found most appealing about it—the participation of nearly an entire generation of McDade's children. On top of that, many of the community's older people viewed the Friday night of Watermelon Festival weekend as a time to socialize with family or old friends who had left McDade but always returned each year for the Watermelon Festival. Many in town feared that a Friday night dance might interfere with these kinds of informal "homecoming" activities.

But the 1984 Watermelon Festival Association decided to proceed with the dance. The tension was palpable in McDade late that Friday afternoon and early evening. The split between those in favor of the dance and those who opposed it was obvious. While the former were uptown getting ready for the big night ahead—putting up fences so they could charge admission, setting up tables and chairs, icing down cases and cases of beer—a smaller group of people was at the school trying to get ready for Saturday. Among the tasks that faced them were peeling and boiling hundreds of pounds of potatoes and then mixing the potato salad, running power lines to various spots around the school yard, building temporary game and craft booths, and watching the children who were there to rehearse the coronation ceremony. Naturally, many of the children wanted to be anywhere other than where they were, especially uptown at the dance. Those working at the school that evening were not as cheerful as the people uptown. In previous years, many more volunteers had been available to perform these jobs, but the dance had drastically reduced their number this year, and those volunteering at the school found themselves having to work longer and harder than ever before to get everything done.

Despite people's misgivings, the dance went on as planned and was an unqualified success. Almost a thousand people paid five dollars apiece to dance on McDade's lone uptown street. A country-and-western band popular among young people in central Texas provided the music, and they kept the crowd up and dancing from the moment they started playing. Despite consuming tremendous amounts of beer, people stayed friendly, and the alcohol-induced fights predicted by dance opponents never materialized, in part because the Watermelon Festival's Dance Committee had recruited several of the town's most imposing men to roam the crowd and act as peacemakers. Nor were there any automobile accidents or arrests for drunken driving afterward, as many had feared. The dance was a financial success as well, clearing almost seven thousand dollars. In fact, only the proceeds from the dance prevented the 1984 Watermelon Festival from losing money. As a result, there was only token resistance to holding a second dance in 1985, and every Watermelon Festival since has included a Friday night street dance which invariably earns the bulk of the festival's profits. In short, financial success has quickly made the dance a Watermelon Festival tradition in its own right. Although a few people in the community voice opposition every year, no one involved with the festival ever seriously considers the possibility of not holding a dance any longer.

Several of McDade's newer residents were instrumental in organizing the first street dance and making it happen. Some members of the Watermelon Festival Association's Board of Directors had been suggesting that the festival hold a dance for years, but they had never been able to overcome the objections of their more conservative neighbors. Nor had they been willing to force the issue. In 1983, the Watermelon Festival had come close to dying; each of its first two meetings that year failed to attract enough people even to elect officers. The following year, some of the town's newcomers got together and, in David Carson's words, "agreed to take [the festival] over." At a meeting in January 1984, Nelson Page was elected president; Laura Maness, vice president; Catherine Wainscott, secretary; and David Carson, treasurer. Only Carson encountered much resistance, narrowly winning out over Henry Grimes, a popular figure in McDade who had served as the festival's treasurer for the past several years. His victory over Grimes, Carson believes, left many people in town "shocked and dismayed" and caused a certain amount of lasting resentment.[3]

The new officers were less sensitive than their predecessors about offending some of their fellow citizens. They encouraged the formation of a dance committee to look into holding a dance and later persuaded the festival board to give the dance its approval. Laura Maness and Clyde Cayton personally shepherded the festival's application for a liquor license through Bastrop County's antiquated bureaucracy, despite encountering resistance from individuals in county government who disapproved of both alcohol and the kind of people who seemed to have taken over McDade's Watermelon Festival. The new officers also knew when (and to whom) to delegate responsibility. They supported those on the dance committee, most of them native to McDade and thus familiar with local preferences, who wanted to risk the money necessary to hire a band with a following, even though they would have to book this band, and pay a sizable deposit, well in advance. Hiring such an expensive band was a gamble, but it paid off. People from all over central Texas attended McDade's first street dance, many of them on the strength of the band's reputation. Much of the dance's success, therefore, was the result of an alliance between newcomers to McDade and the younger generation of local natives, many of them "street people." It was an unlikely alliance, combining the newcomers' organizational abilities and their willingness to sometimes step on toes with the local savvy of some of the town's younger old-timers. In making the first street dance a reality and by providing the Watermelon Festival with a reliable way to turn a substantial profit for years to come, they had accomplished something of lasting importance in McDade. Unfortunately, the alliance itself did not last; almost immediately after the 1984 Watermelon Festival the two groups parted political company. Over the next few years, they opposed each other on several issues of importance to the community, a rivalry that ended only with the eventual disintegration of the newcomers' power bloc into rival subgroups.[4]

The group of newcomers who "took over" the 1984 Watermelon Festival had begun to arrive in McDade in the late 1970s, many of them in search of the peace and quiet they assumed were a routine part of rural life. As noted earlier, the majority had come from cities or suburbs and were better educated and more affluent than most of those who had grown up locally. McDade's old-timers perceived them as "city people" rather than as "country people," an important distinction in places like McDade. At best, the recent arrivals to the area represented a new, unknown quantity in the community, and this alone was more than enough to unsettle some people in town. One long-time resident expressed her anxiety this way: "At one time you could just think in your mind and go down the road from house to house, [and] you could name everybody in McDade. You can't hardly do that anymore. It scares me. It doesn't seem right." Others saw the newcomers as a threat to the local way of life. They seemed rootless, unconcerned with local traditions, and heedless of their neighbors. Their increasing involvement in public affairs also seemed to indicate they had discovered some things they did not like about McDade and that they were going to try to change them. While the newcomers might argue that they had brought new talents and areas of expertise to the community and were simply putting them to work for its betterment, many of McDade's old-timers believed they were consciously scheming to take the town over.[5]

McDade's newcomers tried to get involved in more than just the Watermelon Festival in 1983 and 1984, though none of these other early ventures into public affairs met with as much success. In December 1983, Laura Maness and Barbara Carson tried to revive interest in the moribund McDade Historical Society by organizing a Christmas tea, complete with formal silver tea service, in uptown McDade's old Rockfront Saloon building. This building, which the society had owned since 1964, had housed several museum-style displays over the years but had not been open to the public for some time. Carson and Maness spent most of a week cleaning it, hauling out "truckloads" of accumulated trash, dust, and dirt. The tea was a success, attracting people from throughout the area and adding several hundred dollars to the society's depleted bank account. On the strength of that success, Laura Maness announced that she wanted to be the next president of the McDade Historical Society, claiming that the organization had not "serv[ed] any purpose" or "ma[de] any contribution to the community" for years, primarily because there had been "no real leadership." She would devote herself full time to "get[ting] things moving again," she promised. To her surprise, this announcement elicited howls of angry protest from many of McDade's long-time residents. They saw it as a public insult to Jewell Hudler, the elderly spinster who had been president of the historical society since its inception. They reelected Hudler overwhelmingly, some people in town joining as dues-paying members of the society for the first time just so they could vote for her. In retrospect, Laura believes that she acted "arrogantly, . . . like I came riding up on a white horse," but at the time she thought people would see the benefits of a newly active historical society and vote her in despite the fact that she was relatively new in town. Speaking so bluntly, and so openly, about another person's failings, however, was too great a breach of local etiquette. It was something one just did not do. In their support of Jewell Hudler, McDade's old-timers showed that they would rather have an inactive historical society than insult one of their own. They certainly didn't want their historical society run by someone with so little sense of what was right and proper.[6]

Some of the others who had come to town in recent years thought they could help the community on a broader front. In January 1984, only two weeks after the Watermelon Festival Association had elected Nelson Page, Laura Maness, Catherine Wainscott, and David Carson as its officers, David and Barbara Carson and Kenneth and Catherine Wainscott announced the formation of McDade Community Action, Inc., "a non-profit service organization . . . chartered to serve the community needs." Over the next year or so, this group sponsored the previously mentioned senior lunches at the Baptist Fellowship Hall, distributed government-surplus cheese and butter in McDade, organized several CPR workshops, persuaded the county to put up street signs in town, and published "The Town Crier," a photocopied monthly newsletter. Their future plans included a holiday "Tour of Homes Quilt Show," an autumn arts and craft fair, and a summer recreation program for young people. After a promising start, their projects bogged down: Attendance at the lunches dwindled; few people in town would accept the cheese and butter the organization was giving away; and many of the new street signs were vandalized or stolen shortly after county workers put them up. By early 1985, McDade Community Action was more or less defunct, having been ignored out of existence by most of the rest of the community. Recalling the experience five years later, Barbara Carson felt that she and the others behind McDade Community Action had been "too visible, just too assertive. . . . We weren't clever enough to stay in the background so somebody else could get the credit and be the visible ones." Her husband, David, thought the blame lay elsewhere, believing that many of the town's old-timers waged had "an active campaign against" McDade Community Action, more or less squelching any chance that its programs might succeed.[7]

The newcomers' greatest impact on McDade, however, came through their involvement with the town's school. They had begun to concern themselves with the McDade School in the late 1970s and have continued to do so ever since. Their influence was at its peak, however, between 1983 and 1987, at which point it abruptly diminished, the consequence of a protracted struggle for power between Superintendent and Principal Thomas Baca and various members of the McDade Independent School District's Board of Trustees. This was a dispute rooted in problems with school accreditation and finances dating back to the late 1970s and a 1983 controversy over local property taxes. Several of the town's newcomers played prominent roles in this conflict, as did a number of old-timers, though they were not always on opposing sides, especially in its later stages. One consequence of the controversy was the near dissolution of the McDade Independent School District. Another was the creation of a bitter divisiveness in the community that has yet to fully heal. In a general sense, the struggle was between conflicting visions of McDade—one shared by many of the newer people in town, the other by a good portion of its longtime residents. It would be inaccurate, however, to portray McDade's school controversies of the 1980s primarily as the result of ill will between newcomers and old-timers. Actual events, and the reasons behind them, were far more complicated. Most of the new people in McDade did tend to line up on one side of the fence, at least at first, and most of the old-timers on the other, but there were significant exceptions on both sides from the start. Both sides also experienced defections to the other, as the lengthy, convoluted dispute wore on and gave birth to new alliances and counter-alliances. In fact, the conflict eventually became so drawn out and virulent that by the time it culminated in late 1987 many of McDade's traditional dividing lines had blurred. New factions had developed, and events of the previous four years had provided local citizens with plenty of fuel to keep the fires of personal resentment burning. In short, while the controversies of 1983 and 1986–87 may have determined the immediate future of McDade's school, they also affected the feelings of many in the community toward their neighbors, in some cases even toward family members. All too often, these feelings were hostile, the result of nearly everyone in town having chosen sides in the school dispute.

In 1977, faced with the possible loss of school accreditation if it refused to do so, the McDade Independent School District (ISD) had agreed to a five-year plan proposed by the Texas Education Agency to better the quality of education in McDade. In part, this plan mandated that certain physical improvements, including the construction of a gymnasium, be completed by 1982. In 1980, voters in McDade overwhelmingly rejected a three hundred thousand-dollar bond issue the school board had hoped would finance a combined cafeteria/half-gymnasium and several new classrooms. This left the board little choice but to borrow money to build the required gym, so in 1981 the district secured a loan from the Elgin Bank of Texas. The terms of this note obligated the district to loan payments of approximately thirty-six thousand dollar per year over the next five years. These payments, in combination with a state-mandated increase in teachers' salaries, a hike in the tuition Lexington and Elgin charged McDade for its older students to attend secondary schools in their districts, and a serious overestimation of the previous year's property tax revenues, led to a community crisis late in the summer of 1983, when the school board submitted a budget about 30 percent larger than the previous year's and called for an increase in the local property tax rate that amounted to more than 40 percent.[8]

Partially in protest, partially hoping to find alternatives to the new higher tax rate, local property owners held a public meeting in the school gymnasium on August 30. Superintendent and Principal Thomas Baca, plus several members of the school board, were present to explain and defend the new budget. According to Baca, most of the new expenditures were unavoidable. The district had no choice, he told the gathered crowd, but to make its loan payments, give the teachers their raises, pay tuition for its seventh- through twelfth-graders, and make up the previous year's shortfall in tax revenue. This was not what many of those in attendance wanted to hear. McDade was already spending too much on its school, some believed, pointing out that the district's per student expenditure for the previous year was almost a thousand dollars above the state average. Under the newly proposed budget, that figure would rise to almost twice the state average and become one of the highest in all of Texas. Others at the meeting were concerned about the fairness of local tax assessment. Several people who had come to the area in recent years, especially those who had built new homes, thought their property had been appraised at greater value than comparable properties owned by people who were native to McDade. They seemed to believe that the county tax assessor, a personal friend of Superintendent Baca's, had singled them out for unfair treatment. Some people felt that it was time to do away with the McDade ISD altogether; such a tiny district, consisting of a single elementary school that served fewer than a hundred students, was a modern-day anomaly, they claimed, woefully inefficient and expensive to maintain. McDade would be better off, they argued, consolidating its school district with Elgin's or Bastrop's. In fact, a few among those unhappy with their tax bills had already looked into consolidation, having informally approached the school boards in both Elgin and Bastrop. The president of Elgin's board had reacted favorably, saying that consolidation would probably result in lower taxes for property owners in both communities. He was careful to point out, though, that his comments were unofficial. Before any official discussions of consolidation could begin, he said, the McDade School Board would have to formally request that the Elgin School Board consider such a move.[9]

Two separate, though related, initiatives came out of the August 30 meeting. One was the formation of a committee, subsequently named the "Ad Hoc Committee," whose stated goal was to reduce local property taxes by any means necessary, which most people in town took to mean closing the McDade School. This committee was composed of David Carson, Buddy Hendricks, Margaret Hobbs, Travis McPhaul, and George Seigmund, none of whom had found Thomas Baca's explanation of the new school budget satisfactory. All but McPhaul had come to McDade within the past decade. The committee had no designated chairman, but David Carson was most often its spokesman. Though its members stopped short of saying so in public, there is little doubt that closing the McDade School was the Ad Hoc Committee's aim. Both its supporters and detractors sometimes called it the Padlock Committee, and some committee members had been among the group that had approached Elgin and Bastrop about consolidation. In the aftermath of the August 30 taxpayers meeting, the Ad Hoc Committee urged the McDade School Board to formally approach the Elgin ISD about consolidation, if only to get the process started and keep McDade's future options open. This led to considerable tension in the community. Though no one in town wanted to pay more taxes, many people were adamantly opposed to shutting down the school. Some made the issue a personal one, angrily denouncing anyone who seemed willing to even consider such a course of action.[10]

Another result of the August 30 meeting was a joint effort on the part of many district taxpayers to update and correct the official tax roll. The district's net tax valuation had declined over the past year, dropping from about $13.5 million to $12.5 million, a decrease many in the community could not understand and found difficult to accept. In addition, approximately $26.7 million worth of property was tax-exempt, $19 million of it because its owners had been granted agricultural exemptions. These figures led some in town to question the accuracy of the district's official tax roll and the propriety of some of the exemptions. At a September 19 meeting of the school board, board members and several local property owners sat down with maps, recent aerial photographs, and the tax roll to see if they could find discrepancies. In just a few hours, they discovered "numerous errors." As a result, several such sessions followed over the next few weeks. These sessions were open to anyone who owned property within the boundaries of the McDade ISD. "We used to sit here till after midnight going over that tax roll, making sure that we were getting every dollar that we could," Thomas Baca remembers. "We just got the tax roll on the table and got around in a circle and worked on it." People were shocked by the tax roll's numerous inaccuracies. Clyde Cayton recalls "many, many pieces of property . . . that had had improvements on [them] that had been there for years and [whose owners] had never paid any taxes on [them]. A lot of property wasn't on the tax rolls at all, for that matter." Laura Maness concurs: "People weren't even paying taxes, people that had been living out here for years, their houses were not even being taxed, and people that had agricultural property that wasn't being used for agricultural purposes were paying no taxes, whereas we had people moving in that were paying gigantic taxes." The consensus of opinion was that the district needed to update its tax roll, correct the many long-standing errors the tax roll contained, and balance out its numerous inequities. Some in the community even harbored the hope that "if we straightened up the act, and everybody got their property on the tax roll and everyone paid according to what the use was, that taxes would go down, that it might take a couple years of transition but that when everybody paid their share there would be more money in the kitty. . . . Some people would pay more taxes, some people would pay less, but as a group we would have more revenues." This initiative was supported by newcomers and old-timers alike; some thought they would benefit from a more accurate tax roll, while others saw it as the best chance for McDade to keep its school. A few, shocked at how many mistakes had been found in the old tax roll, felt it needed to be revamped simply as a matter of fairness. Those who wanted to put a major effort into updating and equalizing the tax roll found themselves opposed, however, by the Ad Hoc Committee and its supporters, who, though they agreed that the current tax roll was unfair, saw the move to overhaul it as a smoke screen, a last-ditch attempt to save the McDade ISD from having to consolidate with Elgin. The committee's supporters also counted both newcomers and old-timers among their number.[11]

Updating the tax roll located about eight hundred thousand dollars worth of previously untaxed property. It also resulted in the reappraisal of many properties, usually at higher valuation. In addition, the very process of poring over maps and discussing individual pieces of property led the school board to question whether some of the agricultural exemptions in the district were justified. Whether by coincidence or design, these actions resulted in substantially higher tax bills for all five members of the Ad Hoc Committee. The homes of two committee members were discovered not to have been on the tax roll at all. ("Some of the people that hollered the loudest when taxes went up were some that had not had their property on the tax roll to start with," was one observer's wry comment.) A third member of the committee saw the valuation of his home more than double. In addition, out of the seven agricultural exemptions in the district that the McDade School Board ended up challenging—and, once challenged, the exemptions were immediately removed, the burden of proof in such matters lying with the property owner—three had been for land owned by Ad Hoc Committee members.[12]

At this point the whole controversy became openly personal, often nastily so. More than five years later, David Carson continued to maintain that Thomas Baca engineered the 1983 overhaul of the tax roll as a way of punishing those in the forefront of the move to close down the McDade School, both by making sure the tax appraiser's assessment of their property went up and by seeing to it that the county tax office challenged their agricultural exemptions. Furthermore, according to Carson, the tax roll was updated "selectively," the homes of several Baca supporters continuing to be listed at far below their real value and significant improvements to several of their properties ignored. He also claimed that no one who publicly supported keeping the McDade School open had an agricultural exemption questioned. In Carson's opinion, Baca had been running the McDade ISD as though it were his own personal "fiefdom" for years, and, when the Ad Hoc Committee challenged his authority in 1983, he responded by punishing his enemies and rewarding his friends.[13]

Thomas Baca admits suggesting that the county tax appraisal office "check out" certain properties but denies there was anything improper in his doing so. From his point of view, making sure that the McDade ISD got every tax dollar it was entitled to was part of his job as superintendent, and many in the community agreed with him, whether their taxes turned out to be higher or not. Nor, Baca claims, had he played favorites. All he had done was provide the tax assessor with a list of properties that the process of comparing the tax roll with maps and photographs had indicated might be questionable. The list included properties owned by many local residents, David Carson and other members of the Ad Hoc Committee among them. "Things that were questionable, like [David Carson's agricultural exemption], we let the appraisal district do the questioning. . . . Of course, when they went out there, there wasn't any [agricultural activity] out there. And that started it off, and of course David says, 'Thomas Baca sent them out.' Well, I brought the names down there, but they were from a board meeting, and it was a public meeting. Anybody could have sat in that night. . . . There has never been a personal vendetta out to get someone over taxes, . . . but a lot of people took it personally."[14]

Feelings were running high when the school board met early in October to vote on the proposed new budget and tax rate increase. The gym was packed that night, with the crowd overwhelmingly in favor of accepting Thomas Baca's recommendations and opposed to any suggestion of consolidation. Rancher Merle Rother summarized the sentiments of many in the crowd in two sentences: "A lot of people have lived here all their lives, and they intend to live here the rest of their lives. They certainly don't want to do away with their school." Others expressed anger at the Ad Hoc Committee's apparent desire to shut down the school, verbally attacking individual committee members and their supporters. When Travis McPhaul tried to explain that the committee did not necessarily want to close the school but just wanted the board to look into consolidation as one of several possible options for the future, few in the crowd believed him, and he was shouted down. The weight of public opinion was obviously against the Ad Hoc Committee, and the board voted accordingly, accepting the proposed new budget and tax rate. The meeting ended with David Carson promising that the Ad Hoc Committee would investigate Thomas Baca's "excessive salary" and Travis McPhaul predicting that there would be changes on the school board after April's elections.[15]

The first round of open hostilities had thus concluded with a victory for those who wanted the McDade School to continue operating as it had in the past. The war was not over, though, and battle lines remained drawn. On one side stood the Ad Hoc Committee and its supporters. These people believed that for McDade to continue maintaining a separate school district that consisted of a single elementary school serving fewer than a hundred children was a luxury local residents could no longer afford. They feared that running the school would become more costly each year and would eventually bleed the town dry, themselves along with it. In addition, many among this group felt that Thomas Baca, the school board, and the county tax office had treated them unfairly, further evidence in their minds that the McDade ISD should be eliminated. Generally speaking, those opposed to keeping the school open were people who had come from other places to retire in McDade, plus a good portion of the town's native elderly, many of whom accepted at face value the Ad Hoc Committee's claim that consolidation with Elgin would substantially reduce their taxes.

On the other side were those convinced that McDade needed to keep its school open and operating at all costs. Many perceived this as a matter of community survival. Whether they had school-age children or not, these people saw the school as the town's most vital institution, its only consistent, year-round point of focus. From this point of view, to eliminate the school would be to remove the town's center, the hub of much of its communal social activity, its very heart. If McDade lost its school, they believed, the town's sense of itself as a living, active community would soon atrophy and die. Many were also offended by what they saw as hypocrisy on the part of the Ad Hoc Committee and some of its supporters. Given the fact that none of the committee's members had

been paying as much in taxes as the newly updated tax roll indicated they should, school supporters were appalled that they had dared criticize the school for costing more to run than residents of
the district could afford to pay. They saw the attempt to eliminate the school by people who had not
been paying their full share as uncaring and manipulative, and many of them took it as a personal
insult. Supporters of keeping the school in McDade included most of the families in town that had
children, regardless of how long they had lived in the area. The majority of the community's older
people with school-age grandchildren or great-grandchildren in town also backed the school, as did
most of McDade's German families. Unfortunately, problems that no one could foresee would eventually split this coalition and turn many of its members angrily against each other.

Once the school board voted to accept the proposed new budget and higher tax rate, controversy over the school receded into the background, at least temporarily. In hindsight, it's obvious
that the relative lack of public debate over this issue during most of 1984 and 1985 was misleading.
Important issues concerning the McDade School remained unresolved, especially in the minds of
those who felt the town should not have to support a school. This quieter, less contentious McDade
was the McDade I first visited in February 1984. A major political confrontation had just ended, and
its losers had withdrawn to lick their wounds, plan new strategies, and involve themselves in other
areas of community life. I had little sense of what the town had just been through or that such deeply
divisive feelings existed just beneath its surface. This was also the McDade in which four newcomers, including David Carson, had just assumed top positions in the Watermelon Festival; Laura
Maness and Barbara Carson had recently put on a successful fund-raising tea for the historical society; and the Carsons, along with several others, had just chartered McDade Community Action. All
this activity may have served to camouflage the quieter, more patient tactics the Ad Hoc Committee
and its supporters were prepared to adopt in regard to the school issue. It certainly obscured the
intensity of the dispute over the school—even the fact that such a dispute had occurred—from me.
The conflicts I became aware of during my first year in McDade centered around the senior citizen
lunch program and the Watermelon Festival dance, and I had no idea that funding the community's
school and keeping it open had been recent sources of controversy in McDade.

As Travis McPhaul had promised, members of the Ad Hoc Committee ran for the two positions (out of seven) on the McDade School Board scheduled to be filled in the April 1984 elections.
McPhaul himself narrowly defeated incumbent Doug Pierce (with Laura Maness running a distant
third) for one place, while David Carson lost a close race to Franklin Pohler, a strong supporter of
keeping the school in McDade, for the other. McPhaul received only twenty-two more votes than
Carson polled in his losing effort, a difference probably due to the fact that McPhaul had been born
and raised in McDade. All told, 260 votes were cast in the McPhaul-Pierce-Maness contest, and 248
in the Pohler-Carson race. A year earlier, seventeen votes had been enough to win a seat on the
McDade School Board. Obviously, both sides had made an effort to get out the vote, and members
of the Ad Hoc Committee had done surprisingly well. Their success seems to have stemmed less
from the belief that they would try to close the school than from their ability to convince people
that Thomas Baca was a poor administrator and that the McDade School, as run by Baca, was wast-
ing local tax dollars. Indeed, they had little to say about closing the school as they campaigned for
school board seats, though most people in town assumed that was still one of their priorities. By

and large, the support they received in the school board elections of 1984, 1985, and 1986 came from people who had no direct interest in the McDade School other than wanting to minimize the cost of running it. They got votes from among the town's elderly, from among the sizable portion of the district's rural residents who had no ties to the McDade community, and from individuals who, for one reason or another, disliked Thomas Baca. This was a coalition that during the mid-1980s usually amounted to about half of McDade's voting public. In general, they believed McDade needed to run its school less expensively, though many of them did not want to see the school closed.[16]

Ad Hoc Committee member Buddy Hendricks won one of the two open places on the school board in 1985, and in 1986 David Carson and two committee supporters, Gary Owen and Lloyd Magnuson, won all three available seats. This gave supporters of the Ad Hoc Committee a five-to-two majority on the McDade School Board, and the newly constituted board elected David Carson its president. Rather than signifying a widespread public desire to see the school closed, the election of people associated with the Ad Hoc Committee to the school board seemed to reflect a growing uncertainty in McDade about how effectively the old school board and Thomas Baca had been running the school. There were several reasons for this. In May 1984, the district had been denied a twenty-one thousand-dollar federal grant it had expected to receive, primarily because many of the McDade students designated to be served by the program were not properly documented as being eligible. Justifiably or not, some in the community saw this as evidence of administrative incompetence. The following year, the school board made itself look bad when it voted to switch McDade's official "receiving district" (the district to which McDade would provide free school bus transportation for its secondary school students) from Lexington to Elgin, but then, under pressure from several angry parents, reversed itself just a few weeks later and once again designated Lexington as the receiving district. An arrangement was eventually worked out whereby McDade students would receive free bus transportation to Elgin as well, but the brief controversy had made the school board seem indecisive and unable to withstand public pressure. In addition, there were rumors circulating that Thomas Baca had occasionally gone overboard in his administration of corporal punishment, still a common (and officially approved) form of discipline in rural Texas schools. These rumors were vague and unsubstantiated; they may well have been planted to further community dissatisfaction with Baca's administration of the school. Baca was also criticized for living in Austin instead of McDade, an indication, some said, that he did not care enough about McDade to have the best interests of its children at heart.[17]

After April 1986, with the new school board in place, Thomas Baca's days as superintendent of the McDade ISD and principal of its school seemed numbered. Some of his detractors urged his immediate dismissal, but the majority of the school board members feared a lawsuit if they were to terminate him without specific cause. Instead, they embarked on a course of action apparently designed to make him resign. The new board's first action was to call a public meeting to discuss corporal punishment in the school. Since no one had any specific complaints to voice, the main purpose of this meeting seems to have been to publicly embarrass Thomas Baca and put him on the defensive. Looking back on 1986 and the early part of 1987, Baca remembers being "constantly harassed" by members of the school board, especially David Carson. As board president, Carson sometimes called as many as four meetings a month, rather than the more customary one or two.

According to Baca, several of these extra meetings were called for no other reason than to reconsider questions Carson had not gotten his way on earlier. Others turned into open critiques of Baca's handling of school affairs, with the public invited, in Baca's words, to "take shots at the superintendent." Some were scheduled for weekends, making them especially inconvenient for Baca, who had to travel from Austin. In addition, the new board began scrutinizing his day-to-day management of the school, questioning such matters as the design of the school's stationery (on which Baca's name was printed in larger type than those of board members) and the quantities and kinds of supplies allotted to various teachers. The board also demanded that Baca perform numerous small tasks that, in his opinion, were little more than "busy work," the only purpose of which, as far as he could tell, was to frustrate and annoy him. At the same time, heralding its commitment to reducing "the highest tax rate in Bastrop County," the school board proposed "a frugal budget" for 1987, which called for a substantial pay cut for all administrative personnel, which in McDade meant precisely two people—Thomas Baca and Angie Kanak, the district's bookkeeper and office manager. Baca recalls virtually no discussion of educational matters at board meetings during this time, leading him to conclude that the majority of the school board members were more interested in "screwing operations up" than in educating the town's children. Many in the community saw the board's actions as a calculated strategy to make Thomas Baca resign, and nearly everyone believed—some hopefully, others fearfully—that Baca's resignation would move the McDade ISD toward consolidation with Elgin.[18]

But Baca refused to resign. Finally, in the latter part of February, just a few days before March 1, when his annual contract would automatically renew itself for another year, the school board terminated him, voting to neither renew his old contract nor offer him a new one. By waiting until the last possible moment, this amounted to firing him, but by doing so before the March 1 deadline the board avoided much of its responsibility for showing cause. Baca threatened suit anyway, and attorneys for the two sides met and negotiated a severance settlement totaling half his yearly salary. At this point, Baca seemed resigned to leaving. Once his severance settlement was finalized, he told the *Elgin Courier* that he was "not complaining. . . . I had grounds to put up a heck of a fight, but I agreed not to pursue legal channels if we could work something out, which we did." He then turned most of his attention to winding up his affairs in McDade and trying to find another job.[19]

Much of the rest of McDade, however, reacted angrily, for reasons that varied from person to person. Many thought the school board had mistreated Thomas Baca, dismissing him without good cause and conducting itself less than honorably in the process. Some local residents, especially those who were native to McDade or otherwise had reason to care about the town's reputation, found this disturbing. It reflected badly on the entire community, they felt, making the people of McDade seem petty and vindictive. Others were disgusted that a supposedly cost-conscious school board had been willing to spend more than twenty-five thousand dollars to terminate a longtime employee for reasons that seemed more personal than professional. Some believed the majority of the school board had placed their own private concerns above the educational needs of the town's children. Those convinced that keeping the school open was essential to McDade's survival as a community saw Baca's dismissal as a threat to the town's future, because it increased the power of a school board whose majority, they believed, still thought that McDade would be better off without having to support a school. One thing those unhappy with the school board's termination of Baca could all agree on, however, was that the board had acted counter to the desires of the community as a whole and probably counter to its best interests as well. This provided opponents of the school board majority an issue they could unite around, allowing them to forget the various differences of opinion that had kept them apart in the past.[20]

Immediately after the school board dismissed Thomas Baca, McDade split into two bitterly opposing camps, each made up of about half of the town's citizens. At times, some members of these groups barely seemed able to restrain themselves from violently attacking each other. Early on, a few people in the community tried to act as peacemakers, but they quickly found themselves having to choose between taking one side or another in the controversy or staying out of it entirely. There was no middle ground: one either supported the dismissal of Thomas Baca or one opposed it, a situation that left little room for compromise. A bumper sticker that read "McDade: Love It or Leave It, But Don't Change It!" began showing up around town and quickly became a badge of solidarity among those opposed to the school board's action. It didn't take long for things to turn ugly. David Carson remembers Baca supporters "pack[ing]" the next several school board meetings and demanding that he be reinstated. Sometimes led by a contingent of McDade's street people fresh from drinking beer uptown, the audience at these meetings was often "hostile" and "abusive" toward the five board members who had voted to dismiss Baca, in several instances challenging them to "step outside" to settle their differences "like men." David Carson recalls the spring of 1987 as a "wrenching" and "terribly painful" time, during which he and other board members received threatening phone calls in the middle of the night that made them fear for their safety. His wife, Barbara, recollects that she "didn't feel safe. . . . People were very hostile. . . . I was frightened of those people, and David would go off and spend the night away, and I would say 'don't tell anybody I'm up here alone.' I just really got frightened." She remembers having "to leave our truck [uptown] one night, . . . because they were all sitting around on it drinking beer, all these men, and we were afraid to try to reclaim it."[21]

Nowhere were the tensions that divided McDade more evident than on the town's single uptown street. Almost every day, insults flew back and forth between those who congregated in front of Sam Earl's (especially after they had consumed a few beers) and people going in and out of Seigmund's Grocery, whose owner, George Seigmund, had been one of the original members of the Ad Hoc Committee and was still one of Thomas Baca's harshest critics. The street people even organized a boycott of Seigmund's, which most of those opposed to Baca's dismissal, even if they were not particularly fond of the street people, felt obliged to honor.[22]

Ironically, almost as soon as the McDade School Board refused to renew Thomas Baca's contract, the five-man coalition that had voted to terminate him began to fall apart. The anti-Baca majority lost one seat in the April 1987 elections, when widely respected rancher Morris Kastner, strongly in favor of keeping the McDade School open and operating, but only nominally a supporter of Thomas Baca, defeated incumbent Travis McPhaul, the first member of the Ad Hoc Committee elected to the board back in 1984. The other seat slated to be filled that spring was the one occupied by Franklin Pohler, one of Baca's two supporters on the board. Pohler had tired of public life by this time and declined to run again. This led to a hotly contested three-way race for his seat that ended in a runoff, two weeks after the initial April 4 election, between pro-Baca candidate Clyde Farris and anti-Baca candidate Arthur Behrend. This campaign was a bitter one, full of angry insults, if not always voiced by the candidates themselves, then by their supporters. Farris won the runoff by eleven votes, in a contest marred by election-day accusations of improper vote-counting procedures that eventually required a Bastrop County sheriff's deputy to take possession of the ballot box. This, of course, served to further inflame local resentments, especially when it turned out that the original count had been accurate. In an angry letter to the *Elgin Courier*, Peggy Fisher, who had been tallying votes in local elections for years, seemed to blame some of McDade's newer people for much of the bad feeling in town. "For years," she wrote, "the citizens of McDade had managed to hold honest school board elections with a minimum of fuss, bother and hurt feelings," but more recent campaigns, she complained, had been marked by "outright lies, half truths, and allegations of improper behavior. . . . Unfortunately, some among us seem to believe others would act as dishonestly as they would if given a chance. This is not true. We must remember this community was based on trust and friendship and close our ears to the lies and slander that pass among us." Thus, with considerable hullabaloo, the seat on the school board Franklin Pohler had vacated stayed in the pro-Baca column.[23]

If there had been no other changes in the McDade School Board that spring, Baca's opponents would have retained a four-to-three majority. However, in the two weeks between the April 4 election of Morris Kastner and Clyde Farris's April 18 runoff victory over Arthur Behrend, the anti-Baca majority suffered an additional loss. Out of curiosity about why board member Lloyd Magnuson had not voted in either election, someone discovered that he was not a registered voter; nor had he been registered to vote at the time of his election in 1986. This rendered Magnuson ineligible to sit on the McDade School Board, and he had no choice but to resign. Then, at the April 20 school board meeting, which opened with new board member Clyde Farris being sworn in, Buddy Hendricks, one of the original members of the Ad Hoc Committee, unexpectedly resigned his seat on the school board, citing reasons of poor health. Temporarily reduced to five members, the board proceeded to elect Baca-supporter Buddy Lewis board president by a vote of three-to-two. Lewis then appointed Harold Culp, Lloyd Magnuson's 1986 opponent, to fill Magnuson's vacant seat and Merle Rother, whom everyone knew to be strongly committed to keeping the McDade School open and generally supportive of Thomas Baca, to fill Buddy Hendricks's spot. Just that quickly, only two of the five board members who just seven weeks earlier had voted to terminate Baca remained on the board. Four of the seven current board members had publicly opposed Baca's dismissal, and a fifth, Morris Kastner, opposed it to whatever extent he thought it might threaten the continued existence of the McDade School.[24]

Two weeks later, on May 4, the newly constituted school board rescinded Baca's dismissal and offered him a new three-year contract. The vote was four-to-three, with Lewis, Farris, Culp, and Rother in favor of the new contract and Carson, Owen, and, more on principle than preference, Morris Kastner opposed. At the conclusion of this meeting, Gary Owen angrily resigned his seat, leaving David Carson as the lone board member remaining from the five-man majority that had voted to terminate Thomas Baca. Baca waived his earlier severance settlement and signed the new contract almost immediately. The board's rehiring of Baca caught most of McDade by surprise and sent additional shock waves through a community still reeling from the bitterness and confusion surrounding the sudden changes on the school board. Many people in town were outraged, especially those who had supported Baca's dismissal or otherwise aligned themselves with the majority on the previous board. In a matter of weeks, their control of the McDade School had been wrested away and what most of them considered their single most important accomplishment negated.[25]

Some of the angry response to rehiring Baca, however, came from members of the community the new board majority had assumed would support them. For the most part, these were people who were pleased that the new configuration of the board seemed to guarantee that the McDade School would not close in the immediate future and who generally agreed that the old board had mistreated Thomas Baca. Nonetheless, they also felt that it was time for McDade to close out this troublesome chapter in its history and put the entire affair to rest. The best way to do this, they believed, was by hiring a new principal/superintendent—the district had already received almost forty applications, many of them from people at least as well qualified as Thomas Baca—who would be able to start off afresh, with a clean local slate. More than anything else, this group wanted the McDade School to get back to the business of educating the town's children, and they wanted this done with as little fuss as possible. The school board's surprise decision to rehire Baca hardly seemed a course of action likely to accomplish this. Clyde Cayton, for one, believes that reinstating Baca was "a big mistake. . . . Whether their reasoning was right or wrong, the [old] board made the decision to let Baca go, and [the new board] should have stuck with it. . . . They had a golden opportunity to hire a young, aggressive person who could have helped McDade, and they threw that opportunity away. And by throwing it away, they still have the same attitudes that they had before they decided to let him go." Others were angered that Baca had signed the new contract when he was so obviously a major issue dividing the community. Ed Steinbring, pastor of Faith Lutheran Church at the time, felt that Baca had owed it to McDade not to accept the board's offer: "When the community got so divided, and he knew that he was the stated reason for it, . . . if he had cared about the community he should have left." In any event, by rehiring Thomas Baca, the new school board had guaranteed that the anger and frustration plaguing McDade would not dissipate anytime soon. The town would have to endure more public posturing and bitter hostility in the months to come, not to mention the very real danger that retaliatory action on the part of those opposed to the board's action might, through legal action, result in the abolishment of the McDade ISD. At the end of February, barely two months earlier, the old board's ruling majority had made a serious tactical error by abruptly dismissing Thomas Baca, thereby providing those who feared for the future of McDade's school under the old board's leadership an issue to rally around. Now, by rehiring Baca, the new board had done the same for those opposed to keeping the school open. They had also supplied them with fresh ammunition for renewed attack.[26]

Those unhappy with the board's action reacted swiftly. Within a matter of days, they were circulating a petition on which they began gathering signatures from all corners of the community. The petition read: "We, the citizens of McDade, are shocked and disappointed that you four members of the McDade ISD voted to reinstate Thomas Baca as Superintendent without a public hearing and without public notice. We feel that the McDade community would have been able to unite with one of the other candidates for Superintendent. We feel that you have put your personal feelings for Mr. Baca above the needs of McDade." Though the petition made no call for specific action, the number of people signing it left little doubt that there was widespread public displeasure with the school board's decision to reinstate Baca. By the end of May, it had 277 signatures on it, more than the total number of votes cast in any of the recent school board elections. In response, concerned that the legality of their contract offer to Baca might be questioned because discussion of reinstatement had not appeared on the official agenda for the May 4 meeting, the board scheduled a second vote for the night of June 1, this time making certain that it was listed on the agenda.[27]

The June 1 school board meeting was perhaps the most tumultuous of the entire controversy. Word had spread that McDade was up in arms, and this attracted a reporter from the *Austin American-Statesman* and a news crew from one of Austin's television stations. They went home with stories and videotape that many residents of McDade found embarrassing. The meeting opened with more than an hour of public debate, much of it, in David Carson's words, marked by "insults, verbal brawling, [and] abusive language." There were nearly a hundred people in attendance, many of whom were "discourteous and hostile" toward anyone who disagreed with them. Some argued that there could be "no peaceful coexistence" in McDade as long as Thomas Baca was superintendent, while those in favor of reinstating him claimed that the previous board had dismissed Baca without cause and to let that action stand would unfairly endanger the career of a man who had done nothing to deserve termination and who had faithfully served McDade for more than a decade. Others pleaded with both sides to "consider the children" and quit arguing. Unfortunately, about half of those who said they wanted nothing more than for hostilities to cease thought that would only be possible with Thomas Baca in place as principal and superintendent, while the other half felt the board would have to rescind its decision to rehire him first. After much heated debate, the board once again voted to reinstate Baca, this time by a margin of four-to-two, with Carson and Kastner voting no and Merle Rother abstaining. "[Board president] Buddy Lewis had the votes," David Carson recalls, "and they were just impassive," even in the face of what Carson remembers as overwhelming community sentiment against rehiring Baca. Just before the meeting adjourned, an angry Arthur Behrend announced that he would rather pay tuition for his three children to attend school in Elgin than have them return to the McDade School the following fall. He urged other parents to withdraw their children as well and demanded that at its next meeting the school board consider paying tuition costs for any in the district who wished to transfer their children to schools elsewhere. Essentially, Behrend was proposing a boycott of the McDade School. It was unlikely that the board would agree to pay tuition for the town's elementary students to attend schools in other towns, but, since the level of funding the district received from the state depended on average daily attendance figures, such a boycott could have serious repercussions.[28]

Reaction to the second vote to rehire Baca took several forms. One, seemingly born of frustration, expressed itself in an angry round of name calling. In a letter to the *Elgin Courier*, David Carson accused the school board majority of "a kind of fascism" for reinstating Baca "against the wishes of the people." He went on to disparage Baca in surprisingly personal terms. "Tom Baca is unpopular in McDade, that is certain," Carson wrote. "People have complained to me that he speaks poorly, is often surly, dresses sloppily, writes incorrectly, exhibits no charm, and runs an expensive school few can brag on. He has a reputation for brutality toward his students. He takes his salary and runs home to Austin with little participation in McDade affairs. This is the man four trustees voted to entrust the McDade School to for the next three years at a [total] salary of more $135,000!" In this and other letters, Carson hinted at improprieties on the part of Baca and his supporters on the board. According to Carson, Baca had deposited district funds in "secret" bank accounts only he had access to, a suspicious situation at best. Returning to a theme he had first sounded back in 1983, Carson also suggested that Baca and his supporters on the board had conspired to benefit each other financially, implying that Baca was still using his influence at the county tax office to punish his enemies and reward his friends. Baca's opponents, including himself, Carson claimed, had seen their property valuations rise and had been denied tax exemptions. Conversely, those on the board who backed Baca had received favorable tax treatment, seemingly as part of a quid pro quo arrangement. "If the trustees who voted for the three-year renewal of the contract of Superintendent Baca did not do so in the hope that their taxes will be kept low," Carson asked, "why did they do such an unpopular thing? They don't say."[29]

As expected, the McDade School Board refused to pay tuition for students whose parents wanted them to attend school elsewhere. When school started again the following August, several families withdrew their children anyway. In all, about twenty students transferred, approximately 20 percent of the school's projected enrollment for 1987–88. This eventually resulted in reduced state aid for the district. Other families, unable to afford tuition payments, kept their children in the McDade School unwillingly, making no secret of their unhappiness about it. This created an atmosphere of constant complaint regarding school matters of all kinds and led to resentment among parents, children, teachers, and school staff alike. Thomas Baca believes this contributed to lower morale at the school and generally poor student performance on standardized tests administered during the 1987–88 school year. Joanne Hess, a teacher at the school, agrees that the controversy had a negative impact on McDade's schoolchildren. It "caused a lot of upset," she says. "Children were caught in the middle, having to be on different sides because of what their families said. They couldn't just be normal school kids, because they kept hearing that the school was terrible or that it was okay or that it was going to close or that it wasn't. . . . They didn't know what to think or what was true, and it upset them." Debbie Dunkin, who had three children attending the McDade School at the time and who sometimes worked as a substitute teacher there, remembers that some parents would not let their children be involved in extracurricular activities, go on field trips, or participate in school-sponsored social events. She thinks this was unfortunate for all the students. In a school as small as McDade's, she says, "The kids feel it when someone's missing. . . . It's not the same as having all your friends there."[30]

The most unsettling reaction to the school board's confirmation of its decision to rehire Thomas Baca, however, came in the form of a new petition that began circulating around town shortly after the June 1 board meeting. Citing chapter, subchapter, and section of state law regarding public education, this petition called for a referendum on the outright abolition of the McDade ISD. This was a direct legal challenge to the continued existence of the McDade School. If a majority of the district's voters cast ballots in favor of abolition, the district would be dissolved, irrevocably and without appeal, at the end of the 1987–88 school year. The petition's supporters had no difficulty getting signatures from the required 10 percent of registered voters, though they failed to submit it to county authorities in time for the issue to appear on the ballot during the next scheduled election in August. Instead, it was put on November's ballot.[31]

This delay probably worked to the advantage of those who wanted to keep the school open. It gave them a little breathing room, time they could devote to working on the 1987 Watermelon Festival—a more demanding task than ever that summer because the school controversy had caused many people in McDade to withdraw from community affairs entirely—before mobilizing themselves to deal with this latest, and most serious, threat to the town's school. Throughout the summer and fall of 1987, numerous letters from citizens of McDade appeared on the editorial pages of the *Elgin Courier*, most of them in support of the school district. Some were angry letters directed at David Carson, accusing him of engaging in "a hate battle," of "demonstrat[ing] . . . contempt for the citizens of McDade," of wanting to "exterminate all opposition at any cost," and of not being as familiar as he should with the "old piece of country wisdom 'Don't kick my dog; he knows me but he will bite you,'" this last seemingly a threat, only thinly veiled. Most of the letters, however, were impassioned pleas to the district's voters not to vote the McDade School out of existence. A. D. Sweatt compared closing the school to nuclear holocaust, claiming that there could be "no winners, only losers." Harry Scott wrote that "a community without a school is a community sentenced to wither and die" and accused those who wanted to dissolve the school district of selfishly trying to punish the rest of the town for not letting them have their way. Thad Brown asked, "Can McDade really afford to accept the consequences of closing the school?" Betty Dube decried the "sorry state of affairs in McDade" and pleaded with others in the community to "take a long hard look at what we might be throwing away . . . before it's too late." Janet Brade claimed that the controversy had devastated the town's children, causing them "undue stress and tears over the possible loss of their school." She pleaded with people to "listen to their children and not act out of vengeance. We want to keep our school."[32]

As election day drew closer, supporters of the school district organized a political campaign that was undoubtedly as thorough and energetic as any McDade had ever seen. In an attempt to contact every potential voter, volunteers went from house to house in town, while others drove every mile of the district's many back roads, sometimes encountering people who knew nothing about the controversy over McDade's school. Representatives of the PTA organized a voter registration drive and made countless phone calls in support of the district. Over the protests of some parents, students at the McDade School made posters asking people to vote against dissolution, which were then displayed in various places around town. Full- and half-page advertisements in support of the McDade ISD appeared in the *Elgin Courier* and the *Bastrop Advertiser*, one of which listed the names of 206 McDade citizens committed to keeping the community's school open and operating. Strangely, those who wanted the school district dissolved maintained a much lower profile. Some people in McDade have since theorized that because proponents of abolition knew they could not muster a majority of local voters to support their cause they remained quiet, hoping that an uninformed electorate might assume a "yes" vote to be a vote for the school, whereas, because of the way the proposition was worded, a "yes" vote would actually be a vote for abolition. In any event, the campaign to get out the vote in support of the McDade ISD was a resounding success. Election official Peggy Fisher had ordered three hundred ballots printed for the school referendum and was shocked when 417 people showed up at the polls, 306 of whom voted against abolition. When Fisher announced this result at the end of the day, the crowd that had gathered in the school yard cheered. After almost five years of doubt and conflict, the people of McDade had saved their school, at least temporarily. Once the issue had been disentangled from the confusion surrounding whether one liked or disliked Thomas Baca, or whether one sided with the school board majority that had fired Baca or the board that had rehired him, McDade's voters had not had any trouble deciding what they wanted. Presented with a clear-cut choice between closing its school or keeping it open, the community had overwhelmingly declared itself in favor of the latter. All other issues aside, the people of McDade wanted their children to go to school in town. No matter that the local school did not offer the most sophisticated education available to American children at the end of the twentieth century; most parents were convinced that the McDade School offered more love and support than other towns' schools, and they wanted their children to experience that kind of "hometown feeling" in their early school years. Debbie Dunkin, whose four children all attended grade school in McDade, put it this way: "The love they got [at the McDade School] gives them confidence and security when they go other places. They always thought the school was a nice place to be."[33]

Whether the town would ever be the same again in the wake of such bitter controversy was another question entirely. The anger generated by the school conflict had sorely tested a number of long-standing local institutions and relationships, some of which did not survive intact. As mentioned earlier, there were significant defections from the ranks of those who had always worked hard to put on the town's watermelon festival. These included the resignation of festival board chairman Harry Nesselbeck, who during "many sleepless nights" mourning his hometown's lost sense of "harmony" had sadly concluded that McDade was a place he could "no longer . . . be proud of or . . . work for." As of 1989, some of those who "quit the festival" in 1987 had relented; others, including Nesselbeck, had not. The school controversy caused difficulties within several of McDade's old families as well. These ranged from temporary disaffections that have since been forgotten to more serious estrangements that seem likely to last and may well be permanent. In at least one instance, two men in their fifties, first cousins and best of friends since childhood, have vowed never to speak to one another again. There are probably others in town who feel the same way toward one or more of their brothers or sisters. Nor were McDade's churches spared the bitter fruits of the conflict over the community's school. In the wake of the dissolution election, the congregation of the McDade Baptist Church split into two separate groups that have since had little to do with each other except on Sunday mornings, a situation that has limited the church's effectiveness as a community social institution. Affected even more severely was Faith Lutheran Church, where five families—two on one side of the school controversy, three on the other—quit the church entirely, each group believing that pastor Ed Steinbring had taken the side of the other. These defections amounted to about 20 percent of the congregation, though in terms of financial support they represented a considerably greater portion than that. The fact that the leading figures of the opposing factions within Faith Lutheran were the grandsons of the two men whose 1943 fistfight had resulted in the dissolution of the Siloah Evangelical Lutheran Church is an irony that makes one wonder if things ever really change in places like McDade.[34]

The controversy affected the community in less apparent ways as well. In the years since the dissolution election, the view has developed that the school conflict was the result of new people who had just moved in trying to change the community against the will of its longtime residents, who responded by rallying themselves and successfully resisting. Buddy Lewis, for example, blames the conflict on "strangers moving to town who wanted to change things . . . [while] the old established ones . . . wanted everything left alone." Opal Jones likens the situation to "somebody who comes into your home and tells you how to run your household. It doesn't go over very big." She also feels that the "new people who tried to take over" treated most longtime McDade residents "like we're dumb hicks . . . who don't know what's going on . . . like we're too stupid to know how to do anything," an attitude she thinks many local people sensed in McDade's newcomers and bitterly resented. Wallace Wilson believes the community took offense at "people coming in here and saying, 'We're going to put McDade on the map.' McDade's already on the map. It's been on the map a long time. It doesn't need them to put it on the map. They tried to move in and tell everybody what to do, and people didn't like it." Similarly, though from the opposite side of the fence, David Carson, the most visible of those who had tried to abolish the McDade ISD, tends to look back on the conflict as a struggle between a poorly educated native population and a more sophisticated set of people who had come to town more recently. This tendency to think of McDade's school controversy as primarily a struggle between newcomers and old-timers, however, ignores the fact that many of the people new to the community ended up wanting to retain the school and a significant number of locals signed the petition calling for the school district's abolition. Only at the beginning of the school controversy, before the property tax roll was updated and equalized, could the conflict reasonably be characterized as an issue pitting McDade's newer citizens against residents of longer standing, and even then there were significant exceptions.[35]

It is unfortunate that this perception exists, not only because it ignores the facts, but also because it will perpetuate as local myth. As such, it will serve as a rallying point for town reactionaries anytime they see McDade being challenged by changing circumstances. Rather than considering that change might be beneficial, many in the community will be tempted to take refuge in the belief that change, as represented by the world outside McDade, is something to be resisted, just as it successfully was when the "new people who tried to take over" between 1983 and 1987 were rebuffed in their attempt to shut down the town's school. This is likely to lead to resistance to changes that would benefit the community and unsuccessful resistance to changes that are inevitable, which in turn, no doubt, will result in deeper divisions in town and further bitterness. In 1989, Debbie Dunkin remembered McDade before the school controversy as a place where "the whole town was like a family. . . . Once the school thing got stirred up, though, it was like we had two sides to McDade. . . . It's like all of a sudden we had given up being friends, and the town was full of unfriendliness and coldness. That's when McDade started to lose some of its warmth, and I don't think it's gotten it back." Unless the community can come to a better understanding of its own past, something the town has always resisted, the climate there may yet get colder.[36]

Epilogue
McDade, 1998

Between 1989 and 1998, I visited McDade about once a year, on average. Some of those visits were nothing more than quick detours off U.S. 290 on trips between Austin and east Texas or Louisiana. I stayed in touch with a few town residents through Christmas cards and occasional phone calls. I read Louise Goerlitz's "News from McDade" column every week in the *Elgin Courier* till it stopped appearing in 1994. Once or twice a year, I would see a mention of McDade in the *Austin American-Statesman*, usually on the obituary page. Occasionally it was the obituary of someone I had known, though often not. In 1991, there was a shooting death in McDade, the result of a drunken argument over a minor car accident. I had met the victim once but did not know him; I did not recognize the name of the man who shot him. In November 1995, the *Statesman* carried a story on volunteers helping to rebuild the fire-destroyed Weeping Willow Baptist Church in McDade, though there had been no mention of it having burned the previous July. The paper also noted the filming of parts of the television miniseries *True Women* in McDade in 1996. Occasionally, a letter to the editor from David Carson would appear. Ivy Ann Cronin sometimes sent in recipes.

In the spring of 1998, the University of Oklahoma Press agreed to publish the McDade project, more or less as I had put it together as my doctoral dissertation in 1993. The only major change would be the addition of a brief epilogue that would serve as an update. Though I welcomed this assignment, I also had misgivings. McDade of the 1980s had been a constant presence in my life for more than five years. Researching and writing about its history had taken another four. Since 1993, though, the town had become something of an abstraction to me—more memory, or idea, than flesh and blood—and I wasn't sure how I felt about making it part of my life all over again. For one thing, I was afraid I might not be as welcome there as I had been during the 1980s. I wouldn't be draped in cameras this time or have pictures to give away, but I would once again have a long list of questions to ask. I thought people might resent this, especially since I had not been in contact with many of them for almost a decade. Nor was I sure that people in McDade would be as pleased as I was at the prospect of the project being published. The underlying source of these worries—my own sense of guilt at having dropped out of the community's life, at least publicly, in 1989—was the larger problem, though. I was afraid that I might have offended people, made them feel that their only importance to me was the role they played in my portrayal of McDade, and that my sudden reappearance after such a long absence would only serve to confirm this.

As it turned out, my worries were groundless. No one seemed troubled by my suddenly showing up after having been away so long. In fact, other than the twenty or thirty people I had known best during the 1980s, most town residents did not remember who I was. My face was vaguely familiar to many of them, but until I mentioned that I was the person who used to take pictures around McDade they could not place me. Nor did anyone object to the prospect of the project being published. Many of the town's longtime residents believed McDade to be a special place, so they thought it fitting that books be published about it. Indeed, three fairly popular historical romances—Cindy Bonner's "McDade Cycle," a fictional account of characters and events surrounding the 1883 Christmas-season violence in McDade—were published between 1992 and 1996.

Much of what caught my attention in McDade of 1998 were the kinds of changes that time, as it passes, causes everywhere. People's lives had changed over the years, sometimes radically. Some had married; others had divorced. Some had new, better-paying jobs; some had lost their jobs or retired. Some had started families or had more children; others had died. In terms of the community as a whole, this manifested itself as a kind of "changing of the guard" among successive age groups. Many of those who were schoolchildren in the 1980s are now married and have children of their own (though very few of them have made their homes in McDade). The parents of these now-grown schoolchildren, young adults back then, are now well into middle age, some of them grandparents. While many of them had chafed under the leadership of their elders a decade and more ago, they are now the community leaders a younger generation of adults sometimes wishes would step aside. Many of those who were in upper middle age in the 1980s, at the peak of their influence in the community, are now elderly, their impact on town affairs markedly diminished. And nearly all of the older people I photographed or interviewed during the 1980s are now gone from McDade. Some are in nursing homes, but most have died.

Physically, McDade doesn't look much different than it did in the 1980s. Nor does it feel very different to walk or drive around in. There are a couple of new houses and a few new mobile homes on lots that used to be vacant, but the town doesn't appear any bigger than when I first went there in 1984. Nor does it seem any more affluent. The boom some had predicted would result from Austin building a new airport near Manor, twenty miles west of McDade, had never materialized. (Neither had the airport, for that matter, at least not in Manor. In 1992, after almost a decade of indecision, the Austin City Council vetoed the Manor location once and for all and designated the recently deactivated Bergstrom Air Force Base, just south of the city, as the site of the new airport. Construction began in 1994. The airport is scheduled to open in 1999.) This hasn't left McDade any poorer than it was before, but neither has it helped the community grow, achieve greater diversity, or become any wealthier, all of which might have resulted from construction of the airport in Manor. As I drove around town in 1998, I couldn't help thinking that McDade looked shabbier, even more rundown than it had in the 1980s. In fact, if it weren't for two notable exceptions to the overall aura of neglect, I would have concluded that McDade had been going through another of its stagnant cycles during the 1990s, citing its dilapidated appearance as proof.

The first of these exceptions is on the school grounds, in the form of a handsome new classroom building that stands where the school playground and the Watermelon Festival's outdoor stage used to be. The new building is impressive, housing eight fully equipped classrooms and an up-to-date, twenty-station computer lab. Most people in town are proud of it, confirming as it does the wisdom of not allowing the school to be shut down back in 1987. Completed in December 1996, it was badly needed. Despite McDade's seeming doldrums, at least in what people think of as "town," the surrounding countryside has witnessed a population boom during the 1990s. Along one stretch of "old" Highway 20, about five miles east of McDade, there are now fifty or more mobile homes scattered throughout what used to be a sparsely inhabited stretch of woods. Several smaller, self-contained mobile home parks have sprung up in other parts of the district, and a number of young families have built houses or put mobile homes on scraps of land purchased from local ranchers. This increase in the district's rural population has more than doubled the enrollment at the McDade School since the late 1980s, and prior to construction of the new classroom building—funded in large part by a grant from the Texas Education Agency—McDade's existing facilities, barely adequate even for small numbers of children, had been stretched almost to the bursting point.

Oddly enough, this expanded, high-tech school of the late 1990s no longer seems as central to the McDade community as the smaller, embattled school of the 1980s had been. In large part, this is due to the district's changing demographics, especially the fact that many of the people moving into its rural areas have no previous ties to McDade. It also reflects a trend that many longtime local people find disturbing: very few of those who were students at the McDade School during the 1980s—most of whom are now in their twenties—have remained in McDade. (I know of only four former students at the school with children of their own there now; this is in marked contrast to the mid- and late 1980s, when many more than half of the students at the McDade School were from families with local roots.) What this adds up to in 1998 is a school that seems detached from the community it serves. With many of the students and their families new to McDade, few of them have much contact with the community beyond the school. The old network of long-standing family and social ties no longer seems to connect with the day-to-day life of the town's schoolchildren. Perhaps neither the school nor the traditional cycle of family and/or church-oriented social events are at the center of McDade any longer. At one time, though, they both were, often overlapping considerably.

The second change that belies McDade's shabby appearance is the recent series of improvements made to the property purchased by the Watermelon Festival Association back in 1988. This land, slightly more than two acres, is located two blocks south of uptown, on the spot where A. Y. Field's cotton gin burned in 1940. In 1992, the association erected a multipurpose building on the site. It has several functions. The association's Executive Committee and Board of Directors hold their monthly meetings there; the Watermelon Festival's Saturday-evening barbecue dinner is served in the "festival building"; the parade float is stored there when not in use; and the association's first "casino night" was held there in 1998. It is equipped with a full kitchen, dressing rooms for Queens' Revue and Coronation participants, and an office space. Close by is a covered, state-of-the-art barbecue pit. In 1996, the association built a stage for the Queens' Revue and Coronation ceremonies on the property, in a grove of live-oak trees, which provide welcome shade from the July sun.

The Watermelon Festival remains at the center of McDade's civic and social life, at least during the late spring and early summer. This is especially true for most of those who have been in town for any length of time. The festival has generated handsome profits in recent years: in 1998, the dances cleared about seventeen thousand dollars and the watermelon auction brought in almost twelve thousand dollars. Festival profits are no longer automatically channeled to the school; instead, they are distributed among several organizations working "for the betterment of the community," including the school and the Watermelon Festival Association itself. In 1998, the association established a scholarship fund that they hope will help defray local students' college costs for years into the future.

The Watermelon Festival remains divided between traditionalists who see Saturday night's coronation of the new Watermelon queens as the climax of the weekend and those for whom the Friday night dance and beer party are the high point. In 1998, at the end of June, I attended the Queen's Revue and, at its conclusion, the dance uptown; three weeks later, on festival weekend, I went to the Friday night dance and to the Saturday night coronation ceremony. In both instances, there were only a handful of people who came to both events. This was precisely the situation in the 1980s, when the dances were still controversial breaks with tradition (not only with Watermelon Festival tradition in McDade, but with the deeply ingrained antipathy of rural Southern Baptists and members of the Church of Christ to drinking and dancing). Then, though, the two groups seemed to exist more or less in balance within the festival. In recent years, the dancing and beer-drinking contingent has expanded its influence, as the dances generate more and more money and as an ever greater proportion of those who prefer the Queens' Revue and Coronation become older and have less energy to put into the festival. In fact, ever since the post-parade festivities—the barbecue dinner, the watermelon auction, and the coronation ceremony—have been held on the new festival grounds rather than at the school, beer has been sold there on Saturday afternoon and evening. Unlike at the dances, no one seems to overindulge, but that is little solace to those who find it offensive. Indeed, during a break in the 1998 coronation ceremonies, one of the men in charge of the beer booth—someone I did not know—went onstage and borrowed the microphone to offer a special price on the remaining stock of Coors Light, apparently a slow seller. The shocked revulsion on the faces of many in the crowd, especially among the older people, was evident.

But none of that may matter much longer. McDade's center of gravity is shifting, away from the town's older people, away from those with roots in the community, away from connection with the past. In a general sense that has probably always been happening, but unlike in earlier times of community crisis, there seems no single issue in the late 1990s, whether unifying or divisive, to attach the community's identity to. Though muted in comparison to the explosion over the school conflicts of 1986–87, there remains a certain amount of distrust between many of McDade's "homegrown" residents and more recent "transplants." In 1998, though, this tends to exhibit itself more in terms of style than substance, more on the level of personal insult and/or etiquette than what is good or bad for the community. During the 1998 Watermelon Festival, while waiting for the parade to come by, I overheard one town native complain bitterly to her friends that earlier a man who was helping organize the parade, but whom she had never seen before, had rather brusquely ordered her to get her truck out of the staging area behind Faith Lutheran Church. "I've lived here all my life," she told the group she had said to him, "and I don't know who you are, so what in the hell do you think you're doing, telling me what to do. Get the fuck out of my face, or I'll slap the shit out of you." She went on to say that he had accused her of having "a bad attitude" and had said that he was not interested in "who's lived here longest, [but in] running the festival right . . . What an asshole! We've been doing this festival for a long time now without people like him telling us what to do." The people she was with, all of them "homegrown," shook their heads knowingly. "Yeah, I know who you're talking about," one of them said. "He's a transplant. He doesn't know how to act."

Increasingly, though, the standards by which people are expected "to act" vis-a-vis the community are becoming indiscernible in McDade. The influence of those who were at the core of the community during the 1980s—Baptists and street people alike, both those who wanted to close the school and those who fought to save it, festival traditionalists and those who like to dance uptown— is waning, their numbers thinning out. They are being replaced by people for whom McDade provides little more than a school for their children, a ZIP code, and a telephone exchange. It may be the town they live in, or close to, but many of them see it as a funny little country place that holds a bizarre, tradition-laden outdoor festival in the middle of white-hot July every summer in honor of a crop that hasn't contributed to the local economy for more than forty years, and whose longtime residents bicker among themselves about issues so arcane, personal histories so convoluted and intertwined, as to be incomprehensible. Even if they wanted to, which most of them don't, how could they possibly know the "right way to act"? That's a secret hidden in the rapidly receding past, and no one's very interested in looking for it any longer.

Judy Mayefsky has lived in McDade since the mid-1980s. She is originally from Massachusetts. She once told me that when describing her adopted hometown to old friends who couldn't possibly imagine what life is like there, she would tell them that McDade was thirty-five miles east of Austin and fifty years behind it. I knew what she was saying, but I think I understood it differently than she meant it. I never found McDade's seeming proximity to the past a liability, but neither was I one to gush about how "cute" or "charming" it was. Back in the 1980s, when I was driving back and forth between Austin and McDade several times weekly, I often found the drive restorative—in both directions. Heading east, from Austin to McDade, it lifted me out of my brittle, jangling urban life and forty-five minutes later deposited me in a place that seemed to exist quite normally as part of a calmer, more whole-cloth past. At the end of each visit, though, I was usually happy to be going back to Austin. The drive gave me time to think about what I'd seen or heard in McDade that day and assimilate it into what I already knew. One of the things I thought I knew was that McDade existed no more (or less) in the past than any other place, despite certain appearances to the contrary. But I also knew that the relationship between the past and present there was complicated, and this was a large part of what fueled my interest in the community—in what I was encountering there in the present, in what I was coming to learn about its past, and, especially, in how the two had constantly influenced each other over the years.

In 1998, though, I think the relationship between McDade and its past has changed. Certainly, the community's present has changed, but I think its past has too, at least in the sense of becoming less knowable for many of those who live there now, less accessible to their present-time consciousness. Obviously, this is something that happens every time an older person dies, eliminating another store of firsthand memories of the past, but I'm referring to something else. With McDade's current population being ever less rooted in the local past—not having great-grandparents who can tell them about local farmers shipping hundreds of boxcars full of watermelons from McDade each summer, not having grandparents who know where or what Oak Hill was, not having parents who ever set foot in Sam

Earl's—that past cannot help but lose the luster of its particulars, become dimmer and dimmer all the time, increasingly inaccessible. It loses its specificity, detail by detail, and becomes emptier and more generic with every passing year. And it becomes less useful, less valuable all the time.

This is what I mean when I say that McDade's past has changed. And that, in turn, has altered the community's present, making it a time in which even the recent past is ancient history and has no more lessons to teach. I suppose this renders the town's past simpler, less difficult to understand, and easier to be nostalgic for. But it's no longer a past that belongs to McDade.

————————————

Listed below, in alphabetic order, are the names of most of the people identified in the photographs in chapters 1 through 7 and a little bit about what happened in their lives between 1989 and 1998. In some instances, where it seemed appropriate, I have gone beyond the specifics of people's lives to comment on recent developments in the McDade community more generally.

DONNIE ALANIS (fig. 41) is married to Vicki Long (see fig. 50). Their daughter Bailey was elected Tiny Tot queen in 1998. After working for several years as a carpenter in and around McDade, Donnie decided to change careers. He enrolled at ITT Technical Institute in Austin and eventually received an associates degree in electrical engineering. He now makes "a good living" working for a firm that manufactures semiconductors in Austin.

ALMA ALBRECHT (fig. 61) died in 1994. She was 81.

JOHN ANDERSON (fig. 20) died in 1991. The house he and his wife, RHODE, lived in stood vacant for several years before it was torn down. There is now a small prefab house on the lot, and a new foundation has recently been poured where the Andersons' was, indicating that someone is about to build there.

The Andersons were the last members of the all-black Weeping Willow Baptist Church to live in McDade. Weeping Willow has existed at its current location—about a mile south of uptown McDade (facing U.S. 290 after the highway's completion in 1953)—since about 1910. In the years since World War II, however, nearly all of its members have been residents of Elgin, Bastrop, Taylor, or rural areas associated with those communities. For many years the church doubled as the schoolhouse for African American children from McDade and the surrounding countryside, although the McDade School Board moved a "new" school building (the abandoned schoolhouse from Siloah) next to the church in 1948. "Colored school" continued to be held there until the early 1960s, when it was consolidated with Elgin's black schools. The Weeping Willow Baptist Church burned down on July 31, 1995—a time when African American churches throughout the south were being targeted by arsonists. Investigators found nothing suspicious about the fire at Weeping Willow, however. The following autumn, a construction crew made up of church members, volunteers from McDade, and workers from the Texas Baptist Men's Retired Builders Association poured a new foundation and started framing a new building. They finished in early December. Unfortunately, funds were lacking to complete work on the interior and to install a new septic system. At that point, Evelyn Wolf (figs.

34 and 74) of McDade's Faith Lutheran Church organized a campaign to solicit contributions from churches and other organizations in McDade and surrounding communities. She also secured a matching grant from the Texas Lutheran Brotherhood. Her efforts raised almost ten thousand dollars and enabled the Weeping Willow congregation to finish construction and start worshipping in its own church once again. The new sanctuary was dedicated on June 9, 1996, to an overflow crowd. People from all of McDade's churches attended. Many of them had never before set foot in Weeping Willow.

The reasons there are so few black families in McDade remain obscure. Just as they had in the 1980s, people old enough to remember McDade before World War II—when a number of African American families lived on the southern edge of town (where U.S. 290 went through)—continue to respond vaguely when asked about this. They may, in fact, not know the reason(s) for the absence of African Americans from McDade; or there may have never been anything specific to know. Whatever the facts of the matter, they seem irretrievable. In any event, McDade remains something of an anomaly in this regard. All of the other small towns in the area have sizable black populations

THOMAS BACA (figs. 13 and 95), the focal point of so much controversy in McDade during the 1980s, is still superintendent of the McDade Independent School District. In fact, in early 1998, the McDade School Board voted to offer him a three-year contract that will take him through to retirement.

Some of the anger generated by his firing and rehiring in 1987 has dissipated, though a number of people in McDade still view the conflict as having permanently damaged the town's sense of community. Without question, scars remain: Those families who left Faith Lutheran Church in 1987 have not returned; several individuals who were once close friends have not spoken to one another in more than a decade now; and some people make a point of leaving town during the Watermelon Festival so they won't have to rub elbows with people they disagreed with about Thomas Baca and the future of the McDade School. This kind of ongoing resentment—much of it the consequence of the school controversy—seems to have become a permanent part of the town's social fabric.

For many in the community, though—especially those with the greatest stake in the McDade School of the late 1990s—the conflicts of 1986 and 1987 happened so long ago as to have never taken place. Those children who were students at the McDade School in the late 1980s have all moved on, of course, and most of their parents no longer have children of elementary-school age. Most of the current generation of parents are new to McDade and, ironically, know nothing of the controversy that almost shut the school down a decade ago. So, by virtue of having become "ancient history," the school controversy of the late 1980s gives the appearance of having blown over. Those with longer memories, and deeper roots in the community, know that not to be true. The McDade School of the late 1990s may have escaped its own recent past, but much of the rest of the community has not. So, despite appearances to the contrary, the saying "Time heals" has not proved itself true in McDade, at least not yet.

RUTH BOSTIC (fig. 94) has lived alone since her husband, Shorty (fig. 72), passed away in 1986. For four years after his death, she continued to make her home in the house the two of them had lived in since 1935 and in which they had raised their five children. She was no longer happy there, however. A large house, it was a chore to keep clean, and with no one else living there, it seemed a "big empty barn." At the same time, she felt Shorty "everywhere in that house," and his presence there, she thinks, was prolonging her grief. She also started feeling guilty about living alone in a five-bedroom house while her youngest son Dale and his family were living in a small mobile home down the road. After praying for guidance, the solution appeared to her in the form of a single word—"BUILD." In the autumn of 1990, Mrs. Bostic moved into a compact two-bedroom house she hired a local contractor to build for her on a hilltop on the southern edge of her property. She deeded the old house to Dale, with the stipulation that he could not sell it, but had to pass it on to his children instead. She is more comfortable in her new house. She can clean it "in an hour," and she doesn't feel as burdened by the past. Her only complaint is that on summer nights her son's cows, pastured in the field adjoining her house, gather in her hilltop front yard to catch whatever breezes might be stirring. Every night before she goes to bed in the summer, she goes out to wave towels at the cows to scare them away. If she doesn't, there will be "cow pies" all over when she gets up in the morning.

TANYA BOSTIC (fig. 72) is now in her teens and going through a rebellious phase. After getting into some trouble at Lexington High School, she now attends school in Bastrop, where her mother works.

DAVID BRIGHT (fig. 30) lives with his father's family near Paige. He hasn't seen his mother, Rachel Fisher (see fig. 24), or his grandmother Peggy Fisher in several years.

SONNY BROWN (fig. 69) died in 1993, at age 64.

GRETCHEN (POHLER) BRUNE (fig. 81) and her husband moved back to McDade in the early 1990s, after living in North Carolina for a year or two after their wedding. They have two small children.

Now in her eighties, RUBY CAIN (fig. 64) lives in Elgin. She worked for many years at an Elgin medical clinic, doing the doctors' bookkeeping and keeping their insurance billings straight. The first time she retired she was 75, but she didn't stay retired long, because the doctors begged her to come back. She retired a second, and final, time at age 80.

SHORTY CALHOUN (fig. 60) still lives in McDade. He works at assorted construction jobs in the area.

LAURA CAYTON (fig. 28) now lives in San Antonio, where she works as an elementary school art teacher. She visits her father, Clyde Cayton, at the Cayton Ranch every few months.

MARY CAYTON (fig. 28) died at the Cayton Ranch in the summer of 1997, after a long struggle with brain cancer. She was 76. A memorial service held at the ranch attracted hundreds of guests, with people from throughout central and east Texas arriving to pay their respects. The following Thanksgiving, her husband, daughters, and grandchildren scattered her ashes on the ranch's highest hill, long her favorite spot.

HAZEL CREEL (figs. 78 and 101) is now almost 90. When in good health, she still lives in the small white house that has been her home for almost sixty years. Sometimes, though, when she isn't feeling well, she stays in Bastrop or Smithville, with one of her two daughters.

IVY ANN CRONIN (figs. 53 and 80) still makes her home in McDade but has cut back on her involvement with community affairs. She served as secretary of the Watermelon Festival Association from the late 1980s through the mid-1990s. She was also in charge of the Watermelon Festival's Queens' Revue and Coronation during that time. In 1995, though, someone else was elected secretary. Ivy Ann took offense and withdrew from the Watermelon Festival entirely. She has not participated since.

DAVID DUBE (fig. 77) is retired from his job at the Lower Colorado River Authority power plant in Bastrop.

SAM EARL DUNGAN (fig. 6) closed Dungan Drugs in 1990. Most people in town thought he was just taking a couple of months off and would then reopen the store, but they were wrong. Sam Earl now works for the McDade Water District, maintaining the system, periodically testing water samples, reading water meters, and doing the billing and bill collecting. He is the district's only full-time employee. He says he misses some of the people he used to see at the store—both customers and salesmen, some of whom he'd known since his childhood, when his mother ran the business—but spending so much time there had started to give him a "cooped-up feeling," which he doesn't miss at all.

When Sam Earl's closed, there was no longer a place uptown for McDade's street people to drink beer. For a while they would get together at the JNP Grocery out on U.S. 290, but a disagreement with JNP's owner brought that to an end. As of 1998, their boisterous public gatherings are a thing of the past in McDade. This has made uptown a much less lively place than it used to be. Many in the community are thankful for this. Others miss the easy, informal socializing in front of Sam Earl's.

DEMPSEY DUNKIN (fig. 23) graduated from Elgin High School in 1996. He now lives in Austin, where he works in a day care center. His parents were surprised but not angry when he came home one weekend with an eyebrow ring and several earrings.

FINCH DUNKIN (fig. 23) was Elgin High School's valedictorian in 1994. He attended the University of Texas for a semester but now goes to Texas A&M. He is also in the Texas National Guard.

LEAH DUNKIN (figs. 23 and 83) is now fifteen. She will enter Elgin High School in the fall of 1998. Although an attractive young women, she has never been interested in becoming the McDade Watermelon Festival Queen. This is fine with her parents, who don't want to have to spend their weekends during the spring and summer hauling the Watermelon Festival parade float all over central Texas to other towns' parades.

WALLACE DUNKIN (fig. 23) attends Elgin High School. He was involved in a serious car accident recently. He was lucky not to be badly hurt.

Now 75, SELMA EKLUND (fig. 98) is widowed and lives in Elgin. She spends a lot of time at Alvin and Adeline Eschberger's house, helping Adeline, who is now wheelchair-bound, and sometimes cooking meals for them. Though only three years younger than Alvin, she is his niece.

ADELINE AND ALVIN ESCHBERGER (figs. 19 and 16, respectively) moved into their newly built Elgin retirement home in 1992. The new house is considerably more modern than their house in McDade and accommodates Adeline's wheelchair. Despite that, she misses McDade—less the house that she and Alvin spent nearly fifty years in than feeling she was a part of a community. Even though she has a sister in Elgin and old friends from McDade visit regularly, she says she feels "disconnected." Adeline's health has declined in recent years. She is now confined to a wheelchair. She is rarely strong enough to wheel the chair herself—even from one room to the next—so she has to rely on others, usually Alvin, for mobility. She dislikes being so dependent but knows she has little choice.

Alvin retired from his construction business in 1992, though he still raises cattle on land he owns and leases around McDade. He suffered a heart attack in 1996 and underwent a painful angioplasty procedure. While he was recuperating, the Eschbergers hired a home health nurse to come to the house and help Adeline during the day. In the evening, different family members came to help, usually staying the night.

When her granddaughter Erin Schkade was born with spina bifida, GERTRUDE ESCHBERGER (figs. 43 and 61) quit her job as a school bus driver for the McDade Independent School District and devoted herself to helping her daughter Debbie Schkade care for the baby. At the time, no one knew if Erin would survive infancy. Erin is now twelve, and Gertrude is very proud of her, speaking with open admiration for her tenacity. In the summer of 1998, Gertrude and her husband, Harry, a retired truck driver, accompanied Debbie and her family on a vacation to Arkansas's Ozark Mountains, where Erin and her parents went white-water canoeing down the White River.

LISA ESCHBERGER (figs. 65 and 68) is married and has two boys, ages four and two. She works in an office in Bastrop. Her husband, Steven Wachsmann, stays home on their farm near Paige, where he raises vegetables to sell at his father's grocery store and cares for the children.

CLYDE FARRIS (fig. 87) is retired from a job with the state highway department. He now drives a truck for an oil company in Giddings.

DOUG FARRIS (fig. 31) lives in Elgin with his wife and two children. For a short time, he worked at the brickyard with two of his brothers, but he lost that job after an argument with his supervisor. He has worked at several jobs since but has had trouble keeping any of them for very long.

MARY FARRIS (fig. 25) now lives in west Texas. She visits her husband, Marvin Farris, in McDade only occasionally.

MICHAEL FARRIS (fig. 22) lives with a number of people, including his mother, Doris, in a cluster of four or five mobile homes on a small lot about a mile north of McDade.

Now in her eighties, MINNIE LEE FARRIS (fig. 84) lives alone in her small house in McDade. She still collects dolls.

PEGGY FISHER (figs. 4 and 30) still lives in the small house next door to the house she grew up in. Her parents, Alton and Ruby Greenhaw, are now in a nursing home near Dallas, a location they selected because it was close to where Peggy's brother Paul and his family were living at the time. Unfortunately, Paul has since divorced his wife and moved back to McDade. Unable to make the five-hour drive to see their parents very often, Peggy and Paul considered moving their parents closer to home, but the Greenhaws like the facility they're in and don't want to leave. Peggy's son, Wesley, and his fiancée now live in the Greenhaws' old house. After working at Walmart in Bastrop for several years, Peggy now has a job as a cashier in a Bastrop supermarket. She has gained a reputation for being fast and friendly, and many customers will ignore shorter checkout lines to get in her line instead. Even though she still has several dogs and many cats, she no longer has time for horses. She does keep a cow, though, and has a number of laying hens, whose eggs she sells. She has not seen her two grandchildren, who live with their father's parents in Paige, for several years now.

RACHEL FISHER (figs. 3 and 24) left her husband and children—David and John Bright, now ten and eight—and reassumed her maiden name in 1990. For a short while, she lived with her sister in a mobile home behind their grandparents' house in McDade, but then she moved to Austin, where she took a job as a dancer. In 1998—very much on the spur of the moment, her mother says—she moved to Seattle. Her children live with her husband's family near Paige. Rachel has not seen them for several years.

Now approaching 80, ERHARD GOERLITZ (figs. 3, 35, and 44) remains active in community affairs. He serves as commander of McDade's VFW post, presides over the Three Oaks Cemetery Association, and continues to help out with the Watermelon Festival. Along with Freda Wilson, he manages the local "Meals on Wheels" program, which provides twice-weekly lunches for senior citizens at Faith Lutheran Church. The community honored him and his wife Louise by selecting them to be Parade Marshalls of the 1997 Watermelon Festival parade. That was the first time in many years that Erhard had not carried the American flag as part of the VFW color guard that traditionally leads the parade. In 1998, despite his advancing age and a mid-afternoon temperature of over a hundred degrees, Erhard once again carried the flag at the head of the parade. He thinks by doing so he can be "a good example" for younger people.

Louise Goerlitz (fig. 45) stopped writing her "News from McDade" column for the *Elgin Courier* in 1994. She had been writing the column since 1976. The *Courier* changed hands in 1993, and the new owners hired a new editor. Soon after that, the new editor decided that the *Courier* would no longer print weekly columns of news from the smaller communities around Elgin.

Lida Goodwin (fig. 94) is now 91 and lives in a Giddings nursing home. Ruth Bostic visits her there every week.

Henry Grimes (figs. 41 and 44) has been diagnosed with both throat cancer and prostate cancer in recent years, though he seems to be fighting them pretty effectively so far. Whenever asked, he will tell you that he is feeling fine in a booming, hearty tone of voice. Though he doesn't have much to do with the Watermelon Festival any longer—he was treasurer for many years and master of ceremonies at the Queens' Revue and Coronation—he remains active in the historical society, the VFW, the volunteer fire department, and the Baptist church.

Citing concern for his family's financial future, Jerre Guthrie (figs. 39 and 95) resigned as pastor of the McDade Baptist Church in 1990. He and his wife, Carolyn, now live in Dickinson, Texas—near Houston—where Jerre works for a large construction company and Carolyn is employed as a court reporter. They remain in touch with several members of the McDade Baptist Church, some of whom have visited them in Dickinson. Though they are both still devoutly Christian, Jerre no longer preaches.

When Sam Earl's closed in 1990, Linda Haverland (figs. 11, 26, 41, and 88) had to start looking for a new job. In the spring of 1991, she found one at the Golden Years Nursing Home in Elgin, where she became the activities director, a position she still holds. Always loudly energetic, Linda works hard at making sure that the home's residents have some fun. She dreams up odd-ball contests for them to participate in and has instituted twice-weekly happy hours. She's often willing to take a vanload of people on short trips—out to lunch or for a drive in the country—even on the spur of the moment. She has also coordinated with her counterparts in nursing homes in Bastrop and Giddings to stage quarterly parties for area retirees, whether they are residents of the homes or not. These parties are held at the Faith Lutheran Church in McDade. Several people from McDade—including Frank Kastner (fig. 29), Velma Hoerman (fig. 89), Vlasta Walla (fig. 93), and Lorene Lowery (fig. 102)—live in Golden Years, and they are happy to have Linda's familiar, hometown face there to keep them company. Ironically, now that she socializes for a living, Linda is no longer as socially active in and around McDade as she was during the 1980s, when she worked at Sam Earl's during the afternoons and was one of the main participants in the "street people's" uptown socializing. She looks back on those days with nostalgia; she misses seeing an entire circle of friends several times a week, if not daily. The closing of Sam Earl's "changed our lives," she says.

At age 54, WILLIE HAVERLAND (fig. 41) has worked for the state highway department since 1968. He started at the bottom, on a maintenance crew. He now supervises a team of six maintenance crews. He plans to retire at the end of 1998. He wouldn't mind going to work for the Bastrop County road crew, operating a backhoe or grader, but he doesn't want to be a "boss" any longer.

Now 20, CHRIS HEISER (fig. 33) is in the navy.

Chris's sister, MANDY HEISER (fig. 100), lives in Austin, where she works in telephone sales.

LISA HILCHER (fig. 57) and her family sold their house in McDade and moved to Lexington in 1994. Though they still travel to McDade to visit Lisa's parents, Earl and Inez Haverland, they no longer take part in McDade community affairs. RICKY and SARINA HILCHER (figs. 59 and 57) are now in their teens and attend Lexington High School.

VELMA HOERMAN (fig. 89) now lives at the Elgin Golden Years Nursing Home. A stroke victim, she is confined to a wheelchair and has difficulty making herself understood. She and her husband, Quintus, were named Parade Marshalls of the 1992 Watermelon Festival.

NELLIE HUDLER (fig. 97) died in 1990. She was 90.

LYNN JOHNSON (figs. 48 and 80) now lives in Elgin. Her daughter MICHELLE (fig. 80) lives in Lexington. She is married and has a small baby.

OPAL JONES (fig. 88) still makes her home on the property where she and her twelve brothers and sisters were raised and where the Lewis family continues to hold its annual Easter Sunday reunion. The house she and her siblings grew up in burned down in 1997. Opal and her brother Buddy Lewis, recently divorced from his wife, Chris, were both living there at the time. Opal bought a mobile home and parked it where the house had been. Buddy purchased Alma Kastner's old house, just around the corner, where he now lives with his son, Andrew.

ALMA KASTNER (fig. 63) died in 1997. The house she had lived in since the 1960s is now occupied by Buddy Lewis and his son, Andrew.

DONNY KASTNER (fig. 27) did not become a rancher, as he and other members of his family expected. Instead, after graduating from Texas A&M, he went to medical school. He is now a cardiologist in Temple, Texas. His father, LEONARD RAY KASTNER (fig. 27), continues to raise cattle on his ranch near Lexington.

FRANK KASTNER (figs. 29 and 38) moved into Elgin's Golden Years Nursing Home shortly after his mother's death in 1992. Though only 70, he will probably spend the rest of his life there. Diabetes-related circulation problems have forced doctors to amputate the lower part of his left leg, so he spends most of his waking hours in a wheelchair. He tends to stay up late at night drinking coffee and talking to the night staff, which means he usually sleeps till lunch time. When Frank lived in McDade, he sometimes hung out at Sam Earl's, especially in the afternoons, when Linda Haverland ran the store. The two of them were good friends; they especially enjoyed exchanging humorous insults. Now that Linda is activities director at Golden Years, she sees Frank almost every day. They continue to insult each other, but more gently.

Now retired from a thirty-year career with the Austin Fire Department, MORRIS KASTNER (fig. 38) raises cattle on his ranch north of town. His wife, Vernell, spent many years teaching business courses in several Austin high schools before retiring in 1997. They were selected the Parade Marshalls for the 1996 Watermelon Festival.

STELLA KASTNER (figs. 29 and 78) died in 1992. She was 88 years old.

BARRY KESSLER (fig. 61) lives in Giddings, where he drives an oil truck.

JUSTIN KESSLER (figs. 15, 43, 61, and 65) is now fourteen and attends middle school in Giddings.

Several years after his first wife's death from cancer in the late 1980s, CURTIS LACKER (fig. 77) remarried and moved to his new wife's hometown in Florida.

BUDDY LEWIS (figs. 54, 60, and 85) is now divorced from his wife, Chris. He and their twenty-year-old son, Andrew, now live in Alma Kastner's old house, just around the corner from the house Buddy grew up in. After working for twenty-eight years as a safety inspector for the Texas State Board of Insurance, Buddy took early retirement in 1998. He now has a part-time job with a Houston-area insurance company, doing similar inspection work. He prefers this new job to his old one, because he can do his office work at home and only has to spend a couple of days each week on the road.

Buddy continues to be one of the mainstays of the Watermelon Festival's Dance Committee. He has chaired the committee almost every year since 1985, with his close friend Johnny Sievert stepping in to chair it when Buddy does not. In 1998, the two of them cochaired the committee. The Watermelon Festival has sponsored two dances each year since 1986—one on the night of the Queens' Revue in the latter part of June; the other on the Friday night of the festival, in the middle of July. The dances remain the Watermelon Festival's biggest moneymaker, clearing about seventeen thousand dollars in 1998.

After she and Buddy divorced, CHRIS LEWIS (fig. 88) moved to Austin, where she works for a property management firm. She and Buddy remain on friendly terms. Chris visits McDade frequently, both to see her mother, Sue Field, and to socialize with old friends.

JACK (figs. 10, 41, 85, and 87) and CAROLYN LEWIS (figs. 61 and 88) are also divorced. Carolyn now lives in Paige, where she was born and raised, and works at a bank in Austin. Jack lives in a mobile home in McDade that he rents from Chris Lewis's mother, Sue Field. His son, Randall, lives there with him. Jack has worked as a plumber at the Motorola microprocessor plant in Austin since the early 1990s.

JOE LEWIS (fig. 85) lives in Houston.

RANDALL LEWIS (figs. 10, 43, 68, and 85) lives with his father, Jack Lewis, in McDade. Randall graduated from Elgin High School in 1997. He works for a business in Paige that installs irrigation systems and does landscaping work. He usually works in the immediate McDade-Paige area, though sometimes he goes out with crews that do bigger jobs as far away as Bryan, Austin, and San Antonio. The last of the birthday bashes his parents used to throw for him was in 1995, when he turned sixteen.

VICKI LONG (fig. 50) is married to Donny Alanis (fig. 41). Their daughter Bailey was elected Tiny Tot queen in 1998.

CALVIN LOWERY (figs. 32 and 102) died in 1991. He was 95 years old.

LORENE LOWERY (fig. 102) has lived in Elgin's Golden Years Nursing Home since the mid-1990s.

RAY MCDAVID (figs. 5 and 35) has seen his health decline in recent years. This has forced him to stop farming, though he still raises a few cattle. In 1997, for the first time in many years, he did not prepare the beans that are served with the Watermelon Festival's traditional Saturday night barbecue dinner. Cooking the beans is a big job—eighty pounds of beans, simmering in a huge cast iron pot, require constant attention and take most of a day to cook properly—and Ray no longer felt up to it. So he passed the job on to Franklin Pohler, the festival's main barbecue cook in recent years. Ray and his wife, Thelma, remain active in McDade, however, helping out in other ways with the Watermelon Festival—they are always among those who spend Friday night peeling potatoes for the next day's potato salad—and contributing time, money, and energy to the McDade Historical Society. Their son, Forrest, was president of the Watermelon Festival Association in 1998.

KIMBERLY MERRELL (fig. 59) was elected the Watermelon Festival's Teenage queen in 1991.

Retired from his plumbing business, GEORGE MOORE (fig. 44) now devotes most of his time to raising cattle. He and his wife, Dorothy, were Parade Marshalls in 1990.

JUDY MUNDINE (fig. 50) moved to Lexington after the sudden death of her husband, Royce, in 1989.

MITZI MUNDINE (fig. 50) lives in Austin, where she works as an elementary school teacher.

DEBBIE NEIDIG (fig. 11) has worked at the McDade School since 1989. During that time, she has managed the cafeteria, run the school library, and worked as a teacher's aide. She is one of twenty-seven employees at the school.

Enrollment in the McDade School has more than doubled in the past decade, rising from a low of seventy-seven students in the late 1980s to 180 in 1997–98. Some of this increase is due to additional enrollments in a newly established pre-kindergarten program for three- and four-year-olds. Most of it, however, is the result of new families moving into the district, especially its rural areas. There are a couple of new houses in town, and some previously empty lots that now have mobile homes on them, but not enough to make the town much bigger than during the 1980s. Out in the country, though, there has been a population boom. About five miles east of town, there are now fifty or more mobile homes on the narrow strip of land between "old" Highway 20 and U.S. 290. Perhaps four or five families had homes here in 1989, with the rest being uninhabited woods. Several small mobile home parks have sprung up in other rural parts of the district, and new houses or mobile homes are scattered throughout on rural lots young families have purchased from local ranchers. Other than having contact with the McDade School through their children, very few of these families have involved themselves with other aspects of community life.

Their numbers so swelled the school's enrollment, though, that by the mid-1990s Superintendent Thomas Baca started searching for funds to add a new classroom building. In 1995, McDade was awarded a $425,000 grant from the Texas Education Agency's School Facilities Assistance Program. Construction of the new building was underway in May 1996 and was finished by Christmas. It has eight classrooms—one each for pre-kindergarten, kindergarten, and first through sixth grades—and a computer lab with twenty workstations. It's a handsome brick building, and most people in town are proud of it. Many point to it as proof that closing the McDade School in 1987 would have been a terrible mistake. The only criticism people have of it is that it took up most of the remaining school grounds, so there is now very little outdoor space for the children to play.

HEATH NEIDIG (fig. 76) graduated from Lexington High School in 1998 and joined the navy two weeks later. He is currently stationed at the Great Lakes Naval Recruit Training Station near Chicago.

Heath's grandmother, Hilda Neidig, (fig. 38) drives a rural delivery route for the Elgin Post Office and helps her husband, Richard, run their cattle ranch.

Major Neidig (fig. 76) attends Lexington High School.

Richard Neidig (fig. 38) does maintenance work at Giddings High School, a job he has held for many years. He also raises cattle on his ranch north of McDade, a full-time job in its own right.

After graduating from Lexington High School in 1995, Tori Neidig (figs. 11 and 52) spent a year at the International Travel and Aviation School in the Dallas-Fort Worth area. She hoped to become a flight attendant. When that didn't work out, she took a job as a reservations agent for the Hilton Hotel chain in Dallas. In 1997, feeling homesick, she quit that job and moved closer to McDade. She now lives in Austin, where she works in the office of a shipping company.

Mary Sue Page (fig. 62) lives in Elgin, where she works as an elementary school teacher. Her three children—Lawrence, Mary Ellen, and Gilbert—all graduated from Elgin High School and have stayed in the area. No one I spoke to has heard anything about Nelson Page in several years.

Franklin and Betty Pohler's (fig. 81) four children are all married and live in McDade. They have six grandchildren, with a seventh "on the way."

Gale Rutherford (figs. 36 and 100) lives in Austin, where she has a job with a company that does microfilming.

Debbie Schkade (figs. 15 and 82) and her husband, Kevin, live in Giddings. Debbie works for a bank there, a job she has held since graduating from Giddings High School in 1977. Her first child, a girl named Erin, was born in December 1985 with spina bifida, a congenital deformity of the spinal column. Although not as severely disabled as some victims of spina bifida—Erin attends school, is able to walk and ride a bike (though she cannot run), and in 1998 went white-water canoeing with her parents on Arkansas's White River—her condition still causes her serious problems. She has had nine surgeries thus far and will probably face several more before reaching adulthood. Luckily, Debbie's job provides good medical insurance. She and Kevin also have a seven-year-old son, Ryan.

Les and Debbie Schubert (fig. 37) live several miles north of McDade, in a mobile home on property owned by Debbie's parents, Lawrence and Ernestine Schulz. They have two children, Andrew and Kristen, ages ten and eight. Les works for a company that installs air conditioning systems in Austin. Debbie works in an Austin doctor's office.

Lawrence and ERNESTINE SCHULZ (fig. 53) live about two miles north of McDade, in the house Ernestine grew up in. Lawrence worked as a safety technician for IBM in Austin for twenty-two years. He had hoped to get twenty-five years in, but a heart condition forced him to retire early. Ernestine works as a substitute teacher at the McDade School. She is usually called in two or three days a week, though she will sometimes teach the same class for several weeks running when a teacher is out for an extended period of time. During the early part of the 1990s, Ernestine did a lot of research on the history of McDade. In 1996, she published the results in an 182-page, spiral-bound book entitled *McDade Then and Now*, which she gave to members of her family as surprise Christmas presents that year. She was born Ernestine Wolf. Dan Wolf (fig. 74) is her first cousin. Their properties adjoin, the result of their grandfather Wolf dividing his farm between his two sons, Ernestine's and Dan's fathers.

GENE SCOTT (fig. 86) is retired from his bartending job in Elgin. He now spends a lot of time at the Elgin VFW Post, drinking beer and swapping stories with friends.

GEORGE SEIGMUND (figs. 5 and 18) died of complications resulting from heart surgery in 1990. He was 58. His wife, Jona Lee, continued to run the family grocery business until 1994, when she sold the store to Jesse and Ann Skinner from the Knobbs. The Skinners have renamed it the McDade General Store. Though they still carry a line of groceries, most of the Skinners' business comes from selling feed and supplies to local ranchers. Like the Seigmunds before them, they do not sell beer or wine. Shortly after taking the business over, they had a pay phone installed on the sidewalk out front. There had never been a public phone in McDade before.

JAY SHANNON (fig. 104) lives in Paige and works nights at a Bastrop supermarket.

JOHNNY AND ROBIN SIEVERT (figs. 55 and 60) continue to be active in the Watermelon Festival, especially with the dance. In 1998, Johnny and Buddy Lewis cochaired the dance committee. Having quit his job in Houston several years ago, Johnny now lives in McDade, in the old house next door to Robin's parents' house that he and Robin bought and started fixing up in the mid-1980s. He works for a construction company in Bryan, a seventy-mile drive each way. Robin still spends the working week in Houston, where she has had an office job with the state highway department for more than twenty years. Every Friday night, she drives 120 miles to McDade and doesn't go back to Houston till early Monday morning.

AMY SKUBIATA (fig. 50) is entering her senior year at Elgin High School. She is a good student and hopes to attend Texas Lutheran College in Seguin. She was elected the Watermelon Festival's Teenage queen in 1996, becoming one of twelve girls to have served as both Tiny Tot queen and Teenage queen. Her younger sister, Kayla, was Tiny Tot queen in 1987 and plans to enter the competition for Teenage queen in 1999. Their mother, Melba Skubiata, was Teenage queen in 1972.

Wayne and MELBA SKUBIATA (fig. 50) are both active in McDade. Wayne is currently the chairman of the Congregational Council at Faith Lutheran Church, and Melba teaches Sunday School classes there and helps out with the summer Vacation Bible School. Wayne was vice president of the Watermelon Festival Association in 1998, helping out wherever he was needed, which was sometimes several places at once. Melba took on the job of putting together a special fiftieth-anniversary Watermelon Festival book which includes photographs from many (if not all) past Watermelon Festivals. As well as collecting the pictures from people throughout McDade, deciding which photos to use, and doing the book's layout, Melba sold almost ten thousand dollars worth of advertising space in the book, to both individuals and families (in the form of "Best Wishes from the Smiths") as well as local businesses. She also coordinated the fiftieth-anniversary reunion of former Watermelon queens as part of the 1998 festival. Out of eighty-five former queens, more than fifty attended. Several came from out of state, with the woman who had traveled the farthest—the former Mary Inez Smith, Teenage queen in 1952—having come from Montana.

MARY STAGNER (fig. 62) died in 1996, after several years in Elgin's Golden Years Nursing Home. Toward the end of her life she sometimes confused Linda Haverland, who works at Golden Years, with Linda's mother, whom Stagner had known as a young woman. She would sometimes ask Linda to take her home to McDade with her at the end of the day, often referring to McDade as "God's country."

Even though ED STEINBRING (fig. 47) did not resign as pastor at Faith Lutheran Church till the early 1990s, most people see his departure as stemming from McDade's 1987 school controversy. Eight separate families—about a quarter of the congregation—left the church in 1987. Some of them were angry at fellow church members, but others were upset at Ed because they thought he had taken sides in the conflict. Ed has always denied that he favored one side over the other, though he did sometimes chide members of the congregation for acting in an unchristian manner toward one another. For a while, he even took to wearing black at the church, in mourning for what he saw as a divided, dying congregation. Over time, he alienated much of the membership, and attendance at Sunday morning worship services began to decline. By the early 1990s, just before Ed resigned, it was down to about thirty, after averaging well over a hundred in the mid-1980s.

In 1993, Faith Lutheran became a "joint parish" with the Lutheran church in Paige, and together the two congregations hired veteran Lutheran clergyman Alvin Epperson. Though most of the families who left Faith Lutheran in 1987 have not returned, attendance is up, and the church once again seems to be thriving. It has even gained a number of new members in recent years. Ironically, many of them are "refugees" from the Lutheran church in Bastrop who had conflicts with their newly hired pastor. Among them are several of Bastrop's business leaders, who have been very generous in their financial support of Faith Lutheran.

W. C. Stevens (fig. 86) still lives in McDade and continues to work for Bluebonnet Electric Cooperative.

J. D. Stewart (fig. 94) died in 1998. He was 89 years old.

Mabel Stewart (fig. 94) lives in Elgin. She is in her mid-80s.

John Strong (fig. 41) has worked for Elgin-Butler Brick at the brickyard for forty years, since he was twenty. After their own children had grown up and left home, he and his wife, Margaret, provided a home for foster children in 1990. They have had eleven foster children since then, sometimes as many as four at once. They currently provide a home for two children, the only African American students at the McDade School.

Jack Taylor (fig. 39) was recently diagnosed with throat cancer.

Lisa Taylor (fig. 100) was elected the Watermelon Festival's Teenage queen in 1992. She is now married and lives in Florida. She was among those who returned to McDade in 1998 for the fiftieth anniversary reunion of former Watermelon Festival Queens.

Now 86, Vlasta Walla (fig. 93) is a resident of Golden Years Nursing Home in Elgin.

Fred Wilson (fig. 14) has met with some misfortune in recent years. In 1994, after a twenty-year career with IBM in Austin, he lost his job in a round of corporate down-sizing. This led to financial difficulties for him and his wife, Cindy, which eventually resulted in the breakup of their marriage. As part of their divorce settlement, they had to sell their home. Fred now lives in a mobile home owned by his parents, Wallace and Freda Wilson. His son, Brandon, lives in Austin and works as a mechanic for a heavy equipment dealership in Elgin. Despite his bad luck, Fred remains active in the McDade community. He has served on the school board, is involved with the Watermelon Festival, and is one of the mainstays of McDade Cemetery Association. His luck began to turn in 1996, when, after an often-frustrating job search, he found work in the purchasing department of a technology firm in Austin. He now heads the purchasing department there. In 1998, he and his sister, Deborah Grimmer, accompanied their parents on a three-week visit to friends and family in England.

Wallace and Freda Wilson (figs. 21 and 14, respectively) remain among McDade's most widely respected and well-liked older couples. Now in his mid-eighties, Wallace is becoming a bit forgetful, but his lifelong concern for other people's welfare has not diminished. He is active in the McDade Cemetery Association, and the VFW, and he and Freda are among the core membership of the McDade Baptist Church. The two of them were instrumental in persuading the church to make a generous financial contribution toward rebuilding Weeping Willow Baptist Church after it burned in 1995.

Both Wallace and Freda will tell you that their lives have been "blessed," though sometimes in round-about ways. In 1993, their daughter Deborah's husband, Richard Grimmer, lost his job with RCA, ending a career of more than twenty years that had required their family to relocate twice—from Dallas to St. Louis, and then from St. Louis to New Jersey. When Richard was downsized, Deborah asked her mother to start sending them the Sunday classifieds from the *Austin American-Statesman*. A month or so later, Richard interviewed for a job with an insurance company in Brenham, sixty-five miles east of McDade. ("Pray for him," Deborah told Freda on the phone.) Richard got the job, and he and Deborah moved to Brenham in 1994, a turn of events that delighted everyone. Deborah's daughter, Daphne, and her three children have since joined Richard and Deborah in Brenham. Wallace and Freda are deeply thankful that both of their children and their families have ended up close to McDade.

Now in his early seventies, DAN WOLF (fig. 74) still farms for a living. His main cash crops are peaches, pears, and blackberries. He sells the peaches and pears to grocery stores and at farmers' markets in and around Austin, while most of what he makes from blackberries comes from people who visit the Wolf farm to pick their own. In recent years, Dan's son, William (see fig. 96), has talked about someday planting pecan trees on much of the farm's acreage, a plan that would require investment in an extensive irrigation system. While gratified that William is showing an interest in keeping the farm going—and in the family—Dan is skeptical about switching to pecans. He thinks it would cost too much and that the land is "too poor" to justify the expense.

Dan's wife, EVELYN WOLF (figs. 34 and 74), continues to help with the business end of the farm, as well as staying involved in various community projects. For several years now, she has organized annual rabies vaccination clinics in uptown McDade, which offer convenient and inexpensive vaccinations for the town's many dogs and cats. In 1994, Evelyn embarked on a campaign to get "Expanded Local Calling" for the McDade phone exchange. This required circulating several petitions, collecting dozens of affidavits, and presenting the results—Evelyn had to submit eleven copies of everything, more paper than she could carry to the hearing by herself—to the Public Utilities Commission in Austin. As a result, McDade residents no longer have to pay for every call they make to numbers outside the McDade exchange. Instead, for a small monthly charge, they can now make unlimited calls to Elgin, Bastrop, Paige, Coupland, and Lexington. Evelyn had hoped to get Austin included in the package—Elgin residents can call Austin for free—but the commission denied that part of her request. More recently, in 1996, Evelyn coordinated fund-raising efforts aimed at finishing construction of the new sanctuary for Weeping Willow Baptist Church, whose old sanctuary had burned the previous summer. By soliciting donations from churches and other civic organizations in the area and securing a matching grant from the Texas Lutheran Brotherhood, she helped raise almost ten thousand dollars, which enabled Weeping Willow's new church building to be finished.

In the spring of 1998, Evelyn visited her youngest child, Julie, at Hanau Army Base in Germany, where she works in the base hospital as a nurse. Julie is a civilian, but her husband,

Jason Smith, is an army helicopter pilot whose unit is based at Hanau, though he is currently on duty in Bosnia. Julie and Jason were high school sweethearts at Lexington High School. They married in 1995, shortly after Julie received her nursing degree from the University of Texas Medical Branch at Galveston. She then went to work at the state prison hospital in Huntsville, while Jason finished his degree at Sam Houston State University. The army sent Jason to Germany in 1997, and Julie went with him.

The Wolfs' other children are closer to home. Their oldest, Danna, graduated summa cum laude from Texas A&M in 1987 with a degree in applied mathematical science. She took a job with IBM in Austin right after graduating and has worked there ever since, most recently as a software projects manager. In 1990, Danna married her childhood sweetheart, Scott Rother, whose family has also been in the McDade area for many years. Unfortunately, Evelyn and Scott's mother found themselves on opposite sides of McDade's 1987 school controversy, and even though they were once good friends, they have barely spoken since. This complicates family life for Danna and Scott (and their two children, ages four and one), but they work hard at maintaining a good relationship with both sets of parents. In 1998, Danna and Scott sold their house in Austin and moved into a new house Scott built on land owned by his parents, about halfway between Lexington and McDade.

The Wolfs' second daughter, Monica, lives in Elgin with her husband, who is an Austin fire-fighter, and their two children, ages four and one. After working in the Texas Attorney General's office and attending the University of Texas on a part-time basis, Monica now volunteers a couple of mornings a week at the day-care center her son attends. She says she's very happy as "a full-time mom," at least for the moment. She hopes to go back to school and get a degree in early childhood education when her children are a bit older.

After working for a couple years when he graduated from Lexington High School, Dan and Evelyn's only son, WILLIAM WOLF (fig. 96), attended Sam Houston State University in Huntsville. He majored in criminal justice. For a short while after graduating, he worked as a guard on death row at the state prison there. Among the prisoners he guarded was confessed mass murderer Henry Lee Lucas. William now has a job with the Immigration and Naturalization Service in New Mexico as a Border Patrol Agent. He has a drug-sniffing dog assigned to him, and he keeps the dog with him day and night, on and off the job. William got married in 1996. His wife works as a teacher at the federal prison at Las Cruces, New Mexico.

MARSHALL WOLF (fig. 87) is Dan Wolf's nephew. He works as a construction-site plumber for a contractor in Bryan. He used to do similar work in Austin, only thirty-five miles from McDade, but he quit that job because of the traffic he'd run into every day. He much prefers driving seventy miles each way between Bryan and McDade because there is less traffic. Marshall has worked on several large construction projects at Texas A&M University, including the George Bush Presidential Library and Museum, which opened in 1997.

EMMA WUENSCHE (fig. 103) died in November 1993. She stayed in her small house in McDade until early that year, at which point she went to stay with one of her sons in Houston. The house is now rented out.

Notes

Chapter 8   The Celebrated Past

1. Moore, *Bastrop County*, 191; *The Early Years of Faith Lutheran Church, 1883–1903*, 2.
2. Moore, *Bastrop County*, 191; *Elgin Courier*, May 30, 1968; *Bastrop Advertiser*, July 8, 1971
3. Moore, *Bastrop County*, 191; *Elgin Courier*, May 30, 1968.
4. *Bastrop Advertiser*, July 8, 1971; *Annals of Travis County*, vol. 30, 51; Sonnichsen, *I'll Die*, 169.
5. *Bastrop Advertiser*, July 8, 1971; *The Echo*, 1948–49; Sonnichsen, *I'll Die*, 169; Schulz, *McDade*, 90.
6. *Bastrop Advertiser*, July 19, 1873; September 20, 1873; July 8, 1971; Carter, *Invasion*, 71; *Elgin Courier*, June 24, 1937; July 1, 1971.
7. *Bastrop Advertiser*, July 19, 1873; July 8, 1971.
8. *Elgin Courier*, July 3, 1947; July 1, 1971; *Bastrop Advertiser*, November 22, 1873; December 6, 1873.
9. Sonnichsen, *I'll Die*, 169; Carter, *Invasion*, 71; conversation with Lawrence and Ernestine Schulz, May 5, 1998.
10. Sonnichsen, *I'll Die*, 168; Ficklen, *McDade's Christmas Murders*, 40.
11. Sonnichsen, *I'll Die*, 168; Ficklen, *McDade's Christmas Murders*, 42.
12. Sonnichsen, *I'll Die*, 169; Ficklen, *McDade's Christmas Murders*, 42; interview with Erhard Goerlitz, June 5, 1989.
13. Sonnichsen, *I'll Die*, 170; Ficklen, *McDade's Christmas Murders*, 42; *Austin Weekly Statesman*, January 13, 1875; *Bastrop Advertiser*, May 9, 1874; *Sayersville Historical Association Bulletin*, Spring 1984, 6.
14. Sonnichsen, *I'll Die*, 171–72; *Austin Weekly Statesman*, March 30, 1876; June 1, 1876; July 27, 1876; August 10, 1876.
15. Ficklen, *McDade's Christmas Murders*, 42; Sonnichsen, *I'll Die*, 173–77; *Elgin Courier*, December 25, 1980; *Galveston News*, April 25, 1876; *Austin Weekly Statesman*, August 10, 1876; June 29, 1877; July 4, 1877.
16. Sonnichsen, *I'll Die*, 177–78; *Bastrop Advertiser*, November 25, 1883; *Galveston News*, November 25, 1883; December 4, 1883.
17. Sonnichsen, *I'll Die*, 178; *Galveston News*, December 9, 1883; *Elgin Courier*, December 25, 1980; Schulz, *McDade*, 98.
18. Sonnichsen, *I'll Die*, 178–80; *Austin American*, December 26, 1883; December 27, 1883.
19. Sonnichsen, *I'll Die*, 181–82; *Austin American*, December 26, 1883; December 27, 1883; *Bastrop Advertiser*, January 26, 1884.
20. Sonnichsen, 183–85; *Austin American*, December 26, 1883; December 27, 1883; *Bastrop Advertiser*, January 26, 1884.
21. *Bastrop Advertiser*, January 26, 1884; Schulz, *McDade*, 28.
22. *Austin American-Statesman*, December 27, 1883; December 29, 1883; *Frontier Times*, May 1939 (cited in Schulz, *McDade*, 27–29); *Galveston News*, December 27, 1883.
23. *Austin American-Statesman*, December 26, 1883; *Galveston News*, December 27, 1883.
24. Fecklin, *McDade's Christmas Murders*, 47; *Galveston News*, December 27, 1883; *Elgin Courier*, December 25, 1980.

Chapter 9   The Forgotten Past

1. Carter, *Invasions*, 71; *Elgin: A History of Elgin, Texas, 1872–1972*, 5; Moore, *Bastrop County*, 95.
2. *Elgin Courier*, July 20, 1972.
3. *Bastrop Advertiser*, July 12, 1890; July 26, 1890; August 2, 1890.
4. Ibid., August 2, 1890.
5. Ibid., September 16, 1890.
6. Ibid., August 2, 1890; August 23, 1890.
7. Moore, *Bastrop County*, 171, 119–20; *Elgin Courier*, June 8, 1939; *The Echo*, 1948–49.
8. Moore, *Bastrop County*, 176–77; *Elgin Courier*, May 21, 1936; June 8, 1939
9. Moore, *Bastrop County*, 119–20; Schulz, p. 98, 44; *Elgin Courier*, June 8, 1939; July 2, 1965.
10. *San Antonio Express*, June 14, 1909; *Elgin Courier*, June 20, 1972; *Bastrop Advertiser*, May 21, 1910; *Sixth Annual Announcment*, 1915–16;
11. *Bastrop Advertiser*, May 12, 1910; *Elgin Courier*, June 8, 1939; April 18, 1940; June 29, 1942; February 23, 1961.
12. *Elgin Courier*, December 24, 1964.

Chapter 10   The Other McDade

1. *The Early Years of Faith Lutheran Church, 1883–1903*, 2.
2. Ibid., 3; *Faith Lutheran Church Directory*, 1980.
3. *The Early Years of Faith Lutheran Church, 1883–1903*, 6.
4. Ibid., 7.
5. Ibid.
6. Interview with Adeline Eschberger, June 20, 1989; interview with Dan Wolf, February 24, 1989.
7. *The Early Years of Faith Lutheran Church, 1883–1903*, 8.
8. Bohls, *"From the Record,"* 3.
9. Ibid.
10. *Church Book*, St. Andrew's Lutheran Church.
11. Bohls, *"From the Record,"* 3.
12. Ibid.
13. Ibid.
14. Ibid.
15. Group interview with Selma Eklund, Adeline Eschberger, Alvin Eschberger, Lucy Eschberger, Walter Eschberger, Emilie Goerlitz, Amanda Haverland, Herbert Smith, and Lena Smith, March 15, 1989.
16. Interview with Emilie Goerlitz, June 5, 1989; *Elgin Courier*, April 21, 1917; group interview with Selma Eklund, Adeline Eschberger, Alvin Eschberger, Lucy Eschberger, Walter Eschberger, Emilie Goerlitz, Amanda Haverland, Herbert Smith, and Lena Smith, March 15, 1989.
17. McKay, *Texas Politics*, 38, 42; Sonntag, *Hyphenated Texans*, 47.
18. McKay, *Texas Politics*, 85.
19. Interview with Erhard Goerlitz, June 5, 1989; group interview with Selma Eklund, Adeline Eschberger, Alvin Eschberger, Lucy Eschberger, Walter Eschberger, Emilie Goerlitz, Amanda Haverland, Herbert Smith, and Lena Smith, March 15, 1989. Many of McDade's older German people refer to those living in McDade who are not of German ancestry as "English-speaking people."
20. Interview with Erhard Goerlitz, June 5, 1989; interview with Adeline Eschberger, June 20, 1989.

Chapter 11   Between the Wars

1. Cf. Atherton's discussion of the "predominant middle-class code," Atherton, *Main Street*, 65–108.
2. *Bastrop Advertiser*, November 20, 1881 (reprinted in *Bastrop Advertiser* of November 17, 1927).
3. Ibid., September 30, 1926; May 6, 1926.
4. Ibid., August 20, 1925; November 25, 1926; Bohls, "From the Record," 4.
5. I have heard portions of these stories in various contexts from various sources. In each instance, I was asked not to repeat what I had heard; thus the lack of details.
6. *Bastrop Advertiser*, February 4, 1926; February 11, 1926.
7. Ibid., February 18, 1926; April 21, 1927.
8. Ibid., April 7, 1927; August 17, 1925.
9. Ibid., July 16, 1925.
10. Ibid., February 12, 1925; July 31, 1930; March 25, 1926.
11. Ibid., June 24, 1926; June 23, 1927; February 28, 1929; Dunning, *Tune in Yesterday,* 32–33; interview with an informant who prefers to remain anonymous, 1989.
12. *Bastrop Advertiser*, September 30, 1926; February 11, 1926.
13. Ibid., June 16, 1927; February 11, 1926; April 9, 1925.
14. Ibid., September 3, 1925; February 4, 1926; August 27, 1925.
15. Ibid., August 27, 1925.
16. Ibid., September 30, 1926; April 8, 1926; September 30, 1926; March 4, 1926.
17. Ibid., March 4, 1926; August 6, 1925; August 23, 1928; January 14, 1926.
18. Levine, *Defender of the Faith*, 347, 272.
19. *Bastrop Advertiser*, July 30, 1925; February 26, 1925; April 16, 1925; cited in Cherny, *A Righteous Cause*, 174.
20. *Bastrop Advertiser*, July 21, 1927.
21. Ibid., April 7, 1927; February 12, 1925; February 11, 1926; April 22, 1926; April 7, 1927; July 29, 1926
22. Ibid., June 4, 1925; February 3, 1927; January 17, 1929; July 18, 1929; March 5, 1925; October 29, 1925
23. Ibid., August 5, 1926; August 16, 1928.
24. Cf. Snyder; also the writings of Henry W. Grady, editor of the *Atlanta Constitution* from 1879 to 1889, considered by many as the leading "apostle of the South"; *Bastrop Advertiser*, May 13, 1926; April 22, 1926; May 13, 1926.
25. Cf. Snyder for a brief account of cotton agriculture in the late 1920s and early 1930s; *Bastrop Advertiser*, December 31, 1931.
26. Interview with Tom Dungan, November 9, 1987; interview with Erhard Goerlitz, June 5, 1989.
27. *Bastrop Advertiser*, February 3, 1927; September 27, 1928; October 4, 1928; October 25, 1928; February 28, 1929; Schulz, *McDade,* 146.
28. *Elgin Courier*, June 8, 1939; July 21, 1927; July 3, 1930; January 7, 1926; December 22, 1927; October 30, 1930; November 10, 1927; March 20, 1930; April 7, 1927; April 3, 1930; November 25, 1926.
29. *Bastrop Advertiser*, May 12, 1927; December 22, 1927; July 3, 1930; January 26, 1928; February 9, 1928.
30. Snyder, *Cotton Crisis*, 3–4; *Bastrop Advertiser*, November 6, 1930; December 18, 1930; December 25, 1930.
31. *Bastrop Advertiser*, June 11, 1931; August 6, 1931.
32. Interview with Wallace Wilson, April 21, 1989; interview with Tom Dungan, November 9, 1987.
33. *Bastrop Advertiser*, July 29, 1926.
34. Ibid., August 13, 1931; October 29, 1931; *Elgin Courier*, December 30,1937.
35. *Elgin Courier*, June 8, 1939; April 26, 1979 (interview with John Dube, longtime rancher and farmer in the McDade area); interview with Erhard Goerlitz, June 5, 1989.

36. *Elgin Courier*, June 30, 1938; June 24, 1937; July 1, 1937; August 5, 1937; April 26, 1979 (interview with John Dube, longtime rancher and farmer in the McDade area); November 16, 1939; January 18, 1940; June 5, 1941.

37. *Elgin Courier*, April 25, 1940; December 8, 1938; May 12, 1938; July 23, 1936; September 9, 1937; April 6, 1939; August 1, 1940; November 5, 1940.

38. Ibid., February 20, 1941; April 6, 1939; November 19, 1940; January 20, 1938; December 26, 1940; April 7, 1938.

39. McCarty, *Struggle for Sobriety*, 49; *Bastrop Advertiser*, August 29, 1935; November 12, 1925; March 25, 1926; *Elgin Courier*, June 8, 1939; January 21, 1937; October 27, 1938.

40. *Bastrop Advertiser*, April 30, 1931; *Elgin Courier*, March 28, 1935; August 8, 1940; August 22, 1940; March 6, 1941; March 13, 1941; August 28, 1941.

41. *Elgin Courier*, November 28, 1940; October 31, 1940; August 7, 1941.

42. Storm, *I Ain't down Yet*, 2, 11; McNeil, *Total Television*, 528, 559; *Elgin Courier*, October 26, 1939; January 4, 1940.

43. *Elgin Courier*, November 28, 1940; November 6, 1941.

Chapter 12   Camp Swift

1. *Austin American*, January 19, 1951.

2. Houston and Long, *History*, 6, 8, 10; *Elgin Courier*, January 8, 1942; Freeman, *A Cultural Resource*, 85; *Austin American*, December 19, 1941.

3. *Austin American*, January 8, 1942; March 22, 1942; *Bastrop Advertiser*, January 15, 1942.

4. *Austin American*, February 7, 1942; February 15, 1942; February 22, 1942; March 1, 1942; March 11, 1942; April 3, 1942; *Elgin Courier*, March 12, 1942; conversation with Frank Kastner, June 1985.

5. *Austin American*, February 7, 1942; *Bastrop Advertiser* and *Elgin Courier* (combined "Special Camp Swift Issue"), July 1942.

6. *Austin American*, May 5, 1942; May 24, 1942; June 12, 1942; *Elgin Courier*, May 21, 1942; Houston and Long, *History*, 11.

7. *Elgin Courier*, June 4, 1942.

8. *Austin American*, June 2, 1942; *Elgin Courier*, July 2, 1942; Houston and Long, *History*, 50; interview with Emma Wuensche, April 28, 1989.

9. Houston and Long, *History*, 23–24, 36–38, 43; interview with Tom Dungan, November 9, 1987; interview with Emilie Goerlitz, June 5, 1989.

10. Houston and Long, *History*, 19–20; *Austin American*, October 9, 1942; November 28, 1942; *Bastrop Advertiser*, October 15, 1942.

11. *Austin American*, December 18, 1945; April 26, 1946; January 4, 1947; *Elgin Courier*, December 6, 1945; *Bastrop Advertiser*, May 30, 1946.

12. *Austin American*, March 15, 1947; January 19, 1951; *Bastrop Advertiser*, August 31, 1944; February 20, 1947; *Elgin Courier*, January 16, 1947; interview with Tom Dungan, November 9, 1987.

13. *Bastrop Advertiser*, August 28, 1947.

14. *Austin American*, September 11, 1947; October 13, 1947; *Bastrop Advertiser*, January 30, 1947; August 28, 1947; *Elgin Courier*, September 18, 1947; interview with Tom Dungan, November 9, 1987.

15. *Austin American*, September 11, 1947; October 12, 1947; October 13, 1947; August 2, 1950; *Bastrop Advertiser*, May 30, 1946; *Elgin Courier*, March 25, 1948; interview with Homer Munson, May 6, 1989; interview with Wallace Wilson, April 21, 1989; Freeman, *A Cultural Resource*, 78.

16. *Elgin Courier*, January 15, 1942; October 9, 1947.

17. *Austin American*, January 19, 1951; interview with Homer Munson, May 6, 1989.

18. *Austin American*, January 19, 1951; *Elgin Courier*, July 27, 1939; Carter, *Invasion*, 75; interview with Homer Munson, May 6, 1989.

19. *Austin American*, July 18, 1950; January 19, 1951; *Bastrop Advertiser*, December 28, 1950; interview with Tom Dungan, November 9, 1987.

20. *Austin American*, January 24, 1951.

21. *Austin American*, September, 14, 1947; October 16,1947; July 20, 1950; August 10, 1950; January 25,1951; *Bastrop Advertiser*, January 25, 1951; March 20, 1951.

22. *Austin American*, January 10, 1951; *Bastrop Advertiser*, July 20, 1950; January 18, 1951.

23. *Austin American*, January 25, 1951; *Bastrop Advertiser*, January 25, 1951.

24. *Austin American*, January 24, 1951.

25. *Austin American*, January 28, 1951; August 14, 1951; *Bastrop Advertiser*, March 20, 1951; May 22, 1951.

26. *Elgin Courier*, January 15, 1942; interview with Tom Dungan, November 9, 1987.

27. Interview with Wallace Wilson, April 21, 1989.

28. Interview with Tom Dungan, November 9, 1987.

29. *Bastrop Advertiser*, March 12, 1942; *Elgin Courier*, February 5, 1942; February 19, 1942; February 26, 1942; March 5, 1942; March 12, 1942; conversation with Frank Kastner, June 1985.

30. *Elgin Courier*, February 5, 1942; February 19, 1942; October 8, 1942; March 12, 1947; interview with Tom Dungan, November 9, 1987, interview with Emma Wuensche, April 28, 1989.

31. *Bastrop Advertiser*, February 26, 1942; *Elgin Courier*, February 12, 1942; February 26, 1942; March 5, 1942; March 19, 1942; March 26, 1942; April 16, 1942; April 30, 1942; May 28, 1942.

32. *Elgin Courier*, June 4, 1942; interview with Thelma McDavid, April 21, 1989; interview with Wallace Wilson, April 21, 1989; interview with Homer Munson, May 6, 1989.

33. *Elgin Courier*, July 30, 1942.

34. *Austin American*, January 6, 1942; January 18, 1942; *Elgin Courier*, January 8, 1942; January 15, 1942; interview with Wallace Wilson, April 21, 1989; interview with Emma Wuensche, April 28, 1989.

35. *Elgin Courier*, February 5, 1942; February 26, 1942.

36. Ibid., February 12, 1942; February 26, 1942; March 19, 1942; March 26, 1942; April 16, 1942; May 7, 1942; May 28, 1942.

37. Ibid., May 21, 1942; June 11, 1942.

38. Ibid., June 18, 1942; July 30, 1942; November 6, 1952.

39. Ibid., August 20, 1942; August 27, 1942.

40. Ibid., October 1, 1942; October 29, 1942; February 11, 1943.

41. Ibid., June 4, 1942; interview with Tom Dungan, November 9, 1987.

42. *Elgin Courier*, July 22, 1943; interview with Tom Dungan, November 9, 1987.

43. *Elgin Courier*, September 3, 1942; September 10, 1942; January 21, 1943; August 12, 1943; July 20, 1944; *Bastrop Advertiser* and *Elgin Courier* (combined "Special Camp Swift Issue"), July 1942; interview with Tom Dungan, November 9, 1987; interview with Thelma McDavid, April 21, 1989.

44. *Elgin Courier*, April 8, 1943; July 8, 1943; interview with Tom Dungan, November 9, 1987.

45. *Elgin Courier*, July 16, 1942; February 4, 1943; June 24, 1943; interview with Nellie Hudler, April, 18, 1985.

46. *Elgin Courier*, August 27, 1942; September 3, 1942; November 12, 1942; April 15, 1943; August 24, 1944; interview with Emilie Goerlitz, June 5, 1989; interview with Adeline Eschberger, June 20, 1989.

47. Interview with Tom Dungan, November 9, 1987.

48. Interview with Tom Dungan, November 9, 1987; interview with Adeline Eschberger, June 20, 1989.

Chapter 13   McDade, 1945–1980

1. Interview with Adeline Eschberger, June 20, 1989.

2. *Elgin Courier*, August 1, 1946; September 19, 1946; August 7, 1947; September 18, 1947; November 13, 1947.

3. Holt, "The McDade Baptist Church," 2; *Austin American*, August 5, 1947; *Elgin Courier*, August 12, 1947; October 2, 1947; March 25, 1948; December 23, 1948; April 1, 1948; interview with Wallace Wilson, April 21, 1989; interview with Stella Kastner, May 19, 1989.

4. Interview with Adeline Eschberger, June 20, 1989; interview with Emma Wuensche, April 28, 1989; *Elgin Courier*, September 18, 1941; December 28, 1944; March 14, 1946; January 16, 1947.

5. *Elgin Courier*, March 23, 1946; interview with Adeline and Alvin Eschberger, June 20, 1989; interview with Stella Kastner, May 19, 1989; interview with Emma Wuensche, April 28, 1989.

6. *Elgin Courier*, June 13, 1946, July 18, 1946; interview with Freda Wilson, March 22, 1989; interview with Nellie Hudler, January 21, 1985.

7. *Elgin Courier*, March 6, 1947; May 15, 1947; March 16, 1943; conversation with Ernestine Schulz, June 12, 1998; interview with Adeline Eschberger, June 20, 1989.

8. *Elgin Courier*, August 28, 1947.

9. Ibid., September 2, 1948; McDade Rural Progress Association, "Official Record Book, 1948; *The Echo*; interview with Stella Kastner, May 19, 1989.

10. *Elgin Courier*, May 6, 1948; McDade Rural Neighborhood Progress Association, "Official Record Book," 1948.

11. McDade Rural Neighborhood Progress Association, "Official Record Book," 1948.

12. *Elgin Courier*, May 13, 1948.

13. Ibid., May 27, 1948; June 3, 1948; McDade Rural Neighborhood Progress Association, "Official Record Book," 1948.

14. McDade Rural Neighborhood Progress Association, "Official Record Book," 1948; *Elgin Courier*, June 26, 1948.

15. McDade Rural Neighborhood Progress Association, "Official Record Book," 1948; Haynie's "Voucher Book," cited in Schulz, *McDade*, 113; conversation with Lawrence and Ernestine Schulz, May 5, 1998; conversation with Adeline Eschberger, May 1998; conversation with Erhard Goerlitz, May 1998.

16. McDade Rural Neighborhood Progress Association, "Official Record Book," 1948; interview with Adeline Eschberger, June 20, 1989.

17. McDade Rural Neighborhood Progress Association, "Official Record Book," 1948; interview with Adeline Eschberger, June 20, 1989; interview with Erhard Goerlitz, June 5, 1989.

18. *Elgin Courier*, July 11, 1926; August 5, 1926; July 12, 1928; August 6, 1931; July 11, 1940; June 26, 1941; August 7, 1947; interview with Tom Dungan, November 9, 1987.

19. McDade Rural Neighborhood Progress Association, "Official Record Book," 1948; *Elgin Courier*, July 8, 1948; interview with Adeline Eschberger, June 20, 1989; interview with Stella Kastner, May 19, 1989.

20. Interview with Emma Wuensche, April 28, 1989; interview with Freda Wilson, March 22, 1989; interview with Dan Wolf, February 24, 1989; interview with Adeline Eschberger, June 20, 1989.

21. *Elgin Courier*, July 8, 1948; McDade Rural Neighborhood Progress Association, "Official Record Book," 1948; interview with Alvin Eschberger, June 20, 1989.

22. Wainscott, "Memories, Memories," 1988; interview with Adeline Eschberger, June 20, 1989; McDade Rural Neighborhood Progress Association, "Official Record Book," 1948; *Elgin Courier*, September 9, 1948.

23. *Elgin Courier*, June 11, 1942; September 3, 1942; April 29, 1943; August 12, 1943; May 16, 1946; June 13, 1946; November 7, 1946; November 14, 1946; January 2, 1947; January 23, 1947; May 19, 1948; August 19, 1948; July 20, 1950; November 2, 1950; February 23, 1961. *Bastrop Advertiser* and *Elgin Courier*, combined "Special

Camp Swift Issue," July 1942; interview with Tom Dungan, November 7, 1987; *Austin American*, January 7, 1951.

24. *Elgin Courier*, May 18, 1950; June 6, 1950; November 6, 1952; interview with Adeline Eschberger, June 20, 1989.

25. *Elgin Courier*, November 6, 1941; March 19, 1942; July 7, 1952; *Austin American*, January 4, 1942; January 11, 1942; February 21, 1942; Texas State Department of Transportation Road Maps, 1949, 1950, 1951, 1952.

26. Texas State Department of Transportation Road Map, 1953; interview with Tom Dungan, November 9, 1987; interview with Nellie Hudler, April 18, 1985.

27. *Elgin Courier*, August 17, 1950; July 12, 1951; July 26, 1951; February 21, 1952; interview with Margie Schindler, June 14, 1989; interview with Adeline Eschberger, June 20, 1989.

28. *Elgin Courier*, November 25, 1954; March 3, 1955; August 13, 1959; interview with Tom Dungan, November 9, 1987; interview with Shorty Bostic, June 4, 1985; interview with Dan Wolf, February 24, 1989; interview with Erhard Goerlitz, June 5, 1989; interview with Marshall Wolf, May 1, 1989; interview with Adeline Eschberger, June 20, 1989; interview with Wallace Wilson, April 21, 1989.

29. *Elgin Courier*, July 29, 1954; December 16, 1954; March 17, 1955; September 15, 1955; September 22, 1955; October 20, 1955; February 2, 1956; April 12, 1956; *Dallas Morning News*, February 19, 1956; interview with Stella Kastner, May 19, 1989.

30. *Elgin Courier*, January 16, 1958; March 13, 1958; September 17, 1959; September 24, 1959; January 14, 1960; October 1, 1960; December 24, 1960; January 12, 1961.

31. *Elgin Courier*, June 21, 1951; June 25, 1953; June 24, 1954; July 1, 1954; July 7, 1955; July 21, 1955; August 4, 1955; July 19, 1956; July 11, 1957; July 10, 1958; July 28, 1960; interview with Freda Wilson, March 22, 1989; interview with Tom Dungan, November 9, 1987; interview with Stella Kastner, May 19, 1989.

32. *Elgin Courier*, February 23, 1961; March 9, 1961.

33. *Elgin Courier*, August 11, 1960; August 30, 1962; interview with Tom Dungan, November 9, 1987; interview with Dan Wolf, February 24, 1989, interview with Clyde and Mary Cayton, May 1, 1989.

34. *Elgin Courier*, June 8, 1961; September 7, 1961; April 12, 1962; August 30, 1962; September 12, 1963; August 27, 1964; September 2, 1965; September 7, 1967; August 22, 1968; September 3, 1970.

35. *The Early Days of Faith Lutheran Church*, 14; interview with Erhard Goerlitz, June 5, 1989; *Elgin Courier*, March 22, 1962; interview with Ed Steinbring, April 17, 1989; *Faith Lutheran Church 1980 Directory*, 5; interview with Adeline Eschberger, June 20, 1989.

36. *Elgin Courier*, September 13, 1962; October 3, 1963; April 18, 1963.

37. Moore, *Bastrop County*, 4–5; *Elgin Courier*, November 22, 1962; Interview with Clyde and Mary Cayton, May 1, 1989.

38. *Elgin Courier*, November 29, 1962; July 2, 1965; April 13, 1978; interview with Tom Dungan, November 9, 1987.

39. *Elgin Courier*, June 3, 1963; July 18, 1963; August 8, 1963; April 9, 1964; April 23, 1964; June 4, 1964; July 23, 1964; August 13, 1964; October 29, 1964; December 17, 1964; June 26, 1965; July 2, 1965; August 19, 1965; April 13, 1978.

40. Ibid., December 6, 1962; May 16, 1963; April 16, 1965; June 11, 1965; August 19, 1965.

41. Ibid., April 16, 1965; April 23, 1965; March 16, 1967; interview with Adeline Eschberger, March 8, 1989.

42. *Elgin Courier*, March 16, 1967; December 17, 1970; March 9, 1972; March 30, 1972; May 9, 1968; July 18, 1968.

43. Interview with David Carson, May 24, 1989; interview with Clyde and Mary Cayton, May 1, 1989; *Elgin Courier*, February 10, 1964.

44. Interview with Clyde and Mary Cayton, May 1, 1989.

45. Ibid.

46. Ibid.; interview with Laura Cayton, March 27, 1989.

47. Interview with Clyde and Mary Cayton, May 1, 1989; interview with Thomas Baca, May 16, 1989; interview with Dan Wolf, February 24, 1989; interview with Shorty Bostic, June 4, 1985.

48. *Elgin Courier*, June 8, 1967; June 22, 1967; June 29, 1967; May 16, 1968; interview with Nellie Hudler, April 18, 1985.

49. *Elgin Courier*, January 9, 1969; July 24, 1969; March 6, 1969; April 17, 1969; May 8, 1969; interview with Tom Dungan, November 9, 1987.

50. *Elgin Courier*, May 3, 1969; June 6, 1969; July 24, 1969; November 6, 1969; November 13, 1969; July 16, 1970; July 15, 1971; June 29, 1972; July 25, 1974; July 17, 1975; July 15, 1976.

51. Ibid., November 13, 1969; April 22, 1971; May 6, 1971; February 10, 1972; May 2, 1974; July 15, 1971; June 29, 1972; interview with Ivy Ann Cronin, June 22, 1989.

52. Conversation with Susan Johnson, January 30, 1985.

53. *Elgin Courier*, July 31, 1975; June 28, 1979.

54. Interview with Linda Haverland, March 29, 1989; interview with Tom Dungan, November 9, 1987; interview with Marshall Wolf, May 1, 1989.

55. *Elgin Courier*, June 9, 1977; November 17, 1977; April 13, 1978; interview with Tom Dungan, November 9, 1987; July 26, 1979; March 13, 1980; interview with Stella Kastner, May 19,1989.

56. *Elgin Courier*, January 25, 1979; February 1, 1979; Wainscott, "Memories, Memories"; interview with Ivy Ann Cronin, June 22, 1989; interview with Clyde and Mary Cayton, May 1, 1989; interview with Sam and Debbie Dunkin, May 30, 1989; interview with Freda Wilson, March 22, 1989.

57. *Elgin Courier*, October 21, 1976; November 18, 1976; April 7, 1977; May 19, 1977; March 2, 1978.

58. Ibid., March 3, 1977; August 18, 1977; March 2, 1978; March 9, 1978; interview with Thomas Baca, May 16, 1989.

59. *Elgin Courier*, March 9, 1978; June 22, 1978; interview with Freda Wilson, March 22,1989.

60. Ibid., April 6, 1978; May 4, 1978.

61. Ibid., June 1, 1978; June 22, 1978; July 6, 1978.

62. Ibid., August 24, 1978; August 31, 1978; September 7, 1978.

Chapter 14   McDade in the 1980s

1. Interview with David and Barbara Carson, May 24, 1989.

2. Interview with David and Barbara Carson, May 24, 1989; conversation with Nellie Hudler, January 21, 1985.

3. *Elgin Courier*, March 10, 1983; interview with David and Barbara Carson, May 24, 1989; *Elgin Courier*, January 12, 1984.

4. Interview with Clyde and Mary Cayton, May 1, 1989; interview with Laura Maness, March 27, 1989

5. Interview with Clyde and Mary Cayton, May 1, 1989; interview with Ivy Ann Cronin, June 22, 1989; interview with Tom Dungan November 9, 1987; interview with Freda Wilson, March 29, 1989.

6. *Elgin Courier*, December 1, 1983; interview with Laura Maness, March 27, 1989.

7. *Elgin Courier*, February 2, 1984; "The Town Crier," September 1, 1984; *Elgin Courier*, December 6, 1984; interview with David and Barbara Carson, May 24, 1989.

8. *Elgin Courier*, August 11, 1977; August 7, 1980; October 15, 1981; September 1, 1983; September 22, 1983; interview with Thomas Baca, May 16, 1989.

9. *Elgin Courier*, September 1, 1983; interview with David and Barbara Carson, May 24, 1989; interview with Thomas Baca, May 16, 1989.

10. *Elgin Courier*, September 1, 1983; October 6, 1983; interview with Thomas Baca, May 16, 1989; interview with David and Barbara Carson, May 24, 1989.

11. *Elgin Courier*, September 22, 1983; interview with Thomas Baca, May 16, 1989; interview with Clyde and Mary Cayton, May 1, 1989; interview with Laura Maness, March 27, 1989.

12. *Elgin Courier*, September 29, 1983; February 2, 1984; interview with Laura Maness, March 27, 1989; interview with Thomas Baca, May 16, 1989; interview with Linda Haverland, March 29, 1989.

13. Interview with David and Barbara Carson, May 24, 1989; *Elgin Courier*, June 11, 1987.

14. Interview with Thomas Baca, May 16, 1989; interview with Clyde and Mary Cayton, May 1, 1989; interview with Laura Maness, March 27, 1989.

15. *Elgin Courier*, October 13, 1983; interview with Thomas Baca, May 16, 1989.

16. *Elgin Courier*, April 12, 1984; April 11, 1985; April 10, 1986; *Austin American-Statesman*, June 1, 1987; interview with Dolph and Joanne Hess, June 8, 1989; interview with Linda Haverland, March 29, 1989.

17. *Elgin Courier*, May 2, 1984; April 11, 1985; June 13, 1985; July 11, 1985; April 10, 1986; interview with Linda Haverland, March 29, 1989; interview with Dolph and Joanne Hess, June 8, 1989.

18. Interview with Thomas Baca, May 16, 1989; *Elgin Courier*, August 14, 1986; interview with Dolph and Joanne Hess, June 8, 1989; interview with Buddy Lewis, July 13, 1989.

19. Interview with Thomas Baca, May 16, 1989; *Elgin Courier*, February 26, 1987; March 12, 1987.

20. Interview with Freda Wilson, March 29, 1989; interview with Buddy Lewis, July 13, 1989; interview with Opal Jones, June 9, 1989; interview with Jerre Guthrie, April 28, 1989.

21. Interview with Ed and Sue Steinbring, April 17, 1989; interview with David and Barbara Carson, May 24, 1989.

22. Interview with Linda Haverland, March 29, 1989; interview with Opal Jones, June 9, 1989.

23. *Elgin Courier*, April 9, 1987; April 23, 1987; May 21, 1987.

24. *Elgin Courier*, April 16, 1987; April 30, 1987; *Austin American-Statesman*, April 22, 1987.

25. *Elgin Courier*, May 14, 1987; June 4, 1987; *Austin American-Statesman*, June 1, 1987.

26. Interview with Clyde and Mary Cayton, May 1, 1989; interview with Ed and Sue Steinbring, April 17, 1989.

27. *Elgin Courier*, June 4, 1987; interview with Thomas Baca, May 16, 1989.

28. *Elgin Courier*, June 4, 1987; June 11, 1987; *Austin American-Statesman*, June 3, 1987; interview with Buddy Lewis, July 13, 1989; interview with David and Barbara Carson, May 24, 1989; interview with Thomas Baca, May 16, 1989.

29. *Elgin Courier*, June 11, 1987; May 21, 1987.

30. *Elgin Courier*, July 30, 1987; interview with Thomas Baca, May 16, 1989; interview with Dolph and Joanne Hess, June 8, 1989; interview with Sam and Debbie Dunkin, May 30, 1989.

31. *Elgin Courier*, July 16, 1987; October 8, 1987; photocopy of petition.

32. *Elgin Courier*, June 4, 1987; June 25, 1987; July 2, 1987; July 23, 1987; August 6, 1987; October 1, 1987.

33. Interview with Jerre Guthrie, April 28, 1989; interview with Margie Schindler, June 14, 1989; interview with Dolph and Joanne Hess, June 8, 1989; interview with Tom Dungan, November 9, 1987; *Elgin Courier*, October 29, 1987; November 5, 1987; *Bastrop Advertiser*, October 29, 1987.

34. *Elgin Courier*, June 18, 1987; interview with Ivy Ann Cronin, June 22, 1989; interview with Caroline Guthrie, March 3, 1989; interview with Adeline Eschberger, March 8, 1989; interview with Ed and Sue Steinbring, April 17, 1989.

35. Interview with Buddy Lewis, July 13, 1989; interview with Opal Jones, June 9, 1989; interview with Wallace Wilson, April 21, 1989; interview with David and Barbara Carson, May 24, 1989.

36. Interview with Opal Jones, June 8, 1989; interview with Debbie Dunkin, May 30, 1989.

Bibliography

Newspapers

Austin American, 1883, 1941–51.

Austin American-Statesman, 1883, 1987.

Austin Weekly Statesman, 1875–77.

Bastrop Advertiser, 1873–1942, 1987.

Dallas Morning News, 1956.

Elgin Courier, 1918, 1935–89.

Galveston News, 1876, 1883.

San Antonio Express, 1909.

The Town Crier, 1984.

Books, Other Publications, and Manuscripts

Annals of Travis County, Volume 30. Austin, Tex.: N.p., n.d.

Atherton, Lewis Eldon. *Main Street on the Middle Border*. Bloomington: Indiana University Press, 1954.

Bohls, Alvin. *"From the Record" with Observations*. McDade, Tex: Faith Lutheran Church, n.d. Mimeographed in newsletter format.

Carter, John W. *Invasion and Stagnation: The Role of Local Associations in Community Adaptation to Large Energy Development Episodes in Bastrop County, Texas*. Master's thesis, The University of Texas at Austin, 1981.

Cherny, Robert W. *A Righteous Cause: The Life of William Jennings Bryan*. Boston: Little Brown, 1985.

Church Book, McDade, Tex.: St. Andrew's Lutheran Church, n.d.

Dunning, John. *Tune in Yesterday: The Ultimate Encyclopedia of Old-Time Radio, 1925–1976*. Englewood Cliffs: Prentice Hall, 1976.

"Early Years of Faith Lutheran Church, 1883–1903, The." McDade, Tex.: Faith Lutheran Church, n.d. Mimeographed.

The Echo, 1948–49. McDade, Tex.: McDade School Yearbook, 1949.

Elgin: A History of Elgin, Texas, 1872–1972. Austin: The Elgin Historical Committee, 1973.

Faith Lutheran Church Directory, 1980. McDade, Tex.: Faith Lutheran Church, 1980.

Ficklen, Mary. "McDade's Christmas Murders." *The Cattleman* (December 1967):

Freeman, Martha Doty. *A Cultural Resource Inventory and Assessment at Camp Swift, Texas*. Austin: Texas Archaeological Survey, 1979.

Holt, T. E. "The McDade Baptist Church: Four Steps Forward." McDade, Tex.: McDade Baptist Church, 1947. Mimeographed in newsletter format.

Houston, Oscar Parke, and Walter Ewing Long. "History of Camp Swift,"1958. Ms, Austin/Travis County Collection, Austin History Center, Austin Public Library.

Levine, Lawrence W. *Defender of the Faith: William Jennings Bryan: The Last Decade, 1915–1925.* New York: Oxford University Press, 1965.

McCarty, Jeanne Bozzell. *The Struggle for Sobriety: Protestants and Prohibition in Texas.* El Paso: Texas Western Press, 1980.

McKay, Seth. *Texas Politics 1906–1944.* Lubbock: Texas Tech Press, 1952.

McNeil, Alex. *Total Television: A Comprehensive Guide to Programing from 1948 to the Present.* New York: Penguin Books, 1991.

Moore, Bill. *Bastrop County, 1691–1900.* Wichita Falls, Tex. Nortex Press, 1977.

Nixon, Raymond B. *Henry W. Grady, Spokesman of the New South.* New York: A. A. Knopf, 1943.

Official Record Book. McDade, Tex.: McDade Rural Progress Association, 1948.

Sayersville Historical Association Bulletin. (Spring 1984) Elgin, Texas.

Schulz, Ernestine. *McDade Then and Now.* McDade, Tex.: self-published, 1996.

"Sixth Annual Announcement, 1915–16." McDade, Tex.: McDade School handbook, 1916.

Snyder, Robert E. *Cotton Crisis.* Chapel Hill: University of North Carolina Press, 1984.

Sonnichsen, C. L. *I'll Die Before I'll Run: The Story of the Great Feuds of Texas.* New York: Harper, 1951.

Sonntag, Mark. *Hyphenated Texans: World War I and the German-Americans of Texas.* Master's thesis, The University of Texas at Austin, 1990.

Storm, Gale. *I Ain't Down Yet: The Autobiography of My Little Margie.* Indianapolis: Bobbs-Merrill, 1981.

Wainscott, Catherine. "Memories, Memories." McDade Watermelon Festival Program. McDade, Tex.: McDade Watermelon Festival Association, 1988.

Index

References to people identified in photographs appear in **bold.**